> "America's leading source of self-help legal information." ★★★★
>
> —YAHOO!

 W9-CNB-871

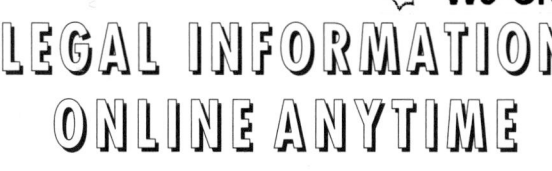

LEGAL INFORMATION ONLINE ANYTIME

24 hours a day

www.nolo.com

AT THE NOLO.COM SELF-HELP LAW CENTER, YOU'LL FIND

Nolo's comprehensive Legal Encyclopedia filled with plain-English information on a variety of legal topics

Nolo's Law Dictionary—legal terms <u>without</u> the legalese

Auntie Nolo—if you've got questions, Auntie's got answers

The Law Store—over 250 self-help legal products including:

Downloadable Software, Books, Form Kits and eGuides

Legal and product updates

Frequently Asked Questions

NoloBriefs, our free monthly email newsletter

Legal Research Center, for access to state and federal statutes

Our ever-popular lawyer jokes

Quality LAW BOOKS & SOFTWARE FOR EVERYONE

Nolo's user-friendly products are consistently first-rate. Here's why:

- A dozen in-house legal editors, working with highly skilled authors, ensure that our products are accurate, up-to-date and easy to use

- We continually update every book and software program to keep up with changes in the law

- Our commitment to a more democratic legal system informs all of our work

- We appreciate & listen to your feedback. Please fill out and return the card at the back of this book.

OUR "NO-HASSLE" GUARANTEE

Return anything you buy directly from Nolo for any reason and we'll cheerfully re-fund your purchase price. No ifs, ands or buts.

An Important Message to Our Readers

3rd edition

IRAs, 401(k)s

& Other Retirement Plans

Taking Your Money Out

by Twila Slesnick, PhD, Enrolled Agent
& Attorney John C. Suttle, CPA

edited by Attorney Amy Delpo

Keeping Up to Date

To keep its books up-to-date, Nolo issues new printings and new editions periodically. New printings reflect minor legal changes and technical corrections. New editions contain major legal changes, major text additions or major reorganizations. To find out if a later printing or edition of any Nolo book is available, call Nolo at 510-549-1976 or check our website at http://www.nolo.com.

To stay current, follow the "Update" service at our website at http://www.nolo.com/update. In another effort to help you use Nolo's latest materials, we offer a 35% discount off the purchase of the new edition of your Nolo book when you turn in the cover of an earlier edition. (See the "Special Upgrade Offer" in the back of the book.)

This book was last revised in: **May 2001.**

Third Edition	MAY 2001
Editor	AMY DELPO
Illustrations	MARI STEIN
Cover Design	TONI IHARA
Book Design	TERRI HEARSH
Production	SARAH HINMAN
Proofreading	SHERYL ROSE
Index	SUSAN CORNELL
Printing	BERTELSMANN SERVICES, INC.

Slesnick, Twila.
   IRAs, 401(k)s, and other retirement plans : taking your money out / by Twila Slesnick and John C. Suttle.--3rd ed.
      p. cm.
   Includes index.
   ISBN 0-87337-752-4
   1. Individual retirement accounts--Law and legislation--United States--Popular works.
   2. Pension trusts--Taxation--Law and legislation--United States--Popular works. I. Title:
IRAs, 401(k)s, and other retirement plans. II. Suttle, John C. III. Title.

KF3510.Z9 S55 2001
343.7305'233--dc21   2001030127

Acknowledgments

Thanks to Nolo editor Robin Leonard for her intelligent and skillful editing on the first edition—and for adding a dose of levity to the entire process. For the second and third editions, thanks to Nolo editor Amy DelPo for her keen eye and clear thinking. We are also grateful to attorney Charles Purnell for reading the entire manuscript more carefully than we had any right to expect. His suggestions were valuable and much appreciated. Thanks also to Robert and Joan Leonard, and Gail Friedlander, for reading parts of the manuscript. And finally, a special thanks to Durf, partner extraordinare, and to Jack and Betty Suttle who have made it possible to balance single parenthood and a profession.

Table of Contents

How to Use This Book

1 Types of Retirement Plans

2 Basic Tax Rules for Distributions

3 Taxes on Early Distributions

7 Distributions to Your Beneficiary If You Die Before Age 70 1/2

8 Distributions to Your Beneficiary If You Die After Age 70 1/2

9 Roth IRAs

Appendixes

A IRS Forms, Notices and Schedules

B Life Expectancy Tables

Index

How to Use This Book

This is not a mystery novel. It is a book about how to take money out of your retirement plan. We are not promising that you will stay up all night breathlessly turning each page to see what happens next. You might, though, because most people will find something useful—perhaps even surprising—in this book.

Let's start with the basics. There are many kinds of retirement plans, and many possible sources for owning one. You might have a retirement plan at work, an IRA that you set up yourself or a plan you've inherited. You might still be contributing to a plan, or you may be retired. No matter what your situation, you will find information to help you through the minefield of rules.

We've included a chapter on Roth IRAs— the hot new type of plan with great retirement savings and estate planning potential. Roth IRAs don't work for everyone, however, so this book helps you figure out if you are eligible to set one up and if it makes sense for you to do so.

There are many reasons to take money out of a retirement plan. You might want to borrow the money for an emergency and pay it back—or not pay it back. Maybe you quit your job and your former employer wants to give you your share of the company's plan. Perhaps you're required by law to withdraw some of your retirement funds.

Here are some FAQs (frequently asked questions) about retirement plans that this book can help you answer:

- How do I know what kind of retirement plan I have? (See Chapter 1.)
- Do I have to wait until I retire to get money out of my plan or my IRA? (See Chapter 3.)
- Can I borrow money from my 401(k) to buy a house? (See Chapters 3, 4 and 5.)
- What should I do with my retirement plan when I leave my company or retire? (See Chapter 2.)
- When do I have to start taking money out of my IRA? (See Chapter 5.)

- How do I calculate how much I have to take? (See Chapter 6.)
- Can I take more than the required amount? (See Chapter 6.)
- What happens to my retirement plan when I die? (See Chapters 7 and 8.)
- Can my spouse roll over my IRA when I die? (See Chapters 7 and 8.)
- What about my children? Can they put my IRA in their names? Do they have to take all the money out of the account right away? (See Chapters 7 and 8.)
- If I inherit a retirement plan, can I add my own money to it? Can I save it for my own children, if I don't need the money? (See Chapters 7 and 8.)
- Am I allowed to set up a Roth IRA? Should I? (See Chapter 9.)
- Can I convert my regular IRA to a Roth IRA? Should I? (See Chapter 9.)

To help you answer these and other questions, we include many examples. They guide you through the decision-making process and step you through calculations. You will also find sample tax forms that the IRS requires, along with instructions for how to complete them.

This book also contains tables to help you calculate distributions. It also contains sample letters and worksheets you can use to communicate with the IRS or with the custodian of your IRA or retirement plan. We've even included some important IRS notices so you can read first-hand how IRS personnel are thinking about certain critical issues.

The tax rules for pensions, IRAs, 401(k)s and other types of retirement plans are notoriously complex, which can be all the more frustrating because they are important to so many people. With this book, it is our goal to make the rules clear and accessible to those people who need to understand them.

Icons Used Throughout

At the beginning of each chapter, we let you know who should read the chapter and who can skip it or read only parts of it.

 Sprinkled throughout the book are planning tips based on strategies that other people have used successfully.

We include several cautions to alert you to potential pitfalls.

Types of Retirement Plans

Who Should Read Chapter 1

→ Read this chapter if you aren't certain which types of retirement plans you have—either through your employer or as a self-employed person. Also read this chapter if you have an IRA but aren't sure which type.

*H*ow many people have warned you that you'll never see a penny of the hard-earned money you've poured into the Social Security system and that you'd better have your own retirement nest egg tucked away somewhere? Perhaps those doomsayers are overstating the case, but even if you eventually do collect Social Security, it is likely to provide only a fraction of the income you will need during retirement.

Congress responded to this problem several decades ago by creating a variety of tax-favored plans to help working people save for retirement. One such plan is set up by you, the individual taxpayer, and is appropriately called an individual retirement account or IRA. Another, which can be established by your employer or by you if you are self-employed, is referred to by the nondescript phrase, a qualified plan. A qualified plan is one that qualifies to receive certain tax benefits as described in Section 401 of the U.S. Tax Code.

There are other types of retirement plans, too, which enjoy some of the same tax benefits as qualified plans but are not technically qualified, because they are defined in a different section of the Tax Code. Many of these other plans closely follow the qualified plan rules, however. The most common of these almost-qualified plans are tax-deferred annuities (TDAs) and qualified annuity plans. (Don't be thrown by the name. Even though it may be called a qualified annuity plan, it is not defined in Section 401 and therefore is not a qualified plan in the purest sense.) Both of these plans are defined in Section 403 of the Tax Code. Because many of the rules in Section 403 are similar to those in Section 401, TDAs and qualified annuity plans are often mentioned in the same breath with qualified plans.

All qualified plans, TDAs and qualified annuity plans have been sweetened with breaks for taxpayers to encourage them to save for retirement. And working people have saved, often stretching as far as they can to put money into their retirement plans. The government's job is to make sure the plans are used as they were intended—to help participants fund their own retirement—not to help them avoid current income tax obligations or to transfer wealth from one generation to another. One way the government ensures that retirement plan money is distributed to the plan participant and taxed during that person's lifetime is to require that the participant take money or assets out of the plan at specified times. To achieve that end, Congress has enacted a host of

Helpful Terms

Adjusted Gross Income (AGI). Total taxable income reduced by certain expenses such as qualified plan contributions, IRA contributions and alimony payments.

Beneficiary. The person or entity entitled to receive the benefits from an insurance policy or from trust property, such as a retirement plan or IRA.

Deductible Contribution. A contribution to a retirement plan that an employer may claim as a business expense to offset income on the employer's tax return. You may know it as simply the employer's contribution. In the case of an IRA, a deductible contribution is one that an individual taxpayer may use to offset income on the individual's tax return.

Distribution. A payout of property (such as shares of stock) or cash from a retirement plan or IRA to the participant or a beneficiary.

Earned Income. Income received for providing goods or services. Earned income might be wages or salary or net profit from a business.

Eligible Employee. An employee who has met certain conditions of an employer's retirement plan, such as years of service, and now qualifies to participate in the plan.

Nondeductible Contribution. A contribution to a retirement plan or IRA that may not be claimed as a business expense or used as an adjustment to offset taxable income on an income tax return.

Nondiscrimination Rules. The provisions in the U.S. Tax Code that prohibit certain retirement plans from providing greater benefits to highly compensated employees than to non-highly compensated employees.

Participant or Active Participant. An employee for whom the employer makes a contribution to the employer's retirement plan.

Tax-Deductible Expense. An item of expense that may be used to offset income on a tax return.

Tax Deferral. The postponement of tax payments until a future year.

Vested Benefit. The portion of a participant's retirement plan accumulation that is nonforfeitable. In other words, the portion a participant may keep after separating from service; or the portion that goes to a participant's beneficiary if the participant dies.

laws dictating the form and timing of distributions.

What does this mean for you? If you or your employer has ever put money into a retirement plan and received tax benefits as a result, then you cannot simply take the money out whenever you want, nor can you leave it in the plan forever. Instead, you must follow a complex set of rules for withdrawing money, or taking distributions, from the plan during your lifetime and even after your death. If you don't follow the rules, you will have to pay penalties—sometimes substantial ones.

But as is so often the case when Congress enacts highly restrictive laws, attached to each is a passel of exceptions. Will you qualify for any of them? Quite possibly. The tax rules, regulations, explanations, guidelines and exceptions relating to distributions from retirement plans fill many unsightly volumes with language far too complex for bedtime reading. And yet every person who has ever contributed to a retirement plan, or who acquires one through inheritance or divorce, needs to know the rules for taking money out of the plan.

This first chapter identifies and briefly describes the types of retirement plans to which these specialized distribution rules apply. If you have a retirement plan at work or if you have established one through your own business, you should find your plan listed below. Also, if you have an IRA, you will find your particular type among those described below.

There is also an entire category of plans known as nonqualified plans to which these rules do not apply. Such plans are used by employers primarily to provide incentives or rewards for particular—usually upper management—employees. These plans do not enjoy the tax benefits that IRAs and qualified plans (including TDAs and qualified annuities) do, and consequently are not subject to the same distribution restrictions. Although this chapter helps you identify nonqualified plans, such plans have their own distribution rules, which fall outside the scope of this book.

Identifying your particular retirement plan probably won't be as difficult as you think. Although there is indeed a large variety of plans earning a mention in the Tax Code, each with its own set of mind-numbing rules and regulations, every plan fits into one of four broad categories:

- qualified plan
- IRA
- plan which is neither an IRA nor a qualified plan, but which has many of the characteristics of a qualified plan, or
- plan which is neither an IRA nor a qualified plan, and which does not have the characteristics of a qualified plan.

A. Qualified Plans

As mentioned above, a qualified plan is one that is described in Section 401 of the

U.S. Tax Code. Practically speaking, it is a forced savings plan established by an employer to benefit its employees. To encourage employers to set up and contribute to these plans, and to encourage employees to direct some of their pay into them when offered the opportunity, the law provides monetary incentives. Perhaps the most significant advantage to the employer is that the contributions it makes to the plan on behalf of its employees are tax deductible.

The advantages to you, the employee, are not only the opportunity to accumulate a retirement nest egg, but also to postpone paying income taxes on money contributed to the plan. Neither the contributions you make nor any of the investment returns are taxable to you until you take money out of the plan. In tax jargon, the income tax is deferred until the money is distributed and available for spending—usually during retirement. Congress built in some safeguards to help ensure that your plan assets are around when you finally do retire. For example, the assets are required to be held in trust and are generally protected from the claims of creditors.

In return for these tax benefits, the plan must comply with a number of procedural rules. First, the plan must not discriminate in favor of the company's highly compensated employees. For example, the employer may not contribute disproportionately large amounts to the accounts of the company honchos. Also, the employer may not arbitrarily prevent employees

from participating in the plan or from taking their retirement money with them when they leave the company. Finally, the plan must comply with an extremely complex set of distribution rules, which is the focus of this book.

Seven of the most common types of qualified plans are described below.

1. 401(k) Plan and Other Profit Sharing Plans

A profit sharing plan is designed to allow employees to share in the profits of the company and to use those profits to help fund their retirement. Despite the plan's title and description, an employer doesn't have to make a profit in order to contribute to a profit sharing plan. Similarly, even if the employer makes a profit, it does not have to contribute to the plan. Each year, the employer has discretion over whether or not to make a contribution, regardless of profitability.

Contributions by the employer are allocated to each participant's plan account based on the participant's compensation. The annual contribution can be as little as zero and as much as 15% of the participant's annual compensation, up to $170,000 of compensation, or a $25,500 contribution, for 2001. (The $170,000 is subject to occasional cost of living adjustments.)

> **EXAMPLE:** Joe and Martha are participants in their company's profit sharing plan. The company contributed 15% of their respective salaries to the plan for 2000. Joe's salary was $120,000 and Martha's was $210,000. The company contributed $18,000 for Joe (15% x $120,000). Martha's salary exceeds the $170,000 threshold, so the company contribution was limited to $25,500 (15% x $170,000).
>
> The company has been struggling financially, however, so the company has decided not to make any contributions to the profit sharing plan for 2001. Thus, no contribution will be made for Joe or Martha or anyone else in the company.

A special type of profit sharing plan, called a 401(k) plan, is named imaginatively after the subsection of the Tax Code that describes it. All 401(k) plans allow you to direct some of your compensation into the plan, and you do not have to pay income taxes on the portion of your salary you direct into the plan until you withdraw it.

The plan may or may not provide for employer contributions. Some employers make matching contributions, depositing a certain amount for each dollar the participant contributes.

> **EXAMPLE:** Fred participates in his company's 401(k) plan. His company has promised to contribute $.25 for each dollar of Fred's salary that he directs into the plan. Fred's salary is $40,000. He directs 5% of his salary, which is $2,000, into the plan for 2001. The company matches with a $500 contribution (which is $.25 x $2,000).

Other employers contribute a fixed percentage of compensation for each eligible employee, whether or not the employee chooses to contribute to the plan.

> **EXAMPLE:** Marilyn's salary for 2001 is $60,000. Her company has a 401(k) plan which does not match employee contributions. Instead, the company contributes a flat 3% of each eligible employee's salary to the plan. Marilyn is saving to buy a house, so she is not currently directing any of her salary into the 401(k) plan. Nonetheless, the company will contribute $1,800 (which is 3% x $60,000) to the plan for Marilyn.

2. Stock Bonus Plan

A stock bonus plan is like a profit sharing plan, except that the employer must pay the plan benefits to employees in the form of shares of company stock.

> EXAMPLE: Frankie worked for the Warp Corp. all her working life. During her employment, she participated in the company's stock bonus plan, accumulating $90,000 by retirement. When she retired, Warp Corp. stock was worth $100 per share. When the company distributed her retirement benefits to her, it gave her 900 shares of Warp Corp. stock.

3. Money Purchase Pension Plan

A money purchase pension plan is similar to a profit sharing plan in the sense that employer contributions are allocated to each participant's individual account. The difference is that the employer's contributions are mandatory, not discretionary. Under such a plan, the employer promises to pay a definite amount (such as 10% of compensation) into each participant's account every year. In that sense, money purchase pension plans are less flexible for employers than are profit sharing plans.

On the other hand, money purchase plans generally permit larger contributions than do profit sharing plans. The maximum contribution to a money purchase plan is 25% of an individual participant's compensation (up to $170,000 of compensation), compared to 15% under a profit sharing plan. However, the annual contribution for each participant is limited to $35,000 per year. (The $35,000 and $170,000 caps are subject to occasional cost of living adjustments.)

> EXAMPLE: Sand Corp. has a money purchase plan that promises to contribute 25% of compensation to each eligible employee's account. Jenna, who makes $45,000, is eligible to participate in the plan, so the company contributed $11,250 (25% x $45,000) to her account for 2001. In 2002, the company lost money. Nonetheless, the company is still bound to contribute 25% of Jenna's salary to her money purchase plan account for 2002.

4. Employee Stock Ownership Plan (ESOP)

An employee stock ownership plan, or ESOP, is a type of stock bonus plan which may have some features of a money purchase pension plan. ESOPs are designed to be funded primarily or even exclusively with employer stock. An ESOP can allow cash distributions, however, as long as the employee has the right to demand that benefits be paid in employer stock.

Because an ESOP is a stock bonus plan, the employer cannot contribute more than

15% of each participant's compensation. For that reason, some employers add a money purchase plan component to increase the maximum contribution to 25%. They can do this by modifying the standard ESOP agreement and adding the technical provisions that are required of all money purchase plans. Then the plan is subject to the other money purchase pension plan rules, including the mandatory fixed contribution requirement for the money purchase plan portion.

5. Defined Benefit Plan

Like money purchase pension plans, defined benefit plans require that the employer make an annual contribution. But unlike a money purchase plan, contributions are not allocated to individual accounts; instead, the plan maintains one large account. Furthermore, the terms of a defined benefit plan always include a promise to pay each participant a specific dollar amount as an annuity beginning at retirement. The promised payment is usually based on a combination of factors, such as the employee's final compensation and the length of time the employee worked for the company. If the employee retires early, the benefit is reduced according to yet another complex formula.

EXAMPLE: Damien is a participant in his company's defined benefit plan. The plan guarantees that if Damien

works until the company's retirement age, he will receive a retirement benefit equal to 1% of his final pay times the number of years he worked for the company. Damien will reach the company's retirement age in 20 years. If Damien is making $50,000 when he retires in 20 years, his retirement benefit will be $10,000 per year (which is 1% x $50,000 x 20 years). If he retires early, he will receive a reduced benefit.

Once the retirement benefit is determined, the company must compute how much to contribute each year in order to meet that goal. The computation is not simple—in fact, it requires the services of an actuary, who uses projections of salary increases and investment returns to determine the annual contribution amount. The computation must be repeated every year to take into account variations in investment returns and other factors and then to adjust the amount of the contribution to ensure the goal will be reached.

Even though, under certain circumstances, defined benefit plans permit much higher contributions than other qualified plans, they are used infrequently (especially by small companies) because they are so complex and expensive to administer.

6. Target Benefit Plan

A target benefit plan is a special type of money purchase pension plan which incorporates some of the attributes of a defined benefit plan. As with a money purchase plan, each participant in a target benefit plan has a separate account. But instead of contributing a fixed percentage of pay to every account, the employer projects a retirement benefit for each employee, as with a defined benefit plan. In fact, the contribution for the first year is computed in the same way a defined benefit plan contribution would be computed—with the help of an actuary. The difference, though, is that after the first year, the contribution formula is fixed. While a defined benefit plan guarantees a certain retirement annuity, a target benefit plan just shoots for it by estimating the required annual contribution in the employee's first participation year and then freezing the formula. The formula might be a specific dollar amount every year, or perhaps a percentage of pay.

If any of the original assumptions turn out to be wrong—for example, the investment return is less than expected—the retirement target won't be reached. The employer is under no obligation to adjust the level of the contribution to reach the original target if there is a shortfall. Conversely, if investments do better than expected, the employee's retirement benefit will exceed the target, and the increased amount must be paid to the employee.

EXAMPLE: Jack is 35 when he becomes eligible to participate in his company's target benefit plan. Jack's target retirement benefit is 60% of his final pay. Assuming Jack will receive wage increases of 5% each year and will retire at 65 after 30 years of service, Jack's final pay is projected to be $80,000. His target retirement benefit, then, is $48,000 (60% of $80,000). In order to pay Jack $48,000 a year for the rest of his life beginning at age 65, the actuaries estimate that the company must contribute $4,523 to Jack's account every year. The company will contribute that amount, even if Jack doesn't receive 5% raises some years, or if other assumptions turn out to be wrong. Thus, Jack may or may not receive his targeted $48,000 during his retirement years. It might be more or it might be less.

7. Self-Employed Plans (Keoghs)

Qualified plans for self-employed individuals are often called Keogh plans, named after the author of a 1962 bill that established a separate set of rules for such plans. In the ensuing years, Keoghs have come to look very much like corporate plans. In fact, the rules governing self-employed plans are no longer segregated, but have been placed under the umbrella of the qualified plan rules for corporations. Nonetheless, the Keogh moniker lingers—a burr in the side of phonetic spellers.

Keogh plans may take the form of a profit sharing, money purchase pension or exist in many forms. Most common is the individual retirement account or individual retirement annuity to which any person with earnings from employment may contribute. These are called contributory IRAs. Some types of IRAs are used to receive assets distributed from other retirement plans. These are called rollover IRAs. Still others, such as SEPs and SIMPLE IRAs, are technically IRAs even though their rules are quite similar to those of qualified plans. Finally, Roth IRAs combine the features of a regular IRA and a savings plan to produce a hybrid that adheres to its own set of rules.

defined benefit plan, and are generally subject to the same rules as corporate qualified plans of the same type, with few exceptions. Thus, if you have income from your own business, you may establish and contribute to one or more of these plans following rules similar to those a corporation would follow. Your contributions to such a plan will be deductible on your individual income tax return and you will not pay income tax on the contributions, or their investment returns, until you withdraw money from the plan.

B. Individual Retirement Accounts

Most people are surprised to learn that individual retirement accounts, or IRAs,

1. Traditional Contributory IRA

If you or your spouse has income from employment or from your own business, you may set up and contribute to an IRA. The only requirement is that you have earned income, which is income you receive for providing goods or services. The IRA can be a special depository account that you set up with a bank, brokerage firm or other institutional custodian. Or it can be an individual retirement annuity that you purchase from an insurance company.

You may contribute a maximum of $2,000 each year. If you contribute more, you could be hit with penalties from the IRS. (See Chapter 3, Section C.1.f.) If you are not covered by an employer's retirement plan, you may take a deduction on your tax return for your contribution. If you are covered by an employer's plan, your IRA might be fully deductible, partly deductible or not deductible at all, depending on how much gross income you have.

For example, in 2001, if you are single and covered by an employer's plan, your contribution is fully deductible if your adjusted gross income, or AGI, is under $33,000 and not deductible at all when your AGI reaches $43,000. Between $33,000 and $43,000 the deduction is gradually phased out. For married individuals, the phaseout range is from $53,000 to $63,000, if the IRA participant is covered by an employer plan. For an IRA participant who is not covered by a plan but whose spouse is covered, the phaseout range is $150,000 to $160,000. (Some of these dollar amounts are scheduled to increase every year through the year 2007. IRS Publication #590 has the details and may be obtained by calling 800-829-3676, visiting the IRS website at http://www.irs.gov or visiting a local IRS office.)

> EXAMPLE 1: Jamie, who is single, works for Sage Corp. and participates in the company's 401(k) plan. In 2001, he made $20,000. Eager to save for retirement, Jamie decided to contribute $2,000 to an IRA as well. Since his income was less than $33,000, Jamie may take a $2,000 deduction on his tax return for the IRA contribution, even though he also participated in his employer's retirement plan.

> EXAMPLE 2: Assume the same facts as in Example 1 except that Jamie's salary was $60,000 in 2001. Although Jamie is permitted to make an IRA contribution, he may not claim a deduction for it on his tax return because his income was more than $43,000.

> EXAMPLE 3: Assume Jamie made $60,000 in 2001, but Sage Corp. did not have a retirement plan for its employees. Because Jamie was not covered by an employer's retirement plan, his $2,000 IRA contribution is fully deductible even though he made more than $43,000.

2. Rollover and Conduit IRAs

If you receive a distribution from a qualified plan, you might decide to put some or all of it into an IRA. (See Chapter 2, Section C.1.b, for information about how and why you might do this.) The IRA that receives the qualified plan distribution is called a rollover IRA.

Rollover IRAs can have special features. For example, you leave your job and the balance of your retirement account is rolled over, or transferred, to you. You deposit it, or roll it over, to a brand new IRA. If you refrain from making any future contributions to that IRA, you may be able to transfer, or roll over, the assets of the IRA into your new employer's qualified plan. Using an IRA for this purpose—as a temporary receptacle—makes it a conduit IRA. If you make additional contributions to the IRA, however, you will not be able to roll any of the assets into a qualified plan.

Conduit IRAs are valuable tools. You can use conduit IRAs to transfer the assets from an old employer's plan to a new employer's plan. Many people do this so that they don't have to make their own investment decisions or manage their own portfolios, since assets in a corporate plan are often managed by professional money managers. In addition, when you pool your assets (for investment purposes) with those of other plan participants, you expand your investment opportunities. For example, some bonds might be sold only in $100,000 increments. If you have only $20,000 in your account, you wouldn't be able to purchase such a bond unless you pooled your assets with other investors. Also, investing on a larger scale (with pooled assets) tends to keep commissions and management fees down.

Conduit IRA limits. Conduit IRAs cannot be used if you mix your old employer's plan with a contributory IRA. In addition, some corporate plan adminis-trators don't permit mixing assets from different types of qualified plans. If you think you might want to transfer assets from one employer's plan to another, it's best to use a new and separate conduit IRA for each plan distribution you receive.

For example, if you receive a distribution from your employer's 401(k) and a sepa-rate distribution from your employer's defined benefit plan, you should establish two conduit IRAs to maximize the prob-ability that at least one of the distributions can be rolled over into your new employer's plan.

3. Simplified Employee Pension

A simplified employee pension, or SEP, is a special type of IRA, which can be established by your employer or by you if you are self-employed. Designed for small businesses, SEPs have many of the characteristics of a qualified plan but are much simpler to set up and administer.

Under a SEP, each participant has his or her own individual retirement account to which the employer contributes. The contributions are excluded from the participant's pay and are not taxable until they are distributed from the plan. If you are self-employed, you may set up a SEP for yourself, even if you have no employees.

The advantage of a SEP over a regular IRA is that contributions are not limited to $2,000 per year. Instead, the limits on contributions are the same as those of a profit sharing plan. They can be as much as 15% of your annual compensation, up to a maximum compensation amount of $170,000.

The disadvantage of a SEP, from an employer's perspective, is that the participation and vesting rules for SEPs are less favorable than those for qualified plans. Participation rules determine which employees must be covered by the plan and must receive contributions to their plan accounts. Vesting rules determine how much an employee is entitled to if the employee leaves the job or dies. An employer who establishes a SEP is required to make contributions on behalf of virtually all employees. Furthermore, the employees must be 100% vested at all times, which means that they must be allowed to take 100% of their plan account with them when they leave the company, no matter how long they have been employed there. Those can be costly requirements for small employers whose staff often includes many short-term part-time employees. By contrast, 401(k) plans (and other qualified plans) can stretch the period before an employee is fully vested to as long as six years.

4. SIMPLE IRA

A Simplified Incentive Match Plan for Employees, or SIMPLE IRA, is yet another type of IRA designed specifically to make it easier for small employers (those with 100 or fewer employees) to establish a retirement plan. A SIMPLE IRA is a salary reduction plan that, like a 401(k) profit sharing plan, allows employees to divert some compensation into retirement savings.

As with a SEP, contributions to a SIMPLE IRA are deposited into a separate IRA for each participating employee. The participant may select any percentage of compensation to defer into the plan—even zero—but the total dollar amount cannot exceed $6,500 per year. Unlike the employee, the employer is absolutely required to make a contribution. The employer has two options:

- It can match the employee's contribution up to 3% of the employee's compensation. (Under certain circumstances, the employer may match less than 3%, but never more.)
- As an alternative to matching, the employer may contribute a flat 2% of compensation (up to a maximum compensation of $170,000) to the accounts of all eligible employees, whether or not the employee directs any salary into the plan.

EXAMPLE 1: Tabor Corp. has four employees, who earned the following salaries in 2001:

Jane	$25,000
Jake	$20,000
Bree	$35,000
Holly	$50,000

Tabor's SIMPLE IRA offers to match employees' contributions up to 3% of compensation. All four employees are eligible to participate. Jane and Jake each direct $6,000 of their salaries into the plan, while Bree and Holly direct none of their salaries into the plan. For

2001, Tabor Corp. contributes $750 (which is 3% x $25,000) for Jane and $600 (3% of $20,000) for Jake. It contributes nothing for Bree or Holly.

EXAMPLE 2: Assume the same facts as in Example 1 except that instead of matching contributions, Tabor's plan requires a contribution of 2% of compensation to the accounts of all eligible employees. For 2001, Tabor contributes $500 for Jane (which is 2% x $25,000) and $400 (2% of $20,000) for Jake. It also contributes $700 (2% of $35,000) for Bree and $1,000 (2% of $50,000) for Holly, even though Bree and Holly did not direct any of their salaries into the plan.

5. Roth IRA

At first glance, a Roth IRA looks a lot like a traditional contributory IRA, because annual contributions are limited to $2,000. Beyond that, though, the similarities are more difficult to see. For one thing, none of your contributions to a Roth IRA are ever deductible on your tax return. Whether or not you are covered by an employer's retirement plan is completely irrelevant. Furthermore, if your AGI exceeds a certain level ($160,000 for joint filers and $110,000 for single filers), you may not make any contribution to a Roth IRA. (Recall that with a traditional IRA, you may make a contribution even if your income is high and you are covered by an employer's plan. You might not be able to deduct the contribution on your tax return, however.)

The big advantage of a Roth IRA is that if you qualify to make contributions, all distributions from the IRA are tax free— even the investment returns—as long as the distribution satisfies certain requirements. Furthermore, unlike traditional IRAs, you may contribute to a Roth IRA for as long as you continue to have earned income. (In the case of traditional IRAs, no contributions are permitted after age 70½.)

Although Roth IRAs belong to the IRA family and are subject to many of the IRA rules, the abundant exceptions and variations in treatment make it difficult to rely on what you know about traditional IRAs when trying to figure out what to do with a Roth IRA. Consequently, we devote all of Chapter 9 to Roth IRAs. In that chapter, we point out the distinguishing characteristics of the Roth IRA and identify which of the distribution rules in this book apply to it and which do not. Before you take any action on a Roth IRA based on what you know about the traditional IRA rules, be sure to read Chapter 9.

C. Almost-Qualified Plans

Tucked into the voluminous Tax Code are a number of hybrid plans that are not strictly qualified plans, but which share many of the benefits and restrictions of qualified plans. The two most common, and the two which most closely mirror the qualified plan rules, are qualified annuity plans and tax-deferred annuities.

1. Qualified Annuity Plan

The rules for qualified plans require that the assets of the plan be held by an administrator in a trust. Congress carved out an exception to this rule by adding Section 403(a) to the Tax Code. Section 403(a) allows employers to use contributions to purchase annuities for employees directly from an insurance company. This alternative to holding the contributions in a trust can simplify administration. In almost every other respect, the rules and regulations that apply to qualified plans also apply to qualified annuity plans.

2. Tax-Deferred Annuity

If you are a university professor or an employee of a public school, odds are that you are covered by an Annuity Plan of Public Charity or Public School, more commonly referred to as a tax-deferred annuity, or TDA. TDAs, defined in Section 403(b) of the Tax Code, are typically funded with individual annuity contracts purchased from an insurance company. When you retire, your benefits are usually paid to you as a monthly annuity for the rest of your life, although some TDAs offer

other distribution options, such as a lump sum payment.

TDAs are not qualified plans and do not track the qualified plan rules as closely as qualified annuity plans do. For example, distributions from TDAs are not eligible for special tax options, such as averaging and capital gains treatment. (See Chapter 2 for more information about tax options.) However, the vast majority of the distribution rules that apply to qualified plans also apply to TDAs. The exceptions are noted where relevant.

D. Nonqualified Plans

Big business being what it is—subject to the sometimes wise and sometimes questionable judgment of the boss—many companies offer special incentives and compensation packages to key employees. The incentives might come in the form of deferred cash bonuses, stock certificates or stock options. Very often, the boss doesn't offer the same deal to everyone.

Because the incentives are not available to everyone, such plans generally do not satisfy the nondiscrimination requirements of qualified plans, and are therefore called nonqualified plans. Because they are nonqualified, they are not subject to the same rigorous vesting, participation and distribution requirements.

Nonqualified plans have some additional distinctive features: an employer may not deduct contributions to the plan, assets of the plan are not required to be held in trust and the assets of the individual participants are not protected from the claims of creditors. Because nonqualified plans are not subject to the same distribution rules as IRAs, qualified plans, qualified annuities and TDAs, they are not covered in this book.

Key Tax Code Sections

§ 401(a)

Qualified Plans in General (including Keoghs): profit sharing, stock bonus, money purchase pension, defined benefit plans.

§ 401(k)

Cash or Salary Deferral Plan: A special type of qualified plan. Can be profit sharing or stock bonus plan.

§ 403(a)

Qualified Annuity Plan: Plan established by employer that is not a public charity or public school. Funded by the employer with purchased annuities.

§ 403(b)

Annuity Plan of Public Charity or Public School: Commonly called tax-deferred annuity or TDA. Usually funded with purchased annuities owned by the employee.

§ 408

IRAs: Contributory, rollover, conduit, SEP, SIMPLE.

§ 408A

Roth IRAs.

Basic Tax Rules for Distributions

Who Should Read Chapter 2

➡️ Everyone will want to read this chapter. It describes the basic tax rules that apply to your retirement plan when you leave your job. (Chapters 3-6 contain more specific rules.) If the only retirement plan you have is an IRA, you can skip Sections C and D of this chapter.

*O*ur tax laws provide both incentive and opportunity to sock away significant sums for retirement. The combination of an up-front tax deduction for contributions to retirement plans, years of tax-deferred growth and eventual taxation at relatively low rates (such as during retirement) can produce dramatic returns on retirement savings.

A. Taxation Fundamentals

To reap maximum benefit from your retirement plan, you must contribute as much as you can through the years, and you must adhere to certain guidelines when you begin drawing money out. Keep in mind that your financial goal should be to maximize your *after-tax* wealth. It won't do you much good to accumulate a comfortable nest egg if you lose the bulk of it to taxes. As you pursue this goal, the following fundamentals will serve you well when you are not sure how to proceed.

1. Defer the Payment of Tax

When you have a choice, it is usually best to delay or defer the payment of income tax for as long as possible. During the deferral period, you will have the use of money that would otherwise have gone to taxes; if you invest it, that money will help generate more tax-deferred income. The easiest way to defer the payment of tax is by deferring the receipt of income. For example, if you have the option of taking a distribution from your retirement plan this year or next, it is often better to wait. As the tables below show, even a one-year delay can be beneficial. Your money grows while the tax man waits.

Many people vastly underestimate the benefits of tax-deferred compounding of investment returns inside a retirement plan account. Take a look at Tables I and II below. Both cases assume a simple 8% return on your investment and a flat 28% tax rate. Table I shows what happens if you take $10,000 out of your IRA, pay tax on it and invest the remainder for 15 years. Because the investment is outside your IRA, each year you will pay tax on your interest, dividends and capital gains.

Now look at Table II, which shows what happens if you leave the $10,000 inside the IRA. The table projects the value of your investment after one year, two years or more. After 15 years, the total value of your IRA will be $31,722, almost twice as much as the balance shown in Table I after 15 years. If you take the money out

Helpful Terms

After-Tax Dollars. The amount of income left after all income taxes have been withheld or paid.

Amortization. The reduction of a debt through periodic payments of principal and interest.

Basis. An amount treated as the purchase price or cost of an asset for purposes of determining the taxable gain or loss when the asset is sold.

Custodian. A person or entity who is in possession of property belonging to another. For example, the custodian of an IRA is the institution that holds the stocks, bonds, cash or other property of the IRA, even though the assets actually belong to the individual who established and funded the IRA.

Distribution. A payout of property (such as shares of stock) or cash from a retirement plan or IRA to the participant or a beneficiary.

Fair Market Value (FMV). The price at which an item could be sold at retail by a willing seller to a willing buyer.

Net Unrealized Appreciation. The amount by which an asset has increased in value before it is sold.

Nondeductible Contribution. A contribution to a retirement plan or IRA that may not be used as a business expense or an adjustment to offset taxable income on an income tax return.

Pre-Tax Dollars. Total taxable income before income taxes have been paid.

Pro Rata. Proportionately. For example, an amount distributed pro rata over four years is distributed evenly over those four years. Property that is distributed pro rata to its owners is distributed according to the percentage of each owner's interest.

Tax Bracket or Marginal Tax Bracket. The rate at which each additional dollar of income will be taxed. Under the Internal Revenue Code, a certain amount of income is taxed at one rate, and additional income is taxed at another. Therefore, it is possible that if you have one more dollar of income it will be taxed at a different rate than the previous dollar. Your marginal rate is the rate at which your next dollar of income will be taxed.

Trustee. A person or entity who holds legal title to the property in a trust. For example, a qualified retirement plan is a trust that is administered by a trustee who manages the trust property for the plan participant.

Table I

Withdraw from IRA: $10,000
Pay income tax: $2,800
Invest remainder: $7,200
Investment return: 8%
Tax Rate: 28%

Year	Initial Investment Beginning of Year	Interest Earned	Current Year Tax on Interest	Total Investment Year End
1	$ 7,200	$ 576	$ 161	$ 7,615
2	7,615	609	171	8,053
3	8,053	644	180	8,517
4	8,517	681	191	9,008
5	9,008	721	202	9,527
6	9,527	762	213	10,075
7	10,075	806	226	10,656
8	10,656	852	239	11,269
9	11,269	902	252	11,919
10	11,919	953	267	12,605
11	12,605	1,008	282	13,331
12	13,331	1,066	299	14,099
13	14,099	1,128	316	14,911
14	14,911	1,193	334	15,770
15	15,770	1,262	353	16,678

Table II

Leave inside IRA: $10,000
Investment return: 8%
Tax Rate: 28%

Year	Initial Investment Beginning of Year	Interest Earned	Current Year Tax on Interest	Total Investment Year End	Tax If Distributed	Net If Distributed*
1	$ 10,000	$ 800	$ 0	$ 10,800	$ 3,024	$ 7,776
2	10,800	864	0	11,664	3,266	8,398
3	11,664	933	0	12,597	3,527	9,070
4	12,597	1,008	0	13,605	3,809	9,796
5	13,605	1,088	0	14,693	4,114	10,579
6	14,693	1,175	0	15,869	4,443	11,425
7	15,869	1,269	0	17,138	4,799	12,340
8	17,138	1,371	0	18,509	5,183	13,327
9	18,509	1,481	0	19,990	5,597	14,393
10	19,990	1,599	0	21,589	6,045	15,544
11	21,589	1,727	0	23,316	6,529	16,788
12	23,316	1,865	0	25,182	7,051	18,131
13	25,182	2,015	0	27,196	7,615	19,581
14	27,196	2,176	0	29,372	8,224	21,148
15	29,372	2,350	0	31,722	8,882	22,840

*Compare last column with last column of Table I

and pay the tax on the distribution, your balance will be $22,840, which is still $6,162 more than you would have if you had paid the tax in year 1 and invested the money outside the IRA. This is true even though in both situations, you start with the same amount of money, earn the same investment return and are subject to the same tax rate.

Occasionally, it may be better not to defer distributions—if you expect to be in a permanently higher tax bracket in the future, for example. Or perhaps the income you earn outside the IRA will be taxed at a capital gains rate that is lower than your ordinary income tax rate. Bear in mind, however, that a slightly higher tax bracket or a temporary spike in your tax rate is not usually enough justification to accelerate distributions. Your tax rate would have to increase significantly to offset the enormous benefits of compounded growth.

2. Pay Tax at the Lowest Rate

Generally, your goal should be to pay tax on all of your retirement income at the lowest possible rate. But how will you know when the time is right to take the money out? Most people will be in a lower tax bracket after retirement, which provides yet another reason to defer distributions as long as possible.

3. Avoid Tax Penalties

A raft of penalty taxes awaits you if you fail to comply with the myriad distribution laws. Some penalties are designed to discourage pre-retirement distributions. Others target individuals who want to leave their retirement funds to their heirs. Penalties are discussed at length in subsequent chapters, but be advised: it is rarely wise to take a distribution and pay a tax penalty, even if it seems like a small amount to you. Not only will you have to pay the penalty when you file your next tax return, but you will also have to report the distribution as income and pay regular income tax on it. When you factor in the loss of tax-deferred compounded growth, you might even be better off borrowing the money you need, rather than dipping into your retirement plan.

At some point, though, you certainly will take money out of your retirement plan, whether it is because your employer distributes it to you when you leave your job, because you need the money or because the law requires you to withdraw it. When that time comes, you must understand how retirement plans are taxed and know your options. You will also need to be aware of potential penalties in order to stay out of harm's way.

B. General Income Tax Rules for Retirement Plans

When you take money out of a retirement plan, whether it is an IRA, qualified plan, qualified annuity or TDA, some basic income tax rules will apply. Although each rule has exceptions, expect the rule to apply in most situations.

1. Distributions Are Taxable Immediately

First and most basic: all distributions will be taxed in the year they come out of the plan. An exception to this rule applies if you roll over your distribution into another retirement plan or an IRA within 60 days, or if your employer transfers the distribution directly into another plan or IRA. In that case, you do not pay income tax until the money is eventually distributed from the new plan or IRA. (Rollovers are discussed in Section C.1.b, below.)

Some money might be withheld!
Beware of rules that require your plan administrator to withhold money to cover income taxes you may owe when you take money out of your retirement plan—even if you plan to roll it over. You can avoid the withholding by having your employer transfer the retirement funds directly into another retirement plan or IRA. (See Section C.5, below, for more information about these withholding rules.)

2. Your Basis Is Not Taxable

If you made contributions to a retirement plan or IRA for which you were not permitted to take a tax deduction on your tax return, then you have what is called "basis" in the plan. In other words, you have contributed money to a plan or IRA that you have already reported as income on your tax return. You will not have to pay taxes on those amounts a second time when you take the money out of your plan, but unfortunately, you usually don't have the luxury of deciding when to withdraw the portion of the money attributable to the basis.

If you have a regular IRA or a Keogh (see Chapter 1 for a description of these plans), your basis generally comes out pro rata, which means that every time you take a distribution, part of it is taxable and part is not. You compute the taxable and non-taxable portions of each distribution on

IRS Form 8606 and submit it with the rest of your tax return at tax time. (A copy of Form 8606 is in Appendix A.) Roth IRAs are different—they have special basis rules. (See Chapter 9 for more information.) In the case of an employer plan, the contributions you made with dollars on which you already paid taxes are usually distributed as a lump sum when you retire—unless you elect to take your retirement benefits as an annuity. If so, you may have to take your basis out pro rata—a little bit with each annuity payment.

EXAMPLE: Over the years, you contributed a total of $10,000 to your IRA. You were not permitted to claim a tax deduction on your tax return for any of those contributions. Thus the $10,000 is all after-tax money, or basis. On December 31, the fair market value of the IRA was $45,000. During the year, you withdrew $5,000 to help cover living expenses. Part of the $5,000 is taxable, and part is not. To determine the tax-free portion, use the following method:

Step 1: Add the distributions you took during the year to the fair market value of the IRA on December 31.

$5,000 + $45,000 = $50,000

Step 2: Divide your total basis in the IRA by the amount from Step 1.

10,000 ÷ $50,000 = .2 or 20%

Step 3: Multiply the result in Step 2 by the amount of the year's distribution.

20% x $5,000 = $1,000

You will not have to pay taxes on $1,000 of the $5,000 distribution, but the remaining $4,000 will be subject to income tax.

Multiple IRAs. If you have more than one IRA, all of your IRAs (including traditional IRA, SEP and SIMPLE IRA but not Roth IRA) are combined and treated as one for purposes of computing the tax-free portion of each distribution.

EXAMPLE: You have two IRAs. Over the years, you made nondeductible contributions of $8,000 to IRA #1. All of your contributions to IRA #2 were deductible. Consequently, your total basis for both IRAs is $8,000. During 2001, you withdrew $5,000 from IRA #1. On December 31, 2001 the fair market value of IRA #1 was $45,000 and of IRA #2 was $30,000. To determine the tax-free portion of the distribution, you must follow these steps:

Step 1: Determine the total fair market value of all of your IRAs as of December 31.

$45,000 + $30,000 = $75,000

Step 2: Add the distributions you took during the year to the total from Step 1.

$5,000 + $75,000 = $80,000

Step 3: Determine the total basis (nondeductible contributions) for all IRAs.

$8,000 + 0 = $8,000

Step 4: Divide the total basis from Step 3 by the amount from Step 2.

$8,000/$80,000 = .1 or 10%

Step 5: Multiply the result in Step 4 by the amount of your distribution.

10% x $5,000 = $500

You will not have to pay tax on $500 of the $5,000 distribution, but the remaining $4,500 will be subject to income tax.

3. You Don't Have to Withdraw Cash

Generally, when you take a distribution from an IRA, you may choose the assets you want to withdraw; you are not required to take cash. For example, suppose you want to withdraw $20,000. Your portfolio consists of $10,000 in cash and the remainder in stocks and bonds. You may take your $20,000 in any combination of cash and property you choose. You may take part of your distribution in cash and part in stocks and bonds, or even all of it in stock. If you take the distribution in property other than cash, the amount of the distribution is the fair market value of the property (such as the stock) on the day it comes out of the IRA.

EXAMPLE: You decide to take a distribution from your retirement account on June 1. On that day, the total value of your account is $50,000, of which $10,000 is in cash and the remainder in 1,000 shares of MacBlue stock valued at $40 per share. The stock was purchased in the IRA for $10 per share. You decide to withdraw all of the cash and 250 shares of MacBlue stock. The total value of your distribution for tax purposes is $20,000 ($10,000 of cash plus 250 shares of MacBlue stock x $40 per share). After the distribution, you will have no cash inside the IRA, but you will have 750 shares of MacBlue stock. The tax basis of the MacBlue stock in your hands will be $40 per share, not its original cost of $10 per share. Therefore, if you sell the stock at some time in the future, the taxable amount will be the sale price less your basis of $40.

When you receive a distribution from your employer's retirement plan, the plan itself usually dictates which assets must be distributed; you frequently have little control.

4. You May Not Claim Losses

You may not claim on your tax return losses you incur inside your IRA or retirement plan. Instead, you simply pay tax on each distribution based on the cash value or the fair market value of the property on the date it is distributed from the plan. For example, if you purchased 100 shares of LM Corp. at $12,000 and the fair market value of the stock is $5,000 when you withdraw all 100 shares from your IRA, you are not permitted to take a loss of $7,000. But before you cry foul, remember that you didn't pay tax on the money you used to purchase the stock, either. It was purchased inside your retirement plan with tax-deferred money. The value of the stock at distribution is $5,000, and that is the entire taxable amount. In fact, you will have obtained a tax benefit from the loss through the reduction of the taxable distribution.

One extremely rare exception to this rule might occur if you have made contributions with after-tax dollars and never managed to withdraw all of your basis. For example, if your basis in your IRA exceeds the fair market value of the entire IRA (or all of your IRAs combined, if you have more than one) when you take a final distribution, you may claim the loss as a miscellaneous itemized deduction on your tax return.

EXAMPLE: In 1990 you made a nondeductible $2,000 contribution to an IRA. You invested all of the money in junk bonds. Because the investment started to go bad immediately, you never made any additional contributions. Now the account is worth $1,500. If you take a distribution of the entire $1,500 and close the account, you may claim a loss of $500 on Schedule A of your tax return.

5. Divorce or Inheritance Doesn't Change the Basic Tax Rules

If you inherit a retirement plan or IRA, or if you receive one from your spouse in a divorce settlement, the four rules just discussed apply to you as though you were the original owner. For example, when you take money or property out of an IRA you inherited from your mother, you pay tax on the fair market value of the assets on the date of distribution. And if your mother had some basis left in the account, that remaining basis is passed on to you.

 Step-up rules don't apply to retirement plans. Many assets receive what is called a step-up in basis when the owner of those assets dies. In other words, the basis of the asset is deemed to be its value when the owner dies rather than what the owner originally paid for it. Because investment assets usually increase in value over time, this benefit is referred to as a step-up.

Assets in IRAs and other retirement plans are not permitted a step-up in basis. The assets in the IRA will be subject to tax at their fair market value whenever they are distributed. Death only determines who will pay the tax. The original owner pays during his lifetime; after that, the beneficiary of the plan pays the tax.

C. Income Tax on Qualified Plans and Qualified Annuities

A variety of circumstances could lead to a distribution from your retirement plan during your working years. Or you might not take money out until you actually retire. If you wait until retirement, you have many options for paying the tax on the money you receive. If you take a distribution before retirement, you will encounter a minefield of restrictions, and you might even have to pay tax penalties.

1. Options for Paying Taxes at Retirement

In general, when you receive a distribution from a qualified plan or qualified annuity, you should consider three tax options:

- You can report the distribution on your return as ordinary income.
- You can roll over the distribution into an IRA or another retirement plan, which means you can continue to delay paying taxes.
- If you qualify, you can use ten-year averaging, which is a method of computing the tax as though the distribution were spread over a ten-year period.

⚠ **Five-year averaging.** Before the year 2000, five-year averaging was also an option. That option has now been phased out.

⚠ **After-tax contributions aren't taxable.** If part of your distribution includes after-tax contributions you made to your plan, those amounts will not be taxable and should not be included when computing your income tax using any of the above methods.

a. Pay Ordinary Income Tax

Some people are tempted to choose the path of least resistance. This is true in life generally, but especially true in that part of life that requires dealing with the IRS. When taking distributions from a retirement plan, the easiest option is simply to take the money, deposit it in your regular bank account and report the amount of the distribution as ordinary income on your tax return at tax time.

Receiving large distributions. If you receive a large distribution from a retirement plan, you ordinarily would not choose to pay tax on the entire amount unless you need the money immediately and don't qualify for any special tax options. Another reason you might have to use the ordinary income tax option is if you made a procedural error when attempting to use one of the other tax options, which left you no choice but to use the ordinary income tax option.

i.   Who Is Eligible?

Anyone who receives a distribution from a retirement plan can choose to have the distribution taxed in this way.

ii.   Which Distributions Are Eligible?

All distributions you receive from a retirement plan that are attributable to pre-tax contributions or to investment returns may be taxed at ordinary income tax rates. This is true whether the distribution represents only part of your account or the entire balance.

iii.   Advantages and Disadvantages

The advantage of this tax option is that once the money comes out of the retirement plan and you pay the taxes owed, you have unrestricted use of the funds. The money that you withdraw is no longer subject to the terms of the plan.

But that peace of mind is expensive. Choosing to subject a distribution to tax at ordinary rates in the same year you receive it is usually the least advantageous option—at least from a financial perspective. If your distribution is large, it could easily push you into a higher tax bracket. It's hardly cheery to think of starting your retirement by handing the government 40% or more of your nest egg.

iv.   Pitfalls

To make matters worse, your problems might not end with the big income tax bite. You could be hit with a tax penalty. Specifically, an early distribution tax might be imposed if you take money out of your retirement plan before you reach age 59½. (See Chapter 3 for more information about the early distribution tax.)

b.   Roll Over Your Distribution

Rather than paying ordinary income tax on your entire retirement plan distribution, you might consider a more versatile and attractive strategy: rolling some or all of the distribution into an IRA or another qualified plan.

A rollover is usually accomplished by having your employer transfer your funds directly to another qualified plan or an IRA through a transaction called a direct rollover. If the funds are distributed directly to you, however, you have 60 days to deposit them into another qualified plan or an IRA. The portion that is rolled over will continue to be tax deferred and will be subject to all the rules of the new plan or IRA. Any portion that is not rolled over within 60 days will be subject to ordinary income tax.

 Rollovers into another qualified plan are unusual. This is because once a person retires, he or she probably doesn't have another plan. Distributions at retirement are usually rolled into an IRA, unless you are taking your benefits as an annuity, in which case no rollover of any kind is permitted.

i.   Who Is Eligible?

Anyone who receives a distribution from a qualified plan or qualified annuity is permitted to roll it over. It doesn't matter how old you are or how long you have been a participant in the plan.

ii.   Which Distributions Are Eligible?

Generally, all distributions and partial distributions from qualified plans and qualified annuities are eligible to be rolled over. The three most significant exceptions are:

* distributions of your after-tax contributions
* distributions that are required to be distributed to you because you have passed age 70½ (see Chapters 5-8 for information about required distributions), and
* distributions in the form of a life annuity or periodic payments that last for ten years or more.

iii.   Advantages and Disadvantages

If you don't need to use your retirement money right away, rolling it over is a big advantage. It allows you to defer paying income tax until you are ready to spend the money (or until you are required to take it out). If you take money out only when you need it, you may be able to withdraw it in small enough chunks to keep yourself in a low tax bracket. Meanwhile, whatever you don't need can be left to grow inside the new plan or IRA.

The disadvantage of rolling over the distribution is that you don't have unrestricted use of the money. As long as it's in an IRA or qualified plan, it is subject to all the rules and restrictions of the plan.

iv.   Pitfalls

If you are about to receive a distribution from a qualified plan or qualified annuity and you want to roll it over into another plan or an IRA, arrange for a direct rollover. In other words, have the funds transferred directly from your old employer's plan into the new plan or IRA. If you don't, and instead receive the funds yourself before delivering them to the new plan, the distribution will be subject to income tax withholding, which could cause you some serious problems. (See Section 5, below, for more information about withholding.) In addition to the withholding problem, you could encounter other traps.

Trap 1: 60-Day Rule. You have 60 days from the time you receive a distribution to roll it over into another plan or IRA, and the clock starts ticking when you have the distribution in hand. The IRS is devilishly unforgiving when it comes to enforcing this rule, so if you're on your way to the bank on the 60th day, don't stop to tie your shoes.

Trap 2: Changing Your Mind. Once you actually complete the rollover of your retirement plan into another plan or IRA, there is no going back.

For example, suppose you instruct the plan administrator of your employer's plan to transfer your retirement money directly into an IRA. A week after the money is deposited to your IRA, you decide that you really should have taken the distribution and elected ten-year averaging (see Section c, below). Unfortunately, you cannot undo a rollover. Once the rollover is complete, you may not pull the money out of the account and elect averaging, even if the 60 days has not yet expired.

If you do pull the money out, it will be treated as another retirement plan distribution, subject to income tax. It might even be subject to an early distribution tax. (See Chapter 3 for information about the early distribution tax.)

Trap 3: Rolling Over Ineligible Funds. Some of the money you receive from a retirement plan might not be eligible to be rolled over. You cannot roll over after-tax contributions you made to the plan, nor can you roll annuity payments or money that must be distributed to you when you are age 70½ or older.

If you accidentally roll over ineligible funds, you have a certain amount of time to correct the problem—usually until the due date of your tax return. (That's April 15th of the following year, unless you request an extension of time for filing your return. In that case, you will have until the extended deadline.) If you do not remove the funds in time, you will be subject to a penalty for each calendar year or part of a year those funds remain in the plan or IRA.

Trap 4: Plan Rules Govern. Sometimes you might find that the law permits you to take certain steps with your retirement plan, but the terms of your plan are more restrictive. In that case, the plan's rules will govern. For example, the law generally allows you to roll over qualified plans and qualified annuities into other qualified plans and qualified annuities. Some plans, however, do not permit mixing and matching. Qualified annuity plan administrators often will not accept rollovers from other qualified annuities. However, you can always roll over a qualified plan or qualified annuity distribution into an IRA.

c. Use Ten-Year Averaging to Compute Tax

It may be that you cannot afford to roll over all of your retirement distribution because you need the money. And if you do need the money, you don't want to give up a large chunk of the distribution to income taxes. Although there is no way to avoid paying taxes if you elect not to roll over the distribution, you may be able to compute the tax using a method called ten-year averaging, which can reduce your total bill.

i.   Who Is Eligible?

You are eligible to use ten-year averaging if you satisfy all of the following conditions:

- you were born before 1936
- you have not used ten-year averaging on any distribution since 1986, and
- you participated in the plan for at least five years, which means you or your employer made a contribution to your plan account in at least five separate years before the year of the distribution.

 Figuring the length of participation. If your account is transferred from one plan to another, you don't have to start the participation clock ticking all over again. The years you participated in the old plan count toward the five-year requirement.

ii. Which Distributions Are Eligible?

Even if you are eligible, you may use ten-year averaging only if your distribution also qualifies. Your distribution will qualify only if both of the following are true:

- The distribution to be averaged must be the entire amount of your qualified plan or qualified annuity. You cannot roll over part of the distribution, and you cannot have rolled over part of it in the past.

- You must receive the distribution all within one tax year, even if you receive more than one payment.

You might have two plans that the IRS treats as one for ten-year averaging. For example, money purchase pension plans and defined benefit plans must be combined and considered one plan for purposes of the ten-year averaging rules. Let's say you receive a distribution of your defined benefit plan one year and roll it over. The next year you receive a distribution of your money purchase pension plan and want to use ten-year averaging. You cannot, however, because the distributions were received in different years.

iii. How Is It Computed?

If you receive a distribution and elect to use ten-year averaging, the tax on the distribution itself is computed on IRS Form 4972 (see Appendix A) and recorded on a separate line of your tax return. You must pay that amount to the IRS even if you owe no other income taxes.

The tax is calculated as though you were a single individual (even if you are married) and as though you received the distribution in ten installments over ten years. Despite this calculation, you pay the total tax due in the year of the distribution, not over ten years. These are the steps:

Step 1: Determine the taxable amount of the distribution.

This is usually the entire amount of the distribution reduced by any after-tax contributions you made. Your employer or the administrator of the plan should provide this information.

Step 2: Determine the Minimum Distribution Allowance.

If your distribution is less than $70,000, you may exclude some of it from your income when computing the tax. The excludable portion is called your minimum distribution allowance, or MDA. To determine the MDA:

1. Reduce the taxable amount of the distribution by $20,000, but not below zero.
2. Multiply the result by 20%, or .2.
3. Subtract the result from $10,000 or from one-half of the taxable amount (the number from Step 1), whichever is less. The result is your MDA.

Step 3: Subtract your MDA from the taxable amount. (Step 1 minus Step 2).

Step 4: Divide the result by 10.

Step 5: Compute the income tax on the amount from Step 4.

You must use the 1986 tax rates for a single person. (A schedule of 1986 tax rates is in Appendix A.)

Step 6: Multiply the result by 10.

EXAMPLE: You receive a lump sum distribution of $50,000 that qualifies for ten-year averaging. You want to use the money to build your retirement dream house, so you decide to pay the tax. Here's how it is computed:

Step 1: Taxable amount = $50,000

Step 2: Since the distribution is under $70,000, you will be entitled to an MDA as follows:

$50,000 - $20,000 = $30,000
$30,000 x .2 = $6,000
$10,000 - $6,000 = $4,000 (your MDA)

Step 3: $50,000 - $4,000 = $46,000

Step 4: $46,000/10 = $4,600

Step 5: Tax on $4,600 at 1986 single rates = $597

Step 6: $597 x 10 = $5,970

Thus, you will owe $5,970 of federal income tax on your $50,000 distribution in the year you receive it. By contrast, if you simply reported the $50,000 as additional income without using the special averaging, you could owe as much as $19,800 of federal income tax on that $50,000, if you are in the top tax bracket.

iv. Advantages and Disadvantages

When should you use averaging? Although it is usually better to roll over a distribution and continue your tax deferral rather than pay a ten-year averaging tax, those guidelines go right out the window if you need the money. In such a situation, ten-year averaging could mean big tax savings.

You might also choose ten-year averaging if your distribution is small enough to be taxed at a rate lower than you are likely to see in the future. But if your distribution is large, ten-year averaging is rarely a good choice. For one thing, you give up substantial compounded growth on the money that would otherwise remain in the retirement account. But also, the tax advantages of averaging decline as the distribution increases in amount. In addition, the top tax rates in 1986 were quite a bit higher than top rates today.

> EXAMPLE: You receive a retirement plan distribution of $100,000. If you use ten-year averaging, the entire tax would be $14,470—all of it taxed at less than 15%, which is the lowest rate today. In contrast, if your distribution is $500,000 and you choose ten-year averaging, more than $150,000 would be taxed at rates higher than any current tax rate. In this case, you may be better off rolling over the $500,000 and spreading distributions out over your retirement years.

Bottom line: it's easy to be seduced by the lure of lower tax rates and ready money. But if your goal is to accumulate substantial sums for your retirement, you are usually better off rolling over your distribution and deferring the payment of tax.

v. Pitfalls

If you still think ten-year averaging is your best option, consider these traps.

Trap 1: One-Time Election. Ten-year averaging is a once-in-a-lifetime election. If you choose to use it on a distribution, you may never again use ten-year averaging on a future distribution from any plan.

Trap 2: Multiple Distributions. If you receive distributions from more than one retirement plan in a single year and want to use ten-year averaging, you must use it on all the distributions you receive that year. If you want to use ten-year averaging on only one distribution, you must arrange to receive the distribution you want to average in a separate year, if possible. This rule is different from the aggregation rule covered in Section C.1.c.ii, above. Under the aggregation rule, if two plans are of the same type, for example both profit sharing plans, they are considered one plan for ten-year averaging purposes. In that case, the distributions from both plans must be received in the same year or you may not use ten-year averaging on either distribution.

d. Use Capital Gain Rates to Compute Tax

If you were born before 1936 and you began participating in your employer's plan before 1974, you have another option available to you in addition to ten-year averaging: you may treat part of your distribution as capital gain subject to a flat 20% tax rate. The amount of your distribution that is eligible for this rate is computed by the plan administrator and is based on the number of years you participated in the plan before 1974. The administrator will report the eligible amount to you so that you can decide if you want to elect the 20% tax option. You may elect to use this special rate whether you choose to use ten-year averaging or ordinary income tax rates on the remaining portion of your distribution.

e. Special Rules for Employer Stock

Your retirement account distribution may include some shares of your employer's stock. If the total current value of the shares of stock purchased in your plan account is greater than the total basis, the difference is called the net unrealized appreciation.

You have several options for paying income taxes on the employer stock that is part of a retirement plan distribution:

- If you elect ten-year averaging, you can exclude the net unrealized appreciation when computing the tax. If you do this, however, when you later sell the stock you will have to include as income the entire net unrealized appreciation and pay taxes using long-term capital gain rates.
- You can include the net unrealized appreciation when calculating your tax using ten-year averaging. You might do this if your tax rate using averaging is lower than the long-term capital gain rate.
- You can pay ordinary income tax (as opposed to using ten-year averaging) on all but the net unrealized appreciation. You would pay ordinary tax, for example, if you did not qualify for ten-year averaging but did not want to roll over all of your employer stock into an IRA. Using this strategy, you would pay capital gains tax on the net unrealized appreciation only when you sell the stock.
- You can roll over your entire distribution, including employer stock, into an IRA. If you do so, the net unrealized appreciation in the stock becomes irrelevant because all future distributions from the IRA will be taxed as ordinary income, not as capital gain.

Paying taxes to preserve capital gains rates. It might be to your advantage *not* to roll over all of your employer stock into an IRA. This might be true if your net unrealized appreciation is large and you would like it to be taxed at low capital gains rates when you sell your employer stock. Remember, once the stock is rolled over into an IRA, all future distributions from the IRA will be taxed at ordinary rates—not capital gains rates.

 No step-up for net unrealized appreciation. Your inclination may be to exclude the net unrealized appreciation from your income tax and keep the stock, passing it on to your heirs when you die. You might do this if you think your heirs will obtain a step-up in the basis of the stock when you die. The step-up would allow them to avoid all tax on the net unrealized appreciation. (See Section B.5, above, for an explanation of a step-up in basis.) But this strategy won't work. The Tax Code specifically denies any step-up in basis for net unrealized appreciation in employer stock.

2. Options for Paying Taxes Before Retirement

It is quite possible that you will receive a distribution from your retirement plan before you retire. Here are some common situations in which that might occur:

- you change jobs
- your company terminates its retirement plan, or
- you are self-employed and terminate your own plan.

The retirement plan rules were written to discourage distributions before retirement. For this reason, you'll find your options for paying taxes somewhat limited if you receive a retirement plan distribution while the government thinks you are too young to be retired.

a. Pay Ordinary Income Tax

If you do not need the distribution you receive from your retirement plan for living expenses, you will almost certainly want to do something with it other than spend it or put it in a regular bank account. If you don't, you will have to report the distribution on your tax return and pay ordinary income tax on it. Furthermore, you might have to pay penalties for withdrawing the money early.

b. Roll Over Your Distribution

If you have not yet reached age 59½ and you receive a distribution from a qualified plan or qualified annuity, you can roll over the distribution into an IRA or another retirement plan to avoid paying an early distribution penalty. One caveat: you cannot roll over any after-tax contributions you made to the plan.

> EXAMPLE 1: You quit your job and have gone to work for a company that, like your previous employer, has a qualified retirement plan. You want to deposit the distribution you receive from your old employer into the plan of your new employer rather than into an IRA. You may do so, as long as both plans are qualified plans and the plans themselves permit such a rollover.

> EXAMPLE 2: You were laid off and haven't yet found a new job. Your former employer needs to know what you want done with your qualified plan distribution. To avoid paying taxes on the money this year, you decide to roll it over into a new IRA. Then, if you don't make any additional contributions to the new IRA, it will qualify as a conduit IRA and you can roll it into your new employer's plan, provided there is a plan and it permits the rollover.

If you roll over the distribution into an IRA to which you have been making annual contributions, or you make additional contributions after the rollover, the IRA will not qualify as a conduit IRA and cannot be rolled into a new employer's plan. You will have deferred the taxes, however.

Arrange a direct rollover. If you receive a distribution from a qualified plan, intending to roll it over into another plan or into an IRA, arrange to have the administrator of your old employer's plan transfer the funds directly into the new plan or IRA instead of sending the money to you. Otherwise, the administrator of the old plan may be required to withhold money to cover taxes you might owe. (See Section 5, below, for more information about withholding.)

c. Use Ten-Year Averaging to Compute Tax

As long as you satisfy the requirements outlined in Section C.1.c, above, then averaging is an option for you.

3. Options for Paying Taxes on Inherited Plans

If you are the beneficiary, rather than the owner, of a qualified plan and you receive a distribution as a result of the owner's death, the rules for paying income taxes are a little different from the general rules described in Section C.1.

a. Pay Ordinary Income Tax

If the plan assets are distributed outright to you and you simply take the money and put it into your regular bank account, then you will have to report the distribution as income on your tax return and pay tax on it, as you might expect. You may be able to reduce the total amount of the tax or gain some breathing room in paying the tax, however, by taking the distribution in installments over a number of years.

There is a bit of good news, too. If you receive a distribution from a plan you inherited, you will not have to pay an early distribution tax, even if you are under age 59½. The penalty is waived for inherited plans. (See Chapter 3 for information about the early distribution tax.)

b. Roll Over Your Distribution

If you inherit a qualified plan or qualified annuity, you cannot roll over the distribution into an IRA or another qualified plan, unless you were the spouse of the deceased owner. If you were not the spouse, the plan must remain in the name of the original (now deceased) owner until the assets are actually distributed from the plan.

If you were the spouse of the original owner, you can roll over the distribution into an IRA in your name, but you cannot roll it over directly into another qualified plan.

c. Use Ten-Year Averaging to Compute Tax

If you inherit a qualified plan or qualified annuity, you can use ten-year averaging provided the distribution is a qualified distribution as described in Section C.1.c, above, and the original owner had satisfied all the eligibility requirements (except the five-year participation requirement) at the time of death.

Meeting the eligibility requirements. It is not you, the person who inherited the plan, who must meet the eligibility requirements; it is the original owner. It doesn't matter how old you are, nor would it matter if you had used averaging on one of your own distributions. As long as the original owner would have qualified for averaging, you qualify.

4. Options for Paying Taxes on Qualified Plans Received at Divorce

Congress has gone to great lengths to protect your qualified plan assets. The cornerstone of that protection is a provision known as the "anti-alienation" rule, which attempts to ensure that you cannot be forced to give away your qualified plan assets.

Divorce presents a unique problem, however. What if you want to use your retirement plan as part of a property settlement? Can you give away some or all of your plan assets in that situation? And if you can, who should be responsible for the taxes and penalties (if any) on the part you give away?

Congress addressed these concerns by giving divorcing couples a vehicle for protecting plan assets and minimizing tax penalties. It's called a Qualified Domestic Relations Order or QDRO (pronounced "Quadro"). The QDRO rules spell out the circumstances under which your qualified plan benefits can go to someone else—an "alternate payee"—such as your soon-to-be ex-spouse.

A QDRO is a judgment, decree or order (including a court-approved property settlement agreement) that satisfies all of the following:

- It relates to child support, alimony or the marital property rights of a spouse, a former spouse, a dependent child or some other dependent of the qualified plan participant.
- It gives an alternate payee, such as a spouse, former spouse, dependent child or other dependent, the right to receive all or a portion of the participant's plan benefits.
- It does not alter the form or the amount of the benefit originally intended for the participant even though the benefit might now go to an alternate payee. For example, the QDRO cannot require the plan to pay a larger annuity to the alternate payee than it would have paid to the participant.
- It contains certain language. Specifically:
  - The alternate payee must be referred to as "the alternate payee" in the QDRO.
  - The QDRO must identify the plan, as well as the amount of each payment and the number of payments to be made.
  - The QDRO must contain the name and address of both the participant and the alternate payee.

If you are in the process of divorcing and you and your spouse agree that you will receive an interest in your spouse's qualified plan, you may be able to preserve some of the tax benefits of the plan for yourself. But this is possible only if there is a QDRO in place. If you and your spouse write up your agreement but it does not meet the above four requirements and is not court-approved, then your agreement is not a QDRO. In such a situation, distributions to a spouse, former spouse or child could be subject to penalties.

In most cases, QDRO payments are made to a spouse or former spouse as alimony or as part of a property settlement. Payments might also be used for child support. If you receive a qualified plan distribution under a QDRO, the rules for how it is taxed and what you can do with it will depend upon your relationship to the original owner or plan participant.

a. Options for a Non-Spouse Alternate Payee

If the recipient of a QDRO payment is not the spouse or former spouse of the plan participant, then the plan participant must report all distributions from the qualified plan as income on the participant's own tax return and pay taxes on them. If the distribution qualifies for special tax treatment, however, the plan participant can opt for the special rules. For example, the plan participant may use ten-year averaging on a distribution to figure the tax liability, provided the participant is eligible. If you are the recipient, you would pay no taxes when you receive the distribution.

Although the tax burden falls heavily on the plan participant, a couple of special rules provide a little tax relief:

- The participant will not have to pay an early distribution tax on any QDRO distribution paid to a non-spouse recipient, no matter how old the participant is or how old the recipient is. (See Chapter 3 for more information about the early distribution tax.)
- If the participant separates the recipient's share of the plan, perhaps by rolling it over into a new IRA, the participant can use ten-year averaging on the remaining portion—provided the remaining portion would have qualified for averaging if it had been the participant's entire plan balance. The participant may not treat the recipient's portion alone as a distribution eligible for averaging, however, unless that portion constitutes the participant's entire plan balance.

b. Options for a Spouse or Former Spouse Alternate Payee

If you are a spouse or former spouse receiving a distribution under a QDRO, you are treated in almost every respect as though you are the plan participant. Specifically:

- You may roll over some or all of the distribution to your own IRA or qualified plan.

- You must pay tax on the distribution if you do not roll it over.
- The distribution is subject to mandatory withholding rules as though you were the plan participant. (See Section 5, below.)

As you might expect, there are exceptions to the general rule that you are to be treated as though you were the plan participant:

- Although you may elect ten-year averaging on the distribution you receive, your eligibility for averaging depends on the participant's eligibility. In other words, if the participant was born before 1936, has not made an averaging election since 1986 and has participated in the plan for at least five years, then you may elect ten-year averaging. If the plan participant does not qualify, neither do you.
- Although you may elect averaging, you are not permitted to use the special capital gain rules for pre-1974 accumulations (see Section C.1.d, above), nor may you exclude from income the net unrealized appreciation in employer stock. (See Section C.1.e, above.)
- Any distribution you keep in a regular account instead of rolling it over will not be subject to an early distribution tax, regardless of your age or the participant's age. (See Chapter 3 for information about early distributions.)

Once you do roll over the distribution into an IRA or a qualified plan in your name, the assets become yours in every respect, as though they never belonged to the original participant.

5. Withholding Money to Pay Taxes

Congress, in its increasingly creative efforts to improve the Treasury's cash flow, passed a mandatory withholding law in 1993 for qualified plans. The law requires your plan administrator to keep 20% of all qualified plan distributions to pay federal income tax before distributing the remainder to you.

> EXAMPLE: You leave your job and plan to travel around the world for six months. Your employer distributes your retirement plan to you. The total value of your account is $10,000. The plan administrator gives you $8,000 and sends the rest to the government to pay the taxes you will owe on the distribution.

a. Exceptions to Mandatory Withholding

There are some exceptions to the mandatory withholding law.

- Amounts that are transferred directly from the trustee of your retirement plan to the trustee of another plan or to the custodian of your IRA are not subject to the withholding. This is called a direct rollover, and is the most appropriate action to take if your intention is to roll over your distribution.

⚠️ **Standard rollovers are not exempt from the mandatory withholding rule.** If you take a distribution of your retirement plan—for example, you receive a check payable to you—intending to roll it over into an IRA, your employer must withhold 20% for taxes. The direct rollover exception only works if the money is delivered directly from your retirement plan trustee to the trustee of another plan or to the custodian of your IRA. (See Section c.i., below, for more information about direct rollovers.)

- Any after-tax contributions you made to the plan are not subject to with-holding when they are distributed to you.
- If you elect to receive your distribu-tion in roughly equal periodic pay-ments over ten or more years, those payments will not be subject to mandatory withholding.
- Small distributions of less than $200 are not subject to mandatory with-holding.

b. Pitfalls of Mandatory Withholding

Unless you use a direct rollover, the withholding law can pose some serious problems for you, and maybe even take a permanent bite out of your retirement nest egg.

i. Reducing Your Retirement Accumulation

If it is your intention to roll over your entire retirement plan distribution into an IRA or another qualified plan and continue the tax deferral, and you don't use a direct rollover, mandatory withholding could put a crimp in those plans. Because the with-holding is usually paid out of the distribu-tion, you will have a smaller amount to roll over.

EXAMPLE: You have just retired. You accumulated $200,000 in your employer's retirement plan. You plan to roll over your distribution into an IRA. However, when you receive the check from your employer, it is only $160,000. Because of the mandatory withholding rules, your employer was required to send 20% or $40,000 to the IRS to cover any income taxes you might owe on the distribution, even if it was always your intention to roll over the entire amount. So now you only have $160,000 in your retirement nest egg. (You may be able to replace the amount withheld, however. See Section c.ii, below.)

ii. Owing Penalties and Taxes

If your distribution was subject to withholding, you may claim a refund of the tax withheld for the portion that was rolled over. However, the portion of the distribution that was sent to the government for taxes was part of your distribution, too, and it wasn't rolled over, so it will be subject to income tax. Worse, if you are not yet 59½, you might have to pay an early distribution tax on the portion withheld for taxes, even though the withholding was mandatory. (See Chapter 3 for more information about the early distribution tax.)

EXAMPLE: You decide to retire in November of the year you turn 61. You have accumulated $300,000 in your employer's retirement plan. When you receive your distribution, the amount is only $240,000 because your employer was required to send 20% or $60,000 to the IRS for taxes. When you file your next tax return, you will report the $60,000 of withholding as tax you have already paid along with any other amounts withheld from your regular paychecks during the year.

In addition, you must report $60,000 of the retirement plan distribution as income. The $240,000 that was rolled over is not subject to tax, but the $60,000 that was sent to the IRS to pay taxes is. Even though the withholding was mandatory, it is still treated as a taxable distribution. In essence you took money out of your retirement account to pay your taxes.

On the plus side, you should be entitled to a big tax refund when you file your tax return, since you paid $60,000 (through withholding) for taxes due on your distribution, but the taxable portion itself was only $60,000. The remaining $240,000 was rolled over.

iii. Selling Assets to Pay Taxes

What happens if there's not enough cash in your account to cover the required withholding? The news is not good. The plan administrator must withhold taxes even if it means selling property in the account to generate enough cash. If you hold stock you don't want to sell, you might be out of luck—unless one of these exceptions applies:

- The plan permits you to come up with the money for withholding from sources outside the plan. This requires that you have a stash of cash.
- If your retirement assets consist solely of cash and employer securities (as opposed to other securities or property) and you don't have enough cash to cover the 20% mandatory withholding, the administrator will withhold only the cash. In other words, you are not required to liquidate employer securities in order to pay the withholding.

EXAMPLE: On the day you retire from Flush Corp., your retirement plan assets consist of $5,000 in cash and 3000 shares of Flush Corp. stock valued at $50 per share or $150,000. The total value of your retirement plan is $155,000, which means that the mandatory withholding is $31,000 (20% x 155,000). Because you do not have $31,000 in cash and you are not required to liquidate employer stock, your mandatory withholding is limited to the amount of cash in your retirement account, which is $5,000.

iv. Repaying Loans From the Plan

If you borrow money from your plan and don't pay it all back by the time you are to receive your distribution, the unpaid loan amount counts as part of your distribution and is subject to both income tax and mandatory withholding. Again, you might need to liquidate assets (except employer securities) in order to cover the withholding.

EXAMPLE: When you retire, you will have $10,000 of cash in your retirement plan and 5000 mutual fund shares valued at $20 per share. The total value of your account is $110,000. However, you also borrowed money from the plan last year and still owe $20,000 on that loan. The plan will report a distribution of $130,000 to the IRS ($10,000 in cash plus $100,000 in mutual fund shares plus the outstanding loan balance of $20,000). The mandatory 20% withholding is based on the full $130,000, and therefore is $26,000. Because you have only $10,000 in cash, the plan must sell 800 of your mutual fund shares to come up with enough cash to cover the withholding. Thus, although a distribution of $130,000 is reported to the IRS, the amount you actually receive will be only $84,000, which is $130,000 reduced by the loan amount and reduced further by the 20% withholding ($130,000 - $20,000 - $26,000 = $84,000).

c. Avoiding or Correcting Mandatory Withholding

Happily, you can avoid the withholding pitfalls altogether. If you don't and instead find yourself in a quagmire, you still might be able to dig yourself out.

i. Direct Rollover

You can avoid mandatory withholding simply by requesting that the plan administrator transfer your entire distribution directly into another qualified plan or an IRA. If you never have access to the funds during the transfer, the administrator is not required to withhold any money. This solution is called a "direct rollover." The rule applies even if your distribution check is sent to you personally, as long as it is payable to the trustee or custodian of the new plan, and not to you.

It is possible to elect a direct rollover for part of your distribution, saving you at least some of the mandatory withholding. Only the portion paid directly to you will be subject to mandatory withholding.

ii. Replace the Withholding Amount

If you fail to request a direct rollover and instead receive a distribution check reduced by the 20% withholding amount, you may be able to make yourself whole. If you can come up with the cash to cover the amount withheld, you can deposit it into the new plan or IRA as though you received it as part of your distribution. Then at tax time, you can claim a refund of the entire withholding amount. You avoid income taxes and penalties, and manage to roll over every dollar of the distribution.

Although this approach works, you must have adequate cash on hand to take advantage of it. And of course, the government has free use of your money until you file your next tax return.

You can use a similar strategy if you have an outstanding loan from your plan. In other words, you can use cash you have outside the plan to roll over the amount of the loan into the new plan.

d. Notification of Mandatory Withholding

Are you worried that if you miss the direct rollover option you'll feel like a fool caught in a radar trap by a camouflaged cop? Take heart: it's not as easy to miss as you might think. Not only must the plan administrator give you the option to elect a direct rollover, but the administrator must notify you of the option at least 30 days (and no more than 90 days, lest you forget) before the distribution is to take place. Failure to give notice will cost the administrator $100 per incidence, up to $50,000 per year. However, once the administrator provides notice, he has satisfied his obligation. The administrator is not required to make sure you read the notice.

6. Loans From Qualified Plans

The law generally permits employees to borrow money from their qualified plans, although some plans do not allow it. Most do, however, because employees consider the ability to borrow from their retirement plan an important benefit. But the borrowing rules are stringent.

a. Loans From Employer's Qualified Plan

A loan from a qualified plan is considered a taxable distribution unless it satisfies certain requirements:

- The loan must be repaid at a reasonable rate of interest with well-defined repayment terms.
- The loan amount cannot exceed $50,000.
- The loan amount cannot exceed the greater of $10,000 or 50% of your vested account balance. (The vested amount is the portion you may take with you when you leave the company.) In other words, the loan is limited to 50% of your vested balance unless your account is under $20,000. Then you may borrow up to $10,000 as long as you have that much in your account and the plan allows it.

EXAMPLE: You have a vested account balance of $70,000 in your employer's retirement plan. You would like to borrow as much as you can from the plan. The loan may not exceed $50,000. But it also may not exceed 50% of your vested account balance, which is $35,000 (50% x $70,000). Thus the maximum you may borrow from the plan is $35,000.

- If you have more than one outstanding loan, the total of all loans from the plan cannot exceed $50,000 reduced by the difference between the highest loan balance for the previous 12 months and the current balance.

EXAMPLE: On January 15, your vested benefit in your employer's retirement plan is $150,000. You borrow $25,000 from the plan. On December of the same year, you realize that you need to borrow some additional money to get through the holiday season. Although you had begun to pay back the first loan, you still owe $20,000. To compute the amount you may borrow now, you begin with the $50,000 limit and reduce it by the amount of money you still owe to the plan. That reduces your limit to $30,000 ($50,000 - $20,000). The $30,000 must be reduced further by the difference between the highest outstanding balance in the last 12 months (which was $25,000) and the current outstanding balance (which is $20,000). That difference is $5,000. Thus the $30,000 is further reduced to $25,000, which is the maximum you may now borrow from the plan.

- The loan must be repaid within five years, using a level amortization schedule (like a home mortgage) with payments to be made at least quarterly. There is an exception to the five-year repayment rule if the loan is used to purchase (but not improve) a principal residence. In that case, you may simply repay the loan in a reasonable amount of time. (The Tax Code does not define "reasonable," however, the IRS has been known to approve loans outstanding for as long as 30 years when they are used to make mortgage payments.)

As long as the above five requirements are met, the amount of the loan will not be considered a taxable distribution to you, either at the time it is made or during the repayment period.

⚠ You may owe taxes on an outstanding loan. If you haven't repaid your loan by the time your share of the plan assets is distributed to you, the loan amount will be subject to income tax. (See Section 5.b.iv, above.)

b. Loans From Self-Employed Plan

The loan rules were enacted to accommodate employees, not owners or self-employed individuals. Consequently, if you have a Keogh plan and own more than 10% of your business, you may not borrow from your plan. If you do, the loan is considered a prohibited transaction and is subject to a 15% penalty on the loan principal for each year any amount remains unpaid. If you own less than 10% of the business, you will be treated just like any other employee even if you're the boss.

Furthermore, by borrowing from the plan, you run the risk of disqualifying the entire plan. If the IRS disqualifies the plan, all of the assets must be distributed and will be subject to income tax and perhaps penalties as well.

You are required to report any improper Keogh plan loan on IRS Form 5330. (A copy is in Appendix A.) You must file the form and pay the prohibited transaction penalty within seven months of the end of the year. If you do not repay the loan, the penalty increases to 100%.

💡 Rules for S-Corporations. Similar rules apply if your business is in the form of an S-Corporation and you own more than 5% of the stock.

7. Hardship Distributions From Qualified Plans

A special relief provision in the Tax Code allows participants in 401(k) plans and other profit sharing plans—but no other type of qualified plan—to withdraw money in the event of hardship. It is not sufficient that the law permits such withdrawals; the plan itself must specifically allow them as well.

The Tax Code defines hardship withdrawal to be a distribution because of "immediate and heavy financial need." The plan must establish objective and nondiscriminatory ways of determining whether such a need exists and measuring the amount of money necessary to satisfy that need.

The IRS provides a list of expenses that qualify as hardship withdrawals. That means that if your expenses fall into one of the listed categories and your plan allows hardship withdrawals, your distribution will generally qualify as a hardship withdrawal. The IRS expenditures are as follows:

- medical expenses for you, your spouse or your dependents
- expenses to purchase a principal residence (but not money to make mortgage payments)
- expenses to pay post-secondary education for a 12-month period, including tuition, room and board, and

- expenses to stave off eviction from your principal residence or to forestall a foreclosure.

Expenses can qualify for hardship withdrawals even if they don't fall into one of the above categories. In that case, the plan document must provide some method of determining whether an expense constitutes immediate and heavy financial need. You must also provide a statement to the IRS declaring that you have exhausted other available resources. For example, if you have a vacation home, you would be required to sell it and use the proceeds before you would qualify to take money out of your plan.

Now the coup de grace. Suppose you jump through all the hoops and are eligible for a hardship withdrawal. What you gain is access to your funds without disqualifying the plan. But a hardship withdrawal is still subject to income tax. And you will also owe a 10% early distribution penalty if you are under age 59½, unless the withdrawal qualifies for one of the exceptions described in Chapter 3.

⚠ Hardship distributions are not eligible to be rolled over into an IRA or another qualified plan. So if you take a distribution from your 401(k) plan under its hardship provisions, and then you decide you don't need the money after all, you are stuck. You cannot roll it into an IRA, nor can you put it back into the plan.

D. Special Income Tax Rules for Tax-Deferred Annuities

Although tax-deferred annuities, or TDAs, closely track the taxation rules for qualified plans, there are some important differences. (See Chapter 1, Section C.2, for more information about TDAs.)

1. Pay Ordinary Income Tax

In general, distributions from TDAs will be taxed along with the rest of your income at normal tax rates unless you roll over the distribution. But you may not exclude from your income the net unrealized appreciation in employer stock, as you can with a qualified plan. (See Section C.1.e, above.)

2. Roll Over Your Distribution

As with qualified plan distributions, you may roll over any portion of a distribution you receive from a TDA.

You may also use an IRA as a conduit if you want to roll a TDA distribution into another plan, but it must be another TDA. Because TDAs are not eligible for averaging (see Section 3, below), the IRS prohibits you from mixing TDAs with qualified plans that are eligible for special tax treatment. Once the plan assets are merged, it would be difficult for the IRS to keep track of which assets were eligible for special treatment and which were not.

If you roll a TDA into a conduit IRA and then decide to withdraw some assets from the IRA (whether to deposit those assets into another TDA or simply to spend), you must empty out the entire conduit IRA. The assets don't all have to go to the same place, however. For example, you could roll half into another TDA and keep half to spend.

3. Averaging and Capital Gain Treatment Not Allowed

Ten-year averaging is not permitted for distributions from TDAs, nor is capital gain treatment for pre-1974 accumulations. (See Sections C.1.c and C.1.d, above.) Distributions from TDAs must be rolled over or they will be subject to ordinary income tax at the tax rates in effect in the year of distribution.

4. Special Rules at Divorce or Separation

The QDRO rules (see Section C.4, above) apply to TDAs just as they do to qualified plans, except that the alternate payee is not permitted to use ten-year averaging or the special capital gain treatment.

5. Hardship Distributions

Hardship distributions from TDAs are permitted and are subject to the same rules as hardship distributions from 401(k) plans. (See Section C.7, above.)

E. Special Income Tax Rules for IRAs

Unlike TDAs, which mimic qualified plans in most respects, IRAs are quite different, and in many ways more restrictive.

Roth IRAs are not standard IRAs. If you have a Roth IRA, the following rules may not apply. See Chapter 9 for a detailed description of Roth IRAs and the taxes, penalties and distribution rules that apply to them.

1. Pay Ordinary Income Tax

All distributions from IRAs are subject to ordinary income tax unless you have made nondeductible contributions to the IRA over the years. In that case, a portion of each distribution will be tax free. (See Section B.2, above, for information about computing the tax-free portion.) The fair market value of the taxable portion is simply included with your income and taxed at your normal rates. You may not use capital gain rates, nor may you claim losses.

2. Roll Over Your Distribution

You may roll over an IRA or part of an IRA into a different IRA or even back into the same IRA, but you must follow two important rules:

- If you take a distribution with the intention of rolling it into a different IRA, you have 60 days from the time you receive the distribution to deposit it into the new IRA. If you miss the deadline, you will owe income tax and perhaps penalties, such as an early distribution tax. (See Chapter 3.)

If you need a short-term loan. It is quite acceptable to take money from your IRA as long as you deposit it into another IRA, or back into the same IRA, within 60 days. Just be careful to redeposit the precise amount of cash you distributed in the first place. Don't buy stock with the distributed funds and then try to deposit the stock into the IRA in lieu of the cash. If cash came out, cash must go back in.

- You are permitted only one rollover per year from each IRA that you own. For example, if your IRA #1 has $50,000 in it and you decide to roll over $20,000 to your IRA #2, you may not roll over any other funds from IRA #1 for 12 months. (Note that the restriction is for a full 12 months, not just a calendar year.)

The same funds can only be rolled over once in a 12-month period. For example, if you roll over $10,000 from one of your IRAs into a new IRA, you may not later roll over that same $10,000 into yet another IRA until 12 months have passed.

 The one-rollover-per-year rule applies only to rollovers. This rule does not apply to transfers that go directly from one IRA custodian to another. For example, if you want to roll funds from IRA #1 to IRA #2, you could simply ask the custodian of IRA #1 to send you a check. When you receive it, you deliver it to the custodian of IRA #2. That is considered a rollover. But if you instruct the custodian of IRA #1 to transfer funds directly to the custodian of IRA #2, so that you never personally receive the funds, that is considered a transfer. The IRS is more lenient with transfers, because you don't have access to the funds and presumably can't do anything improper. The IRS allows you to make as many transfers as you like during the year.

3. Averaging and Capital Gain Treatment Not Allowed

Neither ten-year averaging nor capital gain treatment is permitted on distributions from an IRA.

4. Special Rules at Divorce or Separation

The QDRO rules for qualified plans (described in Section C.4, above) do not apply to IRAs. It is still possible to give a spouse or former spouse an IRA or a portion of an IRA, however, as part of a marital property settlement without subjecting the distribution to current income tax or penalties. To do so, you must have a valid divorce decree, a written instrument incident to divorce, a written agreement incident to a legal separation or a maintenance or alimony decree.

With one of those documents in place, the IRA may be transferred in whole or in part to a spouse or former spouse through one of the following methods:

- The custodian of the participant's IRA may transfer the IRA directly to the trustee of the spouse or former spouse's IRA.
- The participant may direct the custodian to change the title of the IRA to an IRA in the spouse's or former spouse's name.
- The original participant or owner may roll over the IRA into an IRA in the name of the spouse or former spouse.

Under no circumstances, however, should the spouse or former spouse initiate the transfer of the participant's IRA or take possession of the funds before they are deposited into an IRA in the spouse's name. Only the participant may direct the transfer or rollover. Once the funds are in an IRA in the name of the spouse or former spouse, the IRA is treated in every respect as though the spouse or former spouse were the original owner. When assets are later distributed they will be subject to ordinary income tax and perhaps penalties, for which the spouse or former spouse will be liable.

You'll still owe the early distribution tax. Although there is an exception to the early distribution tax for distributions to an alternate payee under a QDRO, that exception does not apply to IRAs. (See Chapter 3.)

5. Mandatory Withholding Doesn't Apply

Distributions from IRAs are not subject to the mandatory withholding rules that apply to distributions from qualified plans. (See Section C.5, above.)

6. Loans Not Allowed

You are not permitted to borrow from an IRA. There are no exceptions. If you do, the consequences are disastrous. If you borrow any amount at all, the entire IRA is disqualified and all assets deemed distributed. The distribution will be subject to income taxes and perhaps other penalties as well, such as the early distribution tax.

7. Hardship Distributions Not Allowed

There is no such thing as a hardship distribution from an IRA—any type of IRA. That's because hardship distributions are not necessary. Unlike a qualified plan, which restricts your access to funds, you can take money out of your IRA any time you want. Of course, you will have to pay income tax and, if you are under age 59½, you'll also have to pay an early distribution tax. But you always have access to the money.

F. How Penalties Can Guide Planning

In this chapter and the previous one, we have defined the most common types of retirement plans, highlighted their differences and discussed the income tax consequences of distributions. In the remaining chapters, we discuss distribution rules that apply across the board—to qualified plans, qualified annuities, TDAs and IRAs. Those rules come with punishing penalties for violations. The penalties are in the form of an additional tax, but are usually avoidable if you understand the rules.

The following two penalty taxes will drive many of the decisions you make about your retirement plan or IRA.

Early Distribution Penalty

You will be hit with an early distribution tax if you take a retirement plan distribution too early—usually before age 59½. This penalty is discussed in depth in Chapters 3 and 4.

Delayed Distribution Penalty

Once you reach a certain age, usually 70½, you will be required to take at least a minimum amount from your retirement plan each year. If you don't, you will be subject to a huge penalty—50% of the shortfall. Similar rules apply after you inherit a retirement plan. These required distributions are discussed in Chapters 5-8.

Historical Note

Before the Taxpayer Relief Act of 1997, two additional penalties threatened individuals who had accumulated large amounts in their IRAs or qualified plans. One tax was called the excess distributions tax and the other the excess retirement accumulation tax. Although the penalties were likely to hit only wealthier taxpayers, they were particularly onerous because they were assessed simply for accumulating large retirement accounts—not for failing to comply with the rules. For this reason, the penalties were dubbed the success tax.

Excess Distributions Tax

Prior law set a limit on how much you could withdraw from your retirement plan or IRA in any one year. In 1996, that amount was $160,000. If you withdrew more, you had to pay a penalty of 15% of the excess.

At first, the law didn't seem so terrible. It was thought that most people should be able to muster the resolve to keep distributions below $160,000. Only later did it become apparent that some individuals would be forced into a penalty situation when it came time for them to take required distributions at age 70½. (See Chapter 5 for information about required distributions.) Some retirees had such large accumulations that the amount they were required to withdraw at age 70½ or later exceeded the $160,000 excess distribution threshold.

Excess Accumulation

But the success tax was not just a lifetime tax. If you had the audacity to die with too much money in your retirement plan, your estate was subject to a 15% tax on the excess. The amount considered "too much" was computed by means of a convoluted formula. The only way to avoid this additional death tax was to pull money out of the account before your death, reducing the retirement account below the penalty tax threshold. But then you had to pay the income tax and lose all future tax deferral.

Purpose of the Success Taxes

The existence of these taxes was entirely consistent with the professed goals of Congress: to encourage individuals to use their retirement assets during their lifetimes, to limit tax deferral so that Congress could collect the tax and to discourage the use of retirement plans for transferring wealth. The effect of these additional taxes was to reduce or eliminate the advantage that deferral provides. Some people did indeed respond by pulling money out of their accounts to avoid the tax at death. But most people found that it still paid to continue the deferral as long as possible, even though the tax would eat away at that benefit.

Repeal of the Success Taxes

The 1997 tax law repealed both the excess distributions and excess accumulation taxes

Historical Note (continued)

retroactively to December 31, 1996. Some affected individuals were elated by the repeal and the prospect of saving thousands of dollars in lifetime taxes and perhaps even more in death taxes. But those who pulled money out of their retirement plans to avoid the success tax were undoubtedly piqued by the repeal, having given up years of additional tax deferral.

What long-term effect will the repeal have? In general, plan participants are less likely to tap into their retirement plans except to the extent necessary to satisfy the required distribution rules. The tax deferral is just too good to pass up—especially for those individuals in the highest income tax brackets. It is now easier than it has been for a long time to use retirement plans to pass wealth to future generations.

Permissible Rollovers		
Original Plan	**Conduit (Optional)**	**New Plan**
Qualified Plan—401(a)	IRA	Qualified Plan—401(a) Qualified Annuity Plan—403(a)*
Qualified Annuity Plan—403(a)	IRA	Qualified Plan—401(a) Qualified Annuity Plan—403(a)*
Tax Deferred Annuity—403(b)	IRA	Tax Deferred Annuity—403(b)
Qualified Plan—401(a)	SEP	Qualified Plan—401(a), SEP
SEP		SEP, Traditional IRA
SIMPLE IRA		SIMPLE IRA (or regular IRA after two years)
Traditional IRA		Traditional IRA (or Roth IRA if certain requirements are satisfied)
Roth IRA		Roth IRA

*403(a) plans often don't permit rollovers to or from any other type of qualified plan even though the law itself permits it.

Key Tax Code Sections

§ 401(a)(31)

Direct Rollover

§ 402

Rollovers; Ten-Year Averaging

§ 414(p)

Qualified Domestic Relations Orders
(QDROs)

§ 3405

Qualified Plan Withholding Rules

§ 4975

Prohibited Transactions

Chapter 3

Taxes on Early Distributions

Who Should Read Chapter 3

➡ Read this chapter if you are younger than 59½ and want to withdraw money from your retirement plan or IRA. If you are older than 59½, this chapter does not apply to you.

*I*f you receive a distribution from a qualified plan, qualified annuity, tax-deferred annuity or IRA (see Chapter 1 for a description of these retirement plans), not only must you report the money as income on your tax return and pay income tax on it, but you must also pay a 10% early distribution tax, unless you are older than 59½ or another exception applies.

That extra 10% may be called a tax, but it looks and feels like a penalty. In fact, the early distribution tax is the cornerstone of the government's campaign to encourage us to save for retirement—or more accurately, to discourage us from plundering our savings before our golden years.

The 10% tax on early distributions is applied to the taxable portion of your distribution. So if you receive a distribution that includes after-tax contributions you made to your retirement plan over the years, the after-tax portion will not be subject to the early distribution tax no matter when you take it. Similarly, if you receive a distribution of employer stock and elect to exclude the net unrealized appreciation from your taxable income, the excluded amount will not be subject to the early distribution tax. (See Chapter 2, Section C.1, for more information about employer stock and net unrealized appreciation.)

EXAMPLE: You retire at age 51 and receive a distribution of $80,000 from your retirement plan. You plan to use the money to buy a vacation home in the mountains. The distribution includes $15,000 of after-tax contributions that you put into the plan over the years. The remaining $65,000 consists of employer contributions and investment returns. At tax time, you will owe regular income tax on the $65,000. You will also owe an early distribution tax of $6,500 (65,000 x 10%).

A. Exceptions to the Tax

Remember, you must pay the early distribution tax unless you qualify for an exception. In other words, you are guilty until proven innocent. Fortunately, there are many chances to prove your innocence—that is, there are many exceptions.

1. Age 59½

The most commonly used exception to the early distribution tax is the age 59½ exception. Any amount you take from your retirement plan on or after the day you

Helpful Terms

Adjusted Gross Income (AGI). Total taxable income reduced by certain expenses such as qualified plan or IRA contributions or alimony payments. Note: Adjusted gross income does not take into account any itemized deductions (see definition below).

After-Tax Contribution. A contribution to a retirement plan or IRA for which no deduction was taken on an income tax return.

Ancestor. A person from whom an individual is descended. For example, an individual's parents, grandparents and great grandparents are among his or her ancestors.

Distribution. A payout of property (such as shares of stock) or cash from a retirement plan or IRA to the participant or a beneficiary.

Itemized Deductions. Expenses, such as medical payments, mortgage interest and charitable contributions, that may be used to reduce AGI to arrive at the total amount of income subject to tax.

Principal Residence. The home in which an individual lives most of the time. ("Most" is not defined in the Tax Code. It is established by your actions.)

Separation From Service. Termination of employment.

Standard Deduction. A fixed dollar amount that may be used instead of itemized deductions to reduce AGI before computing tax liability.

---

turn 59½ escapes the tax. But as simple as it sounds, you can still flub it—so be careful. Interpret the rule literally. If you take a distribution the day before you turn 59½, you will owe the tax. It is not sufficient that you turn 59½ sometime during the year; you must have crossed the age threshold by the time the funds are distributed to you.

 You can't always take your money out when you reach age 59½. Just because you have passed age 59½ doesn't guarantee that you can take money out of your retirement plan. Many qualified plans do not permit distributions before you terminate your employment. Attaining age 59½ simply ensures that if you are able to take money out, it will not be subject to the early distribution tax.

2. Death

Another straightforward exception to the tax, albeit a less attractive one, is death. None of the funds distributed from your retirement plan after your death will be subject to the early distribution tax, as long as the account is still in your name when the distribution occurs.

If you are the beneficiary of your spouse's retirement plan or IRA, then upon your spouse's death you may roll over a distribution from your spouse's retirement plan or IRA to an IRA in your own name. (See Chapters 7 and 8 for more information about post-death distributions.) This benefit is available only to you as a spouse-beneficiary. But once the funds have been rolled over into an IRA in your name, the post-death exception to the early distribution tax no longer applies, because the account is no longer in the deceased owner's name.

If you want to roll over a post-death distribution from your deceased spouse's retirement plan into an IRA in your own name, but need to hold back some of the money for living expenses, this could pose a problem. If you take a distribution from a retirement plan while the plan is still in your deceased spouse's name, the distribution will indeed avoid the 10% tax. But the IRS has ruled that when a surviving spouse invokes this exception, the spouse forfeits

the option to roll over the remainder into an IRA in his or her own name. Although this conclusion arises from a private letter ruling (which means that other taxpayers may not rely on the result when planning their own tax strategies), it serves as a warning.

The logical solution to this problem is for the spouse to roll over only the amount that is not needed for living expenses, leaving the remainder in the deceased spouse's name. The remaining portion could then be tapped to pay expenses without incurring the 10% tax. The IRS has not yet ruled on such a strategy, however.

About Private Letter Rulings

Many taxpayers who are unclear about how to proceed in a murky area of the tax law and who feel they have too much at stake to take a wait-and-see posture with the IRS will request private letter rulings. These rulings are just what their title implies—private—meaning the ruling applies only to the taxpayer who requested it, and only to the situation in question. The result of the ruling will not serve as precedent and cannot be relied upon by anyone else with similar or even identical circumstances. But the rulings can provide valuable insights into which way the IRS leans on a particular issue.

3. Disability

If you become disabled, all subsequent distributions from your retirement plan are free of the early distribution tax. But what does it mean to be disabled? And who decides? The law defines disabled as the inability to "engage in any substantial gainful activity by reason of any medically determinable physical or mental impairment which can be expected to result in death or to be of long-continued and indefinite duration." Is this helpful?

You won't find many answers in the wording of the exception, either. It says the early distribution tax will not apply to distributions that are "attributable to the employee's being disabled." But what does "attributable to" mean? If you take a distribution after becoming disabled, can you use the funds as you please? Must you

have taken the distribution because you are disabled? And if so, does that mean you must use the funds for some medical purpose related to your disability?

This lack of clarity in the Tax Code has spawned a host of cases and rulings. In most of them, the IRS has argued that the taxpayer failed to prove the disability was "irremediable." And because taxpayers must furnish proof of both the existence and permanence of the disability, taxpayers rarely prevail.

The key to the disability exception seems to lie in the permanence of the condition, not the severity. Disability exceptions have been denied for chemical dependence and chronic depression, even when the taxpayers were hospitalized for those conditions. It also appears that the disability must be deemed permanent at the time of the distribution, whether or not it is later found to be permanent. For example, the IRS denied the disability exception for a taxpayer, even knowing that the taxpayer later qualified for Social Security disability benefits.

Successful disability claims have included a dentist who suffered nerve damage to his thumb and who produced documents from four insurance companies declaring his disability permanent. Another successful claim involved a taxpayer who had been granted a disability retirement by his company. The IRS relied on the company's determination of the individual's disability. Although these cases do not tell us how the IRS will rule on the use of distributed funds, they are enlightening in other ways. They reveal that the IRS is most concerned about the timing and the nature of the disability. Using the cases as a guide, if your disability prevents you from working and is deemed permanent at the time you take your retirement plan distribution, then you should qualify for the disability exception. But there are no guarantees in this arena.

The IRS regulations do clarify one point, however. Gainful activity refers specifically to the type of work you were doing before becoming disabled. Thus it would seem that you need not be unfit for all work—just the work you customarily do.

4. Substantially Equal Periodic Payments

The substantially equal periodic payment exception is available to anyone with an IRA or a retirement plan, regardless of age, which makes it an attractive escape hatch. Theoretically, if you begin taking distributions from your retirement plan in equal annual installments, and those payments are designed to be spread out over your entire life or the joint life of you and your beneficiary, then the payments will not be subject to an early distribution tax.

The fly in the ointment is that you are not permitted to compute payments any way you please. The payment method must conform to IRS guidelines, which

sanction three computation methods. Nonetheless, the guidelines are flexible, making the exception at once versatile and complex. For these reasons, Chapter 4 is devoted exclusively to interpreting the IRS's computational guidelines and related rulings.

If you think you might need to tap your retirement plan early, this is the option that is most likely to work for you. One caveat: If you want to begin withdrawing funds from your employer's plan, you must have terminated your employment before payments begin. If the payments are from an IRA, however, the status of your employment is irrelevant.

5. Leaving Your Job After Age 55

If you are at least 55 years old when you leave your job, any distribution you receive from your former employer's retirement plan will not be subject to an early distribution tax. This exception applies only to distributions you receive after you have separated from service, or terminated your employment with the company that sponsors the plan. You don't have to retire permanently. You can go to work for another employer, or even return to work for the same employer at a later date. But you cannot receive a distribution from your employer's retirement plan while you are still employed with the company, if you want to use the age 55 exception to the early distribution tax.

This exception is relevant only if you are between ages 55 and 59½. After age 59½, the early distribution tax does not apply to any retirement plan distribution.

As with other exceptions, you must pay attention to certain details. For example, you need not be age 55 on the day you leave your job, as long as you turn 55 by December 31 of the same year. The strategy falls apart if you retire in a year that precedes the year you turn 55, even if you postpone receiving the retirement benefits until you reach age 55.

> EXAMPLE: You retire at age 53 and convince your employer to keep your retirement plan benefits in the plan until you reach age 55. The day after your 55th birthday, you receive $100,000 from your former employer's plan. You buy a Jaguar and spend the rest of the money on a trip around the world. At tax time, you will owe regular income tax on the $100,000 plus a 10% early distribution tax.
>
> If instead you had retired in the same year you turned 55, the $100,000 would be subject to regular income tax, but you would not have to pay an early distribution tax.

⚠ The age 55 exception is not available for IRAs. See Section C.1, below, for other rules that apply only to IRAs.

6. Dividends From ESOPs

Distributions of dividends from employer stock held inside an ESOP are not subject to the early distribution tax, no matter when you receive the dividend. (See Chapter 1, Section A.4, for more information about ESOPs.)

7. Medical Expenses

If you withdraw money from a retirement plan to pay medical expenses, a portion of that distribution might escape the early distribution tax. But once again, the exception is not as simple or as generous as it sounds. The tax exemption applies only to the portion of your medical expenses that would be deductible if you itemized deductions on your tax return. Medical expenses are deductible if they are yours, your spouse's or your dependent's. But they are only deductible to the extent they exceed 7.5% of your adjusted gross income. Consequently, your retirement plan distribution will avoid the early distribution tax only to the extent it also exceeds the 7.5% threshold.

> EXAMPLE: You are single and your adjusted gross income is $50,000. You had medical bills of $6,000 during the year, which you paid with funds you withdrew from your retirement plan. For income tax purposes, you are permitted to deduct medical expenses

that exceed 7.5% of your adjusted gross income. Thus,

Adjusted gross income (AGI) = $50,000

Nondeductible expenses
7.5% of AGI (.075 x 50,000) = $ 3,750

Deductible expenses
Excess (6,000 - 3,750)   = $ 2,250

Although you took $6,000 from your retirement plan to pay medical expenses, only $2,250 will escape the early distribution tax. The remaining $3,750 will be subject to the 10% additional tax (unless you qualify for another exception). And don't forget that the entire $6,000 is subject to regular income tax, as well.

On the plus side, the medical expense exception is available even if you don't itemize deductions. It applies to those amounts that would be deductible if you did itemize.

> EXAMPLE: As in the preceding example, your adjusted gross income is $50,000. You have $6,000 of medical expenses, which you paid with funds from your retirement plan. Only $2,250 of those expenses are deductible (as calculated above). Your deductible items for the year are as follows:
>
> Deductible medical: $2,250

Deductible taxes: $1,000

Charitable contributions: $ 500

Total $3,750

The standard deduction for a single individual for the year 2000 is $4,400. When computing your tax liability, you are permitted to reduce your adjusted gross income by the larger of your itemized deductions or the standard deduction. In this case, because the standard deduction is larger, you will not itemize deductions on your tax return. You may still exclude $2,250 of your retirement plan distribution from the early distribution tax computation, however.

8. QDRO Payments

If you are paying child support or alimony from your retirement plan, or if you intend to distribute some or all of the plan to your former spouse as part of a property settlement, none of those payments is subject to the early distribution tax as long as there is a QDRO in place that orders the payments. (See Chapter 2, Section C.4, for more information about QDROs.) A QDRO usually arises from a separation or divorce agreement, and involves court-ordered payments to an "alternate payee," such as an ex-spouse or minor child. Although the QDRO exception applies to all distributions from a qualified plan to any named alternate payee, it is critical that the payments arise from a valid QDRO, not just a private agreement between you and your former spouse.

Bear in mind, however, that even though QDRO payments are exempt from the early distribution tax, they are still subject to regular income tax.

⚠️ **The exception to the early distribution tax for QDRO payments does not apply to IRAs.** (See Section C.1.b, below, for more information.)

9. Federal Tax Levy

If you owe back taxes, you can be reasonably certain the government will try to collect them. If you have assets in a retirement plan, the government can take those assets (in other words, the IRS can put a levy on the assets of the plan) to pay your debt. If it does, then those amounts taken for taxes will not be subject to the early distribution penalty even if you happen to be younger than 59½. This shouldn't be too much of a worry for you because IRS policy frowns on the government grabbing retirement plans to satisfy back tax debts unless the debtor is uncooperative and has no other assets.

10. Refunds

If you receive a refund of a contribution to your retirement plan because you contributed more than the law permits, those

"corrective" distributions will not be subject to the early distribution tax, although they might be subject to other taxes and penalties.

B. Reporting the Tax

If you take a distribution from a retirement plan during the year, the trustee or custodian of your retirement plan will send you a copy of IRS Form 1099-R, which reports the amount distributed to you. The trustee or custodian will also send a copy to the IRS. You don't need to attach a copy of Form 1099-R to your tax return unless income tax was withheld from your distribution. In that case, you must attach the 1099-R just as you would attach your W-2 to show how much tax was withheld.

If you are younger than 59½ at the time of the distribution, a Code 1 should appear in Box 7 of the form, indicating that the early distribution tax applies. If you are younger than 59½ but you qualify for another exception (including having left your job after age 55), Box 7 should reflect that information as well. Code 3 indicates a disability exception, Code 4 is a post-death distribution and Code 2 is for all other exceptions.

> EXAMPLE: At age 30, Geoff Sute quit his job with Tech Inc. for a higher paying job with another company. Tech Inc. distributed $1,500 to Geoff, which represented the entire balance of his 401(k) plan account. Geoff de-

Sample: Form 1099-R From Plan Trustee or Custodian to Report Distribution

9898 ☐ VOID ☐ CORRECTED		

PAYER'S name, street address, city, state, and ZIP code	**1** Gross distribution	OMB No. 1545-0119	**Distributions From Pensions, Annuities, Retirement or Profit-Sharing Plans, IRAs, Insurance Contracts, etc.**
Tech Inc 401(k) Plan 786 Chipstone Way Sunburn, California	$ 1,500	**2000**	
	2a Taxable amount $ 1,500	Form **1099-R**	
	2b Taxable amount not determined ☐ Total distribution ☒		**Copy A** **For**
PAYER'S Federal identification number	RECIPIENT'S identification number	**3** Capital gain (included in box 2a)	**4** Federal income tax withheld	**Internal Revenue Service Center**
99-9999	555-55-5555	$	$ 300	File with Form 1096.
RECIPIENT'S name Geoff Sute		**5** Employee contributions or insurance premiums $	**6** Net unrealized appreciation in employer's securities $	For Privacy Act and Paperwork Reduction Act Notice, see the **2000 General Instructions for Forms 1099, 1098, 5498, and W-2G.**
Street address (including apt. no.) 42 Rising Ave		**7** Distribution code IRA/SEP/SIMPLE 1 ☐	**8** Other $ %	
City, state, and ZIP code Sand City, CA		**9a** Your percentage of total distribution %	**9b** Total employee contributions $	
Account number (optional)		**10** State tax withheld $ $	**11** State/Payer's state no.	**12** State distribution $ $
		13 Local tax withheld $ $	**14** Name of locality	**15** Local distribution $ $

Form **1099-R**   Cat. No. 14436Q   Department of the Treasury - Internal Revenue Service

Sample: Form 1040, Page 1, to Report Early Distribution

Form **1040**	Department of the Treasury—Internal Revenue Service **U.S. Individual Income Tax Return** **2000**	(99) IRS Use Only—Do not write or staple in this space.

For the year Jan. 1–Dec. 31, 2000, or other tax year beginning _____, 2000, ending _____, 20 ___ OMB No. 1545-0074

Label

(See instructions on page 19.)

Use the IRS label. Otherwise, please print or type.

Your first name and initial: **Geoff**   Last name: **Sute**
Your social security number: **555 55 5555**

If a joint return, spouse's first name and initial ___ Last name ___
Spouse's social security number

Home address (number and street). If you have a P.O. box, see page 19. **42 Rising Ave**   Apt. no. ___

City, town or post office, state, and ZIP code. If you have a foreign address, see page 19. **Sand City, CA**

▲ **Important!** ▲
You **must** enter your SSN(s) above.

Presidential Election Campaign
(See page 19.)

Note. Checking "Yes" will not change your tax or reduce your refund.
Do you, or your spouse if filing a joint return, want $3 to go to this fund? . . . ▶

You: ☐ Yes ☐ No   Spouse: ☐ Yes ☐ No

Filing Status

Check only one box.

1 ☐ Single
2 ☐ Married filing joint return (even if only one had income)
3 ☐ Married filing separate return. Enter spouse's social security no. above and full name here. ▶ _____
4 ☐ Head of household (with qualifying person). (See page 19.) If the qualifying person is a child but not your dependent, enter this child's name here. ▶ _____
5 ☐ Qualifying widow(er) with dependent child (year spouse died ▶ ___). (See page 19.)

Exemptions

6a ☐ **Yourself.** If your parent (or someone else) can claim you as a dependent on his or her tax return, **do not** check box 6a . . . .
b ☐ **Spouse** . . . .

No. of boxes checked on 6a and 6b ___

c **Dependents:**

(1) First name Last name	(2) Dependent's social security number	(3) Dependent's relationship to you	(4) ✔ if qualifying child for child tax credit (see page 20)
			☐
			☐
			☐
			☐
			☐
			☐

If more than six dependents, see page 20.

No. of your children on 6c who:
• lived with you ___
• did not live with you due to divorce or separation (see page 20) ___

Dependents on 6c not entered above ___

Add numbers entered on lines above ▶ ☐

d Total number of exemptions claimed . . . . 7 ___

Income

Attach Forms W-2 and W-2G here. Also attach Form(s) 1099-R if tax was withheld.

If you did not get a W-2, see page 21.

Enclose, but do not attach, any payment. Also, please use Form 1040-V.

7	Wages, salaries, tips, etc. Attach Form(s) W-2	7
8a	**Taxable** interest. Attach Schedule B if required	8a
b	**Tax-exempt** interest. **Do not** include on line 8a . . . 8b | |	
9	Ordinary dividends. Attach Schedule B if required	9
10	Taxable refunds, credits, or offsets of state and local income taxes (see page 22) . .	10
11	Alimony received	11
12	Business income or (loss). Attach Schedule C or C-EZ	12
13	Capital gain or (loss). Attach Schedule D if required. If not required, check here ▶ ☐	13
14	Other gains or (losses). Attach Form 4797	14
15a	Total IRA distributions . 15a | | **b** Taxable amount (see page 23)	15b
16a	Total pensions and annuities 16a | **1,500 00** | **b** Taxable amount (see page 23)	16b **1,500**
17	Rental real estate, royalties, partnerships, S corporations, trusts, etc. Attach Schedule E	17
18	Farm income or (loss). Attach Schedule F	18
19	Unemployment compensation	19
20a	Social security benefits . 20a | | **b** Taxable amount (see page 25)	20b
21	Other income. List type and amount (see page 25) _____	21
22	Add the amounts in the far right column for lines 7 through 21. This is your **total income** ▶	22

Adjusted Gross Income

23	IRA deduction (see page 27) 23	
24	Student loan interest deduction (see page 27) . . . 24	
25	Medical savings account deduction. Attach Form 8853 . 25	
26	Moving expenses. Attach Form 3903 26	
27	One-half of self-employment tax. Attach Schedule SE . 27	
28	Self-employed health insurance deduction (see page 29) 28	
29	Self-employed SEP, SIMPLE, and qualified plans . . 29	
30	Penalty on early withdrawal of savings 30	
31a	Alimony paid **b** Recipient's SSN ▶ ___ 31a	
32	Add lines 23 through 31a	32
33	Subtract line 32 from line 22. This is your **adjusted gross income** . . . . . . ▶	33

For Disclosure, Privacy Act, and Paperwork Reduction Act Notice, see page 56.   Cat. No. 11320B   Form **1040** (2000)

Sample: Form 1040, Page 2, to Report Early Distribution

Form 1040 (2000)			Page **2**

Tax and Credits

34 Amount from line 33 (adjusted gross income) . . . . | **34** |

35a Check if: ☐ **You** were 65 or older, ☐ Blind; ☐ **Spouse** was 65 or older, ☐ Blind.
Add the number of boxes checked above and enter the total here . . . ▶ **35a** ☐

b If you are married filing separately and your spouse itemizes deductions, or
you were a dual-status alien, see page 31 and check here . . . . . ▶ **35b** ☐

Standard Deduction for Most People

Single: $4,400

Head of household: $6,450

Married filing jointly or Qualifying widow(er): $7,350

Married filing separately: $3,675

36 Enter your **itemized deductions** from Schedule A, line 28, **or standard deduction** shown on the left. **But** see page 31 to find your standard deduction if you checked any box on line 35a or 35b **or** if someone can claim you as a dependent . . . . | **36** |

37 Subtract line 36 from line 34 . . . . | **37** |

38 If line 34 is $96,700 or less, multiply $2,800 by the total number of exemptions claimed on line 6d. If line 34 is over $96,700, see the worksheet on page 32 for the amount to enter . . | **38** |

39 **Taxable income.** Subtract line 38 from line 37. If line 38 is more than line 37, enter -0- . | **39** |

40 **Tax** (see page 32). Check if any tax is from **a** ☐ Form(s) 8814   **b** ☐ Form 4972 . . . | **40** |

41 Alternative minimum tax. Attach Form 6251 . . . . | **41** |

42 Add lines 40 and 41 . . . . ▶ | **42** |

43 Foreign tax credit. Attach Form 1116 if required . . . | **43** |

44 Credit for child and dependent care expenses. Attach Form 2441 | **44** |

45 Credit for the elderly or the disabled. Attach Schedule R . . | **45** |

46 Education credits. Attach Form 8863 . . . . | **46** |

47 Child tax credit (see page 36) . . . . | **47** |

48 Adoption credit. Attach Form 8839 . . . . | **48** |

49 Other. Check if from **a** ☐ Form 3800   **b** ☐ Form 8396
c ☐ Form 8801   **d** ☐ Form (specify) _____ | **49** |

50 Add lines 43 through 49. These are your **total credits** . . . . | **50** |

51 Subtract line 50 from line 42. If line 50 is more than line 42, enter -0- . . . . . . ▶ | **51** |

Other Taxes

52 Self-employment tax. Attach Schedule SE . . . . | **52** |

53 Social security and Medicare tax on tip income not reported to employer. Attach Form 4137 | **53** | 150

54 Tax on IRAs, other retirement plans, and MSAs. Attach Form 5329 if required . . . . | **54** |

55 Advance earned income credit payments from Form(s) W-2 . . . . . . | **55** |

56 Household employment taxes. Attach Schedule H . . . . | **56** |

57 Add lines 51 through 56. This is your **total tax** . . . . ▶ | **57** |

Payments

If you have a qualifying child, attach Schedule EIC.

58 Federal income tax withheld from Forms W-2 and 1099 . . | **58** |

59 2000 estimated tax payments and amount applied from 1999 return | **59** |

60a **Earned income credit (EIC)** . . . . | **60a** |

b Nontaxable earned income: amount . . ▶ _____ and type ▶ _____

61 Excess social security and RRTA tax withheld (see page 50) | **61** |

62 Additional child tax credit. Attach Form 8812 . . . . . | **62** |

63 Amount paid with request for extension to file (see page 50) | **63** |

64 Other payments. Check if from **a** ☐ Form 2439 **b** ☐ Form 4136 | **64** |

65 Add lines 58, 59, 60a, and 61 through 64. These are your **total payments** . . . . ▶ | **65** |

Refund

Have it directly deposited! See page 50 and fill in 67b, 67c, and 67d.

66 If line 65 is more than line 57, subtract line 57 from line 65. This is the amount you **overpaid** | **66** |

67a Amount of line 66 you want **refunded to you** . . . . ▶ | **67a** |

▶ b Routing number ☐☐☐☐☐☐☐☐☐ ▶ c Type: ☐ Checking ☐ Savings

▶ d Account number ☐☐☐☐☐☐☐☐☐☐☐☐☐☐☐☐☐

68 Amount of line 66 you want **applied to your 2001 estimated tax** . ▶ | **68** |

Amount You Owe

69 If line 57 is more than line 65, subtract line 65 from line 57. This is the **amount you owe.**
For details on how to pay, see page 51 . . . . ▶ | **69** |

70 Estimated tax penalty. Also include on line 69 . . . . . | **70** |

Sign Here

Joint return? See page 19.

Keep a copy for your records.

Under penalties of perjury, I declare that I have examined this return and accompanying schedules and statements, and to the best of my knowledge and belief, they are true, correct, and complete. Declaration of preparer (other than taxpayer) is based on all information of which preparer has any knowledge.

Your signature	Date	Your occupation	Daytime phone number ( )
Spouse's signature. If a joint return, **both** must sign.	Date	Spouse's occupation	May the IRS discuss this return with the preparer shown below (see page 52)? ☐ Yes ☐ No

Paid Preparer's Use Only

Preparer's signature ▶	Date	Check if self-employed ☐	Preparer's SSN or PTIN
Firm's name (or yours if self-employed), address, and ZIP code ▶		EIN	
		Phone no. ( )	

Form **1040** (2000)

cided to spend the $1,500 on a new suit. At tax time, Tech Inc. sent Geoff the following Form 1099-R, reporting the distribution. Note that Box 7 correctly shows a Code 1.

If the Form 1099-R is accurate, your only responsibility is to compute and pay the extra 10%. This early distribution tax is reported as an additional tax under "other taxes" on page 2 of Form 1040, your regular income tax form. Even if you do not owe the IRS any regular income tax, you must still report the early distribution tax on your tax return and pay it at tax time.

EXAMPLE: Using the same facts as in the previous example, Geoff should report his $1,500 distribution on lines 16a and 16b of Form 1040, as shown below. Then he should report the early distribution tax of $150 on line 50.

If the Form 1099-R is not properly coded, you must still compute and pay the additional tax, but you must also complete IRS Form 5329 to show your computation of the tax. Include it with your other forms when you file your tax return. (A copy is in Appendix A.)

EXAMPLE 1: The facts are the same as in the previous example except that Tech Inc. failed to enter Code 1 in Box 7 of Form 1099-R. As a result, Geoff must complete Part I of Form

5329 and include the form when he files the rest of his tax return. Part I should be completed as shown in Sample 1, below.

EXAMPLE 2: Irwin retired from Tech Inc. at age 56. The company distributed $25,000 to Irwin, which represented the entire balance in his 401(k) plan. When Irwin received his Form 1099-R from Tech Inc. at tax time, the form showed a Code 1 in Box 7, indicating that Irwin had received an early distribution. Because Irwin left the company after age 55, his distribution is not subject to an early distribution tax. He must complete and attach Form 5329 to his tax return to tell the IRS which exception applies. The instructions for Form 5329 indicate that the age 55 exception is number 01. Irwin must enter 01 on line 2 of Part 1. Irwin completes the rest of the form as shown in Sample 2, below.

C. Special Rules for IRAs

The early distribution tax applies to IRAs in much the same way it applies to qualified plans, with just a few exceptions and variations which are described in this section. Bear in mind, however, that the Roth IRA is not a typical IRA, so the following rules do not necessarily apply to it. For a complete discussion of the Roth IRA rules, see Chapter 9.

Sample 1: Form 5329 to Report Early Distribution, No Code on 1099-R

Form **5329**	**Additional Taxes Attributable to IRAs, Other Qualified Retirement Plans, Annuities, Modified Endowment Contracts, and MSAs**	OMB No. 1545-0203
	(Under Sections 72, 530, 4973, and 4974 of the Internal Revenue Code)	**2000**
Department of the Treasury Internal Revenue Service	▶ Attach to Form 1040. ▶ See separate instructions.	Attachment Sequence No. **29**

Name of individual subject to additional tax. (If married filing jointly, see page 2 of the instructions.)	Your social security number
Geoff Sute	555 55 5555

Fill in Your Address Only If You Are Filing This Form by Itself and Not With Your Tax Return	Home address (number and street), or P.O. box if mail is not delivered to your home	Apt. no.
	City, town or post office, state, and ZIP code	If this is an amended return, check here ▶ ☐

If you **only** owe the 10% tax on early distributions, you may be able to report this tax directly on Form 1040 without filing Form 5329. See **Who Must File** on page 1 of the instructions.

Part I	**Tax on Early Distributions**

Complete this part if a taxable distribution was made from your qualified retirement plan (including an IRA other than an education IRA), annuity contract, or modified endowment contract before you reached age 59½. If you received a Form 1099-R that incorrectly indicates an early distribution (with no known exception to the additional tax) or you received a Roth IRA distribution, you also may have to complete this part. See page 2 of the instructions.

Note: You must include the taxable amount of the distribution on Form 1040, line 15b or 16b.

1	Early distributions included in gross income. For Roth IRA distributions, see page 2 of the instructions	**1**	1,500
2	Early distributions not subject to additional tax. Enter the appropriate exception number from page 2 of the instructions: _____	**2**	0
3	Amount subject to additional tax. Subtract line 2 from line 1	**3**	1,500
4	**Tax due.** Enter 10% (.10) of line 3. Also include this amount on Form 1040, line 54	**4**	150

Caution: If any part of the amount on line 3 was a distribution from a SIMPLE retirement plan, you may have to include 25% of that amount on line 4 instead of 10%. See page 3 of the instructions.

Part II	**Tax on Certain Taxable Distributions From Education (Ed) IRAs**

Complete this part if you had a taxable amount on Form 8606, line 30.

Note: You must include the taxable amount of the distribution on Form 1040, line 15b.

5	Taxable distributions from your Ed IRAs, from Form 8606, line 30	**5**	
6	Taxable distributions not subject to additional tax. See page 3 of the instructions	**6**	
7	Amount subject to additional tax. Subtract line 6 from line 5	**7**	
8	**Tax due.** Enter 10% (.10) of line 7. Also include this amount on Form 1040, line 54	**8**	

Part III	**Tax on Excess Contributions to Traditional IRAs**

Complete this part if you contributed more to your traditional IRAs for 2000 than is allowable or you had an excess contribution on line 16 of your 1999 Form 5329.

9	Enter your excess contributions from line 16 of your 1999 Form 5329. If zero, go to line 15		**9**	
10	If your traditional IRA contributions for 2000 are less than your maximum allowable contribution, see page 3. Otherwise, enter -0-	**10**		
11	Taxable 2000 distributions from your traditional IRAs	**11**		
12	2000 withdrawals of prior year excess contributions included on line 9. See page 3	**12**		
13	Add lines 10, 11, and 12		**13**	
14	Prior year excess contributions. Subtract line 13 from line 9. If zero or less, enter -0-		**14**	
15	Excess contributions for 2000. See page 3. Do not include this amount on Form 1040, line 23		**15**	
16	Total excess contributions. Add lines 14 and 15		**16**	
17	**Tax due.** Enter 6% (.06) of the **smaller** of line 16 **or** the value of your traditional IRAs on December 31, 2000 (including contributions for 2000 made in 2001). Also include this amount on Form 1040, line 54		**17**	

For Paperwork Reduction Act Notice, see page 4 of separate instructions.   Cat. No. 13329Q   Form **5329** (2000)

Sample 2: Form 5329 to Report Exception to Early Distribution Tax

Form **5329**	**Additional Taxes Attributable to IRAs, Other Qualified Retirement Plans, Annuities, Modified Endowment Contracts, and MSAs** (Under Sections 72, 530, 4973, and 4974 of the Internal Revenue Code) ▶ Attach to Form 1040. ▶ See separate instructions.	OMB No. 1545-0203
Department of the Treasury Internal Revenue Service		20**00** Attachment Sequence No. **29**

Name of individual subject to additional tax. (If married filing jointly, see page 2 of the instructions.) Irwin Hirsh	Your social security number 444 : 44 : 4444

Fill in Your Address Only If You Are Filing This Form by Itself and Not With Your Tax Return	Home address (number and street), or P.O. box if mail is not delivered to your home	Apt. no.
	City, town or post office, state, and ZIP code	If this is an amended return, check here ▶ ☐

If you **only** owe the 10% tax on early distributions, you may be able to report this tax directly on Form 1040 without filing Form 5329. See **Who Must File** on page 1 of the instructions.

Part I   Tax on Early Distributions

Complete this part if a taxable distribution was made from your qualified retirement plan (including an IRA other than an education IRA), annuity contract, or modified endowment contract before you reached age 59½. If you received a Form 1099-R that incorrectly indicates an early distribution (with no known exception to the additional tax) or you received a Roth IRA distribution, you also may have to complete this part. See page 2 of the instructions.
Note: *You must include the taxable amount of the distribution on Form 1040, line 15b or 16b.*

1	Early distributions included in gross income. For Roth IRA distributions, see page 2 of the instructions	**1**	25,000
2	Early distributions not subject to additional tax. Enter the appropriate exception number from page 2 of the instructions: _____	**2**	25,000
3	Amount subject to additional tax. Subtract line 2 from line 1	**3**	0
4	Tax due. Enter 10% (.10) of line 3. Also include this amount on Form 1040, line 54	**4**	0
	Caution: *If any part of the amount on line 3 was a distribution from a SIMPLE retirement plan, you may have to include 25% of that amount on line 4 instead of 10%. See page 3 of the instructions.*		

Part II   Tax on Certain Taxable Distributions From Education (Ed) IRAs

Complete this part if you had a taxable amount on Form 8606, line 30.
Note: *You must include the taxable amount of the distribution on Form 1040, line 15b.*

5	Taxable distributions from your Ed IRAs, from Form 8606, line 30	**5**	
6	Taxable distributions not subject to additional tax. See page 3 of the instructions	**6**	
7	Amount subject to additional tax. Subtract line 6 from line 5	**7**	
8	Tax due. Enter 10% (.10) of line 7. Also include this amount on Form 1040, line 54	**8**	

Part III   Tax on Excess Contributions to Traditional IRAs

Complete this part if you contributed more to your traditional IRAs for 2000 than is allowable or you had an excess contribution on line 16 of your 1999 Form 5329.

9	Enter your excess contributions from line 16 of your 1999 Form 5329. If zero, go to line 15 . .	**9**	
10	If your traditional IRA contributions for 2000 are less than your maximum allowable contribution, see page 3. Otherwise, enter -0- .	**10**	
11	Taxable 2000 distributions from your traditional IRAs	**11**	
12	2000 withdrawals of prior year excess contributions included on line 9. See page 3	**12**	
13	Add lines 10, 11, and 12	**13**	
14	Prior year excess contributions. Subtract line 13 from line 9. If zero or less, enter -0-	**14**	
15	Excess contributions for 2000. See page 3. Do not include this amount on Form 1040, line 23	**15**	
16	Total excess contributions. Add lines 14 and 15	**16**	
17	Tax due. Enter 6% (.06) of the **smaller** of line 16 **or** the value of your traditional IRAs on December 31, 2000 (including contributions for 2000 made in 2001). Also include this amount on Form 1040, line 54 . .	**17**	

For Paperwork Reduction Act Notice, see page 4 of separate instructions.   Cat. No. 13329Q   Form **5329** (2000)

1. Rules Applicable to All IRAs Except Roth IRAs

Six special rules apply to rollover IRAs, contributory IRAs, SEP IRAs and SIMPLE IRAs.

a. No Age 55 Exception

Employees who are at least age 55 when they terminate their employment will not be subject to an early distribution tax on distributions from their former employer's qualified plan. This rule does not apply to IRAs, however. If you have an IRA, you must be at least 59½ to use the age exception to the early distribution tax. Of course, you may still qualify for an exception that is unrelated to your age.

b. No QDRO Exception

The special QDRO rules in the Tax Code do not apply to IRAs. This means the QDRO exception to the early distribution tax is available for qualified plan distributions, but not for IRA distributions. Even if your divorce agreement or court order mandates child support or alimony payments from an IRA, the payments will be subject to an early distribution tax unless one of the other exceptions applies. Sometimes the divorce agreement simply requires the distribution to a spouse of his or her interest in the IRA (for example, a community property interest), but in that case, too, the distribution could be subject to an early distribution tax.

There is one way around this, but it is available only to the former spouse of the IRA participant, and only if the spouse is to receive some or all of the IRA as directed by a divorce or maintenance decree, or a written separation agreement. The IRA participant may direct the custodian of the IRA to transfer some or all of the IRA assets directly into an IRA in the former spouse's name. Alternatively, the participant could roll over the spouse's share into a new IRA in the participant's name and then direct the custodian to change title on the new IRA to the spouse's name. The participant might even roll over the spouse's interest into an IRA in the spouse's name (instead of using a direct transfer). The key in each case is for the spouse not to take possession of the funds before they are deposited into an IRA in the spouse's own name.

Once the funds are in an IRA in the spouse's name, however, they belong to the spouse in every way. Thereafter, all IRA rules apply to the assets as though the spouse had been the original IRA participant. If the spouse takes a distribution, the spouse will have to pay an early distribution tax unless an exception applies.

Get it in writing! The transfer of IRA assets to an account in the name of a spouse or former spouse must be as a result of a written divorce or separation agreement. You may not transfer funds from your IRA into your current spouse's IRA simply because you want to increase the value of his or her account for some reason.

⚠ **Child support cannot go into an IRA.** The above transfer strategy is available only for payments that are made to a separated or former spouse. Child support payments may not be transferred to an IRA in either the child's name or the former spouse's name.

c. Health Insurance Premiums

An early distribution tax exception unique to IRAs concerns health insurance premiums. If you are unemployed or were recently unemployed and use money from your IRA to pay health insurance premiums, the IRA funds used specifically for that purpose will not be subject to an early distribution tax, as long as you satisfy the following conditions:

- you received unemployment compensation for at least 12 consecutive weeks
- you received the funds from the IRA during a year in which you received unemployment compensation or during the following year, and
- the IRA distribution is received no more than 60 days after you return to work.

EXAMPLE: You are 45. You lost your job in 2000 and began receiving unemployment compensation on September 22, 2000. You want to main-

tain your health insurance even during your unemployment. You pay $400 per month on the first day of each month beginning October 1. Because you are short of cash, you withdraw the $400 from your IRA each month to cover the cost of the premiums. You land a job and begin working on March 15, 2001. Unfortunately, your new employer does not provide any health benefits, so you continue to pay premiums of $400 per month, withdrawing the money from your IRA each time. Only the premiums you pay after December 15, 2000 (12 weeks after your unemployment compensation payments began) and before May 15, 2001 (60 days after you began work) are eligible for the exception to the early distribution tax. Thus your distributions of $400 on January 1, February 1, March 1, April 1 and May 1 totaling $2,000 all escape the early distribution tax. Distributions after May 15 are subject to the early distribution tax unless another exception applies.

You may also make a penalty-free withdrawal from your IRA to pay for health insurance if you were self-employed before you stopped working, as long as you would have qualified for unemployment compensation except for the fact that you were self-employed.

d. Higher Education Expenses

Distributions that you use to pay higher education expenses will not be subject to the early distribution tax, as long as those distributions meet the following requirements:

- The distributions are used to pay for tuition, fees, books, supplies and equipment. They may also be used for room and board if the student is carrying at least half of a normal study load (or is considered at least a halftime student).
- The expenses are paid on behalf of the IRA owner, spouse, child or grandchild.
- The distributions do not exceed the amount of the higher education expenses. Furthermore, the total expenses (tuition, fees and so on) must be reduced by any tax-free scholarships or other tax-free assistance the student receives, not including loans, gifts or inheritances.

e. First Home Purchase

A long-awaited exception to the early distribution tax was finally enacted in 1997. Its purpose was to make it easier for people to buy their first homes. When the dust settled, the benefit was not as dramatic as people had hoped—not because it was difficult to qualify, but because the lifetime distribution limit was only $10,000. Here are the details.

- The IRA distribution must be used for the acquisition, construction or reconstruction of a home.
- The funds must be used within 120 days of receipt. If it happens that the home purchase is canceled or delayed, the funds may be rolled over into another IRA (or back into the same one) as long as the rollover is complete within 120 days of the initial distribution.
- The funds must be used to purchase a principal residence for a first-time home buyer. A first-time home buyer is someone who has had no interest in a principal residence during the two years ending on the date of purchase of the new home. If the individual happens to be married, then neither the individual nor the spouse may have owned any part of a principal residence during the preceding two-year period.
- The first-time home buyer must be the IRA owner, or the owner's spouse, or an ancestor (such as a parent, grandparent or great grandparent), child or grandchild of either the IRA owner or the owner's spouse.
- The lifetime limit of $10,000 applies regardless of whose home is purchased or improved. If the IRA owner withdraws $10,000 and gives it to his or her child, the lifetime limit for the IRA owner is used up. The IRA owner may not invoke the first home exception for any future distri-

bution even if it is to buy a house for a different relative or for himself. The $10,000 does not have to be distributed all at once or even in a single year. For example, the IRA owner could withdraw $5,000 one year, giving it to a qualified person for a home purchase, and then withdraw another $5,000 in a later year.

f. Refunds

There is a limit to how much you may contribute to an IRA each year. If you contribute too much, then you have made an "excess contribution." If you withdraw the excess by the time you file your tax return (including extensions, if you filed a request and were granted an extension), the excess will not be subject to the early distribution tax. You must also withdraw the income earned on the excess while it was in the IRA, however, and that portion will be subject to the early distribution tax, unless it qualifies for another exception.

EXAMPLE: You are self-employed. In January you open an IRA and contribute $2,000 for the current tax year. On December 31, when you compute your net income for the year, you discover that you only made $1,500 in self-employment income. Because your IRA contribution is limited to the lesser of $2,000 or your net income, you have made an excess contribution of $500. Also, you earned 10% on the IRA investment during the year. To correct the excess contribution, you must withdraw not only the $500, but the $50 of earnings on that excess (10% of $500) as well. If you withdraw these amounts by April 15 (or the due date of your tax return, if you received an extension of time for filing the return), there will be no penalty on the $500 distribution. The $50 of earnings will be subject to ordinary income tax and a 10% early distribution tax of $5.

If you fail to correct an excess contribution to an IRA by the time you file your tax return, but make a corrective distribution later, the entire amount of the distribution is subject to the early distribution tax unless it qualifies for another exception.

2. Rule Applicable Only to SIMPLE IRAs

SIMPLE IRAs are described in Chapter 1, Section B.4. All the special IRA rules discussed above apply to SIMPLE IRAs, but there is one additional rule. If you are a participant in a SIMPLE IRA and you receive a distribution within two years of the date you began contributing to it, the early distribution tax increases from 10% to 25%. At the end of two years, it falls back to 10%. Of course, if the distribution qualifies for an exception, the early distribution tax will not apply at all.

Key Tax Code Sections and IRS Pronouncements

§ 72(t)
Early Distribution Tax

§ 402(g)(2)(C)
Distribution of Excess Deferrals

§ 4972
Nondeductible Contributions to Qualified Plans

§ 4973
Excess Contributions to IRAs

§ 4979
Excess Contributions to Qualified Plans (in Violation of Nondiscrimination Rules)

Revenue Procedure 92-93
Treatment of Corrective Distributions

■

Chapter 4

Avoiding the Early Distribution Tax: Substantially Equal Periodic Payments

Who Should Read Chapter 4

➡ Read this chapter if you are under age 59½ and want to learn about one method you can use to draw on your retirement plan or IRA without incurring penalties.

*A*s explained in Chapter 3, you are eligible for an exception to the early distribution tax (assuming your plan permits early distributions) if you receive substantially equal periodic payments from the plan. The payments must be distributed at least annually over your life expectancy (or over the joint life expectancy of you and your beneficiary). The silver lining on this exception is that there are no age restrictions. You could be 25 and start payments from your retirement plan without incurring a penalty.

There is one significant restriction, however. If you elect to take substantially equal periodic payments from a qualified plan, qualified annuity or tax-deferred annuity (see Chapter 1 for a description of these plans), the payments must begin after you have terminated your employment with the company sponsoring the plan. You may not begin periodic payments from your company's retirement plan while you are still working there if you want the early distribution exception to apply.

💡 **This restriction does not apply to IRAs.** If you need to use some of your retirement funds while you are still employed, you can begin substantially equal periodic payments from your IRA and avoid an early distribution tax. Of course, this won't help you if all your retirement money is in a company plan and you don't have an IRA.

A. General Rules for Computing Payments

Although the Tax Code itself does not offer a blueprint for computing periodic payments, the IRS has issued some guidelines. Those guidelines don't provide all the answers, but they help. And they also suggest that the IRS will accept a wide range of periodic payments.

1. Black and White Area of the Law

The law is clear about certain aspects of the periodic payment exception:

- The payments must be substantially equal, which means you cannot alter the payment each year to suit your needs, perhaps by taking a few dollars one year and a few thousand the next.

- You must compute the payments as though you intend to distribute the retirement plan over your entire life,

Helpful Terms

Amortize. To liquidate or reduce (as in the case of a debt) through periodic payments of principal and interest.

Annuity. A contract, sold by an insurance company, that promises to make monthly, quarterly, semiannual or annual payments for life or for a specified period of time.

Distribution. A payout of property (such as shares of stock) or cash from a retire-ment plan or IRA to the participant or a beneficiary.

Joint Life Expectancy. The number of years that is expected to pass before the second of two individuals dies.

Recalculated Life Expectancy. Life expectancy that is revised each year according to statistically accurate measures of mortality.

---

or over the joint life of you and your beneficiary.

- Payments from your employer's plan must begin after you leave your job. (This rule does not apply to IRAs.)

- You may not discontinue payments or alter the computation method for at least five years. And if you have not reached age 59½ at the end of the five-year period, you must wait until you do reach that age before making a change. If you modify payments too soon, the early distribution tax (plus interest) will be applied retroactively to all of the payments you have received. (See Section D, below, for more information about the consequences of modifying payments.)

2. Gray Area of the Law

IRS Notice 89-25 broadly describes three computation methods that will pass muster. (The relevant portion of Notice 89-25 is in Appendix A.) All three methods are discussed in detail in Section B, below. But even Notice 89-25 doesn't answer all questions. Two particularly murky issues remain.

Issue 1: Is there a limit to how large or how small the payments can be?

Although this question has never been answered directly, IRS guidelines and private letter rulings suggest that the agency is more concerned about large payments than small ones. The guidelines caution against using a method that will result in unreasonably large payments, but are silent on the advisability of using a method that produces an exceptionally small payment. This bias in favor of small payments is consistent with the government's goal of encouraging you to preserve your retirement plan assets for your retirement years.

Issue 2: What if you don't want to withdraw all your funds?

Even if you find you need to draw on your retirement plan early, you may not need all of it—perhaps just a little to help with cash flow through some lean years. If that is the case, you won't want to take any more than necessary, because you will have to report the distribution as income and pay income tax on it, giving up valuable tax-deferred growth.

If you have two or more retirement plans, you might be able to solve your problem by taking periodic payments from one and leaving the other(s) intact. IRS rulings have consistently allowed taxpayers to take periodic payments from one or more plans and not others.

But what if you have only one plan? IRS rules don't say. Some taxpayers have inferred from the rulings on multiple plans that the IRS will not object if they split an existing plan or IRA into two separate accounts in such a way that one is just large enough to produce the precise payment desired. A couple of the IRS's private letter rulings even support this particular

approach, and none has yet forbidden it. Although no one knows for certain if the IRS will routinely condone it, the strategy may well be a viable one.

3. Rollovers and Withholding

Payments that are part of a series of substantially equal periodic payments are not eligible to be rolled over. Perhaps in your zeal to withdraw from your retirement plan precisely the amount you need and no more, you devise a plan to begin periodic withdrawals and then roll over into an IRA the portion of each payment you don't use. That strategy is creative, logical, reasonable—and prohibited. The Tax Code specifically denies rollover treatment to periodic payments. You should be able to achieve a similar result by splitting the account first (as described in Issue 2, above) before beginning periodic payments. At least that strategy is not specifically forbidden.

Periodic payments are also exempt from the mandatory income tax withholding rules for qualified plan distributions. (See Chapter 2, Section C.5, for more information about withholding.) Mandatory withholding applies only to those distributions from pension plans that are eligible to be rolled over. Because periodic payments are not eligible to be rolled over, they are not subject to mandatory withholding.

B. Computing Periodic Payments

The basic requirement for periodic payments is that they be spread over your lifetime in roughly equal payments. This is trickier than it first appears. For one thing, you probably don't know how long you are going to live, and you also probably don't know how your investments are going to do over the years. If you did (and more important, if the IRS did) the calculation would be simple.

But because most of us have pretty murky crystal balls, the IRS requires us to use some generally accepted life expectancy assumptions and interest rates. Although the IRS does not hand us the numbers we are to use, the agency has put its stamp of approval on three methods for computing required distributions. These are the minimum distribution, amortization and annuity factor methods. Each has its own set of guidelines for determining life expectancy and selecting an interest rate or an expected investment return.

You are permitted to use any of the methods you want, but before you choose, you should be aware of the principles that are common to all three computation methods:

Principle 1: Using a joint life expectancy instead of your single life expectancy will reduce the size of your payments.

Principle 2: Using a low interest rate assumption will reduce the size of your payments.

Principle 3: The IRS is more likely to object to large periodic payments than small ones.

1. Minimum Distribution Method

The first method approved by the IRS is a relatively simple one. Each year you determine your retirement account balance and divide it by a life expectancy factor. The result is your periodic payment for that year. The life expectancy factor can be plucked right out of tables provided by the IRS. (See Tables I and II in Appendix B.) You don't have to worry about choosing an interest rate because your year-end account balance reflects the actual investment returns you earned during the year.

As simple as this method is, you must still decide whether to use your single life expectancy or joint life expectancy with your beneficiary. A joint life expectancy will produce a smaller payment than a single life expectancy will. The size of the payment you need should be the only factor in your decision, given that your choice will affect no other aspect of your retirement plan.

After you make your decisions about life expectancies, follow the steps below, to arrive at a payment.

Step 1: Determine your life expectancy factor.

If you use your single life expectancy, you will look up your age each year in Table I in Appendix B, and use the number from the table.

If you use a joint life expectancy with a spouse, look up the life expectancy factor for both of your ages each year in Table II in Appendix B.

You may also use a joint life expectancy with a beneficiary other than your spouse. If you do, it would seem that the IRS does not intend to impose any restrictions on the age of the beneficiary you may use to compute substantially equal periodic payments. You might want to name a young beneficiary to keep your payments low. But the beneficiary used for this purpose must be your actual beneficiary, not merely a convenient young person.

Step 2: Determine your account balance.

Determine the balance of your retirement plan as of December 31 of the year before the periodic payments are to begin. This means you cannot calculate your yearly payment in advance. You must wait until January 1 of each year to know exactly what the balance was on the preceding December 31.

Step 3: Calculate the payment.

Divide the account balance by your single or joint life expectancy factor. The result is the amount that must be distributed during the first year. For the second year, you follow a similar procedure, using the account balance as of December 31 of the first payment year.

EXAMPLE: You quit your job last year and rolled over your retirement plan into an IRA. The balance of your IRA at the end of the year you retired was $100,000. This year, you will turn 50. You need to draw on the IRA to help make ends meet, so you plan to begin periodic payments.

Year 1

Step 1: From Table I you see that your single life expectancy (for age 50) is 33.1 years.

Step 2: Your December 31 balance for the year before payments are to begin was $100,000.

Step 3: Your first annual periodic payment is $3,021, or $100,000 divided by 33.1.

Year 2

Assume that the balance of your IRA at the end of the first year of periodic payments was $110,000. (You earned more in interest than you withdrew the first year.) Follow these steps to compute the second year payment.

Step 1: Refer again to Table I. You will turn 51 this year. Thus, your life expectancy is 32.2.

Step 2: Your account balance as of December 31 of the first year of periodic payments was $110,000.

Step 3: Your second periodic payment is $3,416, or $110,000 divided by 32.2.

Be exact. Although this method is referred to as the minimum distribution method, the payment does not represent the minimum you must take, but the exact amount. Once you compute your periodic payment for the year, you must distribute precisely that amount—no more, no less.

a. Advantages of Minimum Distribution Method

The IRS has declared that payments computed under minimum distribution rules will be considered substantially equal periodic payments. Nonetheless, the payments could vary significantly from one year to the next, depending on how well or poorly your portfolio performs. Thus, the advantage of this method is that it reflects your actual investment returns. And if your intention is to spread payments over your lifetime, this method can accomplish your goal. Not to be overlooked is the fact that this calculation method is simple and straightforward. And if you choose it, the IRS is unlikely to challenge your payment size or your methodology.

b. Disadvantages of Minimum Distribution Method

Although this method might accurately reflect your investment returns, it is the least flexible. Except by choosing a joint or single life expectancy, there is no way to tweak payments to produce the distribution you want. And because of market fluctuations, you might find your payments too large one year and not quite large enough the next. Even without market fluctuations, this method will tend to skew payments so that they are small in the early years and larger in later years. That's fine if you expect to need more income later, but if you need more now, there's no way to skew payments in the other direction.

2. Amortization Method

The amortization method is favored by many taxpayers because it is flexible enough to produce a range of payments, and the computation is straightforward. First you must decide if you will use a single or joint life expectancy. (Remember, a joint life expectancy produces lower payments.) Then you follow these steps.

Step 1: Choose an interest rate.
This is where most of the flexibility—but also the uncertainty—comes in. IRS guidelines say specifically that the interest rate you choose may not "exceed a reasonable interest rate on the date payments commence." But nothing specifically forbids a very low rate. (Higher interest rates produce higher payments.)

Some of the interest rates approved in IRS private letter rulings include:

- Specific interest rates ranging from 5% to 10.6%. In these private letter rulings, the taxpayers did not specify how the interest rates were selected. It was left to the IRS to judge them reasonable or unreasonable. But if you choose an interest rate you like, be prepared to defend it as a reasonable expected return on your investments. For example, if your entire IRA is invested in 30-year Treasury bonds yielding 6% interest, you might have difficulty defending a 10% interest rate if you are audited. You don't have to match current rates, but you should be in the ball park.

- The long-term applicable federal rate (published monthly by the Treasury Department). This rate is based on the average market yield on outstanding marketable obligations of the United States (such as Treasury notes and bonds) with maturities of more than nine years (meaning the notes or bonds are due to be redeemed after at least nine years).

- 120% of the midterm applicable federal rate (published monthly by the Treasury). Midterm rates are based on U.S. obligations with maturities from three to nine years.

In private letter rulings, the long-term federal rate and 120% of the midterm rate are both cited frequently and appear to be acceptable to the IRS. Another advantage of using these rates is that they are easy to find. You can find them on the Internet (http://www.pmstax.com/afr) and in many public libraries. Of course, you can always call your accountant and ask him or her to find the rate for you.

Step 2: Determine your life expectancy.

Look up your life expectancy in Table I (if you are using your single life) or Table II (if you are using a joint life) as of your respective birthdays in the year payments are to begin.

Step 3: Determine your account balance.

Although the IRS has not prescribed the date as of which the account balance is to be determined, using the December 31 account balance for the year prior to your first distribution is most consistent with the overall guidelines. Note, however, that some rulings have allowed the use of account balances for the month before the first distribution, and others have allowed the use of account balances sometime during the same month as the first distribution. Although the sketchy guidelines offer no guarantees, it seems likely that the IRS will approve account balances determined at any of those times.

Step 4: Calculate the payment.

Amortize your account balance using the life expectancy and interest rate you have chosen. Use the same method you would use to amortize a home mortgage or other loan. You can make the computation with a financial calculator, on a computer spreadsheet or with an amortization program that might be included with other financial software you have. Fortunately, Nolo and

several financial sites on the Internet have free calculators you can use for this purpose:

- Nolo.com, http://www.nolo.com/calculator/index
- FinanCenter, http://financenter.com/calcs.html
- First Source Bank, http://www.1stsrce.com /phtml/finance/financl.htm, and
- Credit Union One, http://www.cuone.com.

Enter your account balance when asked for the loan amount and your life expectancy when asked for the number of years or months you will take to repay the loan. Then enter the interest rate you have chosen. The calculator then computes the payment amount.

> **EXAMPLE:** You have decided to start taking substantially equal periodic payments annually from your IRA beginning in the year you turn 52. Your IRA account balance as of December 31 of the preceding year was $82,000.
>
> **Step 1:** You decide to use the long-term applicable federal rate for December of the year before you begin distributions. That rate is 7%.
>
> **Step 2:** You will take distributions over your own single life expectancy, which is 31.3 (from Table I) for age 52.

Step 3: Your account balance on December 31 of the year before payments are to begin was $82,000.

Step 4: Using a financial calculator, you compute your annual payment to be $6,525 ($82,000 amortized over 31.3 years at 7%). Your payment for the second and future years will also be $6,525. If you are using Hewlett Packard's financial calculator—the HP–12C—you will reach a slightly different result: $6,681 instead of $6,525. This is because the HP–12C rounds up to the next integer when you use a fractional period (number of years) in the equation.

a. Advantages of Amortization Method

One significant attraction of this method is its simplicity. Once you determine your payment, you never have to compute it again. No looking up numbers in tables every year, or trying to remember computation formulas. You do it once and it's done.

Along with the simplicity comes a great deal of flexibility. You can choose from a wide range of interest rates, and you may use a joint or single life expectancy. That flexibility should get you close to the payment you want unless you need an exceptionally large amount. And because your choice of interest rate is the only variable open to scrutiny by the IRS, you can have a certain amount of confidence that your payments will fly—as long as you don't choose a rate, like 20%, which is significantly higher than prevailing rates.

b. Disadvantages of Amortization Method

The amortization example in the IRS guidelines, as well as in most of the favorable private letter rulings, computes a fixed payment—one that doesn't vary at all from year to year. Fixed payments, by definition, do not take into account recalculation of life expectancies, actual investment returns on your account or inflation. The payments are constant. Consequently, if inflation surges, you might find yourself stuck with a payment that is too low for your needs and that doesn't reflect either the real returns on your investments or the changing economic climate.

3. Annuity Factor Method

Although the underlying arithmetic in the annuity factor method is essentially the same as in the amortization method, the computation is performed simply by dividing your account balance by an annuity factor. The annuity factor comes from a table that has the amortization formula built in, so most of the number crunching is done for you.

There is one more way the annuity factor method differs from the others. The minimum distribution and amortization methods require the use of life expectancy tables found in the Income Tax Regulations. (See Appendix B.) But if you use the annuity factor method, you are permitted to use any reasonable life expectancy assumption.

Although the IRS doesn't define "reasonable" for us, it isn't likely that you can select the age that you yourself expect to die. Instead, you must choose a generally accepted figure for your life expectancy. In private letter rulings, the IRS has generally approved the use of mortality figures used by insurance companies and pension plan administrators. Those figures are then converted by actuaries to a table of annuity factors. Such tables are not widely published, but if you call your friendly insurance agent, he or she might be able to find one for you.

The IRS also publishes an annuity factor table generated from its own life expectancy figures. (See Table S in Appendix A for a sampling of IRS annuity factors.) Because the Tax Code and Regulations are widely published, many taxpayers have relied on those figures when choosing the annuity factor method. And there is little chance the IRS would reject its own mortality figures.

If you decide to use this method, follow these steps.

Step 1: Choose an interest rate.

Your criterion for choosing an interest rate should be no different for this method than for the amortization method. Higher rates will produce higher payments; but if the rate is too high, it might not pass muster with the IRS, and you might not qualify for the early distribution exception.

Step 2: Find your annuity factor.

Using an annuity factor table, such as the IRS's Table S, look up the factor for your age in the year you will begin receiving payments. If you are using a joint life expectancy, look up your age and your beneficiary's age for the year payments begin.

Step 3: Determine your account balance.

The IRS has routinely permitted the use of the December 31 account balance for the year prior to the first payment. You may also use the account balance for the month before the first payment, or even the month of the first payment.

Step 4: Compute the payment.

Divide the account balance by the annuity factor to arrive at your payment.

Although the example in the IRS guidelines computes a fixed payment, several private letter rulings in which the annuity factor method was used approved some variation in the payments. Variations permitted by the IRS included redetermining the annuity factor each year by recalculating life expectancies and using the revised retirement plan balances, much as you would if you were using the minimum distribution method.

EXAMPLE: You will turn 52 this year. You decide to begin substantially equal periodic payments from your IRA, and you plan to use your own single life expectancy. Your IRA account balance as of December 31 of the preceding year was $82,000. Assume that at the end of this year (after distributions) it will be $80,000.

Year 1

Step 1: You choose an interest rate of 7%, which is the long-term applicable federal rate.

Step 2: You use the IRS's annuity factor table, Table S. For age 52 and an interest rate of 7%, you come up with an annuity factor of 11.2231.

Step 3: Your account balance on December 31 of last year was $82,000.

Step 4: Your periodic payment for this year, your first payment year, is $7,306 (Step 3 divided by Step 2; or $82,000 divided by 11.2231).

Year 2

If you choose to use a fixed payment, you will withdraw the same amount, $7,306, every year, and there is little chance the IRS will reject your methodology, provided the IRS deems 7% a reasonable interest rate.

If you choose to recompute the annuity factor in subsequent years by using your current life expectancy, then you would compute the second year's payment as follows:

Step 1: Your interest rate is 7%.

Step 2: Using the same table you used for year 1, you find the annuity factor for age 53 and an interest rate of 7%. The factor is 11.0770.

Step 3: Your account balance on December 31 of the first payment year was $80,000.

Step 4: Your periodic payment for the second year is $7,222, or $80,000 divided by 11.0770. In future years, you repeat Steps 1 through 4.

⚠ **Only fixed payments are officially approved by the IRS.** Bear in mind that although some private letter rulings sanction variable payments under the annuity factor method, only fixed payments have been approved officially by the IRS.

a.   Advantages of Annuity Factor Method

The only substantive difference between the annuity factor method and the amortization method is that the annuity factor method allows you to use mortality figures other than those provided by the IRS. Thus, theoretically, you have the flexibility to choose a table that accurately reflects your situation or produces a payment that better suits your needs.

Private letter rulings also suggest the IRS takes a more flexible stance on payments computed under this method. Although rulings on the amortization method seem to heavily favor fixed payments, rulings on the annuity factor method have permitted recalculation of life expectancies and the use of updated account balances. These variations have not been embodied in official IRS policy, but they do provide guidance for those taxpayers who want to perform more creative calculations.

b. Disadvantages of Annuity Factor Method

If you decide to receive a fixed payment under the annuity factor method, then the disadvantages are the same as those under the amortization method: your payment will not reflect a changing economy or the actual performance of your investments. If you choose to receive a payment that reflects annual changes in your account balance and your updated life expectancy, then you increase both the complexity of the computation and the risk that the IRS will not approve your method.

C. Implementing and Reporting Your Decision

Once you have selected your computation method, prepare a worksheet illustrating the computation. (See sample, below.) Keep it with your other important tax papers in case the IRS should ever ask you to explain the methodology you chose. Next, arrange with your plan administrator or IRA custodian to begin periodic payments. Your only remaining task is to report the payments on your tax return.

Sample Worksheet for Your Tax Files

Computation of Substantially Equal Periodic Payments Using Amortization Method
Annual distributions to be made each January 1, beginning in the year 2001.
December 31, 2000 value of IRA Account # 01234: $100,000.
My single life expectancy in the year 2001 (from IRS Publication 590, Appendix E, Table 1): 40 years.
Long-term applicable federal rate for December 2000: 6%.
Annual payment ($100,000 amortized over 40 years at 6%): $6,646.

After the end of the year, you will receive a Form 1099-R from the trustee of your plan or the custodian of your IRA. It will report the total amount of distributions you received during the year. If the form shows a Code 2 in Box 7, you do not need to file any special forms with your tax return. (Code 2 means that the distribution qualifies for an exception to the early distribution tax.) You will simply report your periodic payments as ordinary income on your tax return. (See Chapter 3, Section B, for more information about Form 1099-R codes and the reporting requirements for IRA and qualified plan distributions.)

If Box 7 of Form 1099-R does not show Code 2, you must complete Part 1 of Form 5329 and file it with the rest of your tax return. Part 1 of Form 5329 asks you to report the total amount of your early distributions (on line 1) and the distributions that are eligible for an exception to the early distribution tax (line 2). Line 2 also provides a space for you to write in the exception number. The exception number for substantially equal periodic payments is 02. Exception codes can be found in the instructions for Form 5329, which is in Appendix A.

> EXAMPLE: At age 52, you began receiving substantially equal periodic payments of $2,000 per month from your IRA. After the end of the year, you receive your 1099-R from your IRA custodian, reporting distributions of $24,000 from your IRA. Box 7 incorrectly shows a Code 1. Consequently, you must complete Part 1 of Form 5329 and file it with the rest of your tax return. Lines 1-4 of Form 5329 should look like the sample form on the next page.

D. Modifying the Payments

In general, the substantially equal periodic payment exception will save you from the early distribution tax only if you do not discontinue your payments or alter your

Sample: Form 5329 to Report Incorrectly Coded 1099-R

Form **5329**	**Additional Taxes Attributable to IRAs, Other Qualified Retirement Plans, Annuities, Modified Endowment Contracts, and MSAs** (Under Sections 72, 530, 4973, and 4974 of the Internal Revenue Code) ▶ **Attach to Form 1040.** ▶ **See separate instructions.**	OMB No. 1545-0203
Department of the Treasury Internal Revenue Service		**2000** Attachment Sequence No. **29**

Name of individual subject to additional tax. (If married filing jointly, see page 2 of the instructions.)	Your social security number

Fill in Your Address Only If You Are Filing This Form by Itself and Not With Your Tax Return ▷	Home address (number and street), or P.O. box if mail is not delivered to your home	Apt. no.
	City, town or post office, state, and ZIP code	If this is an amended return, check here ▶ ☐

If you **only** owe the 10% tax on early distributions, you may be able to report this tax directly on Form 1040 without filing Form 5329. See **Who Must File** on page 1 of the instructions.

Part I	**Tax on Early Distributions**

Complete this part if a taxable distribution was made from your qualified retirement plan (including an IRA other than an education IRA), annuity contract, or modified endowment contract before you reached age 59½. If you received a Form 1099-R that incorrectly indicates an early distribution (with no known exception to the additional tax) or you received a Roth IRA distribution, you also may have to complete this part. See page 2 of the instructions.

Note: *You must include the taxable amount of the distribution on Form 1040, line 15b or 16b.*

1	Early distributions included in gross income. For Roth IRA distributions, see page 2 of the instructions	**1**	24,000
2	Early distributions not subject to additional tax. Enter the appropriate exception number from page 2 of the instructions: ___02___	**2**	24,000
3	Amount subject to additional tax. Subtract line 2 from line 1	**3**	0
4	Tax due. Enter 10% (.10) of line 3. Also include this amount on Form 1040, line 54	**4**	0

Caution: *If any part of the amount on line 3 was a distribution from a SIMPLE retirement plan, you may have to include 25% of that amount on line 4 instead of 10%. See page 3 of the instructions.*

Part II	**Tax on Certain Taxable Distributions From Education (Ed) IRAs**

Complete this part if you had a taxable amount on Form 8606, line 30.

Note: *You must include the taxable amount of the distribution on Form 1040, line 15b.*

5	Taxable distributions from your Ed IRAs, from Form 8606, line 30	**5**	
6	Taxable distributions not subject to additional tax. See page 3 of the instructions	**6**	
7	Amount subject to additional tax. Subtract line 6 from line 5	**7**	
8	Tax due. Enter 10% (.10) of line 7. Also include this amount on Form 1040, line 54	**8**	

Part III	**Tax on Excess Contributions to Traditional IRAs**

Complete this part if you contributed more to your traditional IRAs for 2000 than is allowable or you had an excess contribution on line 16 of your 1999 Form 5329.

9	Enter your excess contributions from line 16 of your 1999 Form 5329. If zero, go to line 15		**9**	
10	If your traditional IRA contributions for 2000 are less than your maximum allowable contribution, see page 3. Otherwise, enter -0-	**10**		
11	Taxable 2000 distributions from your traditional IRAs	**11**		
12	2000 withdrawals of prior year excess contributions included on line 9. See page 3	**12**		
13	Add lines 10, 11, and 12		**13**	
14	Prior year excess contributions. Subtract line 13 from line 9. If zero or less, enter -0-		**14**	
15	Excess contributions for 2000. See page 3. Do not include this amount on Form 1040, line 23		**15**	
16	Total excess contributions. Add lines 14 and 15		**16**	
17	**Tax due.** Enter 6% (.06) of the **smaller** of line 16 **or** the value of your traditional IRAs on December 31, 2000 (including contributions for 2000 made in 2001). Also include this amount on Form 1040, line 54		**17**	

For Paperwork Reduction Act Notice, see page 4 of separate instructions.   Cat. No. 13329Q   Form **5329** (2000)

computation method (other than in the approved ways, such as recalculation based on annual changes in life expectancy or account balance) once payments have begun. If you change your computation method, the early distribution tax can be applied retroactively to all distributions.

Fortunately, Congress didn't intend that your payments remain fixed until your death—just for a well-defined period of time. And, of course, there are exceptions to the no-modification rule which would allow you to change the payments under certain circumstances, even if you don't satisfy the time-period requirement.

1. What Constitutes a Modification?

Once you establish a schedule and begin receiving substantially equal periodic payments, the payments may not be modified or discontinued for five years or until you attain age 59½, whichever period is longer. For example, if you are age 49 when you begin receiving payments, you will be only 54 after five years. Therefore, you must continue the payments until you reach 59½. On the other hand, if you begin payments when you are 58, you must continue them for five full years, even though you will have passed the age 59½ milestone in the meantime.

The time-period requirement is quite literal. If you begin monthly payments at 49 and wish to stop at age 59½, you must take your last payment on or after the day you reach age 59½. You may not simply stop payments on January 1 of the year you turn 59½. Similarly, if you begin monthly payments on your 58th birthday, you must continue them at least until your 63rd birthday, when five full years will have passed.

There are two exceptions to the requirement that payments not be modified:

- If you die before the required period has passed, your beneficiary may discontinue the payments.
- If you become disabled, you are no longer tied to your periodic payment schedule, and subsequent distributions will not be subject to the early distribution tax. For this exception to apply, you must satisfy the IRS's definition of disabled. (See Chapter 3, Section B.3, for more information on the disability exception.)

2. Penalties for Modification

If you modify your payments before the required period has expired, then all distributions you have received since you initiated periodic payments will be subject to the early distribution tax. Because a modification invalidates the substantially equal periodic payment exception, all of the payments are treated (retroactively) as though they were normal discretionary distributions. Therefore, funds that were distributed before you turned 59½ are subject to an early distribution tax, but amounts received after age 59½ are not.

The cumulative payments for all years must be reported on your tax return for the year in which you first modify the payments. The taxes must be paid with that return. You must also pay interest on any early distribution taxes that would have been due from and after the year of the first periodic payment.

EXAMPLE 1: You began taking substantially equal periodic payments of $6,000 per year on July 1 of the year you turned 49. You took the last one on July 1 of the year you turned 54. Then you stopped the payments altogether. Because you were required to continue payments until you reached age 59½, the substantially equal periodic payment exception became invalid in the year you turned 55 when you failed to take a payment. When you file the tax return for that year, you must report all distributions received and pay the early distribution tax with your tax return. The tax is 10% of all distributions that would have been subject to the early distribution tax if you had not been using the substantially equal periodic payment exception. The total of all distributions is $36,000 (six payments multiplied by $6,000). The early distribution tax is $3,600 ($36,000 x .10).

In addition, you will owe interest retroactively on the early distribution

tax itself, as if the tax had been imposed on the due date of the tax return for the year in which you received the early distribution. In this example, your early distribution tax for each year was $600. You didn't pay any of it until the year you turned 55. For the distribution you took during the year you were 49, you owe six years of interest on the $600. For the distribution you took during the year you were 50, you owe five years of interest on $600. You get the idea. The rate used to compute the interest you owe is the IRS's standard rate on underpayment of tax. The rate is based on the applicable federal short-term rate and therefore changes from time to time. As of January 1998, the rate for underpayment of tax was 9%.

EXAMPLE 2: Your birthday is August 1. You began taking substantially equal periodic payments of $6,000 per year on December 31 of the year you turned 58. You took an identical payment every December 31 through the year you turned 61 and then stopped. Because you were required to continue payments for five full years, you will be subject to an early distribution tax of 10% on distributions that would have been subject to the tax if you had never invoked the substantially equal periodic payment exception. You took four payments of $6,000, the last one in December of the year you turned 61. However, if you had not been using the substantially equal period payment exception, only the distributions you took in the years you turned 58 and 59 would have been subject to an early distribution tax. All other distributions occurred after age 59½ and thus would not have been subject to penalty. (Note that because your birthday is August 1, you didn't turn 59½ until the same year you turned 60, so the distribution you took in December of the year you turned 59 was an early distribution, because you weren't yet 59½.)

Your early distribution tax will be $1,200 ($6,000 x 2 years x .10), plus interest.

Key Tax Code Sections, Regulations and Notices

§ 72(t)(2)(A)(iv)
Substantially Equal Period Payment Exception

§ 72(t)(3)(B)
Separation From Service Requirement for Age 55 Exception

§ 1.72-9
IRS Life Expectancy Tables

§ 402(c)(4)
Prohibition Against Rollover of Periodic Payment

§ 1.401(a)(9)
Regulations for Minimum Distribution Calculation

Notice 89-25
IRS Guidelines for Computing Substantially Equal Payments

Chapter 5

When Must You Begin to Take Your Money?

Who Should Read Chapter 5

➡ This chapter gives an overview of the situations in which you are required to take money out of your retirement plan or IRA. Chapters 6, 7 and 8 provide the details you will need to compute required distributions during your lifetime. Those chapters also provide the information your heirs will need to compute distributions after your death.

Someone once said that the government's strategy for encouraging people to use their retirement money is a lot like herding cattle through a gate. If a cow heads off to the left of the gate, a cattle prod nudges her back on track. Similarly, if you wander off the retirement trail and withdraw your funds too early, you're brought up short with an early distribution tax. If our proverbial cow meanders too far to the right, she receives another painful poke, just as you are hit with another penalty if you wait too long to withdraw your retirement money. That penalty—for waiting too long—is the focus of this chapter.

To avoid being penalized for delaying distributions, you must comply with what are called the required distribution rules. Those rules mandate that you take at least a minimum amount from your retirement plan each year, beginning in the year you turn 70½ or, under certain circumstances, in the year you retire if you work past age 70½. The minimum amount is calculated according to a formula in the income tax regulations. You may take more than the minimum, but you may not take less. If you do take less, you will be fined 50% of the amount that should have come out of your plan but didn't—the shortfall, in penalty parlance.

The required distribution rules evolved from Congress's desire that you use up your retirement funds during your own retirement, instead of passing the assets on to your heirs. The law presents you with a date by which you must start withdrawing money from your retirement plan. It also answers questions like: What happens if you die before the date you are supposed to begin distributions? Ordinarily, your assets would simply go to your beneficiary, but if your entire retirement plan is distributed upon your death, the income tax burden on your beneficiary might be enormous. Should the law provide income tax relief to your heirs? Should your beneficiary be allowed to defer distributions from your plan even though the funds were never intended for his or her retirement? Should your spouse have special privileges?

As if those issues didn't complicate matters enough, there is a flip side to the premature death issue: What happens if you die after you have started receiving required distributions but before you have used up all your retirement money? Does this change anything? Should your heirs be given relief in this situation? And, again, should your spouse have special privileges?

Helpful Terms

Beneficiary. The person or entity entitled to receive the benefits from insurance or from trust property, such as a retirement plan or IRA, usually after the insured or the owner of the property dies.

Deferral Period. The number of years over which distributions from a retirement plan or IRA can be spread.

Distribution. A payout of property (such as shares of stock) or cash from a retirement plan or IRA to the participant or a beneficiary.

Grandfather Provision. A part of a new law that exempts an individual or entity from the new law and allows the individual or entity to use the old law or special transitional laws.

TDA or Tax-Deferred Annuity. Many university professors and public school employees are covered by a TDA, which is a retirement annuity plan for public charities or public schools. These retirement plans are usually funded with individual annuity contracts purchased from an insurance company. Retirement benefits are frequently paid as a monthly annuity for life.

Waiver. Intentional dismissal, as of a penalty.

The required distribution rules attempt to address all of these questions and more. In this chapter, we offer a summary of those rules. In Section A, we discuss the "New Rules," which came about through regulations that the IRS issued in January 2001. In Section B, we discuss the "Old Rules," which are the rules that were in place prior to the January 2001 regulations. Why do we discuss both? Because anyone who must take a required distribution in 2001 has the option of using either the old rules or the new rules.

Choose the new rules. Almost without exception, the new rules are more favorable than the old rules. If you have a choice, you should almost certainly opt to use the new rules for your 2001 required distribution.

New rules do not look back. If you took a required distribution for the year 2000, you do not have a choice and cannot use the new rules. (See Section B, below, for a discussion of the old rules.)

A. New Rules

As we explained above, the IRS issued regulations in January 2001 that created a new set of required distribution rules. On the whole, these rules are much more favorable than the old ones. If you are required to take a distribution for the 2001 tax year, you have the option of using these rules.

![triangle warning icon] **Qualified plans versus IRAs.** If you are taking required distributions from a qualified plan, you may use the new rules only if the plan administrator amends the plan documents to incorporate the new regulations. If you are taking required distributions from an IRA, however, you may use the new rules for year 2001 distributions, even if the IRA documents have not been amended.

1. Required Distributions During Your Lifetime

You don't have to worry about taking required distributions from your own retirement plan until the year in which you turn 70½. At that time, you must start taking distributions under one of the following two scenarios:

- You may withdraw everything by your required beginning date, or RBD, which for most people is April 1 of the year after turning 70½, but for some people will be April 1 of the year after they retire. (See Chapter 6, Part I, Section A for more information about determining your RBD.)
- Alternatively, you may distribute your retirement plan money over a period of years. Most people will use what the IRS calls the "uniform table" (see Table III in Appendix B) to determine the number of years over which they may spread distributions. If your spouse happens to be more than ten years younger than you are, however, you may use a different and more favorable table called the "joint life expectancy table." (See Table II in Appendix B.)

When faced with those two distribution options, few people would choose the first—to distribute the entire amount of their retirement plan at once—because of the income tax implications. A whopping distribution all in one year could put you in the top tax bracket for that year, allowing the government to take a huge tax bite out of your nest egg.

In contrast, the second option allows people to spread distributions over a period of years, thereby keeping their tax burden lower. As an added bonus, the second option is flexible: If people want to take only the minimum required amount, they can, but they also have the option of taking more money out when they need it.

Chapter 6 describes the steps involved in determining your required distributions during your lifetime.

2. Death Before Required Beginning Date

If you die before your RBD, your beneficiary generally may spread distributions from your retirement plan over his or her life expectancy. Or he or she may take distributions according to the five-year rule (depending on whether your retirement plan requires or permits this). Under the five-year rule, your retirement plan assets must be completely distributed by December 31 of the year containing the fifth anniversary of your death. The law does not prescribe a distribution method. In order to mitigate the tax impact, your beneficiary might choose to take money out of the plan in annual installments over that five-year period. This strategy is perfectly acceptable as long as the plan administrator will allow it. But the plan has the authority to determine the distribution method during the five-year period. Some plans will permit installment payments; others will require a lump sum payment.

If you have no beneficiary, the five-year rule is mandatory.

If your sole beneficiary is your spouse, he or she has some additional privileges. After your death, your spouse may defer distributions from your retirement plan until you would have been 70½. At that point, the distributions will be spread over his or her own life expectancy. Alternatively, your spouse can roll over your retirement plan (whether a qualified plan or an IRA) into an IRA in his or her own name. Your spouse would then name new

beneficiaries and begin distributions in the year he or she turns 70½.

⚠ If there are other beneficiaries. If your spouse is not the sole beneficiary but is instead one of several, then he or she cannot take advantage of these special privileges.

Chapter 7 describes the implications of premature death on your retirement distributions, and it includes a detailed explanation of the life expectancy rule, the five-year rule and the special privileges accorded a surviving spouse.

3. Death After Required Beginning Date

If you survive to your RBD, you must begin taking required distributions as described in Section 1, above. If there is still some money in your retirement plan when you die, your beneficiary must continue to take distributions every year—generally based on his or her life expectancy. Your beneficiary can elect to receive more than the prescribed amount, but not less.

If you did not name a beneficiary, the assets will generally be distributed to your estate over your own remaining life expectancy as of the year of your death.

Some special rules apply if your spouse is your sole beneficiary. For example, your spouse may take distributions as though he or she were a non-spouse beneficiary. Alternatively, your spouse can roll over your retirement plan into an IRA in his or her own name. After the rollover, the IRA belongs to the spouse in every respect, and the required distribution rules apply as though the spouse had been the original owner.

Chapter 8 explains your beneficiary's options if you die after you begin receiving required distributions.

B. Old Rules

The old rules are optional for required distributions that you take in 2001. As mentioned above, however, you will almost surely decide against this option, since the old rules are less favorable. If you can, go with the new rules as described in Section A, above.

Some people, however, will be stuck with the old rules. If you are still dealing with distributions taken in 2000, you must use the old rules. And if you are taking required distributions from a qualified plan and the plan has not been modified to permit use of the new rules, you will be stuck with the old rules until the plan is amended.

Different rule for IRAs. Remember: Your IRA plan documents do not have to be amended for you to take advantage of the new rules. You can start using the new rules immediately for distributions from IRAs, regardless of what the documents say.

1. Required Distributions During Your Lifetime

You must begin taking required distributions from your own retirement plan in the year you turn 70½. At that time, you will have two choices as to how to go about taking the distributions:

- You may withdraw everything by your required beginning date, or RBD, which for most people is April 1 of the year after turning 70½, but for some people will be April 1 of the year after they retire. (See Chapter 6, Part II, Section A for more information about determining your RBD.)
- Alternatively, you may distribute your retirement plan money over a period of years but no longer than either your life expectancy or the joint life expectancy of you and your beneficiary.

Chapter 6 describes the steps involved in determining your required distributions during your lifetime.

2. Death Before Required Beginning Date

If you die before your RBD, then all of your retirement plan assets must be distributed by December 31 of the fifth year after your death—unless an exception applies. Although this is the same five-year rule described in Section A.2, above, it applies by default to non-spouse beneficiaries under the old rules with one exception: Beneficiaries who satisfy certain requirements can spread distributions over their life expectancies.

Your spouse has some additional privileges, but only if he or she is your beneficiary. After your death, your spouse may defer distributions from your retirement plan until you would have been 70½ and then spread distributions over his or her own life expectancy. Alternatively, your spouse can roll over your retirement plan (whether a qualified plan or an IRA) into an IRA of his or her own, naming new beneficiaries and beginning distributions in the year your spouse turns 70½.

Chapter 7 describes the ramifications of your premature death, including a detailed explanation of the five-year rule, the exception to the five-year rule and the special privileges accorded a surviving spouse.

3. Death After Required Beginning Date

If you survive to your RBD and begin taking required distributions, the five-year rule will not apply to you at all.

Once you die—having survived your RBD and commenced required distributions—your beneficiary must continue to receive at least the amount you would have received each year if you had survived. Although the beneficiary can elect to receive more, he or he cannot take out less. In other words: Your beneficiary must deplete the account as fast as or faster than you were depleting it.

Some special rules and exceptions apply either if your beneficiary is more than ten years younger than you are or if your beneficiary is your spouse.

Your spouse may continue your pattern of distributions or roll over the plan or IRA to his or her own IRA. If your spouse rolls over the plan or IRA, the assets will thereafter belong to the spouse in every respect, and the required distribution rules will apply as though the spouse had been the original owner.

For beneficiaries who are more than ten years younger than you are, a quirk in the law allows them to extend the period over which they can take distributions after you die, rather than simply maintain your schedule of distributions.

Chapter 8 discusses beneficiary's options if you die after you begin receiving required distributions.

C. Special Rules for Tax-Deferred Annuities

If you were a participant in a tax-deferred annuity (also known as a TDA or 403(b) annuity) established before 1987, some special required distribution rules apply. Specifically, all contributions and earnings added to your account after 1986 are subject to the same required distribution rules described in Sections A and B, above.

But the amount in your account on December 31, 1986 was grandfathered in under an older set of rules, and is not subject to the current required distribution rules.

! **Plan must be amended to use the new rules.** As is the case with qualified plans, people who take required distributions from a TDA in 2001 will be able to use the new regulations for distributions of the post-1986 accumulations only if the plan has been amended to incorporate the new rules.

Because of this grandfathering, when it comes time for you to start required distributions from your TDA, you may subtract your pre-1987 balance and compute your required distribution on the difference. You may continue to subtract the pre-1987 balance when computing required distributions every year until you reach age 75, at which time your entire account, including the pre-1987 balance, will be subject to current required distribution rules.

! **Grandfathering rules are strict.** Although you may exclude the pre-1987 balance when computing required distributions, you may not exclude any subsequent earnings attributable to the grandfathered amount. The grandfathered portion is a fixed dollar amount—the precise balance of your account on December 31, 1986.

EXAMPLE: On December 31, 1986, the balance in your TDA was $130,000. You are retired and will turn 70½ this year. The total value of your account is $220,000. Because you are not yet 75, you may exclude $130,000 (your pre-1987 balance) when you compute your first required distribution, which means the required distribution will be based on an account balance of $90,000 ($220,000 – 130,000). You may use this approach until the year you turn 75. From that year forward, you must use the total value of your account when computing your required distribution.

All required distributions you take before age 75 are deemed to come from your post-1986 accumulation. Any amount you withdraw in excess of the required amount, however, is deemed to come from the pre-1987 portion.

EXAMPLE: As in the previous example, your pre-1987 account balance is $130,000, and your post-1986 accumulation is $90,000. You compute your first required distribution to be $5,625, but decide to take an extra $5,000 to pay some unexpected medical expenses. Your total distribution for the year is $10,625. The minimum required amount of $5,625 is deemed to come from your post-1986 account (the $90,000 portion). The remaining $5,000 is deemed to come from your pre-1987 accumulation. Therefore, next year when you subtract your pre-1987 balance before computing your required distribution, you will subtract $125,000 (which is $130,000 - $5,000), instead of $130,000.

⚠️ **Be careful not to forfeit your option to defer.** If at any time before you reach age 75 you roll over your entire TDA into an IRA, then you forfeit the option to defer until age 75 distributions on your pre-1987 accumulation. In addition, if the trustee or custodian of your TDA at any time ceases to keep accurate records of the year-end balances of your grandfathered and nongrandfathered portions, the entire balance of your TDA will be subject to current required distribution rules and you will no longer have the option of deferring distributions on your pre-1987 accumulation.

D. Special Rules for Roth IRAs

Roth IRAs conform to some of the required distribution rules described in Sections A and B, above, but not others. Specifically,

you are not required to take lifetime distributions. But if you die leaving a balance in your Roth IRA, the post-death rules introduced in Sections A.2 (new rules) and B.2 (old rules) and described fully in Chapter 7 will apply whether you die before or after your RBD. Chapter 9 contains a detailed discussion of the Roth IRA rules.

E. Penalty

The penalty for failing to take a required distribution is one of the worst in all the Tax Code: 50% of the shortfall. Some call it onerous, others call it Draconian, but everyone calls it punitive. If you were required to take a $10,000 distribution but took only $4,000, you would owe the IRS $3,000 for your mistake—50% of the $6,000 you didn't take.

1. Failure to Distribute

When meting out punishment for failure to comply with a rule or regulation, enforcers of the law sometimes attempt to discern your intent so that the punishment better fits the crime. For example, in the case of a required distribution violation, did you make an inadvertent error? A once-in-a-blue-moon blunder? Or are your failures chronic? Perhaps you attempted to cash in on a perceived loophole? The more egregious the violation or the intent, the more severe the penalty is likely to be.

a. Innocent Blunders

If you simply forget to take your required distribution one year, the 50% penalty is probably the worst you'll face. And as painful as it is, at least it only hits once. So even if you don't correct the shortfall the next year, the excise tax will not be assessed again with respect to the first transgression.

> EXAMPLE: You forgot to take your required distribution of $6,000 for the year 2000. In 2001 you computed your required distribution for 2001 and withdrew it, but you still hadn't discovered your error for the year 2000. Your mind cleared sometime in the year 2002 and you withdrew the $6,000 for 2000 along with your distribution for the year 2002. You must pay a penalty of $3,000 (50% of $6,000) plus interest for the year 2000 mistake. However, you only have to pay it once, even though the mistake remained uncorrected through 2001. (See Section 2, below, for information on how to report the distribution and penalty.)

Once you stumble and are faced with an unavoidable penalty, you might think there is nothing to be gained by distributing the required amount. But here are two good reasons to withdraw it:

- Only if you correct your mistake can you hope to obtain an official waiver of the penalty. (See Section C,

below, for more information about waivers.)
- If you don't correct the shortfall, you risk disqualifying the plan, which would force a total distribution of the account and loss of all future tax-deferred growth. The Tax Code states that a plan will not be a qualified plan unless it complies with the required distribution rules. Arguably you will not be in compliance for as long as a shortfall remains uncorrected.

b. Chronic Errors

Make no mistake, the IRS will look askance at the taxpayer who habitually fails to take proper required distributions, whether those distributions are late, incorrect or nonexistent. Once a problem becomes chronic, not only will the IRS's sympathy wane, but plan disqualification becomes a serious risk. It's not as though the IRS monitors all required distributions for all taxpayers. But if you should be audited one year and the IRS discovers a flaw in your minimum distribution calculations, the IRS might stick a red flag on your file and keep an eye on you for a while. Certainly, failing to take any distribution at all when you reach age 70½ is likely to raise a flag or two.

c. Ineligible Rollovers

There is one more way for you or the trustee of your retirement plan to mess up your required distribution. You might roll it over. Required distributions from plans and IRAs are not eligible for rollover. (See Chapter 2 for more information about rollovers.) If they were, you would be able to withdraw your required distribution each year and roll what you don't need into another plan or IRA. That strategy might fit in with your financial and estate planning goals, but it flies in the face of Congressional intent, which is to encourage you to deplete your retirement account during your retirement, instead of preserving the assets for your heirs.

When Congress enacted the no-rollover rule, lawmakers recognized the rule would be difficult to enforce without help. Consequently, income tax regulations were fashioned to push the rule a step further, tacking on penalties for ineligible rollovers and requiring trustees of qualified plans to lend a hand in enforcement. The regulations for IRAs and TDAs are slightly different from those for qualified plans and qualified annuities.

i.   Qualified Plans and Qualified Annuities

If you decide to roll over an amount from one qualified plan to another qualified plan or to an IRA during a year you are required to take a distribution, then only the amount that exceeds the required distribution is eligible for rollover. The amount of the required distribution itself must be distributed to you, and if it is not, it must be included in your taxable income for the year anyway.

EXAMPLE: When you retired, you left your 401(k) assets with your employer. When you turned 70½ several years ago, your employer began distributing your minimum required distributions to you. On January 1 of this year, you decide to roll over your remaining 401(k) account balance into an IRA so that you can manage your own investments. The balance of your 401(k) is $500,000. Your minimum distribution for the current year is $40,000. When you receive your 401(k) distribution, you are permitted to roll over only $460,000, because your required distribution for the current year is not eligible for rollover. If you roll over the entire $500,000 anyway, you must still report $40,000 of income on your tax return as though you had not rolled over the required distribution. And there could be other penalties, as well.

If you roll over an ineligible amount into an IRA, the consequences extend beyond including the ineligible portion in your income for the year. The ineligible amount is considered an excess contribution to the IRA. If it is not promptly withdrawn, it will be subject to excess contribution penalties in the year of the contribution (rollover) and again each year the excess remains uncorrected. (See Section d, below, for more about excess contributions.)

To help ensure that the required distribution is not rolled over, the regulations require trustees of retirement plans to compute required distributions for all participants. There is good reason for placing this burden on a trustee: The portion of any distribution that exceeds the participant's required distribution is eligible for rollover. When a trustee distributes any amount that is eligible for rollover, the trustee must comply with a host of procedural rules and regulations related to withholding, disclosure and participant notification of tax options. In order to comply with these administrative rules, the trustee must determine whether or not some or all of a distribution is eligible for rollover. That in turn requires computation of the required distribution.

⚠ **Required distributions are not only ineligible for rollover, they are also ineligible for transfer.** This means that a trustee must compute the minimum required distribution not only during a rollover, but also when benefits are being transferred by the trustee directly to a new plan. Consequently, the trustee must distribute the required amount to the participant either at the time of transfer or before the required distribution deadline for the year.

ii. IRAs and TDAs

Required distributions from IRAs and TDAs also are ineligible for rollover, but compliance can be a little tricky. If you have more than one IRA (whether traditional, SEP or SIMPLE IRA), you must compute the required distribution for each one. You are then permitted to withdraw the total required amount from one or more of the IRAs. This aggregation rule applies to TDAs as well. So if you have more than one TDA, you may calculate the required distribution for each and withdraw the total from only one. Note, however, that you may not mix and match. You may not calculate a required distribution from your IRA and withdraw it from your TDA, or vice versa.

EXAMPLE: You have two IRAs and a TDA. Your required distribution from IRA #1 is $3,000 and from IRA #2 is $2,500. Your required distribution from your TDA is $4,000. You may total the required distributions from your two IRAs and withdraw the entire $5,500 from either IRA #1 or IRA #2 (or part from both). But the $4,000 required distribution from the TDA must be distributed from the TDA, not from one of the IRAs.

⚠ **Aggregation applies only to IRAs and TDAs.** Aggregation does not apply to qualified plans or qualified annuities. For example, if you have more than one 401(k) plan, you must compute the distribution for each and withdraw the required amount from the respective plan.

Because of this aggregation option for IRAs and TDAs, the IRS cannot really require the custodian of these plans to distribute the required amount before rolling over funds. What if you have already computed and withdrawn the requisite amount from another IRA or TDA—or you intend to do so? Because of this potential problem, compliance rests on the shoulders of the participant. Thus, it will be your responsibility to ensure that your required distribution from an IRA or TDA is not rolled over. Your safest approach will be to withdraw your required distribution before initiating a rollover. Otherwise, if no funds have yet been distributed for the year, a reasonable interpretation of the law might be that the first dollars distributed from any IRA are required distributions to the extent the cumulative distribution for the year does not exceed the required amount. If you roll over those first dollars, the IRS could argue you have made an excess contribution.

> **EXAMPLE:** You have three IRAs. Your required distribution from IRA #1 is $3,000, from IRA #2 is $2,500 and from IRA #3 is $3,500. You have not yet withdrawn any amount for the year from any of your IRAs. You plan to take the required distributions for all IRAs (a total of $9,000) from IRA #3. You are also planning to consolidate your IRAs during the year by rolling over IRA #1 into IRA #2.
> You should withdraw the $9,000 from IRA #3 before rolling IRA #1 into IRA #2. If you roll over IRA #1 before completing your required distribution, the IRS might argue that $3,000 of the rollover (which is the required distribution for IRA #1) is ineligible for

rollover and constitutes an excess contribution. (See Section d, below, for more about the excess contribution penalty.)

d. Excess Contributions

One of the most intimidating characteristics of the tax law is that penalties sometimes seem to come out of nowhere. One seemingly small mistake can turn a manageable tax liability into a financial albatross.

A rollover into a plan or IRA of an amount that is not permitted to be rolled over can lead to catastrophe. Unless the mistake is corrected promptly, usually by the filing deadline for the tax return, the IRS will consider the rollover an excess contribution to the plan or IRA. Excess contributions are subject to a penalty—6% for excess contributions to an IRA or 10% for excess contributions to a qualified plan. This penalty is assessed in addition to any other penalties or taxes that might apply, and it will be imposed every year until the excess is removed.

> **EXAMPLE:** In 2000 you received a required distribution of $6,000 from your 401(k) plan and rolled it over into an IRA. Because required distributions are ineligible for rollover, the $6,000 is an excess contribution. You were unaware of the problem until the IRS audited your 2000 tax return in late 2002. You removed the $6,000 in

December 2002. The $6,000 must be reported as income on your tax return for the year 2002. In addition, you will owe an excess contribution penalty of $360 (6% of $6,000) for each of the years 2000 and 2001. Because you distributed the excess before filing your year 2002 tax return, you will owe no penalty for the year 2002.

2. Reporting the Penalty

If you owe a penalty for failing to take your required distribution, you must complete IRS Form 5329 (see Appendix A) and include it when you file your tax return. If you have already filed your tax return for the year, then you must file an amended tax return for the year of the error and pay the penalty plus interest.

EXAMPLE: You began taking required distributions from your IRA in 1995 and took them regularly until 1999. In 1999, you inherited some money, so you didn't need to draw on the IRA for living expenses as you had in the past. Consequently, you simply forgot to take your required distribution of $6,000. In fact, you forgot to take your 2000 distribution, too, which would have been $6,500. Finally, in February of 2001, you realized your error.

For 1999, you must file an amended tax return and include a completed Form 5329. You must also pay a penalty of $3,000 (50% of $6,000), plus

interest, for which the IRS will bill you.

For 2000, because you have not yet passed the filing deadline for your tax return, you may simply file as usual by April 15, 2001 and include a completed Form 5329. Along with any regular income tax you owe, you will owe a penalty of $3,250 (50% of $6,500). You will not have to pay interest, though, as long as the tax return and payment are filed on time.

Finally, you should correct the distribution errors by withdrawing the required amounts for both 1999 and 2000. If you correct the problem in 2001, you must report the distributions of $6,000 (for 1999) and $6,500 (for 2000) on your 2001 tax return. In addition, you will have to take a required distribution for 2001 and include it as income on your tax return.

In general, you have until December 31 to take your required distribution for any given year. If you miss the deadline, you must pay the penalty when you file your tax return (or pay the penalty with an amended return). The one exception to the December 31 deadline is the first year of required distributions. A grace period gives you until April 1 of the following year to withdraw your first required distribution. (See Chapter 6, Section A, for more information about when distributions must begin.) Thus, if you don't take a distribution by December 31 of the first year of required distributions, you won't owe a penalty unless you miss the April 1 deadline as well. If you happen to miss that one, too, you must pay the penalty, but you would pay it when you file your tax return for the following year—the year containing the extended distribution deadline.

> **EXAMPLE:** You turned 70½ in 1999, so your required beginning date (with the grace period) was April 1, 2000, although your first distribution year is officially 1999. This means that you were supposed to take your first required distribution by April 1, 2000 and your second distribution by December 31, 2000. Unfortunately, you forgot to take any distribution at all until January 2001. You will owe penalties for 1999 and 2000, because you missed the deadline for both required distributions. But because both distribution deadlines were in 2000, you can simply complete a Form 5329 and attach it to your tax return for the 2000 tax year (which is due by April 15, 2001). At that time, you must pay the 50% penalty on the required distribution shortfalls for both 1999 and 2000. You do not have to file an amended return for 1999, because the distribution for 1999 did not have to be made until April 1, 2000.

F. Waiver

Mistakes happen. Even Congress knows it. That's why a waiver has been written into the penalty provisions of the required distribution law.

1. Terms of the Waiver

There are four short paragraphs in the Tax Code section that assesses a penalty for delaying distributions from your retirement plan. But the entire fourth paragraph is devoted to a waiver of the penalty. It says that if you demonstrate that your failure to withdraw the proper amount was due to reasonable error and you are taking steps to correct the shortfall, the penalty may be waived. "May" is the operative word, though. The IRS is not required to waive the penalty; it simply has the authority to do so.

Sometimes, the penalty will be waived. If a beneficiary inherits a retirement plan, he or she will generally take distributions over his or her life expectancy beginning in the year after the original participant's death (the life expectancy rule). But if the beneficiary fails to take the first distribution on time, he or she can fall back on the five-year rule to avoid a penalty. The five-year rule requires that all assets be distributed by December 31 of the year containing the fifth anniversary of the participant's death. To fall back on the five-year rule, the plan must permit the five-year rule as an option. If it does and if the beneficiary chooses to use it, the penalty for failing to take a distribution under the life expectancy rule will be waived automatically. (See Chapter 7 for more information about the life expectancy rule and the five-year rule.)

2. Requesting a Waiver

To request a waiver, you must first explain how the mistake came about. Perhaps you didn't understand the computation formula. Or maybe you wrote a letter to the custodian of your plan requesting a distribution, but you broke your leg on the way to the post office to mail the letter and forgot to drop the letter in a mail box after you were released from the hospital.

Your excuse must accompany a description of the steps you have taken to correct the mistake. For example, you might report that as soon as you discovered you didn't take the appropriate amount from your IRA, you asked the custodian to distribute the funds, which the custodian did the following week.

These explanations must be attached to a completed Form 5329 and filed along with the rest of your return at tax time. If you are submitting an amended return, send it in right away. There is one catch: even though you intend to request a waiver, you must still pay the 50% penalty and mail it with your tax return. If the IRS accepts your explanation and approves the waiver, you will receive a refund.

The IRS has been generous with these waivers, so don't assume your excuse is too lame to pass muster. For example,

taxpayers have argued that they didn't understand the formula for computing the required distribution or that they made an arithmetic error. One taxpayer claimed that he signed the request for a distribution but forgot to mail it to his custodian. In all of those cases, the taxpayers had corrected their mistakes by the time they reported the error to the IRS, and they were all granted waivers.

If you have a plausible explanation for your error and you have taken steps to correct it, you stand a good chance of obtaining a waiver. Even the IRS is aware that 50% is a stiff penalty, and the agency is more interested in curbing abuse than punishing the computationally challenged. But if you consistently fail to take appropriate distributions, or if the IRS discovers your mistake during an audit, the IRS is likely to be less forgiving.

Key Tax Code Sections
§ 401(a)(9)   Required Distributions From Qualified Plans
§ 402(e)(4)   Eligible Rollover From Qualified Plan
§ 408(d)(3)(E)   Ineligible Rollover From IRA
§ 4974   50% Excise Tax on Required Distributions
§ 1.403(b)-2   Treatment of Pre-1987 Accumulation in TDA

Chapter 6

Distributions You Must Take During Your Lifetime

Who Should Read Chapter 6

➡️ Most everyone will need to read this chapter. It tells you precisely when you are required to begin taking money out of your own retirement plan or IRA, how you compute the amount to withdraw and what other decisions you must make at that time.

*C*omedians and accountants have long pondered the origin of the numbers that appear in the Tax Code—the ones that don't seem to make any sense. Why must we start taking money out of our retirement plans at age 70½? Why not 70? Or even 71? Some of us like to think Congress has a sense of humor, although cynics believe there's a conspiracy to keep the Tax Code complex. More likely, it's the result of a compromise.

Whatever its history, 70½ has become an important milestone; it's the age when most people must crack open their retirement nest eggs, even if they don't want to. Before age 59½, you have to worry about penalties for tapping your retirement money too early. (See Chapter 3 for information on the early distribution penalty.) Age 59½ to 70½ is the penalty-free zone. You can take distributions any time you want—or not—without penalty. But once you reach 70½, you are required to begin taking distributions.

Some or all of your retirement plan nest egg might be paid to you as an annuity after you retire, which means you will receive your money in installments—usually in the form of monthly payments. The payments might continue for a fixed number of years (a term certain) but more often will be spread over your lifetime. Annuities are a common form of payment if you were covered by your employer's defined benefit plan while you were working.

Annuity payments must also satisfy the required distribution rules described in this chapter. Annuity plan administrators are aware of the distribution rules, and the plans are generally structured to ensure that your payments satisfy the requirements; however, ultimately the responsibility is yours.

If, instead of an annuity, some or all of your nest egg is in an IRA or another type of retirement plan account, then when it is time for you to begin required distributions it is your responsibility to compute and withdraw the appropriate amount each year.

In this chapter, we discuss in detail the rules governing required distributions that you must take during your lifetime. You may recall from Chapter 5 that there are two sets of rules to contend with: The so-called new rules, which came about through regulations that the IRS issued in January 2001, and the so-called old rules, which are simply the rules that were in place prior to the January 2001 regulations.

Helpful Terms

Annuity. A contract, sold by an insurance company, that promises to make monthly, quarterly, semiannual or annual payments for life or for a specified period of time.

Contingent Beneficiary. A person or entity who is entitled to receive the benefits of a retirement plan or IRA only if and when a specific event occurs, such as the death of a primary beneficiary.

Distribution. A payout of property (such as shares of stock) or cash from a retirement plan or IRA to the participant or a beneficiary.

Irrevocable Trust. A trust that cannot be changed or terminated by the person who created it. Once assets are transferred to an irrevocable trust, the assets are subject to the terms of the trust for as long as the trust exists.

Life Expectancy Factor. The divisor used for determining a required distribution. An account balance is divided by a life expectancy factor to arrive at the required distribution for a given year.

Primary Beneficiary. A person or entity entitled to receive benefits from a retirement plan or IRA upon the death of the original participant.

Recalculated Life Expectancy. Life expectancy that is revised each year according to statistically accurate measures of mortality.

Revocable Trust. A trust whose terms allow the creator of the trust to alter its provisions, cancel it or remove some or all of the property from the trust and return the property to the creator.

Term Certain or Period Certain. A fixed, identifiable period, such as a specific number of years. For example, a retirement plan that is distributable over a term certain of 20 years must be completely liquidated (distributed) after 20 years.

We discuss the new rules in Part I and the old rules in Part II. As you read this chapter, please keep in mind that:

- The new rules are more favorable, so you will want to start using them as soon as possible. Even if you started taking required distributions some years ago, you can still use the new rules for distributions that you take in 2001. (But read on for a special wrinkle pertaining to qualified plans.)

- If you have an IRA, you can start using the new rules immediately. If you have a qualified plan, however, the plan must be modified (amended) to incorporate the new rules before you can use the new rules (this is the wrinkle that we mentioned above). If you are not sure whether the plan has been modified, ask the plan administrator.

- As you read through parts I and II, be careful that you don't lose track of which part you are reading. Some of the changes are subtle, but significant.

Part I: New Rules

A. Required Beginning Date

The absolute deadline for taking your first required distribution (withdrawal) from your retirement plan is called your "required beginning date," or RBD. If you are the original owner of your retirement plan (as opposed to the beneficiary of someone else's plan), then your RBD is April 1 of the year after you turn 70½.

> EXAMPLE: You were born January 1, 1932. You will turn 70½ on July 1, 2002. Your RBD is April 1, 2003.

Your RBD marks the deadline for taking the required distribution for your first distribution year only. For all subsequent years, the deadline is December 31.

You can defer your RBD for an employer plan if you work past age 70½. In that case, your RBD for that particular plan is April 1 of the year after you retire, no matter what age you are.

! Self-employed people beware. This special deferral option is not available if you own 5% or more of the business that sponsors the retirement plan, which of course includes virtually all self-employed individuals.

You generally cannot defer your RBD for any IRAs you have. There are exceptions for people who are covered by a federal or state government plan or by a church plan. (A church plan is one maintained by a church for church employees. This would include any type of religious organization or house of worship, as long as the organization qualifies as a tax-exempt organization.) If neither of those situations applies, the RBD for an IRA is April 1 of the year after you turn 70½, even if you continue to work.

As you can see, it's possible to have more than one RDB if you work beyond age 70½—one for an employer plan and one for an IRA.

💡 If you inherit a retirement plan. You must use a different set of rules to determine your RBD for plans that you inherit. We discuss those rules in Chapters 7 and 8.

Because April 1 of the year after age 70½ is the RBD for most people, that is the date we will use for discussion purposes in this chapter.

1. First Year

You must withdraw at least the required minimum amount from your retirement plan account by your RBD or you will face a stiff penalty. To satisfy this requirement, you may count all distributions that take place between January 1 of the year you turn 70½ and April 1 of the following year (which is your RBD). In other words, you have 15 months to complete your first distribution.

Although you are permitted to take the required distribution in one big chunk, you don't have to. You can take it out as you need it, for example in monthly installments, as long as you have removed the minimum required amount for the first year by your RBD.

It is important to remember that amounts distributed before January 1 of the year you turn 70½ do not count toward your first required distribution, nor do amounts distributed after your RBD.

EXAMPLE 1: You turn 70½ in 2002, which means that 2002 is your first distribution year. Although you were not required to take money out of you IRA in 2001, you took $20,000 on October 1, 2001, to buy a car. In 2002,

your required minimum distribution is $10,000. You may not count the $20,000 you took in 2001 toward your 2002 required distribution.

EXAMPLE 2: You turn 70½ in 2002, and your RBD is April 1, 2003. Your required distribution for 2002 is $10,000. You decide to wait until 2003 to take the distribution for your first year. You take $9,000 on March 1, 2003, and another $1,000 on May 1, 2003. Because the $1,000 that you took on May 1 is after your RBD, you cannot use it as part of your required distributions. Because you are $1,000 short of the amount required to be distributed, you will owe the IRS penalties on the $1,000 shortfall.

2. Second Year and Beyond

For the second and all future distribution years, you must take at least the required amount out of your retirement account between January 1 and December 31. There are no more three-month grace periods.

Waiting can be costly. If you decide to wait until your RBD (which is April 1 of your second distribution year) to take your first required distribution, you must still take the full required distribution for the second year by December 31. That means you would have to take two required distributions in the same year, which could push you into a higher income tax bracket. For example, let's say you turn 70½ in 2002, which is your first distribution year, and your RBD is April 1, 2003. Your required distribution for your first distribution year is $20,000 and for the second year is $22,000. You are single and have no other taxable income. You also use the standard deduction. If you take your first distribution in 2002 and the second in 2003, you will pay a 15% tax rate on both distributions. If take both distributions in the same year, however, your gross income will be $42,000. At that level, some of your distributions will be taxed at a 28% rate.

Again, you may take the distribution in bits and pieces during the 12-month period, or you may take the entire amount on December 31. If you happen to take more than the required amount in one year, which is permissible, you may not count the excess toward your required distributions for the next year (or beyond).

EXAMPLE: Your required distribution for your second distribution year is $10,000 and for your third distribution year is $12,000. If you take $16,000 in your second distribution year, you may not apply the extra $6,000 to your third distribution year and withdraw only $6,000. Instead you must withdraw the full $12,000 during the third year.

B. Computing the Required Amount

To compute your required distribution for a given year, simply divide your account balance by what the IRS calls the "applicable distribution period," or ADP (see Section 2, below). The resulting number is the minimum amount you must withdraw from the account for that year.

You must compute this required minimum distribution separately for each retirement plan that you have. When it comes to actually withdrawing the computed amounts, however, you have some flexibility. For example, you may be able to withdraw the total amount from only one account. (See Section 4, below, for more information about this strategy.)

1. Determining the Account Balance

According to Tax Regulations, the account balance for computing your required distribution each year is determined as of "the last valuation date in the calendar year before the distribution calendar year." For the vast majority of people who are computing their own required distributions, this would be December 31 of the year before the distribution year.

If your retirement assets are in a qualified plan when you begin required distributions instead of in an IRA, however, it is possible that the plan itself specifies a date other than December 31 for valuing the plan assets and computing require distributions. Nevertheless, we will use December 31 for discussion purposes in this book.

> **EXAMPLE:** You turn 70½ in 2002. To compute the required distribution for your first distribution year (2002), you use your account balance as of December 31, 2001. To compute the required distribution for the year 2003, you look at your account balance as of December 31, 2002, and so on.

Recall that you are permitted to take your first required distribution in the year after you turn 70½, as long as you take it on or before your RBD (which is April 1 of the year after you turn 70½). Deferring your first distribution, however, does not alter the date for determining the appropriate account balance. For example, if you turn 70½ in 2002 and decide to take your first distribution in March of 2003, you must still use your account balance as of December 31, 2001, to compute the amount of your first distribution.

If you decide to take advantage of the grace period and take your first required distribution after December 31, things get a little complicated when it's time to compute the distribution for the second year. In that case, you must subtract the amount of your first year's distribution from the account balance.

> **EXAMPLE:** You turn 70½ in 2002. On December 31, 2001, your account balance was $41,200 and you computed your required distribution to be $2,000. You decided not to withdraw the required distribution for your first distribution until March 1, 2003, which is well before your RBD of April 1, 2003. Your December 31, 2002, account balance is $50,000. But you don't use that amount to calculate the distribution for the second distribution year (2003). Instead, you use $48,000 ($50,000 – $2,000)—just as if you had taken your 2002 distribution during 2002.

This extra subtraction is not necessary if you withdraw the entire minimum required amount by December 31 of the year you turn 70½. And because you cannot defer your second (or any future) required distribution beyond December 31 of the distribution year, no adjustments to the year-end account balance will be necessary (or permitted).

2. Determining the Applicable Distribution Period

Once you have determined the appropriate account balance to use for a particular distribution year, you must divide it by the applicable distribution period (or ADP) to arrive at your required distribution.

a. First Year

To find your ADP for your first distribution year, you must use one of two tables provided by the IRS. Most people will use what the IRS calls the "uniform table" (Table III in Appendix B), but some people will be able to use the "joint life and last survivor expectancy table" (Table II in Appendix B). The table you use depends on whom you designate as your beneficiary. (See Section C, below, for more information about designating a beneficiary.)

i.   General Rule

The vast majority of people will use the uniform table to find their ADP. The only time a person will not do this is when a spouse is the sole beneficiary of the retirement account and is also more than ten years younger than the owner of the account.

In all other cases, you will use the uniform table. Thus, if your beneficiary is a child, grandchild, friend, charity, your estate or a spouse who is not more than ten years younger than you are, you will use the uniform table. And if you haven't yet named a beneficiary, you will use the uniform table.

To find the ADP for your first distribution year, determine your age as of your birthday in the year you turn 70½. If that age is 70, then find the ADP next to age 70 in the uniform table (Table III in Appendix B). That number is 26.2.

If your age is 71 on your birthday in the year you turn 70½, the ADP from the table is 25.3.

! It depends on when your birthday is. You are not always age 70 in your first distribution year. If your birthday falls after June 30, you will turn 70½ in the same year in which you turn 71. In that case, you must use age 71 when looking up the ADP for your first distribution year.

ii. Spouse More Than Ten Years Younger

If your beneficiary is your spouse and he or she is more than ten years younger than you are, the rules are slightly more favorable. You do not use the uniform table to find your ADP. Instead, you use the joint life table (Table II in Appendix B) to find it. This is because the ADP is the actual joint life expectancy of you and your spouse.

To determine your ADP, look up the number that corresponds to your age and your spouse's age on your respective birthdays in your first distribution year. For example, if you are age 70 on your birthday in your first distribution year (the year you turn 70½) and your spouse is age 55 in that year, your ADP from Table II is 29.9.

Be careful, though. In order to use Table II for your ADP, you must satisfy both of the following requirements:

- your spouse must be more than ten years younger than you are, and

- your spouse must have been the sole designated beneficiary of the retirement account for the entire year. (See Section C, below, for more information about designating a beneficiary.)

b. Second Year and Beyond

Determining the ADP for the second and future distribution years is done in precisely the same way you determined the ADP for the first year.

i. General Rule

In your second distribution year, you will again use the uniform table, or Table III, to find your ADP—unless your spouse-beneficiary is more than ten years younger than you are. (In that case, see Section ii, below.) For the second year calculation, use your age as of your birthday in the second year. If your age in that year is 71, find the ADP next to age 71 in Table III. That number is 25.3. For the third year, assuming you are age 72 on your birthday, your ADP is 24.4, and so on.

ii. Spouse More Than Ten Years Younger

If your spouse is more than ten years younger than you are, and if he or she was the sole designated beneficiary of your retirement plan or IRA for the entire year, then you use Table II to find the ADP for your second distribution year. Look up the number that corresponds to your age and your spouse's age on your respective birthdays in your second distribution year. For example, if you are age 71 on your birthday in your second distribution year and your spouse is age 56 in that year, Table II indicates that your joint life expectancy—your ADP—for the second year is 29.

EXAMPLE: You turned 70½ in 2002. At that time, your brother was the beneficiary of your IRA. In November of 2002, you married someone 20 years younger than you and changed the beneficiary designation of your IRA to your new spouse. For 2002, you must use the uniform table—Table III—to compute your first required distribution. For 2003, you may use Table II to find your ADP, as long as your new spouse remains the beneficiary for all of 2003.

3. Computing the Required Distribution

Once you have determined the appropriate account balance and ADP, you simply divide the account balance by the ADP to arrive at your required minimum distribution. You can withdraw more than the required amount each year, but you may not withdraw less without incurring a penalty. (See Chapter 5 to learn more about the penalty.)

EXAMPLE: You turn 70 on March 1, 2002, and your IRA account balance on December 31, 2001, is $50,000. Your niece is the beneficiary of your IRA. Your ADP for your first distribution year is 26.2 (from Table III). Therefore, your first required distribution is $1,908 ($50,000 divided by 26.2).

Special opportunity for after-tax contributions. If you retire and receive a lump sum distribution from your employer's plan, any after-tax contributions that you made to the plan may not be rolled over into an IRA, but must be distributed to you. Because these amounts are not taxable, you have an interesting planning opportunity if your retirement date is in the year you turn 70½ or later. Specifically, you may count the distribution of after-tax amounts as part of your required distribution from the plan for that particular year. By doing so you can reduce your income tax while leaving additional pre-tax amounts in the account to grow for another year.

EXAMPLE: You retire in 2002, which is also the year you turn 70½. Over the years, you created quite a nest egg of pre-tax dollars inside your employer's qualified retirement plan. You have also made $10,000 in after-tax contributions. Your required distribution for your first distribution year is $19,000. When you retire in 2002, your employer distributes your retirement benefits to you as a lump sum. You decide to take your first required distribution by December 31, 2002. Your intention is to roll over into an IRA all but your required distribution for 2002. You keep out your after-tax contributions of $10,000, which you may not roll over anyway. You keep an additional $9,000. You then roll over the remainder of the lump sum into an IRA. Thus, you have distributed from your retirement plan the entire amount of your first required distribution ($19,000), but only $9,000 of it is taxable.

4. Special Aggregation Rule for IRAs and TDAs

If you have more than one IRA, you must compute the required distribution for each IRA separately, but then you may add up all the computed amounts and take the total from only one or several IRAs, as long as the aggregate or total amount is distributed before the deadline.

This strategy also works if you have more than one TDA (tax deferred annuity) plan. You may compute the required distribution for each plan, and then distribute the total from just one or more of the plans. You may not mix and match IRAs and TDAs, however. If you have one IRA and one TDA, you must calculate and distribute the required amount from each separately.

⚠️ **No aggregation for other types of plans.** You are only allowed to use the aggregation rule for IRAs and TDAs. If you have another type of plan (such as an employer plan or Keogh), you must compute the required amount for that plan and take the computed amount from that particular plan.

5. Reporting Distributions

Each year, the custodian or trustee of a plan or IRA from which distributions must be taken must report to the IRS and to the participant of the plan or IRA the amount of the required distribution. The custodian or trustee will determine the amount based on the account balance and the life expectancy of the designated beneficiary.

Just because the custodian is reporting the required minimum distribution to the IRS doesn't mean you must take the distribution from that account. For example, you can take a different amount if you use the aggregation rule described in the previous section. If you have more than one IRA, you might be calculating the total distribution from all, but taking the distribution from only one.

The IRS expects it will be able to total the amounts reported by all custodians and see a matching number on your tax return. Presumably, the IRS will not attempt to track which account the distribution came from.

C. Designating a Beneficiary

In the old days, if you did not name a person as beneficiary of your IRA or retirement plan, you would feel the impact of that decision as soon as you reached age 70½. That's because, without a designated beneficiary, you would be required to distribute your retirement plan a lot faster than you would if you had named a designated beneficiary.

But the IRS has relaxed that requirement. Now it doesn't matter who your beneficiary is when you start taking required distributions. You are permitted to use the uniform table, even if you fail to name any beneficiary at all.

Even though the IRS won't punish you for not naming a beneficiary by your RBD, naming a designated beneficiary is still important. First, if your spouse is more than ten years younger than you are and you want to use Table II to compute required distributions, you can only do so if your spouse is your designated beneficiary.

Second, if you die without a designated beneficiary of your retirement plan or IRA, the distribution of the plan or IRA assets could be accelerated after your death, possibly leaving your heirs with significant tax problems. (See chapters 7 and 8 for more information about what happens if you die without a designated beneficiary.)

Bear in mind that you may name any person or entity as the beneficiary of your retirement plan. But not all beneficiaries are "designated" beneficiaries. If you choose a beneficiary who does not fall within the definition of designated beneficiary, you are deemed to have no beneficiary at all for required distribution purposes.

1. Definition of Designated Beneficiary

A designated beneficiary must be a "natural person," as opposed to an entity such as a charity or a corporation. There is one exception to this natural person rule: a trust that has certain qualifications (known as a qualified trust—see Section c, below) can be a designated beneficiary.

If you fail to name a natural person or a qualified trust as your beneficiary and instead name your estate, a charity, a corporation or a non-qualified trust, then you are deemed to have no designated beneficiary for required distributions purposes.

Just because you do not complete a beneficiary designation form and record the name of a beneficiary does not necessarily mean that you have no designated beneficiary. Some plans provide for a default beneficiary, usually a spouse, when the owner does not name a beneficiary. Be sure to find out if your plan has such a default provision. If it does not, then you are deemed to have no designated beneficiary even if the laws of your state dictate who should receive your assets.

Designated beneficiaries fall into the following three categories: spouse, non-spouse natural person and qualified trust. We look at each category in the following sections.

a. Spouse

If you are married, you can name your spouse as your designated beneficiary. If your spouse is your designated beneficiary, your spouse will have certain privileges after your death—such as a rollover option—that other beneficiaries will not have. (See Chapters 7 and 8.)

b. Non-Spouse Natural Person

Any human being—what the Tax Code calls a "natural person"—qualifies as a designated beneficiary. For example, your designated beneficiary could be a friend, relative or a non-marital partner.

c. Qualified Trust

A trust can be a designated beneficiary if it meets all of the following requirements:

- The trust must be valid under state law, meaning the terms must be enforceable.
- The trust must be either irrevocable while you are alive (meaning you cannot change its terms or cancel it) or irrevocable upon your death.
- The beneficiaries of the trust must be natural persons (humans) and must be identifiable. They don't have to be identified by name, however. For example, you may use the terms "spouse" or "children."
- You must provide a copy of the trust to the trustee or custodian of your retirement plan or IRA. If the trust is revocable (meaning you can change or amend it), you must give the trustee or custodian a copy of any subsequent amendments. As an alternative to submitting the entire trust agreement, you may also provide a list of beneficiaries with a description of the amount each is to receive and the conditions, if any, under which they will receive benefits.

If the trust meets all of the above qualifications, then the beneficiary of the trust is treated as the designated beneficiary for purposes of computing your required distributions. The trust must satisfy all of the above for any period during which the trust is named beneficiary and during which the beneficiary of the trust is being used to determine required distributions. If your spouse is sole beneficiary of the trust and is more than ten years younger than you are, you can use Table II to find your ADP each year when computing required distributions. If there is more than one beneficiary of the trust, however, the multiple beneficiary rules of Section 2, just below, will apply.

2. Multiple Beneficiaries

If you want to name more than one person as the beneficiary of your retirement plan, you should be aware of the consequences.

a. Primary Beneficiaries

You can name several primary beneficiaries of your retirement plan who may or may not share equally in the plan assets after your death. If any one of the primary beneficiaries fails to qualify as a designated beneficiary, then you are deemed to have no designated beneficiary at all. This is true even if all other beneficiaries would qualify as designated beneficiaries. For example, if you name your sister to receive

50% of your IRA and a charity to receive the rest, you are deemed to have no designated beneficiary (because the charity is not a natural person).

You can avoid this problem by setting up a separate IRA for each beneficiary. For example, you can direct the custodian of the IRA, in writing, to set up a second IRA and transfer half of your existing IRA assets into the new IRA. You would name the charity as sole beneficiary of the new IRA and your sister as sole beneficiary of the old IRA.

 Sometimes, your heirs can cure the problem. If you die having named multiple beneficiaries of your retirement plan and if one of those beneficiaries is not a designated beneficiary, all is not lost. Your heirs might be able to cure the problem by splitting the account or by distributing assets to one or more beneficiaries by December 31 of the year after your death. For more information about these strategies, see the "Multiple Beneficiaries— One Account" sections of Chapters 7 and 8.

b. Contingent Beneficiaries

A contingent beneficiary is a beneficiary you name to receive your retirement plan assets in the event your primary beneficiary does not qualify to receive the benefits. Usually a primary beneficiary fails to qualify because he or she has already died. If you name a primary beneficiary and then name a contingent beneficiary who will receive the retirement benefits

only if the primary beneficiary predeceases you, then the contingent beneficiary has no effect on required distributions.

If the contingent beneficiary could become the primary beneficiary for any reason other than the death of the original primary beneficiary, then the contingent beneficiary is treated as one of multiple beneficiaries (along with the primary beneficiary) when determining required distributions.

EXAMPLE: You have instructed the custodian of your IRA in writing that you name your spouse, who is 15 years younger than you, as primary beneficiary of your IRA, but only if you are married at the time of your death. In the event you and your spouse divorce, your father will become the primary beneficiary of your IRA. Because your father's interest is not contingent solely on the death of your spouse, both your spouse and your father are considered beneficiaries of your retirement plan. Consequently, because your spouse is not the sole designated beneficiary, you may not use Table II to compute required distributions. Instead you must use the uniform table—Table III.

D. Special Rules for Annuities

If you are taking some or all of your retirement plan benefits in the form of an annuity, those annuity payments must also satisfy the required distribution rules described in this chapter.

Although the required distribution rules for annuities are essentially the same as those for IRAs and other retirement plans, there are some differences worth noting.

Types of Annuities

In order to understand how the required distribution rules apply to your annuity, you must first know what type of annuity you have:

Life Annuity: A life annuity makes payments to you or to you and your beneficiary for your entire life. You might have a single life annuity or a joint and survivor annuity. Payments from a single life annuity continue throughout your lifetime and stop when you die, regardless of how much has been paid. No further payments are made to any heirs or to your estate. In the case of a joint and survivor annuity, payments continue until your death or the death of your beneficiary—whichever occurs later—and then the payments stop. No additional payments are made to any other heirs or to your estate.

Term Certain Annuity: A term certain annuity makes payments for a fixed number of years regardless of when you die or when your beneficiary dies. If you die before the term is over, payments will be made to your beneficiary, your estate or your heirs for the remainder of the term.

Life Annuity With Term Certain: A life annuity with a term certain will make payments for your lifetime or for a term certain if you die before the term is up. For example, assume you are taking a single life annuity with a term certain of ten years. If you live more than ten years, the annuity payments will continue throughout your life and stop when you die. If you die after five years, the annuity will continue payments for five more years. Similarly, if you have a joint and survivor annuity with a term certain, and both you and your beneficiary die before the term is up, the annuity will continue to be paid to your heirs for the remainder of the term.

1. Form of Payment

To satisfy the required distribution rules, annuity payments must come at regular intervals of at least once a year. For example, you can receive payments monthly, quarterly, semi-annually or annually, but not every 18 months.

The payments may be in the form of either a life annuity or a term certain.

If you choose a life annuity, the payments must last for your lifetime or the joint lifetime of you and your beneficiary.

If you choose a term certain, the term must satisfy one of the following:

- it must be the shorter of the ADP for your age (from Table III) or the joint life expectancy of you and your beneficiary (from Table II), or
- it must be no longer than the joint life expectancy of you and your spouse beneficiary (from Table II), if your spouse beneficiary is more than ten years younger than you are.

Once payments begin, the term certain may not be lengthened and payments generally must be level, although they might be increased to reflect changes in cost of living, benefit increases under the plan or investment gains in your annuity portfolio.

2. Required Beginning Date

When you receive your retirement benefits as an annuity, the first payment must be made on or before your RBD to satisfy the required distribution rules. The amount of the first required payment is simply your regular annuity payment for that period. For example, if the terms of your annuity require that you be paid $2,000 per month for life, then you must receive your first $2,000 payment on or before your RBD. You are not required to receive any payments before that date.

3. Starting Early

If you elect to start receiving your annuity before your RBD and if you comply with the "Form of Payment" rules described in Section 2, above, then the start date of your annuity becomes your RBD for all purposes. For example, the start date is the irrevocable deadline for naming a designated beneficiary whose life expectancy can be used to determine your minimum required annuity payment.

4. Young Beneficiaries

If the beneficiary of your annuity is more than ten years younger than you are (and is not your spouse), then you must use special tables to determine whether or not your annuity satisfies the required distribution rules. You will need to know what type of annuity you have in order to determine which table to use.

a. If You Have a Term Certain Annuity

If you have elected to take your annuity over a term certain and have named a non-spouse beneficiary who is more than ten years younger than you are, you may still use Table II to find your joint life expectancy, but only until your RBD. Once you reach your RBD, you must satisfy the required distribution rules, which means you must use the MDIB rules. Specifically, the term certain may not exceed the period found in Table III (see Appendix B) beginning in the year you turn 70½ and for all subsequent years.

> EXAMPLE: You were born March 1, 1937. You retire and begin taking your annuity in 2002 when you are age 65. You name your grandson as beneficiary. In 2002, he was 35 years old and your joint life expectancy, according to Table II, was 47.7 years. You elected to begin taking distributions over a term certain of 47.7 years. Five years later, when you turn 70½, the remaining term certain is 42.7 years (47.7 – 5). According to Table III, however, which you must use when you reach age 70½, the remaining term certain may not exceed 26.2 years. In order to satisfy required distribution rules, your annuity plan must automatically adjust your payments beginning in the year you turn 70½ so

that the annuity is paid out over 26.2 years (instead of 42.7 years).

b. Joint and Survivor Annuity

If you elect to receive a life annuity (without a term certain) over the joint life of you and a non-spouse beneficiary who is more than ten years younger than you are, then at all times from and after your first distribution year (the year you turn 70½), the projected payment to your beneficiary cannot exceed a certain percentage of the payment you are currently receiving. The percentage is based on the difference in your ages and is determined from Table IV (see Appendix B).

As in the case of a term certain annuity, if you begin receiving payments before your RBD and they do not satisfy the required distribution rules, the payments must be adjusted beginning in the year you turn 70½.

> EXAMPLE: You were born on March 1, 1932. You are taking your retirement benefits as a joint and survivor annuity over the joint life of you and your daughter. Your daughter was born in 1953. In 2002, the year you turn 70½, your monthly payment is $3,000. The age difference between you and your daughter is 21 years. From Table IV, you see that, beginning in 2002, your daughter's projected benefit when you die cannot exceed 72% of your current

benefit—that is, it cannot exceed $2,160 per month ($3,000 x .72). So when you die, the payment to your daughter must drop from $3,000 per month to no more than $2,160 per month.

If you name more than one beneficiary of your annuity, then you must use the youngest beneficiary to determine the percentage from Table IV. And similarly, if you change your beneficiary to a younger beneficiary (for any reason other than the death of a primary beneficiary), your payments may need to be adjusted so that projected payments to the beneficiary satisfy the percentage requirements from Table IV.

c. Joint and Survivor Annuity With Term Certain

If you have a life annuity with a term certain, you must satisfy both the term certain requirements described in Section a, above, as well as the survivor benefit limitations described in Section b, above. In other words, the term of your annuity may not exceed the number corresponding to your age in Table III, and the projected payments to your beneficiary after your death may not exceed the percentage in Table IV.

It's not always this difficult.
Although the annuity rules seem (and can be) complex, most people's annuities take the form of a single life annu-

ity or a joint life annuity with a spouse. If you have selected either of these forms of payment, then you should not have to make new computations every year. It is only when you use a much younger non-spouse beneficiary or when you change beneficiaries that your situation could become more complicated.

E. Divorce or Separation

If you are divorced or separated, part of your qualified plan, qualified annuity or TDA might be payable to an "alternate payee" (such as a spouse, former spouse or child) under the terms of a QDRO—a court-approved divorce or maintenance agreement. (See Chapter 2, Section C.4, for more information about QDROs.)

When you reach your RBD, the required distribution rules will apply to the alternate payee's portion, as well as to your own. And because you are the plan participant, it is your RBD that determines when distributions must begin. Furthermore, if the required amount is not withdrawn in timely fashion, you, not the alternate payee, must pay the penalty. As for other required distribution rules, the way in which they are applied will depend on whether or not the alternate payee's portion is in a separate account.

Alternate payee must wait. The terms of your QDRO might provide that the alternate payee is to receive immediate and total distribution of his or her share of the plan. Unless the plan itself permits such a distribution, however, the alternate payee must wait to receive his or her share until the time when you distribute assets from the plan, either at your retirement or when you begin required distributions or at some other time specified by the plan.

1. Separate Account

A QDRO might require that an alternate payee's portion be "divided" and separately accounted for. If so, the following variations in the required distribution rules apply:

- The alternate payee's separate share is not to be combined, or aggregated, with the rest of your plan benefits when you compute required distributions. In other words, you would separately compute the required distribution amount for your portion and the alternate payee's portion. You would then distribute the alternate payee's portion from his or her share.
- In computing the required distribution from the alternate payee's portion, you may use one of the following to determine the ADP:
- the uniform table (Table III) based on your age
- the joint life of you and the alternate payee, if the alternate payee is your ex-spouse and is more than ten years younger than you are, or

- The alternate payee's single life expectancy.

The decision about which ADP to use belongs to you—not to the alternate payee—even though the distribution will come from the alternate payee's portion and will be distributed to the alternate payee. (See Section B.2, above, for more information about ADP.)

⚠️ **If the alternate payee dies.**
Although you have several options for selecting a distribution period to compute required distributions from the alternate payee's portion, one option that you do not have is to use the joint life expectancy of the alternate payee and his or her beneficiary. If the alternate payee dies before your RBD, however, the alternate payee's beneficiary will be treated as the beneficiary for required distribution purposes.

EXAMPLE: Your ex-husband is entitled to half of your pension plan under the terms of your QDRO. The pension plan administrator separated your ex-husband's share into a separate account, and your ex-husband named his sister as beneficiary of his separate share of the pension. The plan provides that no distributions can be made until you retire or reach your RBD. If your ex-husband dies before your RBD, then your ex-husband's sister becomes the designated beneficiary when computing distributions from your ex-husband's portion of the pension.

Even if a QDRO mandates dividing the retirement benefit between you and the alternate payee, the terms of the plan might not permit physically separating the shares. The plan administrator can get around this using a reasonable method to separately account for the alternate payee's portion. For example, a reasonable method would be to allocate on a pro rata basis all investment gains and losses, as well as contributions and forfeitures (if applicable).

2. No Separate Account

In some instances, you will not physically separate your share from the alternate payee's share. Some QDROs do not require an actual separation of the alternate payee's share, and some plans don't permit actual separation.

In either case, the retirement plan remains undivided, and a portion of each distribution goes to the alternate payee. Under this scenario, the alternate payee's portion does not have to separately satisfy the minimum distribution requirement. Instead, it is combined, or aggregated, with your other plan assets for purposes of determining the account balance and calculating your required distribution for the year.

Thus, aggregation means that the required distribution rules work as though there was no alternate payee. When calculating required distributions, you may use

either the uniform table or Table II (if your spouse-beneficiary is more than ten years younger than you are). But you may not use the alternate payee's single life expectancy.

3. Income Taxes and Penalties

Generally speaking, the rules governing the payment of taxes and penalties on QDRO distributions are essentially the same whether the alternate payee is a spouse, former spouse or child.

There are, however, two exceptions to that general rule. We explain those in the following sections.

a. Spouse or Former Spouse Alternate Payee

If the alternate payee named in the QDRO is your spouse or former spouse, the alternate payee must pay all income taxes on distributions he or she receives. But you are responsible for penalties on any shortfall in required distributions, even though the alternate payee is receiving a portion.

b. Non-Spouse Alternate Payee

If the alternate payee is someone other than your spouse or former spouse (for example, your child), you must pay all income taxes, as well as any penalties that might apply. This is true even though the distribution actually goes to the alternate payee.

4. Rollovers

The option to roll over a distribution from a qualified plan into an IRA or another qualified plan is a big tax benefit. Traditionally, the benefit has been reserved for plan participants, and occasionally the participant's spouse. Under the QDRO rules, the privilege is extended to a former spouse.

a. Spouse or Former Spouse Alternate Payee

A spouse or former spouse may roll over any distributed portion of his or her interest in your plan if there is a QDRO in place. This is the case whether or not the spouse or former spouse's portion was held in a separate account. Once the spouse or former spouse completes the rollover to an account in his or her name, the account belongs to the spouse or former spouse in every way, and the required distribution rules apply to that account as though the alternate payee were the original owner.

⚠ The plan has the final word.
Although the QDRO rules permit your spouse or former spouse to roll over an interest in your retirement plan, some plans will not permit it. Furthermore, some plans will not make any distribution at all until you have reached a certain retirement age—one that is specified in the plan. Be-cause the plan rules ultimately govern distributions, spouses and former spouses often have little control over how they receive QDRO payments.

b. Non-Spouse Alternate Payee

Non-spouse alternate payees may not roll over their interest in your retirement plan under any circumstances. The law does not allow it.

⚠ When the rules don't apply.
Remember: The special rules described in this section apply only to qualified plans, qualified annuities and TDAs, and they only apply if there is a QDRO in place. If there is no QDRO, your retirement plan is treated as though it is entirely yours for required distribution purposes. If your divorce agreement states that your former spouse is to share in your plan, you must generally give your former spouse his or her share as it is distributed from the plan. In other words, a portion of each distribution would go to your former spouse and you would keep your share. As for IRAs, there are no corresponding QDRO rules. As long as the IRA remains in your name, the required distribution rules apply as though your former spouse had no interest in the IRA. But if some or all of your IRA is transferred into your former spouse's name as a result of a written divorce or separation agreement, then from the time the transfer is complete, the transferred portion be-

longs to your former spouse in every respect. That means the required distribution rules apply as though your former spouse were the original owner. (See Chapter 2, Section E.5, for more information about IRAs and divorce.)

Part II: Old Rules

Because the old rules are optional for 2001 distributions, we are including them in this book. As mentioned above, it is almost certainly to your advantage to begin using the new rules as soon as possible. The new rules are described in Part I, above.

Some people may not be able to use the new rules, however. If you are taking required distributions from a qualified plan that has not been modified or amended to permit use of the new rules, you will be stuck with the old rules described in this part. (Remember, this restriction does not apply to IRAs. If you have an IRA, you can begin using the new rules immediately.)

In addition, if you are dealing with distributions that you took in 2000, then you are limited to the old rules described in this part.

A. Required Beginning Date

The year you turn 70½ is a very important year when it comes to your retirement plan distributions. It is known as your first distribution year, and it contains your required beginning date (RBD). If you are the original owner of your retirement plan (as opposed to the beneficiary of someone else's plan), then your RBD is April 1 of the year after you turn 70½.

> **EXAMPLE:** You were born January 1, 1930. You will turn 70½ on July 1, 2000. Your RBD is April 1, 2001.

Your RBD is crucial because it is the absolute deadline for three important tasks:

- You must take your first required distribution (withdrawal) from your retirement plan.
- You must decide whether or not to recalculate life expectancies. Recalculating means looking up your life expectancy in a table every year instead of simply reducing your life expectancy by one each year. (See Section B, below, for more on recalculation.)
- You must identify one or more "designated" beneficiaries for your retirement plan. Although you might already have named a beneficiary, that beneficiary might not qualify as a "designated" beneficiary. (See Section 3, below, for more about designated beneficiaries.)

A special rule allows you to defer required distributions from your employer's plan if you work past age 70½. In that case, your RBD for that particular plan is April 1 of the year after you retire, no matter what age you are. This special deferral option is not available if you own 5% or more of the business that sponsors the retirement plan, which of course includes virtually all self-employed individuals.

In addition, you generally cannot defer your RBD for any IRAs you have. There are exceptions for people who are covered by a federal or state governmental plan or by a "church" plan. (A church plan is one maintained by a religious organization or house of worship for its employees, as long as the organization qualifies as a tax-exempt organization under the Tax Code.) If neither of those situations applies, the RBD for an IRA is April 1 of the year after you turn 70½, even if you continue to work.

As you can see, it's possible to have two plans, each with a different RBD, if you work beyond age 70½. For example, if you have a qualified plan with your employer and you maintain an IRA, your RBD for the IRA will be April 1 of the year after you turn 70½; the RBD for your employer-sponsored plan will be April 1 of the year after you retire, if you retire after age 70½.

If you inherit a retirement plan, you must use a different set of rules to determine your RBD. Those rules are discussed in Chapters 7 and 8. If you inherit a retirement plan from your spouse and elect to treat it as your own, your RBD will be determined as though you were the original owner—with some exceptions. These rules are also discussed in Chapters 7 and 8.

Because April 1 of the year after age 70½ is the RBD for most people, that is the date we will use for discussion purposes in this chapter.

1. Deadlines for Required Distribution

Your RBD marks the deadline for taking the required distribution for your first distribution year only. For all subsequent years, the deadline is December 31.

a. First Year

You must have withdrawn at least the required minimum amount from your retirement plan account by your RBD or you will be subject to a stiff penalty. To satisfy this requirement, you may count all distributions that take place between January 1 of the year you turn 70½ and April 1 of the following year (which is your RBD). In other words, you have 15 months to complete your first distribution.

Although you are permitted to take the required distribution in one big chunk, you don't have to. You can take it out as you need it, for example in monthly installments, as long as the minimum required amount for the first year has been removed from your account by your RBD.

It is important to remember that amounts distributed before January 1 of the year you turn 70½ do not count toward your first required distribution, nor do amounts distributed after your RBD.

> **EXAMPLE 1:** You turn 70½ in 2000. Because 2000 is your first distribution year, you were not required to take money out of your IRA in 1999; but you took $20,000 on October 1, 1999 to buy a car. In 2000, your required minimum distribution is $10,000. You may not count the $20,000 you took in 1999 toward your 2000 required distribution, even though you were not required to take any amount out of your IRA in 1999.

> **EXAMPLE 2:** You turn 70½ in 2000; your RBD is April 1, 2001. Your required distribution for 2000 is $10,000. You decide to wait until 2001 to take the distribution for your first year. You take $9,000 on March 1, 2001 and another $1,000 on May 1, 2001. The $1,000 that you took on May 1, 2001 is after your RBD, however. Because you were $1,000 short of the amount required to be distributed, you will owe the IRS penalties on the $1,000 that should have come out by April 1.

b.   Second Year and Beyond

For the second and all future distribution years, you must take at least the required amount out of your retirement account between January 1 and December 31. There are no more three-month grace periods.

⚠ A delay could cost you! If you decide to wait until your RBD (which is April 1 of your second distribution year) to take your first required distribution, you must still take the full required distribution for the second year by December 31. That means you would have to take two required distributions in the same year, which could push you into a higher income tax bracket.

> **EXAMPLE:** You turn 70½ in 2000, which is your first distribution year, and your RBD is April 1, 2001. Your required distribution for your first distribution year is $20,000, and for the second year is $22,000. You are single and have no other taxable income. You also use the standard deduction. If you take your first distribution in 2000 and the second in 2001, the distributions will both be taxed at the 15% tax rate. However, if you don't take the distribution for the first year until your RBD in 2001, then because you must also take your second distribution in 2001, your gross income will be $42,000. At that level, some of your

distribution will be taxed at 28% (instead of 15%).

Again, you may take the distribution in bits and pieces during the 12-month period, or you may take the entire amount on December 31. If you happen to take more than the required amount in one year, which is permissible, you may not count the excess toward your required distributions for the next year (and beyond).

> **EXAMPLE:** Your required distribution for your second distribution year is $10,000 and for your third distribution year is $12,000. If you take $16,000 in your second distribution year, you may not apply the extra $6,000 to your third distribution year and withdraw only $6,000. Instead, you must still withdraw the full $12,000 during the third year.

2. Election Deadline for Recalculating Your Life Expectancy

Your RBD is also the deadline for deciding whether or not to recalculate your life expectancy. So what does that mean? Actuaries like to say that the longer you live, the longer you can expect to live, but what they really mean is that your life expectancy doesn't decrease by a full year for each 12 months that pass. Here is an example of what they are talking about: At

age 70, your life expectancy, according to IRS mortality tables, is 16 years. But once you turn 71, your life expectancy is re-determined, and you are expected to live another 15.3 years, not 15 years.

To understand this apparent paradox, think back to the days when infant mortality was extremely high. Including infants' life expectancies with those of other segments of the population dragged down the average. But if infants were not included in the computation (in other words, if only those who survived infancy were tallied), then the average life expectancy increased dramatically. Similarly, your life expectancy at age 40 is 42.5 years. But if you survive all of life's dangers and are still alive at 82.5, then the actuaries (and the IRS) expect you to live another 8.4 years—they don't say your life is over.

Turning our attention back to retirement plan distributions, the minimum amount you must withdraw beginning at age 70½ is based on your life expectancy or the joint life expectancy of you and your beneficiary. Joint life expectancy is an estimate of how many years will pass before the second of you dies.

The IRS permits you to determine your life expectancy each year in one of two ways:

- For each year beginning with the year you turn 70½, you can look up your life expectancy in a table provided by the IRS. This method is known as "recalculating" your life expectancy, because each year the table provides a new, statistically accurate estimate of your life expectancy. Using this method, your life expectancy will not reach zero until you die.

- You can look up your life expectancy in the year you turn 70½ and then simply subtract one each subsequent year without using a table. This is called the term certain method because life expectancy is fixed—it is not recalculated every year. Using this method, if you live beyond your term-certain life expectancy, your retirement plan will be completely distributed. This is because your term-certain life expectancy will eventually reach one. And because your required distribution is computed by dividing your account balance by your life expectancy, when you divide by one, the required distribution will be the entire remaining account balance. (See Section C.3, below, for more about computing your required distribution.)

As the owner of your retirement plan, you are permitted to recalculate your own life expectancy. If your spouse is your beneficiary, you can recalculate your spouse's life expectancy as well. You may not recalculate the life expectancy of a non-spouse beneficiary, however. The life expectancy of a non-spouse beneficiary must be reduced by one every year. This complicates the task of determining the joint life expectancy if you are recalculating and your beneficiary is not. You can't simply use a table as you would if both lives were being recalculated, and you can't simply reduce the life expectancy by one each year as you would if neither life was being recalculated. Section C.2, below, provides more information on how to determine life expectancies.

The decision as to whether or not you or your spouse-beneficiary will recalculate your life expectancies must be made by your RBD and, once made, becomes absolutely irrevocable for the remainder of your lifetime. If you do nothing and simply ignore the whole issue, you are deemed to have elected to recalculate your life expectancy and your spouse-beneficiary's life expectancy each year. This is very often the wrong choice, as you will see in Section B, below.

If you do not want to recalculate and instead want to subtract one each year, then on or before your RBD you must "make an election," or notify the IRS, of your decision. (Section B.3, below, describes how to make the election.)

3. Deadline for Naming Designated Beneficiary

Finally, your RBD is the deadline for naming a "designated" beneficiary of your retirement plan. Although you may name any person or entity you choose, not every beneficiary qualifies as a "designated" beneficiary as defined by the Tax Regulations. Any person qualifies as a designated beneficiary, and so do some trusts. Charities, corporations and estates do not. (Section D, below, provides more information about designated beneficiaries.) Only if you name a designated beneficiary may you use a joint life expectancy with that beneficiary for determining your required distributions. If your beneficiary is not a designated beneficiary, or if you haven't named a beneficiary at all, then you must use your own single life expectancy when calculating required distributions. That is the only consequence of failing to name a designated beneficiary. But the restriction can have a significant effect on the size of required distributions, as illustrated in Section C.2, below.

It is important to remember that although you may change your beneficiary at any time, the beneficiary named as of your RBD will affect how your required distributions are calculated from that time until your death, with certain rare exceptions.

B. Recalculating Life Expectancies

Because your choice of whether or not to recalculate your life expectancy becomes irrevocable on your RBD, it is important to know the benefits and consequences of your decision. If you elect not to recalculate, you simply reduce your life expectancy by one each year after your first distribution year, regardless of your age or health. On the other hand, if you recalculate, you must look up the life expectancy for your current age in the appropriate table each year.

The quirky aspect of the recalculation rule is that your decision survives your death—that is, it remains in place after you die. If you choose not to recalculate, then your life expectancy will continue to be reduced by one each year even though you are dead. This means your beneficiary will have the option to continue to calculate distributions in the same way until the divisor is reduced to one. This option would save the beneficiary from having to take a distribution of the entire remaining amount in one year and paying a lot of tax. (Your beneficiary can always accelerate distributions, or take more than the required amount. If a beneficiary chooses to deplete the account as slowly as possible, however, the maximum period over which distributions can be spread is your remaining term-certain life expectancy.) On the other hand, if you had been recalculating and using the tables each year, your recalculated life expectancy goes to zero in the year after you die, which generally accelerates the distribution of your retirement account.

Your spouse has another option.
Although these rules also apply when you name your spouse as beneficiary, your spouse, and only your spouse, has the option to roll over your account when you die. A rollover can mitigate the risks inherent in a recalculation election. (See Chapter 7 for more about a spouse's rollover option.)

1. Advantages of Recalculation

There is really only one advantage to recalculating life expectancies, but it can be a big advantage. Recalculating allows you to use a larger divisor when computing required distributions, which produces a smaller required amount. (Recall that your required distribution is your account balance divided by the appropriate life expectancy.) Because you are always permitted to withdraw more, keeping the required amount at the lowest possible level increases your financial flexibility. For example, if you don't need to draw on

your IRA for living expenses during retirement, you would like to withdraw the minimum required amount in order to keep your income taxes down and to leave more of your assets to grow tax-deferred inside the IRA.

It's easy to see that the benefits of recalculation increase as you grow older. At 70, your life expectancy is 16 years. If you use a term-certain method for computing required distributions, your entire IRA will be distributed by the time you reach age 86. But if you are recalculating, when you reach age 86, you will still have a remaining life expectancy of 6.5 years. Instead of having to distribute the entire IRA, you could continue to spread distributions over your remaining life expectancy. Using this method, your IRA will never be completely distributed as long as you are alive.

2. Consequences of Recalculation

In spite of the significant computation advantage recalculation might give you, it could still be the wrong choice. Here's why.

a. Single Life Expectancy

If you must use your single life expectancy to compute your required distribution (if, for example, you did not designate a beneficiary) and choose not to recalculate your life expectancy, then your retirement account will be distributed over a term certain whether you survive the term or not. Assume you begin distributions at 70 for a period of 16 years (your life expectancy at that time), but you die at age 75. Your heirs may continue to take distributions from your retirement account over the remaining 11 years of the term, rather than all at once.

On the other hand, if you are recalculating each year and you die at age 75, your life expectancy automatically goes to zero in the year after your death, and the entire remaining balance of the account must be paid out. In that case, a greater portion of the retirement plan account is likely to be lost to taxes.

b. Joint Life Expectancy with Non-Spouse Beneficiary

If your beneficiary is not your spouse, you must use one of two sets of rules depending on the age of your non-spouse beneficiary.

i. Beneficiary No More Than Ten Years Younger

Recall that life expectancy is only reduced to zero if the life expectancy was being recalculated. Also, recalculation is available only to you and a spouse beneficiary. Therefore, if you have a non-spouse beneficiary, you have only two options: you can recalculate your own life expectancy and use a term certain for your beneficiary; or you can use a term certain for both of you.

Let's assume that the joint life expectancy for you and a non-spouse beneficiary on your first distribution year is 25 years.

If you elect not to recalculate, the retirement plan can be paid out over 25 years regardless of who dies when. If you elect to recalculate your life expectancy and you die after ten years, however, your life expectancy becomes zero in the year after your death and the beneficiary may use only his or her remaining single life.

EXAMPLE: Your sister is the beneficiary of your IRA. Your joint life expectancy in your first distribution year, when you were 70 and she was 68, was 21.5 years. You elected to recalculate your life expectancy. Nine years later you die, and your life expectancy is reduced to zero in the tenth year. Your sister must use her remaining single life expectancy, 7.6 years, to compute the required distribution for the tenth year. That number must then be reduced by one each subsequent year. Thus if the IRA balance was $100,000, the required distribution would be $100,000 divided by 7.6, or $13,158.

On the other hand, if you had elected not to recalculate, your joint life expectancy would be reduced by one each year, no matter who died when. In the tenth year—the year after your death—your joint life expectancy would have been 11.5 (21.5 - 10), rather than 7.6. The required distribution would be only $8,696, instead of $13,158. (See Section C.2, below, for more about determining life expectancy. See Section C.3 for more about computing the required amount.)

ii. Beneficiary More Than Ten Years Younger

If your non-spouse beneficiary is more than ten years younger than you are, a special rule called the Minimum Distribution Incidental Benefit (MDIB) rule applies. It requires that you use a special table (Table III in Appendix B) to find your joint life expectancy.

Minimum Distribution Incidental Benefit Rule

It's worth a digression here to explain why there is a special table for this situation. As mentioned briefly in Chapter 1, Congress initiated tax-favored treatment of retirement plans to encourage people to save. At the same time, Congress wanted to ensure that those favorable laws wouldn't simply be used by the rich to avoid current taxation and to pass wealth to their heirs. Congress intended that retirement plans be used by their owners during retirement and that the retirement money be taxed during the owner's lifetime.

Wealthy people could violate the spirit of the law by naming a very young person, such as a great grandchild, as a beneficiary. The resulting long joint life expectancy would have the effect of dramatically reducing required distributions and leaving the retirement plan essentially intact for future generations.

Congress attempted to close this loophole with the enactment of the Minimum Distribution Incidental Benefit (MDIB) rule. It provides that if you name a beneficiary (other than your spouse) who is more than ten years younger than you are, then for purposes of computing required distributions during your lifetime, the beneficiary is deemed to be only ten years younger. The IRS even went so far as to create a separate table (Table III in Appendix B) to be used by retirement plan owners who name such young beneficiaries.

Note that the MDIB rule does not apply to your spouse no matter how much younger he or she is, unless your spouse is one of several designated beneficiaries on the same account. In that situation, if your spouse and all the other beneficiaries are more than ten years younger than you are, the MDIB rules apply.

If you name a beneficiary who is more than ten years younger, you still need to decide by your RBD whether or not you will recalculate your life expectancy. Although using the special table during your lifetime makes your recalculation decision temporarily irrelevant, at your death the special MDIB rules cease to apply, and your beneficiary must compute distributions for future years as though the MDIB rules had never been applicable. That's when the consequence of your recalculation decision will rear its head.

EXAMPLE: Your daughter is the beneficiary of your IRA. She was age 45 in 1995. Also, 1995 was your first distribution year, and you elected to recalculate your life expectancy. You die in 2001, and the MDIB rules cease to apply beginning in the year 2000. That means your daughter no longer has to use the special MDIB table. Because you had been recalculating, your life expectancy goes to zero. Your daughter may use her remaining life expectancy to compute required distributions. Her life expectancy in 1995 was 37.7 years, so in 2000 her remaining life expectancy is 32.7, or 37.7 - 5. If you had elected not to recalculate your life expectancy, your daughter would use your joint life expectancy (instead of her single life expectancy) as of your first distribution year, reduced by one each year. In 1995, when you were 70 and she was 45,

your joint life expectancy (without the MDIB rule) would have been 38.3. So in 2000, the remaining term-certain joint life expectancy would be 33.3, or 38.3 - 5. (See Section C, below, for more about computing required distributions.)

c. Joint Life Expectancy With Spouse Beneficiary

If your spouse is your beneficiary and you elect not to recalculate your life expectancies, your joint life expectancy is reduced by one each year even after the death of either or both of you. So if your initial joint life expectancy was 20 years and you both die eight years later, leaving your son as sole heir, your son may spread distributions over the remaining 12 years of your term-certain life expectancy.

Because your spouse is the only beneficiary whose life may be recalculated, you have the option to use a joint life expectancy and recalculate both your life and your spouse's. If you do so, however, when the first of you dies, that person's life expectancy goes to zero. But worse, if your spouse dies first, then when you die (or if both of you die at the same time), both life expectancies will have been reduced to zero and the retirement plan account must be paid out entirely in the following year.

Fortunately, if you die first, your spouse has some additional options which could mitigate the consequences of your recalculation election. Specifically, your spouse could roll over your plan into an IRA in his or her own name. This strategy is discussed in Chapters 7 and 8.

3. Making the Election

Once you choose between recalculating life expectancy and using a term certain, how do you make the election official? The regulations are clear that if you make no election and your retirement plan itself is silent on the issue, then you and your spouse (if your spouse is your beneficiary) are deemed to have elected to recalculate your life expectancies.

Therefore, if you do not want to recalculate, you must make a specific election not to. The regulations are distressingly mum on the precise manner in which the election should be made, but several methods are likely to pass muster:

- You might simply calculate and withdraw the appropriate amount, keeping a record of both the method used and the amount of the distribution. In the event of an IRS audit, use those records to demonstrate that you have consistently applied one method.

- You might show the calculation for the first distribution year in a statement attached to your tax return (and filed before your RBD) along with a signed statement indicating that you choose to "make recalculation inapplicable" to your life expectancy. If you are making a similar election for your spouse, both of you would sign and attach similar statements. (See sample statement, below).

- You might send (before your RBD) the signed statement described above in the form of a letter to your plan administrator or IRA custodian, indicating your intention to not recalculate your life expectancy or your spouse's. (See sample letter to custodian, below.)

- You could cover all bases and use all three of the above methods.

Sample Letter to Custodian

November 23, 20xx
Christopher DeJesus
14th National Bank
1000 Main Street
Cincinnati, OH 40000

Re: Nonrecalculation Election for Minimum Required Distributions
     from Individual Retirement Account

Dear Mr. DeJesus:

My date of birth is January 14, 19xx and my spouse-beneficiary's date of birth is July 12, 19xx. My required beginning date for distributions from the above-referenced IRA is April 1, 20xx. The Joint Life and Last Survivor Expectancy of my spouse and me for my first distribution calendar year, as set forth in IRS Regulation Section 1.72-9, is 21.2 years.

Pursuant to IRS Proposed Treasury Regulation Section 1.401(a)(9)-1, E-7, I hereby make the following elections:

1. IRC Section 401(a)(9)(D) shall be inapplicable to me, and my life expectancy shall not be recalculated annually.

2. IRC Section 401(a)(9)(D) shall be inapplicable to my spouse, and her life expectancy shall not be recalculated annually.

The applicable life expectancy for each calendar year after my first distribution calendar year shall be determined by reducing the prior year's applicable life expectancy by one.

Please acknowledge receipt of this letter in the space provided below on the enclosed copy of this letter and return it to me. Please place the original of this letter with my IRA Custodial Account Agreement.

Thank you for your assistance.

Very truly yours,

Herbert H. Wilcox
_____
Herbert H. Wilcox, IRA Owner

Marla Sinclair-Wilcox
_____
Marla Sinclair-Wilcox, Spouse

Receipt is hereby acknowledged this _____ day of _____,
20___.

By: _____
    Christopher DeJesus

Sample Statement to Attach to Tax Return

IRA Owner: Herbert H. Wilcox
Date of Birth: January 14, 19xx
Beneficiary: Marla Sinclair-Wilcox, spouse
Date of Birth: July 12, 19xx
Joint Life Expectancy: 21.2 years

12/31/xx Value of All IRAs	Minimum Required Distribution	Actual Distribution
$155,000	$8,311	$8,500

Pursuant to IRS Proposed Treasury Regulation Section 1.401(a)(9)-1, E-7, I hereby make the following elections:

1. IRC Section 401(a)(9)(D) shall be inapplicable to me, and my life expectancy shall not be recalculated annually.
2. IRC Section 401(a)(9)(D) shall be inapplicable to my spouse, and her life expectancy shall not be recalculated annually.

Herbert H. Wilcox
Herbert H. Wilcox, IRA Owner

Marla Sinclair-Wilcox
Marla Sinclair-Wilcox, Spouse

This is not likely to be an issue while you are alive. As a practical matter, it seems unlikely that the IRS would examine the details of your calculation method until after your death—because that's when the election will have the biggest impact on your tax liability. For example, if you were recalculating your single life expectancy, then after your death the entire account must be distributed, and the IRS would be able to collect a large amount of tax all at once.

C. Computing the Required Amount

Computing your required distribution for a given year is simply a matter of determining an account balance for your retirement plan and dividing that balance by the appropriate life expectancy. The resulting number is the minimum amount you must withdraw from the account for that year. This required minimum distribution must be computed separately for each retirement plan that you have. When it comes to actually withdrawing the computed amounts, however, you have some flexibility. For example, you may be able to withdraw the total amount from only one account. (See Section 4, below, for more information about this strategy.)

1. Determining the Account Balance

According to Tax Regulations, the account balance for computing your required distribution each year is determined as of "the last valuation date in the calendar year before the distribution calendar year." For the vast majority of people who are computing their own required distributions, this would be December 31 of the year before the distribution. If your retirement assets are in a qualified plan when you begin required distributions instead of an IRA, it is possible that the plan itself specifies a date other than December 31 for valuing the plan assets and computing required distributions. Nevertheless, we will use December 31 for discussion purposes in this book. For example, if you turn 70½ in 2001, to compute the required distribution for your first distribution year (2001), you use your account balance as of December 31, 2000. When computing the required distribution for the year 2002, you look at your account balance as of December 31, 2001, and so on.

![icon] **You are permitted to take your first required distribution in the year after you turn 70½.** But you must do so on or before your RBD—April 1 of the year after you turn 70½. Deferring your first distribution, however, does not alter the date for determining the appropriate account balance. For example, if you turn 70½ in 2000 and decide to take your first distribution in March of 2001, you must still use your account balance as of December 31, 1999 to compute the amount of your first distribution.

If you decide to take advantage of the grace period and take your first required distribution after December 31, things get a little complicated when it's time to compute the distribution for the second year. In that case, you must subtract the amount of your first year's distribution from the account balance.

EXAMPLE: You turn 70½ in 2000. On December 31, 1999 your account balance was $41,200, and you computed your required distribution to be $2,000. You decided not to withdraw the required distribution for your first distribution until March 1, 2001—well before your RBD of April 1, 2001. Your December 31, 2000 account balance is $50,000. But you don't use that amount to calculate the distribution for the second distribution year (2001). Instead, you use $48,000 ($50,000 - $2,000)—just as if you had taken your 2000 distribution during 2000.

This extra subtraction is not necessary if you withdraw the entire minimum required amount by December 31 of the year you turn 70½. And because your second (or any future) required distribution may not be deferred beyond December 31 of the distribution year, no adjustments to the year-end account balance will be necessary (or permitted).

2. Determining Life Expectancy

Once you have determined the appropriate account balance to use for a particular distribution year, you must divide it by a life expectancy to arrive at your required distribution. The life expectancy is your own single life expectancy if you have no designated beneficiary or a joint life expectancy if you do.

a. First Year

You will use a table to determine the appropriate life expectancy ("divisor") for your first distribution year. But you need to know which table to use.

Single Life Expectancy. If you must use your own single life expectancy to compute required distributions, then use Table I (in Appendix B) to find the appropriate divisor. Your age is determined as of your birthday in the year you turn 70½. If that age is 70, then your divisor is 16. If your age is 71 on your birthday in the year you turn 70½ (which is the case if your birthday is after June 30), then the divisor is 15.3.

Joint Life Expectancy. If you use a joint life expectancy with a designated beneficiary who is no more than ten years younger than you are, or with your spouse (regardless of your spouse's age), then use Table II (in Appendix B) to determine your divisor. For example, if you are age 70 on your birthday in your first distribution year (the year you turn 70½) and your designated beneficiary is age 65 in that year, Table II indicates that your joint life expectancy, or divisor, is 23.1.

Joint Life Expectancy With Young Beneficiary. If you use a joint life expectancy with a designated beneficiary (other than your spouse) who is more than ten years younger than you are, then the MDIB rules apply and you must use Table III (in Appendix B). For example, if you are age 70 in your first distribution year and your non-spouse beneficiary is more than ten years younger than you are, Table III indicates that your joint life expectancy is deemed to be 26.2, regardless of the actual age of your beneficiary.

⚠ **You are not always age 70 in your first distribution year.** If your birthday falls after June 30, you will turn 70½ in the same year in which you turn 71.

b. Special Option for First Year

A special computation option is available for your first distribution year only. If you change your designated beneficiary after December 31 of the year you turn 70½, but before your RBD, you may use the life expectancy of either the old beneficiary or the new beneficiary when computing your first distribution. For the second and all future years, however, you must use the beneficiary named as of your

RBD, computing life expectancies as though the new beneficiary's life had been used from the start. This rule can be used to reduce the required distribution for the first year, in turn reducing income taxes for that year and allowing additional amounts to continue to grow tax deferred inside your retirement plan.

> EXAMPLE: You want your spouse to be the beneficiary of your IRA for the long term. Both you and your spouse are age 70 in 2000, your first distribution year. Your joint life expectancy (divisor) for the first year would be 20.6 years. Your account balance is $1 million, and your first required distribution would be $48,544 based on your joint life expectancy. Instead, you name your son as your beneficiary, switching to your spouse after December 31, 2001 but before your RBD of April 1, 2002. When you calculate your first year's distribution, you use the divisor based on the joint life expectancy of you and your son, which is 26.2 years (using the MDIB table). The required distribution is $38,168—more than $10,000 less than if you had used the joint life expectancy of you and your spouse.
>
> For the second and future years, you must use the joint life expectancy of you and your spouse for determining the divisor, as though your spouse had been the beneficiary from the start. If neither you nor your spouse is

recalculating, then the divisor for the second year will be 19.6 (20.6 - 1).

⚠ Don't forget to make the second change. If it is critical to your estate plan that your spouse be the beneficiary of your retirement plan when you die, then be careful when taking advantage of this special rule. Keep the period of time during which a non-spouse is named beneficiary as short as possible, to minimize the chances that you will die during that period. If you can arrange it so that your son is your beneficiary on January 1 and your spouse is your beneficiary on January 2, it will be safe for you to die on January 3, as long as you are sure all the paperwork has been completed properly.

c. Second Year and Beyond

How you determine the appropriate divisor for the second and future distribution years depends on whether or not you elect to recalculate life expectancies. Here are the various possibilities.

i. Single Life Expectancy—Not Recalculating

If you are using your single life expectancy and not recalculating your life expectancy each year, then to determine the current year's divisor, simply reduce the prior year's divisor by one. For example, if your life expectancy in your first distribution year is 16, the divisor for the second distribution year is 15, and so on.

ii. Single Life Expectancy—Recalculating

If you elect to recalculate your life expectancy, look at Table I every year, using your age to locate the applicable divisor. For example, if you were age 70 on your birthday in your first distribution year, you will be age 71 in your second distribution year. Using Table I, you will see that your divisor for the first year is 16 and for the second year is 15.3.

iii. Joint Life Expectancy With Spouse—Neither Spouse Recalculating

If you choose not to recalculate either life expectancy, you simply reduce the prior year's divisor by one. For example, if you are age 70 and your spouse is 65 in your first distribution year, your joint life expectancy for that year (taken from Table II) is 23.1. Your divisor for the second distribution year is 22.1, for the third year 21.1, and so on.

iv. Joint Life Expectancy With Spouse—Both Spouses Recalculating

If you elect to recalculate both life expectancies, you must continue to use Table II each year. For example, if you are age 70 and your spouse is age 65 in your first distribution year, then your joint life expectancy is 23.1 for that year. For the second distribution year, when you are 71 and your spouse is 66, your divisor (taken from Table II) is 22.2. In the third year (when you are 72 and your spouse is 67) your divisor is 21.3, and so on.

v. Joint Life Expectancy With Spouse—One Spouse Recalculating

Although you may choose to recalculate one life expectancy and not the other, the resulting computation is complex and provides little advantage, unless you both survive to a very ripe old age. Nonetheless, if that is your choice, here's how the computation works. In this example, assume you elect to recalculate your own life but not your spouse's. But the example works the same way if the reverse is true.

1. Reduce your spouse's single life expectancy for the previous year by one.

2. Using Table I, find the age associated with that new life expectancy. This number is your spouse's "imputed" age. The imputed age might or might not be your spouse's actual age, but it is the one you must use to compute required distributions. If the imputed

age falls between two numbers, you must use the higher.

3. Using the imputed age from Step 2 and your own age as of your birthday in the current year, find your joint life expectancy from Table II.

EXAMPLE: You are age 70 and your spouse is 68 in your first distribution year. Your joint life expectancy (from Table II) for your first distribution year is 21.5. Your spouse's single life expectancy in the first distribution year is 17.6 (from Table I). To determine your joint life expectancy for the second distribution year, follow these steps:

1. Reduce your spouse's single life expectancy for the previous year by one. In this case, the result is 16.6 (17.6 - 1).

2. Using Table I, find the age associated with the life expectancy 16.6. Since that age falls somewhere between 69 and 70, you must use the higher age, which is 70. This is your spouse's imputed age. (Note that your spouse's actual age for year two would be 69.)

3. Using your spouse's imputed age from Step 2 (age 70) and your own age for your second distribution year (age 71), find a joint life expectancy from Table II. That number is 20.2.

vi. Joint Life Expectancy With Non-Spouse—Beneficiary Not More Than Ten Years Younger—Not Recalculating

If your beneficiary is no more than ten years younger than you are and if you elect not to recalculate your life expectancy each year, simply use Table II to determine your joint life expectancy for the first year. For all future years, you reduce the prior year's divisor by one.

vii. Joint Life Expectancy With Non-Spouse—Beneficiary Not More Than Ten Years Younger—Recalculating

If your beneficiary is no more than ten years younger than you are and if you elect to recalculate your life expectancy each year, the computation becomes more complicated. You cannot simply reduce your divisor by one each year, because you are recalculating. Furthermore, you cannot use Table II after the first year, because it assumes both you and your beneficiary are recalculating—which is only permissible if your spouse is your beneficiary. Instead, you must use the following procedure. (Note: this is the same procedure described just above where your spouse was your beneficiary and you choose to recalculate only one of your life expectancies.)

1. Reduce your beneficiary's single life expectancy for the previous year by one.

2. Using Table I, find the age associated with that new life expectancy. This number is your beneficiary's "imputed" age. The imputed age might or might

not be the beneficiary's actual age, but it is the one you must use to compute required distributions. If the imputed age falls between two numbers, you must use the higher.

3. Using the imputed age from Step 2 and your own age as of your birthday in the current year, find your joint life expectancy from Table II.

EXAMPLE: You are age 70 and your non-marital partner, who is your beneficiary, is 68 in your first distribution year. Your joint life expectancy (from Table II) for your first distribution year is 21.5. Your beneficiary's single life expectancy in the first distribution year is 17.6 (from Table I). To determine your joint life expectancy for the second distribution year, follow these steps:

1. Reduce your beneficiary's single life expectancy for the previous year by one. In this case, the result is 16.6 (17.6 - 1).

2. Using Table I, find the age associated with the life expectancy 16.6. Since that age falls somewhere between 69 and 70, you must use the higher age, which is 70. This is your beneficiary's imputed age. (Note that your beneficiary's actual age for year two would be 69.)

3. Using your beneficiary's imputed age from Step 2 (age 70) and your own age for your

second distribution year (age 71), find a joint life expectancy from Table II. That number is 20.2.

viii. Joint Life Expectancy With Non-Spouse—Beneficiary More Than Ten Years Younger

If your beneficiary is more than ten years younger than you are, the MDIB rules apply and you must use Table III for all years.

3. Computing the Required Distribution

Once you have determined the appropriate account balance and life expectancy, you simply divide the account balance by the life expectancy to arrive at your required minimum distribution. You can withdraw more than the required amount each year, but you may not withdraw less without incurring a penalty. (See Chapter 5 to learn more about the penalty.)

EXAMPLE: You turn 70 on March 1, 2001 and your IRA account balance on December 31, 2000 is $50,000. You use your single life expectancy to compute required distributions. The life expectancy factor for your first distribution year is 16. Therefore, your first required distribution is $3,125 ($50,000 divided by 16).

If you retire and receive a lump sum distribution from your employer's plan, any after-tax contributions you made to the plan may not be rolled over into an IRA, but must be distributed to you. Because these amounts are not taxable, you have an interesting planning opportunity if your retirement date is in the year you turn 70½ or later. Specifically, you are permitted to count the distribution of after-tax amounts as part of your required distribution from the plan for that particular year. By doing so you can reduce your income tax and leave additional pre-tax amounts in the account to grow for another year.

EXAMPLE: You retire in 2001, which is also the year you turn 70½. Over the years, you have built up quite a nest egg of pre-tax dollars inside your employer's qualified retirement plan. You have also made $10,000 in after-tax contributions. Your required distribution for your first distribution year is $19,000. When you retire in 2001, your employer distributes your retirement benefits to you as a lump sum. You decide to take your first required distribution by December 31, 2001. Your intention is to roll over into an IRA all but your required distribution for 2001. You keep out your after-tax contributions of $10,000, which you may not roll over anyway. You keep an additional $9,000. You then roll over the remainder of the lump sum into an IRA. Thus you have

distributed from your retirement plan the entire amount of your first required distribution ($19,000), but only $9,000 of it is taxable.

4. Special Aggregation Rule for IRAs and TDAs

If you have more than one IRA (whether traditional IRA, SEP or SIMPLE IRA), you must compute the required distribution for each IRA separately, but then you may add up all the computed amounts and take the total from only one or several IRAs, as long as the aggregate or total amount is distributed before the deadline.

This strategy also works if you have more than one TDA (tax-deferred annuity) plan. You may compute the required distribution for each plan, and then distribute the total from just one or more of the plans. You may not mix and match IRAs and TDAs, however. If you have one IRA and one TDA, you must calculate and distribute the required amount from each separately.

⚠ **Aggregation is permissible only for IRAs and TDAs.** If you have another type of plan, you must compute the required amount for that plan and take the computed amount from that particular plan.

D. Designating a Beneficiary

You may name any person or entity you choose to be the beneficiary of your retirement plan. Unless the beneficiary falls under the definition of a "designated" beneficiary and is named on or before your RBD, however, you won't be able to use a joint life expectancy to compute required distributions. Using a joint life expectancy gives you the flexibility to reduce required distributions in order to keep taxes low and allow your plan to grow.

1. Definition of Designated Beneficiary

A designated beneficiary must be a "natural person," as opposed to an entity like a charity or a corporation. There is one exception to this natural person rule: a trust that has certain qualifications (described in Section c, below) can also be a designated beneficiary.

If you fail to name a natural person or a qualified trust as your beneficiary and instead name your estate, a charity, a corporation or a trust that does not satisfy certain requirements, then you are deemed to have no designated beneficiary and must use your own single life expectancy to compute required distributions.

Silence doesn't necessarily mean no beneficiary. Just because you do not complete a beneficiary designation form and record the name of a beneficiary does not necessarily mean that you have no designated beneficiary. Some plans provide for a default beneficiary, usually a spouse, when no beneficiary is named by the owner. Be sure to find out if your plan has such a default provision. If it does not, then you are deemed to have no designated beneficiary even if the laws of your state dictate who should receive your assets.

Designated beneficiaries fall into the following three categories.

a. Spouse

If you are married, you can name your spouse as your designated beneficiary. Then you can use a joint life expectancy and recalculate either your life expectancy, your spouse's life expectancy or both.

When you name your spouse as sole beneficiary, you are not restricted by the MDIB rules if your spouse is more than ten years younger than you are. In other words, you do not have to use Table III. Instead you use Table II to determine your joint life the first year (and for all subsequent years as well, if you are both recalculating). But if your spouse is one of several beneficiaries, the MDIB rule will apply if your spouse and the other beneficiaries are all more than ten years younger than you are. (See Section 2, below.)

b. Non-Spouse Natural Person

Any human being—what the Tax Code calls a natural person—qualifies as a designated beneficiary. If you name a friend, relative (other than your spouse) or non-marital partner who is no more than ten years younger than you are, you may use a joint life expectancy with that beneficiary. You can recalculate your own life expectancy, but not the beneficiary's. If the person you name is not your spouse and is more than ten years younger, you may still use a joint life expectancy, but the life expectancy number must come from Table III (see Appendix B).

c. Trust

A qualified trust is the one exception to the requirement that a designated beneficiary be a natural person. To figure out if the trust is qualified, you must consider the trust's status as of either your RBD or the date the trust is named your beneficiary, whichever comes later. As of that date, the following must all be true:

- The trust must be valid under state law, meaning the terms must be enforceable.
- The trust must be irrevocable, meaning you cannot change its terms or cancel it. You could name a revocable trust—one that can be altered, or

amended, at any time—as long as it becomes irrevocable upon your death.

- The beneficiaries of the trust must be natural persons (humans) and must be identifiable. They don't have to be identified by name, though. You may use descriptive terms such as "spouse" or "children."
- You must provide a copy of the trust to the trustee or custodian of your retirement plan or IRA. If the trust is revocable, you must give the trustee or custodian a copy of each subsequent amendment, if any. As an alternative to submitting the entire trust agreement, it is permissible to simply provide a list of beneficiaries with a description of the amount each is to receive and the conditions, if any, under which they will receive benefits.

If the trust meets all of the above qualifications, then the beneficiaries of the trust are treated as designated beneficiaries for purposes of computing your required distributions, provided the beneficiaries would otherwise qualify as designated beneficiaries (for example, are natural persons). If there is more than one beneficiary of the trust, the multiple beneficiary rules of Section 2, below, will apply. This generally means that you must use a joint life expectancy with the oldest beneficiary of the trust.

2. Multiple Beneficiaries

It is not uncommon to name more than one beneficiary of a retirement plan, but if you do, be aware of the consequences.

a. Primary Beneficiaries

You can name several primary beneficiaries of your retirement plan who may or may not share equally in the plan assets after your death. Regardless of the percentage allocated to each beneficiary, if you name more than one primary beneficiary of a single retirement plan account, you may use only one beneficiary—the one with the shortest life expectancy (the oldest person)—for purposes of computing required distributions. If that beneficiary is more than ten years younger than you are, the MDIB rules will apply even if the beneficiary is your spouse.

Furthermore, if any one of the primary beneficiaries fails to qualify as a designated beneficiary, then you are deemed to have no designated beneficiary at all, and you may not use a joint life expectancy when computing required distributions. This is true even if all other beneficiaries would qualify as designated beneficiaries. For example, if you name your sister to receive 50% of your IRA and a charity to receive the rest, you are deemed to have no designated beneficiary because the charity is not a natural person; and you may not use a joint life expectancy to compute

required distributions, even for your sister's portion of the account.

 If you have no designated beneficiary. Remember, when you die, the assets of your IRA will still be divided among your beneficiaries even if you are deemed to have no "designated beneficiary." For example, in the previous paragraph, 50% of the assets would go to charity and 50% to your sister. Having no designated beneficiary simply means you must use your own single life expectancy to compute required distributions.

You can avoid this problem by setting up a separate IRA for each beneficiary. For example, you can direct the custodian of the IRA, in writing, to set up a second IRA and transfer half of your existing IRA assets into the new IRA. You would name the charity as sole beneficiary of the new IRA and your sister as sole beneficiary of the old IRA. Then you could use the joint life expectancy of you and your sister when computing required distributions from the old IRA. For the new IRA that names a charity as beneficiary, you may only use your own single life expectancy when computing required distributions. The required distribution would then be computed separately for each account.

b. Contingent Beneficiaries

A contingent beneficiary is a beneficiary you name to receive your retirement plan assets in the event your primary beneficiary does not qualify to receive the benefits. Usually a primary beneficiary fails to qualify because he or she has already died. If the contingent beneficiary will receive the retirement benefits only in the event that the primary beneficiary predeceases you, then the contingent beneficiary's age and life expectancy have no effect on the computation of required distributions.

> EXAMPLE: You have instructed the custodian of your IRA in writing that you name your spouse as primary beneficiary of your IRA. You indicate further that if your spouse dies before you do, your mother shall be the beneficiary of the IRA. Because your mother's interest in the IRA is contingent only upon the death of your spouse, you will use the joint life expectancy of you and your spouse when computing required distributions. You are not required to use the shorter life expectancy of your mother.

If the contingent beneficiary could become the primary beneficiary for any reason other than the death of the original primary beneficiary, then the contingent beneficiary shall be treated as one of multiple beneficiaries (along with the primary beneficiary) when determining required distributions.

> EXAMPLE: You have instructed the custodian of your IRA in writing that you name your spouse as primary beneficiary of your IRA, but only if you are married at the time of your death. In the event you and your spouse divorce, your father shall become the primary beneficiary of your IRA. Because your father's interest is not contingent solely on the death of your spouse, you must consider the ages of your spouse and your father and use the one with the shortest life expectancy when computing required distributions.

Similarly, if you name a contingent beneficiary that does not qualify as a designated beneficiary, for example a charity, you do not have to use your single life expectancy to compute required distributions unless the charity's interest was contingent on some occurrence other than the death of the primary beneficiary.

3. Changing Beneficiaries After Your RBD

You can always change the beneficiary of your retirement plan. It would indeed be awful if you could not change your mind after your RBD. How would you otherwise keep recalcitrant heirs in line? But although you can change beneficiaries, the method for computing required distributions does become irrevocable on your RBD with one significant exception: If you change your beneficiary after your RBD and your new beneficiary is *older* than the previous beneficiary, you must use the new beneficiary's shorter life expectancy when computing future required distributions. Future distributions are computed as though the new beneficiary had been the beneficiary since your RBD. If the new beneficiary is *younger* than the previous beneficiary, you make no change.

> EXAMPLE: You were age 70 in your first distribution year. You named your 65-year-old brother as beneficiary of your IRA as of your RBD, and you elected not to recalculate your life expectancy. Four years later, you decide that your sister is likely to need your IRA money more than your brother will, so you change the beneficiary designation to name your sister. Your sister is one year older than you are and therefore has a shorter life expectancy than your brother. Consequently, you must use her life expectancy to compute all future distributions, beginning with the fifth year after your first distribution year. If she had been your designated beneficiary on your RBD, your joint life expectancy (age 70 for you and 71 for her) would have been 20.2 years. When you change the designated beneficiary to your sister,

you put aside all calculations done with your brother. Thus, the divisor for computing the required distribution in the fifth year after beginning required distributions is 15.2 (20.2 - 5). You will reduce the divisor by one in all subsequent years.

a. Spouse Beneficiary

If your new beneficiary happens to be your spouse, the above general rule still applies. That is, if your spouse is older than the previous beneficiary, you must use your spouse's shorter life expectancy when computing all future distributions.

In addition, if you were married to your spouse on your RBD (even if your spouse was not your beneficiary at the time), then recalculation would apply to your spouse's life expectancy when your spouse does become your beneficiary. However, if your new beneficiary is a spouse whom you married after your RBD, then recalculation for your spouse is not an option.

> EXAMPLE: On your RBD you named your plumber's grandson as beneficiary of your IRA. Five years later, at age 75, you finally married your college sweetheart and named him as beneficiary of your IRA, replacing the plumber's grandson. For all future required distributions you will use the joint life expectancy of you and your new spouse, because your new spouse's

life expectancy is shorter than the life expectancy of the plumber's grandson. You cannot elect to recalculate your spouse's life expectancy, however, because he was not your spouse on your RBD.

b. Contingent Beneficiary

When the primary beneficiary changes because the original primary dies and a contingent beneficiary steps in, there is no change in the method of computing required distributions.

c. No Designated Beneficiary

The rules described in the preceding paragraphs of this section presume that when you change beneficiaries, the new beneficiary qualifies as a designated beneficiary. If you add a beneficiary after your RBD that is not a designated beneficiary—a charity, for example—then distributions for all future years must be based on your single life expectancy.

d. Consolidating IRAs

Sometimes, a change in beneficiaries occurs as a result of consolidating IRAs that have different beneficiaries. If you roll over one IRA into another after your RBD, the general rule for changing beneficiaries will apply whether all beneficiaries stay on the account or not. For example, if the receiving IRA has a beneficiary with a shorter life expectancy than that of the distributing IRA (the IRA being rolled over), the entire receiving IRA (including the amounts rolled over) will now be subject to the distribution computations of the receiving IRA.

On the other hand, if the receiving IRA's beneficiary has a longer life expectancy, you must keep a separate accounting of the amount rolled over and calculate separate distributions for each portion of the combined IRA, as though the IRAs had not been combined and the beneficiaries had not changed. The result is the same whether or not you drop one or more of the beneficiaries after the IRAs are combined. These rules provide a pretty compelling reason for keeping the IRAs separate. Any administrative costs saved as a result of consolidation are likely to be lost to the inefficiencies of these intricate record-keeping requirements.

E. Special Rules for Annuities

If you are taking some or all of your retirement plan benefits in the form of an annuity, those annuity payments must also satisfy the required distribution rules described in this part.

Although the required distribution rules for annuities are much the same as those for IRAs and other retirement plans, there are some differences worth noting.

Types of Annuities

In order to understand how the required distribution rules apply to your annuity, you must know what type of annuity you have.

Life Annuity. A life annuity makes payments to you or to you and your beneficiary for your entire life. You might have a single life annuity or a joint and survivor annuity. Payments from a single life annuity continue throughout your lifetime and stop when you die, regardless of how much has been paid. No further payments are made to any heirs or to your estate. In the case of a joint and survivor annuity, payments continue until your death or the death of your beneficiary—whichever occurs later—and then the payments stop. No additional payments are made to any other heirs or to your estate.

Term Certain Annuity. A term certain annuity makes payments for a fixed number of years regardless of when you die or when your beneficiary dies. If you die before the term is over, payments will be made to your beneficiary, your estate or your heirs for the remainder of the term.

Life Annuity With Term Certain. A life annuity with a term certain will make payments for your lifetime or else for a term certain if you die before the term is up. For example, assume you are taking a single life annuity with a term certain of ten years. If you live more than ten years, the annuity payments will continue throughout your life and stop when you die. If you die after five years, the annuity will continue payments for five more years.

Similarly, if you have a joint and survivor annuity with a term certain, and both you and your beneficiary die before the term is up, the annuity will continue to be paid to your heirs for the remainder of the term.

1. Form of Payment

To satisfy the required distribution rules, annuity payments must come at regular intervals of at least once a year. You can receive payments monthly, quarterly, semi-annually or annually, but not every 18 months. The payments may be in the form of either a life annuity or a term certain. If you choose a life annuity, the payments must last for your lifetime or the joint lifetime of you and your beneficiary.

If you choose a term certain, the term must be equal to or shorter than your single life expectancy or the joint life expectancy of you and your beneficiary. Once payments begin, the term certain may not be lengthened and life expectancies may not be recalculated, even if you change beneficiaries. Furthermore, payments generally must be level, although they might be increased to reflect changes in cost of living, benefit increases under the plan or investment gains in your annuity portfolio.

2. Required Beginning Date

If your annuity is a life annuity with no term certain or a life annuity with a term certain of 20 or fewer years, then the first *payment* must be made on or before your RBD to satisfy the required distribution rules. The amount of the first required payment is simply your regular annuity payment for that period. For example, if the terms of your annuity require that you be paid $2,000 per month for life, then you must receive your first $2,000 payment on or before your RBD. You are not required to receive any payments before that date.

If your annuity is a life annuity with a term certain of more than 20 years, or if it is just a term certain with no life annuity component, then you may not simply begin your annuity on your RBD. Instead, you must have received the *entire annual amount* for your first distribution year by your RBD.

> EXAMPLE: You turn 70½ in 2000. You have elected to take your qualified plan benefits in the form of a term certain annuity with a 16-year period. Your monthly payment is $2,000. Therefore, your required distribution

for 2000 (your first distribution year) is $24,000. That amount must be distributed to you no later than your RBD (April 1, 2001). In other words, distributions to you between January 1, 2000 and April 1, 2001 must be no less than $24,000. Furthermore, you must receive distributions of at least another $24,000 during 2001 to satisfy your required distribution for your second year.

3. Starting Early

If you elect to start receiving your annuity before your RBD and if you comply with the "Form of Payment" rules described in Section 1, above, then the start date of your annuity becomes your RBD for all purposes. For example, the start date is the irrevocable deadline for naming a designated beneficiary whose life expectancy can be used to determine your minimum required distributions.

4. Young Beneficiaries

If the beneficiary of your annuity is more than ten years younger than you are (and is not your spouse), then the MDIB rules apply. That means you must use special tables to determine whether or not your annuity satisfies the required distribution rules. You will need to know what type of annuity you have in order to determine which table to use.

a. Term Certain Annuity

If you have elected to take your annuity over a term certain and have named a non-spouse beneficiary who is more than ten years younger than you are, you may still use Table II to find your joint life expectancy, but only until your RBD. Once you reach your RBD, you must satisfy the required distribution rules, which means you must use the MDIB rules. Specifically, the term certain may not exceed the period found in Table III (see Appendix B) beginning in the year you turn 70½ and for all subsequent years.

EXAMPLE: You were born March 1, 1935. You retire and begin taking your annuity in 2000, when you are 65 years old with a 35-year-old grandson. You name your grandson as beneficiary. In 2000, your joint life expectancy, according to Table II (which you use because you are not yet 70½), was 47.7 years. You elect to begin taking distributions over a term certain of 47.7 years. Five years later, when you turn 70½, the remaining term certain will be 42.7 years (47.7 - 5). According to Table III, however, which you must use when you reach age 70½, the remaining term certain may not exceed 26.2 years.

In order to satisfy required distribution rules, your annuity plan must automatically adjust your payments beginning in the year you turn 70½ so that the annuity is paid out over 26.2 years (instead of 42.7 years).

b. Joint and Survivor Annuity

If you elect to receive a life annuity (without a term certain) over the joint life of you and a non-spouse beneficiary who is more than ten years younger than you are, then at all times from and after your first distribution year (the year you turn 70½), the projected payment to your beneficiary cannot exceed a certain percentage of the payment you are currently receiving. The percentage is based on the difference in your ages and is determined from Table IV (see Appendix B).

As in the case of a term certain annuity, if you begin receiving payments before your RBD that do not satisfy the required distribution rules, the payments must be adjusted beginning in the year you turn 70½.

EXAMPLE: You are taking your retirement benefits as a joint and survivor annuity over the joint life of you and your daughter. In the year you turn 70½, your monthly payment is $3,000. The difference in age between you and your daughter is 21 years. From Table IV, you see that, beginning in the year you turn 70½, your daughter's projected benefit when you die cannot exceed 72% of your current benefit— that is, it cannot exceed $2,160 per month ($3,000 x .72). So when you die, the payment to your daughter must drop from $3,000 per month to no more than $2,160 per month.

If you name more than one beneficiary of your annuity, then you must use the youngest beneficiary to determine the percentage from Table IV. And similarly, if you change your beneficiary to a younger beneficiary (for any reason other than the death of a primary beneficiary), your payments may need to be adjusted so that projected payments to the beneficiary satisfy the percentage requirements from Table IV. (See Section D.3, above, on changing beneficiaries.)

c. Joint and Survivor Annuity With Term Certain

If you have a life annuity with a term certain, you must satisfy both the term certain requirements described in Section a, above, as well as the survivor benefit limitations described in Section b. In other words, the term of your annuity may not exceed the number corresponding to your age in Table III, and the projected payments to your beneficiary after your death may not exceed the percentage in Table IV.

Real life is rarely as complex as these rules. Although the annuity rules seem (and can be) complex, most people's annuities take the form of a single life annuity or a joint life annuity

with a spouse. If you have selected either of these forms of payment, then you should not have to make new computations every year. It is only when you use a much younger non-spouse beneficiary or when you change beneficiaries that your situation becomes more complicated.

F. Divorce or Separation

If you are divorced or separated, part of your qualified plan, qualified annuity or TDA might be payable to an "alternate payee" (such as a spouse, former spouse or child) under the terms of a QDRO—a court-approved divorce or maintenance agreement. (See Chapter 2, Section C.4 for more information about QDROs.) Nonetheless, when you reach your RBD, the required distribution rules will apply to the alternate payee's portion, as well as to your own. And because you are the plan participant, it is your RBD that determines when distributions must begin. Furthermore, if the required amount is not withdrawn in a timely fashion, you, not the alternate payee, must pay the penalty. As for other required distribution rules, their application will depend on whether or not the alternate payee's portion is in a separate account.

Read your QDRO carefully. Your QDRO might provide that the alternate payee is to receive immediate and total distribution of his or her share of the plan. Unless the plan itself permits such a distribution, however, the alternate payee must simply wait and receive his or her share as the assets are distributed from the plan, either at your retirement or when you begin required distributions, or at some other time specified by the plan.

1. Separate Account

A QDRO might require that an alternate payee's portion be "divided" and separately accounted for. If so, the following variations in the required distribution rules will apply:

- The alternate payee's separate share is not to be combined, or aggregated, with the rest of your plan benefits when you compute required distributions. In other words, you must separately compute the required distribution amount for your portion and the alternate payee's portion and then distribute the alternate payee's portion from the alternate payee's separate share.

- In computing the required distribution from the alternate payee's portion, you may use your own single life expectancy, the single life expectancy of the alternate payee or the joint life expectancy of you and the alternate payee. The decision belongs to you—not to the alternate payee— even though the distribution will come from the alternate payee's

portion and will be distributed to the alternate payee. (See Section C.2, above, for more information about life expectancies.)

⚠ **Remember your limited options.** Although you have several options for selecting a life expectancy to compute required distributions from the alternate payee's portion, one option you do not have is to use the joint life expectancy of the alternate payee and his or her beneficiary. If the alternate payee dies before your RBD, however, you can use the life expectancy of the alternate payee's beneficiary in place of the alternate payee's life expectancy.

EXAMPLE: Your ex-husband is entitled to half of your pension plan under the terms of your QDRO. The pension plan administrator separated his share into a separate account, and your ex-husband named his sister as beneficiary of his separate share of the pension. The plan provides that no distributions can be made until you retire or reach your RBD. If your ex-husband dies before your RBD, then you may use the joint life expectancy of you and your ex-husband's sister when computing distributions from your ex-husband's portion of the pension.

- If the plan permits the employee to choose whether or not to recalculate life expectancies and a former spouse is the alternate payee, then the participant may choose whether or not to recalculate life expectancies when computing distributions from the participant's share, but only the former spouse may choose whether to recalculate life expectancies when computing distributions from the alternate payee's portion.

• If your QDRO requires that the alternate payee's portion be separated, and if the plan complies, the MDIB rules will *not* apply, even if the alternate payee is a non-spouse (or non-ex-spouse) such as your child, and is more than ten years younger than you are. (See Section B.2 for more information on the MDIB rules.)

EXAMPLE: Under the terms of a QDRO, you are required to divide your retirement plan benefits into two equal shares. One share is payable to you upon distribution and the other share is payable to your daughter. You begin to take required distributions in the year you turn 70 and your daughter turns 45. When computing required distributions from your daughter's segregated share, you may use the joint life expectancy of you and your daughter. Although your daughter is more than ten years younger than you are, you are not required to use the MDIB rule, because the retirement benefits are payable to your daughter under a QDRO and are separated from the rest of your retirement benefits.

Instead, you may use Table II. The joint life expectancy for you and your daughter at ages 70 and 45 respectively is 38.3 years. (If you had been required to use the MDIB table—Table III—the joint life expectancy would have been 26.2.)

Even if a QDRO requires that a retirement benefit be divided, it might not be possible to physically separate the alternate payee's share. The terms of the plan may not permit it. The share may be deemed separate in the eyes of the IRS, however, if the plan administrator uses a reasonable method to separately account for the alternate payee's portion. For example, a reasonable method would be to allocate on a pro rata basis all investment gains and losses, as well as contributions and forfeitures (if applicable). But if all the funds are kept in the same account and the administrator's accounting fails to show any allocation to an alternate payee, it would be hard to argue that the alternate payee's portion is separate. Other rules are explained below in Section 2.

2. No Separate Account

Some QDROs do not require an actual separation of the alternate payee's share, or perhaps the plan won't permit it. In either case, your retirement plan would remain undivided and a portion of each distribution would be paid to the alternate payee. Under this scenario, the alternate payee's portion need not separately satisfy the minimum distribution requirement. Instead, it would be combined, or aggregated, with your other plan assets for purposes of determining your account balance and calculating your required distribution for the year.

The effect of this aggregation on the required distribution rules is simply that the rules are applied as though there were no alternate payee. Specifically:

- When calculating required distributions, you will use your single life expectancy or the joint life expectancy of you and your beneficiary, but not the alternate payee's single life expectancy.
- The authority to make a recalculation election (see Section B, above) belongs to you, not the alternate payee, assuming the plan itself gives you the authority to make an election. Thus, when you compute the amount of the required distribution from your interest and the alternate payee's interest, the decision as to whether your life expectancy or your beneficiary's life expectancy is to be recalculated is entirely yours.
- There will be no exception to the MDIB requirements for a non-spouse alternate payee. If a non-spouse beneficiary is more than ten years younger than you are, you must use Table III when computing required distributions. Furthermore, if a spouse or former spouse is the alternate payee and if you have named

multiple beneficiaries on the account, the exception to the MDIB rule for a spouse or former spouse will not apply and Table III must again be used if any beneficiary is more than ten years younger than you.

3. Income Taxes and Penalties

The rules concerning the payment of taxes and penalties on QDRO distributions are essentially the same whether the alternate payee is a spouse, former spouse or child. But there are two exceptions.

a. Spouse or Former Spouse Alternate Payee

If the alternate payee named in the QDRO is your spouse or former spouse, the alternate payee is liable for all income taxes on distributions paid to the alternate payee. But you are responsible for penalties on any shortfall in required distributions, even though the alternate payee is receiving a portion.

b. Non-Spouse Alternate Payee

If the alternate payee is someone other than your spouse or former spouse (for example, your child), you are liable for all income taxes, as well as any penalties that might apply. This is true even though the distribution is payable to the alternate payee.

4. Rollovers

The option to roll over a distribution from a qualified plan into an IRA or another qualified plan is a big tax benefit. Traditionally, the benefit has been reserved for plan participants, and occasionally the participant's spouse. Under the QDRO rules, the privilege is extended to a former spouse.

a. Spouse or Former Spouse Alternate Payee

A spouse or former spouse is permitted to roll over any distributed portion of his or her interest in your plan if there is a QDRO in place. (See Chapter 2, Section C.4, for information about QDROs.) This is the case whether or not the spouse or former spouse's portion was held in a separate account. Once the spouse or former spouse completes the rollover to an account in his or her name, the account belongs to the spouse or former spouse in every way and the required distribution rules apply to that account as though the alternate payee were the original owner.

 Your actions may be limited by the plan terms. Although the QDRO rules permit your spouse or former spouse to roll over an interest in your retirement plan, some plans will not permit it. Furthermore, some plans will not make any distribution at all until you (the employee) have reached a certain retirement age—

one that is specified in the plan. Because the plan rules ultimately govern distributions, spouses and former spouses often have little control over how they receive QDRO payments.

b. Non-Spouse Alternate Payee

Non-spouse alternate payees may not roll over their interest in your retirement plan, under any circumstances. The law does not allow it.

 You must have a QDRO in place. The special rules described in this section apply only to qualified plans, qualified annuities and TDAs, and only if there is a QDRO in place. If there is no QDRO, your retirement plan is treated as though it is entirely yours for required distribution purposes. (If your divorce agreement states that your former spouse is to share in your plan, you must generally give your former spouse his or her share as it is distributed from the plan. In other words, a portion of each distribution would go to your former spouse, and you would keep you share.)

 QDRO rules don't apply to IRAs. So as long as the IRA remains in your name, the required distribution rules apply as though your former spouse had no interest in the IRA. But if some or all of your IRA is transferred into your former spouse's name as a result of a written divorce or separation agreement, then from the time the transfer is complete, the transferred portion belongs to your former spouse in every respect. This means the required distribution rules will apply as though your former spouse were the original owner. (See Chapter 2, Section E.4, for more information about IRAs and divorce.)

Key Tax Code And Regulations Sections

§ 401(a)(9)

Required Distributions From Qualified Plans

§ 1.401(a)(9)

Required Distribution Regulations

§ 1.408-8

Required Distributi8on Rules for IRAs

Chapter 7

Distributions to Your Beneficiary If You Die Before Age 70$^{1}/_{2}$

Who Should Read Chapter 7

Read this chapter if you want to know what happens to your own retirement plan after you die or if you inherit a retirement plan or IRA from someone who died before reaching age 70½. This chapter describes how the account must be distributed and explains other administrative procedures to help avoid unnecessary penalties and taxes.

The law says you must start taking money out of your retirement plan by a certain date—your "required beginning date" (RBD). But what if you never make it to that date? What would your premature death mean for your beneficiaries (other than the obvious sadness), and how can you prepare for it?

As you may recall from Chapters 5 and 6, the IRS issued in January 2001 new regulations simplifying and liberalizing the required distribution rules. To allow taxpayers to take advantage of the beneficial changes, the IRS has made the new rules optional for 2001. Because the new rules are more favorable than the old rules, we think that virtually anyone who can use the new rules should do so.

As we describe immediately below, however, some taxpayers won't be able to use the new rules. For that reason, we discuss both sets of rules in this chapter. Part I discusses the new rules, and Part II discusses the old rules. As you read this chapter, please keep the following in mind:

- It bears repeating: The new rules are more favorable, so you will want to start using them as soon as possible.
- If you have an IRA, you can start using the new rules immediately for 2001 distributions.
- If you have a qualified plan, you can only use the new rules for 2001 distributions if the plan has been modified (amended) to incorporate the new rules. To find out whether your plan has been modified, contact the plan administrator.
- If you are still dealing with distributions that you took in 2000 for any type of plan or IRA, then you must use the old rules.
- If you inherited an IRA in 2000 or later, you can use the new rules for distributions that you receive in 2001 and beyond. If you inherited a qualified plan in 2000 or later, you can use the new rules for distributions that you receive in 2001 and beyond if the plan has been modified to incorporate the new rules.
- If you inherited an IRA or other retirement plan before 2000, it is not yet clear whether you can switch to the new rules. To be safe, you should continue to use the old rules until the IRS clarifies this issue.
- As you read through Parts I and II, be careful that you don't lose track of which part you are reading. Some

Helpful Terms

Annuity. A contract, sold by an insurance company, that promises to make monthly, quarterly, semiannual or annual payments for life or for a specified period of time.

Contingent Beneficiary. A person or entity who is entitled to receive the benefits of a retirement plan or IRA only if and when a specific event occurs, such as the death of a primary beneficiary.

Deferral Period. The number of years over which distributions from a retirement plan or IRA can be spread.

Disclaimer. A renunciation of or a refusal to accept property to which a person is entitled by gift, by law or under the terms of a will or a trust.

Distribution. A payout of property (such as shares of stock) or cash from a retirement plan or IRA to the participant or a beneficiary.

Estate. All property that a person owns.

Irrevocable Trust. A trust that cannot be changed or terminated by the person who created it. Once assets are transferred to an irrevocable trust, the assets are subject to the terms of the trust for as long as the trust exists.

Primary Beneficiary. A person or entity entitled to receive benefits from a retirement plan or IRA upon the death of the original participant.

Recalculated Life Expectancy. Life expectancy that is revised each year according to statistically accurate measures of mortality.

Revocable Trust. A trust whose terms allow the creator of the trust to alter its provisions, cancel it or remove some or all of the property from the trust and return the property to the creator.

Term Certain. A fixed, identifiable period, such as a specific number of years. For example, a retirement plan that is distributable over a term certain of 20 years must be completely liquidated after 20 years.

of the differences are subtle, but significant.

Part I: New Rules

A. Determining the Designated Beneficiary

If you die before your RBD, which for most people is April 1 of the year after they turn 70½ (see Chapter 6 for information about determining your RBD), your designated beneficiary (if you have one) generally must begin taking distributions from your retirement plan in the year after your death, with some exceptions. Just how rapidly the assets must be distributed and according to what schedule depends primarily on who the designated beneficiary is. So before we look at distribution methods, let's see how the IRS will determine who your designated beneficiary is.

Recall that you can name any person or organization you want as the beneficiary of your retirement plan or IRA. However, when determining how your retirement plan assets should be distributed after your death, only designated beneficiaries are taken into account. (See Chapter 6 for more information about designated beneficiaries.) If one or more of your named beneficiaries is not a designated beneficiary, you are deemed to have no designated beneficiary and distributions must be accelerated.

1. Deadline for Determining Designated Beneficiary

The designated beneficiary of your retirement plan is determined as of December 31 of the year after your death. Although the determination date occurs after you die, this doesn't mean that someone can come along and name beneficiaries to your retirement plan after you have passed away. If you fail to name any beneficiary of your retirement plan, you generally will be deemed to have no designated beneficiary.

But if nobody can add a beneficiary after your death, why, you might ask, is the deadline for determining the beneficiary so long after your death? That's the issue that we address in the following section.

2. Changing Beneficiaries Before the Deadline

Even though no one can add beneficiaries to your retirement plan after you die, your beneficiary could change after your death. For example, suppose you name your spouse as primary beneficiary and your children as contingent beneficiaries. After your death, your spouse decides she has enough to live on for the rest of her life without using any of your retirement plan assets. She might disclaim (renounce) her interest in your retirement plan. In that case, the plan assets would go to your children as contingent beneficiaries.

The IRS inserted this extended deadline into the regulations as a relief provision. It gives beneficiaries an opportunity to do some post-mortem planning, whether to make administration of your distributions easier or to "clean up" a disadvantageous situation you left behind.

For example, suppose you named your wife and your favorite charity as equal beneficiaries on your retirement account. When you die, if the charity and your spouse are still equal beneficiaries on December 31 of the year after your death, you are deemed to have no designated beneficiary (because the charity isn't a designated beneficiary) and distributions to all beneficiaries are accelerated. (See Section B.2, below.) This could have disastrous tax consequences for your spouse.

As a clean-up measure, however, the charity can receive its entire distribution before December 31 of the year after death, leaving only your spouse as beneficiary. Then the post-death rules apply as though your spouse were sole beneficiary—and therefore the designated beneficiary—of the account. This would produce a much more favorable result. (See Section C, below.)

B. Distribution Methods

If you die before your RBD, your retirement plan benefits will be distributed using one of three methods: the life expectancy rule (see Section 1, below), the five-year rule (see Section 2, below) or a spousal rollover (see Section 3, below).

1. Life Expectancy Rule

The life expectancy rule allows your beneficiary to spread distributions over his or her life expectancy after your death, if both of the following conditions are met:

- the beneficiary of your plan or IRA as of December 31 of the year after your death is a designated beneficiary; and
- the plan itself either permits the life expectancy rule or is silent (meaning it doesn't indicate one way or another which rule should be used).

Distributions under the life expectancy rule generally must begin in the year after your death and continue until the entire account has been depleted. (Some unusual twists apply if your spouse is your beneficiary. See Section C, below.)

Sections C through I, below, provide detailed information about calculating distributions for each type of designated beneficiary.

2. Five-Year Rule

The five-year rule is mandatory in cases where both of the following are true:

- you die before your RBD, and
- your retirement plan or IRA is deemed to have no designated ben-

eficiary as of December 31 of the year after your death. (See Chapter 6 for more information about which beneficiaries qualify as designated beneficiaries.)

If the five-year rule applies, all of your retirement plan assets must be distributed within five years.

 Actually, it's five years plus. Practically speaking, your beneficiary has a little more than five years to withdraw the assets. This is because the official distribution deadline is December 31 of the year containing the fifth anniversary of your death. For example, if you die on March 3 in the year 2002, your retirement plan need not be completely distributed until December 31, 2007—five years and almost ten months later.

a. Required Beginning Date

The five-year rule applies only if you die before your RBD. If you live past that milestone, a different set of rules will apply when you die without a designated beneficiary. If you have passed your RBD, you can forget about the five-year rule (and you should be reading Chapter 8). But be careful: It is your RBD that counts—not the year you turn 70½. For example, if your RBD is April 1, 2002, but you die on March 15, 2002, the five-year rule will apply even though you have already passed age 70½ and even if you have already taken a distribution for your

first distribution year. Technically, you have not begun required distributions until you pass your RBD.

> **EXAMPLE:** You turned 70½ in June 2002, which makes your RBD April 1, 2003. On December 30, 2002, you withdrew $6,000 from your IRA, which was the amount of your first required distribution. But then you died on March 15, 2003, before reaching your RBD. Because you died before your RBD, the five-year rule will apply even though you had already withdrawn an amount that would have satisfied your first required distribution.

b. Distributing the Account

The five-year rule mandates that all assets be distributed from your retirement plan by December 31 of the year containing the fifth anniversary of your death, but it places no restriction on the form of payment. This means, for example, that your beneficiary could receive the entire amount as a lump sum in the month after your death, monthly installments spread over the five-year period or perhaps nothing at all until the December 31 deadline in the fifth year.

Although the IRS would accept any of those approaches, the retirement plan itself might have more stringent distribution requirements—and the plan controls how payments will be made. (See Section 4, below, for more about plan rules.) Some plans allow beneficiaries to receive installment payments or to leave the funds in the plan until the five-year period is up. If the plan requires immediate distribution of the entire account, however, then that's what your beneficiary will be stuck with.

3. Spousal Rollover

If your beneficiary is your spouse and if he or she is the sole beneficiary of your retirement plan, your spouse will generally have an alternative to the life expectancy rule or the five-year rule. That alternative is to roll over your retirement plan into an IRA in the spouse's own name.

Spouses only. This option is available only to spouses who are the sole beneficiaries for the plan. (See Section C, below, for more information about spousal rollovers.)

4. Effect of the Retirement Plan's Rules

Although the law provides a framework for required distributions within which retirement plans may operate, the plan's own rules can be—and usually are—more restrictive. In that case, the plan's rules govern. For example, even though the law allows a designated beneficiary to use the life expectancy rule and take distributions

over his or her life expectancy, the plan itself might require that even designated beneficiaries use the five-year rule. Or sometimes the plan will allow the designated beneficiary to choose a method of distribution.

a. Optional Provisions

Sometimes, plans give beneficiaries a choice of which rule to use. For example, in the best of all worlds (from the taxpayer's perspective), plans would allow beneficiaries to choose between the five-year rule and the life expectancy rule. And if a beneficiary didn't have a choice and was saddled with the five-year rule, the beneficiary would certainly like to be able to choose how the assets were distributed over that five-year period.

If you do get to choose. Generally, a beneficiary who has the option to use the life expectancy rule would choose it and not the five-year rule. However, if a beneficiary failed to take a timely distribution under the life expectancy rule, he or she might want to fall back on the five-year rule to avoid the hefty penalty for failing to take a required distribution.

But this isn't the best of worlds, and plan administrators don't always put taxpayers' needs first. In fact, some plans offer no options at all to beneficiaries, instead mandating distribution of the entire plan in the year of death. At the other extreme, some plans might distribute nothing at all until the end of the fifth year.

Furthermore, many plans have different policies for different beneficiaries. For example, the terms of a plan might require that non-spouse beneficiaries receive a distribution of the entire plan immediately following the participant's death (without the five-year grace period), but allow a spouse beneficiary to use the life expectancy rule.

b. Default Provisions

If the plan is resolutely silent on how distributions will occur after the death of the plan participant, certain default provisions kick in by law. Specifically, if the plan has a designated beneficiary, the life expectancy rule applies by default.

C. Spouse Beneficiary

If your spouse is the sole beneficiary of your retirement plan, he or she has three options for taking distributions from your retirement plan after your death. Your spouse can:

- leave the account in your name and use the life expectancy rule to take distributions over his or her own life expectancy beginning in the year after your death (see Section 1, below)
- leave the account in your name and use the life expectancy rule to take distributions beginning in the year you would have been 70½ (see Section 2, below), or
- roll over the plan or IRA into an IRA in his or her own name (see Section 3, below).

1. Life Expectancy Rule: Beginning in Year After Your Death

One option for your spouse is to leave your retirement account in your name and begin taking required distributions by December 31 of the year after your death. If your spouse chooses this method, he or she would use the following steps for computing the first minimum distribution from your account:

Step 1: Determine the Account Balance
Your spouse must use your retirement account balance as of December 31 of the year of your death to compute the first required payment.

Step 2: Determine the ADP

Using his or her age in the year after your death, your spouse must look up the appropriate life expectancy factor in Table I (see Appendix B). That factor is the applicable distribution period—or ADP—for the first year.

Step 3: Calculate the Required Distribution:

To determine the first required distribution, your spouse divides the account balance by the ADP—which is Step 1 divided by Step 2. The resulting amount must be distributed by December 31 of the year after your death.

> EXAMPLE: You died on March 15, 2002, before reaching your RBD. Your spouse is the sole beneficiary of your retirement plan, and she turns 68 in 2003. Your account was valued at $100,000 on December 31, 2002. To calculate the first required distribution, she must go through the following steps:

Step 1: Determine Account Balance

To compute the first distribution, your spouse must use the account balance as of December 31, 2002, which is the year of your death. That amount is $100,000.

Step 2: Determine the ADP

Your spouse will be age 68 on her birthday in the year after your death (2003). Her single life expectancy at age 68 (from Table 1 in Appendix B) is 17.6 years.

Step 3: Calculate the Required Distribution

Your spouse's first required distribution is $100,000 divided by 17.6 (Step 1 divided by Step 2) or $5,682. Your spouse must withdraw at least that amount by December 31, 2003.

For the second and future years, your spouse would find the ADP from Table I each year, using his or her age for the current year. Your spouse would then divide the account balance as of December 31 of the previous year by the new ADP.

> EXAMPLE: Continuing the example, above, for the year 2004, your spouse will use the December 31, 2003, balance of your retirement account and divide it by her ADP. The ADP for age 69 (from Table I) is 16.8.

2. Life Expectancy Rule: Beginning in Year You Would Have Turned 70½

Alternatively, if your spouse is the sole beneficiary of your retirement account, your spouse can wait until the year you would have turned 70½ to begin receiving required distributions. Recall, that your spouse is the sole beneficiary of the account if he or she is the sole beneficiary on December 31 of the year after your death. This additional deferral—until the deceased participant would have been 70½—is only available to a spouse.

> EXAMPLE: Ed was born on March 15, 1935, and died June 1, 2000, at the age of 65. Ed's spouse Bertha is the sole beneficiary of his retirement account, and she elects to defer distributions from the plan until December 31, 2005, the year Ed would have been 70½. At that time, she may begin taking annual distributions based on her single life expectancy (or more quickly, if she prefers). To determine the minimum distribution for 2005, she looks up the ADP for her age that year (from Table I) and divides the ADP into the account balance for December 31, 2004. In subsequent years, she looks up the ADP (in Table I) for her age in the current year. She then divides the account balance on December 31 of the previous year by the new ADP.

If your spouse is older than you are.
Your spouse may defer distributions until you would have been 70½ even if your spouse has already turned 70½, as long as your spouse leaves the account in your name.

3. Rollover

If a spouse is the sole beneficiary of a qualified plan or IRA, the spouse has another quite valuable deferral option. The spouse can roll over the plan assets into an IRA of his or her own. (Note: This option is available only to a spouse.)

If your plan is a qualified plan, the only way your spouse can make the plan her own is by rolling the plan assets over into an IRA in the spouse's own name.

But if your retirement plan is an IRA, your spouse has several ways to make your IRA her own. She can do so by:

- rolling over the assets into a new or pre-existing IRA in her own name (see Section a, below)
- failing to take one of your post-death required distributions at the proper time (see Section b, below), or
- contributing additional amounts of her own to your retirement account.

a. Convert to Spouse's IRA by Rollover

A spouse can roll over a deceased participant's retirement plan into an IRA in the spouse's own name. This method is the cleanest because there is a clear record of what happened and when.

Once the account becomes the spouse's own, it belongs to the spouse in every way—as though he or she were the original owner. Required distributions will begin when the spouse reaches his or her own RBD and will be based on the ADP for the spouse's age at that time.

EXAMPLE: Grace died in 2002 at the age of 69. Her husband, George, was the sole beneficiary of her retirement plan, and he turned 64 on February 14, 2002. At the end of 2002, George rolls over Grace's retirement plan into an IRA in his own name. George will not need to begin required distributions until his own RBD, which is April 1 of the year after he turns 70½, or April 1, 2009.

⚠ **Not for qualified plans.** A spouse may not roll over a deceased person's retirement plan into a qualified plan in the spouse's name; the rollover can only be to a new or an existing IRA of the spouse's own.

If a surviving spouse rolls over a deceased participant's retirement plan into a new IRA, the spouse may name a new beneficiary of his or her own choosing.

EXAMPLE: Your husband is the primary beneficiary of your retirement plan, and your brother will inherit the plan if your husband dies before you do. You die in 2002. Your husband decides to roll over your retirement plan into an IRA in his own name. He completes the rollover in December 2002 and names his sister as primary beneficiary. His action is completely legal under the rollover rules. Once he rolls over your retirement plan, the assets are his. His sister will receive the IRA assets; your brother will not.

Your spouse may roll over your retirement plan and name a new beneficiary after you die, even if your spouse has passed his or her RBD at the time of the rollover. Your spouse's RBD for purposes of the new IRA is December 31 of the year after the rollover, and required distributions must begin at that time.

EXAMPLE: You died in 2002 at the age of 69. Your wife turned 72 in 2002, and so was past her RBD. In December 2002, she rolled over your retirement plan into an IRA in her name and designated your children as beneficiaries. Your wife must take her first required distribution by December 31, 2003.

b. Convert to Spouse's IRA by Failing to Take Required Distribution

If you die before your RBD, and your spouse fails to take a required distribution on your behalf under the life expectancy rule—either by December 31 of the year after your death or by December 31 of the year you would have been 70½—your spouse is deemed to have made an election to treat your account as his or her own. The retirement plan becomes your spouse's own on December 31 of the year of the failure, and your spouse will not be required to take a distribution until his or her own RBD.

> **EXAMPLE:** Your wife died in the year 2000 at age 63. You were the sole beneficiary of her IRA. You did not take any distributions in 2001, nor had you taken any distributions by December 31, 2007—the year your wife would have been 70½. Therefore, by missing all of the deadlines for taking a distribution from your wife's retirement account, the account is deemed to be your own as of December 31, 2007.

c. Timing

The IRS imposes no deadline for a spouse to elect to treat a deceased participant's retirement plan as the spouse's own IRA. That means a spouse can begin taking distributions as a beneficiary under the life expectancy rule and then some years later roll over the assets into an IRA of the spouse's own.

As a practical matter, if a spouse is past age 59½ and intends to roll over a participant's retirement plan, there is nothing to be gained from waiting. If the spouse needs money, the spouse can take it freely from the IRA even after rolling it over, because there is no penalty for taking distributions after age 59½.

If the spouse is younger than 59½, however, free use of the IRA funds could be dicey. Recall that one of the exceptions to the early distribution tax is a distribution to a beneficiary after the death of the original participant. (See Chapter 3 for more information on the early distribution tax.) But that particular exception is not available to a spouse after the spouse rolls over the deceased person's plan into an IRA in the spouse's name. Once it is rolled over, it is the spouse's IRA and because the spouse is still alive, the after-death exception does not apply. Thus, the spouse must generally postpone distributions until age 59½ to avoid the early distribution tax.

Consequently, if the spouse is younger than 59½ and needs to use the retirement plan money to live on, the spouse might be better off leaving the plan in the name of the deceased so that the after-death exception can be used. The one disadvantage of this approach is that, according to at least one IRS private letter ruling, once a spouse invokes the after-death exception to the early distribution tax, the spouse forever forfeits the right to roll over the account into an IRA in the spouse's own name.

4. Death of Spouse Beneficiary

If a spouse beneficiary inherits a retirement plan or IRA and begins taking required distributions on December 31 of the year after the participant's death (or December 31 of the year the deceased participant would have turned 70½) but dies before all assets of the retirement account are distributed, the spouse's beneficiary must take distributions in the following way:

- In the year of the spouse's death, the spouse's beneficiary will divide the account balance as of December 31 of the year before the spouse's death by the ADP for the spouse in the year of the spouse's death (using the spouse's age on his or her birthday in the year of death and looking up the respective ADP in Table I in Appendix B).

- In the second year and beyond, the spouse's beneficiary will reduce the ADP determined in the previous paragraph by one and divide it into the account balance as of the previous December 31. The computation continues in this way each year until the entire account is depleted.

EXAMPLE: You died in 2002 at age 69. Your wife was the sole beneficiary of your IRA and began taking required distributions from your IRA in 2003. She died in 2005. She would have been 64 on her birthday. Her sister is the sole beneficiary of her estate. On December 31 2004, the balance in the IRA was $60,000. Your wife's ADP in 2005 (for age 64) is 20.8 (from Table I). The required distribution for 2005 is $2,885 ($60,000 divided by 20.8).

In the second year—2006—the ADP will be reduced by one. On December 31, 2005, the balance in the IRA was $63,000. The ADP for 2006 is 19.8 (which is 20.8 – 1). Therefore, the sister's required distribution for 2006 is $3,182 ($63,000 divided by 19.8).

If a spouse beneficiary dies after the participant, but before beginning required distributions under the life expectancy rule (and before rolling over the account into an IRA in the spouse's own name), then the following rules apply:

- In general, the life expectancy rule or the five-year rule will apply to the spouse's beneficiary as though the spouse had been the original participant. Specifically, the age of the spouse's beneficiary will determine how required distributions are computed under the life expectancy rule. (If the spouse remarries and names his or her new spouse as beneficiary, however, the new spouse will be treated as a non-spouse beneficiary. See the next bullet point.)

EXAMPLE: You die in 2002 at age 65. Your wife is the sole beneficiary of your retirement plan account and therefore is not required to begin distributions until you would have been age 70½ (in the year 2007). Her sister is the sole beneficiary of your wife's estate. Your wife died in 2005 before beginning required distributions from your retirement account. The life expectancy rule will apply to distributions to her sister, the beneficiary. Under the life expectancy rule, you wife's sister must begin distributions by December 31, 2006, and take them over her life expectancy. For her first distribution, she would use her age in 2006 and find the ADP in Table I. For subsequent years, she would reduce the ADP by one.

- If your spouse remarried and named his or her new spouse as beneficiary, the special additional deferral option, described in Section 1, above, is not available to the new spouse beneficiary. Specifically, the spouse's new wife or husband is not permitted to wait until the spouse would have been 70½ to begin required distributions. The spouse's beneficiary is simply treated as a non-spouse and is subject to the rules in the previous bullet point.

EXAMPLE: You die in 2002 at age 65. Your wife is the sole beneficiary of your retirement plan account and therefore is not required to begin distributions until you would have been age 70½ (in 2007). Your wife remarried in 2004 and named her new husband as beneficiary of her entire estate. She died in 2005 before beginning required distributions from your retirement account. The life expect-

ancy rule applies and your wife's new husband must begin distributions by December 31, 2006, and take them over his life expectancy. He is not entitled to use the special deferral option of a spouse, however. He may not wait until his spouse (your wife) would have been 70½ to begin distributions.

D. Non-Spouse Beneficiary

As a participant in a retirement plan, or as the spouse of a participant, it is easy to take for granted the special privileges, exceptions and additional distribution options the Tax Code offers. But when the beneficiary is a non-spouse beneficiary, that person typically has only one option—the life expectancy rule.

If there is more than one beneficiary. The rules in this section only apply only if there is one beneficiary named on the account. If there is more than one beneficiary, a different set of rules applies. See sections F and G, below, for more about the multiple beneficiary rules.

1. Life Expectancy Rule

The law allows a non-spouse beneficiary to use the life expectancy rule to calculate required distributions after the plan participant's death. Those distributions must begin no later than December 31 of the year after the participant's death. No additional deferral is permitted.

Don't forget, however, to check the plan to see what it says. Remember: When the plan rules are more restrictive than the law, the plan controls. For example, the plan can require that benefits be paid out according to the five-year rule, in which case the beneficiary is stuck with it. On the other hand, if the plan is silent on post-death distributions, the life expectancy rule applies by default.

EXAMPLE: You died on March 15, 2002, before reaching your RBD. Your son is the beneficiary of your retirement plan, and he turns 48 in 2003. Your account was valued at $100,000 on December 31, 2002. Your son will use the life expectancy rule to compute required distributions.

Step 1: Determine the Account Balance

To compute the first payment, your son must use the account balance as of December 31, 2002, the year of your death. That amount is $100,000.

Step 2: Determine the ADP

Your son will be age 48 on his birthday in the year after your death (2003). His single life expectancy — or ADP—at age 48 (from Table 1 in Appendix B) is 34.9 years.

Step 3: Calculate the Required Distribution

Your son's first required distribution is $100,000 divided by 34.9 (Step 1 divided by Step 2) or $2,865. Your son must withdraw at least that amount by December 31, 2003.

For distributions in years after the first year, a non-spouse beneficiary must reduce the previous ADP by one. A non-spouse beneficiary is not permitted to use Table I for any year but the first year of required distributions.

EXAMPLE: Continuing the above example, for the year 2004, your son will use the December 31, 2003, balance of your retirement account and divide it by the new ADP, which is 33.9 (34.9 − 1).

Remember, too, that a beneficiary can always take more than the minimum amount each year, but not less.

2. No Rollover

A non-spouse beneficiary is never permitted to roll over a deceased person's retirement plan. Ever. If the beneficiary attempts to do so, the entire rollover could be considered a taxable distribution and an excess contribution to an IRA—and it would be subject to penalties. Even if the excess contribution is corrected, the retirement plan assets cannot be re-deposited into the deceased participant's account. Consequently, the beneficiary will owe income tax on the entire amount, whether or not penalties are assessed as well.

A non-spouse beneficiary really has only one option: to leave the retirement account in the name of the deceased participant until the account is completely distributed under the life expectancy rule (or more rapidly). (See Section G.3.b for more information about titling accounts.)

3. Death of Non-Spouse Beneficiary

If a non-spouse beneficiary dies after the participant has died, but before the retirement plan has been completely distributed, the distribution method remains the same. For example, if distributions were made under the life expectancy rule, distributions will still be made over the life expectancy of the deceased beneficiary, using the beneficiary's age on his or her birthday in the year after the participant's death, reduced by one in each subsequent year.

> EXAMPLE: Sara named her brother, Archie, as beneficiary of her retirement plan. She died in 2002 at the age of 68. Archie intended to begin taking distributions over his life expectancy beginning in 2003. He would have turned 55 on March 1, 2003, but he died on February 15, 2003. Nonethe-

less, distributions will be made to his beneficiary as though he were still alive. Archie's ADP at age 55 would have been 28.6 years (from Table I). The ADP will be reduced by one each year until the entire account is distributed.

If the plan had required the beneficiary to use the five-year rule, the entire account must still be distributed by December 31 of the year containing the fifth anniversary of the original participant's death, even though the beneficiary has since died.

Who is the beneficiary's beneficiary? When a primary beneficiary dies after the original participant has died but before all the retirement plan assets have been distributed, where does the remainder go? The answer depends on the laws of your state. If the primary beneficiary had designated a beneficiary, the path is clear. If not, typically, the retirement plan will be distributed according to the terms of the primary beneficiary's will. In the absence of a will, the assets would be distributed to the heirs of the primary beneficiary according to state law.

E. No Designated Beneficiary

If you have no designated beneficiary for your retirement account, then payout options at your death are restricted. Recall that a designated beneficiary must usually be a natural person, although it may also be a special type of trust. (See Chapter 6 for more information about designated beneficiaries.) And although you are permitted to name any beneficiary you choose, whether a person or an entity, some privileges are reserved for beneficiaries that qualify as designated beneficiaries.

1. Five-Year Rule

If the beneficiary of your retirement plan is not a designated beneficiary and if you die before your RBD, the five-year rule applies and the entire account must be distributed by December 31 of the year containing the fifth anniversary of your death.

2. No Life Expectancy Rule

If your beneficiary is not a designated beneficiary, the life expectancy rule is never an option under any circumstances. The five-year rule is mandatory, and all of the assets in the plan must be distributed by December 31 of the year containing the fifth anniversary of your death.

The law allows installments. Even if the life expectancy rule is not an option, it is still permissible for the beneficiary to take distributions in installments over the five-year period, if the plan will allow it.

F. Multiple Beneficiaries, Separate Accounts

If you have several IRAs or retirement plans, each with a different beneficiary, then each plan is treated separately for purposes of the required distribution rules. You are not considered to have multiple beneficiaries.

But suppose you have only one retirement account and you want to name more than one beneficiary. In that case, it is probably best to split the account into separate accounts, naming only one beneficiary on each. With separate accounts, your beneficiaries would be able to manage their money as they pleased. Each beneficiary could also take distributions over his or her own life expectancy instead of using the life expectancy of the oldest beneficiary, as would be required if there were no separate accounts. (See Section G, below, for more about multiple beneficiaries with one account.)

If you do name multiple beneficiaries of a single retirement plan, however, your beneficiaries still have a chance to get the benefits of a separate account. If the plan administrator or custodian agrees to do so, he or she can segregate each beneficiary's share and treat each as a separate account payable to one beneficiary. And even if the administrator does not segregate the shares, the shares may be treated as separate accounts if the administrator or custodian sets up separate accounting procedures (under which, for example, investment gains and losses are allocated to beneficiaries on a pro rata basis). Under either of these scenarios, each beneficiary could take distributions over his or her own life expectancy rather than using the life expectancy of the oldest beneficiary. (See Section G.3, below, for a discussion of how to split accounts.)

EXAMPLE: You have two IRAs, IRA #1 and IRA #2. Your daughter is beneficiary of IRA #1 and your son is beneficiary of IRA #2. If you die before your RBD, your daughter may distribute IRA #1 over her single life expectancy and your son may distribute IRA #2 over his. If you had only one IRA and if your son and daughter were both beneficiaries, they could ask the plan administrator to segregate their shares and begin treating each share as separate account by December 31 of the year after your death. If they do that, your daughter could distribute her share over her life expectancy, and your son could distribute his share over his life expectancy.

 Don't count on administrators allowing separate accounting. As a practical matter, many qualified plan administrators are reluctant to shoulder the burden of separate accounting or even to physically split the account. Consequently, the beneficiaries may be stuck with the multiple beneficiary/one account rules described in the next section. IRA custodians,

too, are often unwilling to provide a separate accounting for each beneficiary when multiple beneficiaries are named on one account. In the case of an IRA, however, there is nothing to prevent you from splitting the account during your lifetime into separate IRAs, one for each beneficiary. If you do split your IRA, however, be careful of the one-rollover-per-year rule. (See Chapter 2, Section E.2, for more information about rollovers.) You can avoid this one-rollover-per-year rule by asking the custodian to transfer the funds directly from one IRA to another. There is no limit to the number of direct transfers you can make in one year.

G. Multiple Beneficiaries, One Account

The rules change significantly if there is more than one person named as beneficiary of a single retirement account. Bear in mind, the date for determining whether or not there are multiple beneficiaries is December 31 of the year following your death. If you name multiple beneficiaries and all of those beneficiaries are still named on a single account as of that deadline, the beneficiaries are no longer free to use their own life expectancies to take distribution of their respective shares. Even a spouse may lose some special privileges if you name both your spouse and a child as primary beneficiaries on a single account.

When you have multiple beneficiaries, for purposes of the life expectancy rule and the five-year rule, all beneficiaries are treated as non-spouse beneficiaries, even if one of them is your spouse. As a result, the most restrictive rules—those that pro- duce the worst result—will apply to all beneficiaries. For example, if you name your spouse and your children, the benefi- ciaries must choose from the options avail- able to your children because children have fewer options than spouses.

1. Life Expectancy Rule

The life expectancy rule still applies when there are multiple beneficiaries on a single account (as long as the plan does not re- quire accelerated payments). But the least favorable distribution period is the one your beneficiaries must use: The account must be distributed over the single life ex- pectancy of the oldest beneficiary. This will yield the largest distribution and de- plete the account most rapidly—exactly what Congress wants. The oldest beneficiary's life expectancy is determined (from Table I) as of his or her age in the first distribution year—the year after your death. Once the distribution amount is cal- culated and withdrawn, it is divided among the beneficiaries in proportion to their interest in the account.

EXAMPLE: You name your mother and your three children as equal beneficia- ries of your retirement plan. You die in 2002. Under the terms of the plan, your beneficiaries are permitted to use the life expectancy rule when distrib- uting your retirement account. Be- cause your mother is the oldest beneficiary, the account must be dis- tributed over her life expectancy. She will turn 85 in 2003, the first distribu- tion year. Her life expectancy—or ADP—at that time will be 6.9 years (from Table I). To compute the first distribution, your beneficiaries must divide the December 31, 2002, account balance by 6.9. That amount will then be distributed and divided equally among your mother and your three children. Each will get a fourth. The ADP will drop by one each subse- quent year, and the account will be completely distributed in just seven years.

2. Five-Year Rule

Again, it's important to remember that the plan can require that distributions be made according to the five-year rule. If the plan provides that the five-year rule applies to non-spouse beneficiaries, but the life ex- pectancy rule is available for a spouse, the spouse is nonetheless prohibited from us- ing the life expectancy rule if the spouse is one of multiple beneficiaries.

3. Splitting Accounts

If you die before your required beginning date having named multiple beneficiaries of your single retirement account, your beneficiaries have until December 31 of the year after your death to separate their respective shares. If they complete the separation in time, the distribution rules will apply separately to each beneficiary and his or her respective share. (See Section F, above, for a discussion of those rules.)

As we explained in Section F, above, the biggest benefit will be that each beneficiary will be able to use his or her own life expectancy to calculate distributions from his or her share. Furthermore, the separation will give each beneficiary autonomy over investment decisions and will also simplify accounting and other record-keeping. As long as the plan itself permits the separation, the law won't prevent it.

> EXAMPLE: You name your mother and your three children, Holly, Herman and Hank, as equal beneficiaries of your retirement plan. You die in 2002. At that time, your mother was 85 and your children were 34, 36 and 38 respectively. Your mother and the three children instructed the custodian to split your IRA into 4 separate but equal IRAs. By March 2003, there were four IRAs—all still in your name. Now, however, one of the IRAs names only your mother as beneficiary, one names

Holly, one names Herman and one names Hank. Because your IRA was split into separate IRAs for each beneficiary before December 31, 2003 (the year after your death), each beneficiary can take all future distributions from his or her share of the IRA over his or her own life expectancy, beginning in 2003. Your mother, who is 86 in 2003, must take distributions over 6.5 years (from Table 1). In contrast, your children can spread distributions over 47.3, 45.4 and 43.5 years (for ages 35, 37 and 39, respectively). If the account had not been separated by December 31, 2003, the entire account would have to be distributed over your mother's life expectancy (6.5 years) because she is the oldest beneficiary.

You should split accounts when you reach your RBD. A strict reading of the IRS Regulations suggests that this option to split accounts by December 31 of the year after the participant's death applies only if the participant dies before his or her RBD. If the participant dies after his or her RBD with multiple beneficiaries named on a single account, it would appear that the beneficiaries would not have the option of splitting accounts, and the rules of sections 1 and 2 above would apply. For this reason, it might be wise to split your account once you reach your RBD.

a. Transfer

When separating each beneficiary's share into a separate account after your death, assets must be transferred directly from the trustee or custodian of the original single plan account to the trustee or custodian of each separate account. The beneficiary must not have control of the funds at any time. If the beneficiary is deemed to have control, the IRS will consider the assets fully distributed and fully taxable in the current year.

Furthermore, in the case of non-spouse beneficiaries, the account must remain in the name of the deceased (see Section b, below), so it cannot be transferred to one or more of the beneficiaries' existing retirement plans or even into a new retirement account in a beneficiary's name. If a spouse is one of the beneficiaries, however, the spouse could presumably separate his or her share and roll it over to either an existing or a new IRA in the spouse's name.

b. Name on Account

When transferring a portion of the plan assets to a new account, the IRS requires that the new account also be in the original participant's name. But financial institutions generally do not like to maintain accounts, let alone set up new ones, in the name of a deceased person. To accommodate both the IRS requirements and their own internal accounting procedures, many custodians construct account titles that identify both the original participant (now deceased) and the beneficiary who is to receive distributions.

EXAMPLE: Joe Corpus died leaving a substantial IRA equally to his three children, Dan, Irwin and Bruce. The children want to split the IRA into three separate IRAs so that each can manage his own investments. The IRA custodian set up three new IRA accounts in Joe's name and transferred a third of Joe's original IRA into each one. The title on Dan's account reads: "Joe Corpus, Deceased, for the benefit of (or FBO) Dan Corpus." The other two accounts are titled "Joe Corpus, Deceased, FBO Irwin Corpus" and "Joe Corpus, Deceased, FBO Bruce Corpus."

Reporting Requirements

The IRS has issued what is called a "revenue procedure" outlining a set of reporting requirements that IRA custodians must adhere to after an IRA participant dies. The custodian must file IRS Form 5498 (see Appendix A) for each beneficiary. The form reports the name of the original owner, the name of the beneficiary, the beneficiary's tax ID or Social Security number and the value of the beneficiary's share of the IRA as of the end of the year.

With this information, the IRS can trace the source of the IRA for income tax purposes and determine who is liable for the deferred tax. The form must be filed every year until the account is depleted.

⚠️ **No rollover allowed.** Some non-spouse beneficiaries and, unfortunately, even some custodians are under the mistaken impression that a beneficiary may roll over a deceased participant's retirement plan into an IRA in the beneficiary's own name. This option, however, is available only to a spouse beneficiary. (See Section C.3, above, for more information about spousal rollovers.) Non-spouse beneficiaries are never permitted to roll over retirement plan assets into a new or existing IRA in their own names.

c. Choosing the Distribution Option

As we explained above, the effect of naming multiple beneficiaries of one retirement plan account (assuming the account is not split by December 31 of the year after death) is to limit the deferral period to the life expectancy of the oldest beneficiary. As long as the plan permits, however, there is nothing to prevent one beneficiary from accelerating distributions of his or her share while the remaining beneficiaries use the life expectancy rule. The remaining beneficiaries' deferral period would be limited to the life expectancy of the oldest, even if the oldest had already withdrawn some or all of his or her share.

EXAMPLE: Mary, Paul and Peter inherited an IRA from their father, Jake, who died in 2002. The children had not split the account by December 31,

2003. Now, Mary, the oldest child, wants to take her share and use it to buy a house. The boys don't need the money right now and want to take their portions out slowly, spreading distributions over as many years as possible. Mary may take her share outright, and the boys may continue to spread distribution of their shares over Mary's life expectancy.

4. When a Spouse Is One of the Beneficiaries

If your spouse is one of several (or even just two) beneficiaries of your retirement account as of December 31 of the year after your death, your spouse loses both the option to defer distributions until you would have been 70½ and the option to roll over the account into an IRA in his or her own name. Instead, distributions under the life expectancy rule must begin by December 31 of the year after your death.

5. Designated and Non-Designated Beneficiaries

If as of December 31 of the year after your death, any one of the beneficiaries of your retirement account is not a designated beneficiary, the account is deemed to have no designated beneficiary, even if one or more of the other beneficiaries on the account would otherwise be a designated beneficiary. If the account is deemed to have no designated beneficiary, the life expectancy rule is not available. Instead, the assets must be distributed under the five-year rule. Many a charitably inclined taxpayer, wanting to leave a portion of his or her retirement plan to charity and a portion to a spouse or child, has been blindsided by this unfavorable application of the rules.

> EXAMPLE: Paul named his son and the American Cancer Society as equal beneficiaries of his IRA. Paul died in 2002. The beneficiaries did not get around to splitting the account before December 31, 2003. Because the American Cancer Society is not a natural person or a qualified trust, it is not considered a designated beneficiary. Therefore, the IRA is deemed to have no designated beneficiary, even though Paul's son would have qualified had he been the sole beneficiary. As a result, the entire account must be distributed by December 31, 2006, with half going to Paul's son and half to the American Cancer Society.

Remember, though, this problem can be cured by separating the account or by distributing the charity's share before December 31 of the year after death.

H. Trust Beneficiary

Generally, a beneficiary must be a "natural person" to qualify as a designated beneficiary and be eligible for the life expectancy rule. The exception to this general rule applies when the beneficiary is a trust that meets certain stringent requirements. As explained in Chapter 6, if the trust satisfies all of the requirements, then the beneficiaries of the trust will be treated as designated beneficiaries for purposes of the life expectancy rule. In other words, the trustee or custodian of the retirement plan may "look through" the trust to find the designated beneficiary whose life expectancy can be used to compute required distributions.

Bypass Trusts and Estate Planning

You must jump through a raft of hoops to name a trust as beneficiary of a retirement plan and feel confident that you have accomplished what you intended. Sometimes, you never do achieve a high level of confidence. So with all the risk and uncertainty, why would anyone bother?

People name trusts as beneficiaries for all kinds of reasons, and one of the most significant of those is to fund what is called a "bypass" trust to minimize death taxes.

The use of trusts in estate planning to minimize death taxes and other costs is complex, but here's a brief summary of what it means to use a retirement plan to fund a bypass trust.

The law allows each individual to leave a certain amount, called an "exclusion amount," to his or her heirs free of death taxes. (The exclusion amount is scheduled to increase incrementally from $675,000 in 2001 to $1,000,000 by the year 2006.) In addition, an individual may leave an unlimited amount to a spouse. If an individual leaves everything outright to a spouse, however, some or all of the individual's exclusion amount could be wasted.

For example, assume a husband and wife have a combined net worth of $1 million. The husband dies in January 2001 and leaves everything to his wife, never using his $675,000 exclusion amount. Although there will be no death taxes when the husband dies, when the wife dies, she can only leave her own exclusion amount tax free to the children. The remainder will be subject to death taxes. If the wife dies in December 2001 and the estate is still worth $1,000,000,

she leaves $675,000 tax free to the children, but the remaining $325,000 is subject to death taxes. If the husband had given his $675,000 to the children when he died, instead of to his spouse, the entire estate could have passed to the children tax-free.

Many people choose not to give large amounts to their children outright because they don't want to risk leaving a spouse strapped for cash. That's where the bypass trust concept comes in. When the husband dies, he can direct his exclusion amount to a trust which is accessible to the wife during her lifetime and which flows to the children upon her death. Technically, the assets in the trust do not belong to the wife, so when she dies, she can give additional amounts equal to the exclusion to the children—all of it tax free.

Now, what role does the IRA or retirement plan play in all of this? For many people, a retirement plan is their most substantial asset, and a bypass trust couldn't be fully funded unless the plan assets were used. In other words, many people don't have enough assets outside the plan to put the exclusion amount into a bypass trust. But the law won't allow a trust to "own" a retirement plan, which means it is not possible to simply transfer the plan into the trust. To fund the trust, a person would have to name the trust as beneficiary so that after-death distributions from the plan would be directed into the trust every year until the trust is fully funded. The spouse could then have access to the funds once they have been distributed from the retirement plan to the trust.

1. Non-Spouse Beneficiary of Trust

If you do name a trust as beneficiary and if it meets the requirements of a designated beneficiary (see Chapter 6), distributions under the life expectancy rule or the five-year rule will be computed as though there were no trust in place—as though the beneficiary of the trust had been named beneficiary of the retirement plan. Therefore, if the beneficiary of the trust is not your spouse, the life expectancy rule would apply and the beneficiary may spread required distributions over the beneficiary's life expectancy beginning in the year after your death. In any case, all distributions would go into the trust and become subject to the terms of the trust, which may or may not call for an immediate distribution to the beneficiary.

2. Spouse Beneficiary of Trust

If your spouse is sole beneficiary of the trust, your spouse will be treated as the designated beneficiary for purposes of the life expectancy rule. That means your spouse could take distributions over his or her life expectancy beginning on December 31 of the year after your death—or your spouse could delay distributions until the year you would have been 70½. In either case, your spouse would use his or her age each year to find the corresponding ADP in Table I.

Rollovers may not be permitted.
Even if your spouse is sole beneficiary of the trust, the IRS regulations state that he or she cannot roll over the retirement plan assets into an IRA in the spouse's own name. (See Section C.3, above, for more information about spousal rollovers.) Some private letter rulings suggest a rollover is still possible in certain circumstances (see Section 4, below), but it's not something you should count on.

3. Multiple Beneficiaries of Trust

If a trust has multiple beneficiaries and meets the criteria for looking through the trust for a designated beneficiary, then for purposes of applying the life expectancy rule, the multiple beneficiary rules described in Section G, above, will apply as though the individuals themselves were named beneficiaries of the retirement plan.

4. Trust Beneficiary and Spousal Rollovers

Recall that a trust—called a bypass trust—is often named the beneficiary of a retirement plan in order to minimize estate taxes. This method usually works in the following way: The plan participant names a trust as the beneficiary of the plan and names his or her spouse as the beneficiary of the trust. When the participant dies, distributions from the plan go into the trust, and then the trust makes distributions to the spouse.

But sometimes the surviving spouse discovers after the participant dies that the retirement plan assets are not needed to fund the trust after all. In that case, the surviving spouse might prefer to get rid of the trust and roll over the assets into his or her own IRA, name his or her own beneficiary and begin a new schedule of required distributions.

The legality of this sort of rollover is in question. This is because the law says that only a spouse beneficiary may roll over assets. Generally, a trust beneficiary may not roll over assets.

But taxpayers have argued that if the spouse is the sole beneficiary of the trust, then for all intents and purposes, the assets do pass directly from the deceased plan participant to the spouse—and thus the rollover complies with the intent, if not the letter, of the law. Similarly, if the spouse has complete control over the assets of the trust and can distribute all of the assets without interference from any third party, then again the assets arguably pass directly from the deceased to the spouse—and thus the rollover is essentially within the law.

Despite the lack of explicit legal approval of these rollover strategies, the IRS in the past established a pattern of approving such actions in a number of its private letter rulings.

In regulations issued in January 2001, however, the IRS changed its position. Those regulations state specifically that a spouse cannot make a deceased participant's IRA her own if a trust is named primary beneficiary of the IRA—even if the spouse is sole beneficiary of the trust.

Some practitioners believe, however, that if the spouse has the power to distribute all the assets of the trust, he or she could distribute the IRA assets to the trust and then distribute the assets from the trust to the spouse. Having done so, the spouse could then roll over the assets into an IRA of his or her own. Although this strategy is not specifically sanctioned by the IRS, some practitioners believe it will pass muster, even under the new regulations.

We believe you should proceed with caution. If you name a trust as beneficiary of your retirement plan with the expectation that your spouse can fall back on a rollover, you are taking a risk.

If you plan to pursue this approach, you may want to do some research of your own. If so, you will need access to a law library to review some of the IRS private letter rulings, or PLRs. Here are some of the favorable ones to start with: PLRs 9633043, 9623056, 9611057 and 9608036. In each of these PLRs, a trust was named beneficiary and the spouse was the beneficiary of the trust. Upon the participant's death, the plan assets were distributed to the trust, and then from the trust to the spouse, and finally to an IRA in the spouse's name. Bear in mind, however, that all of these PLRs were issued before the new regulations.

As an alternative to taking this risk, consider naming your spouse as primary beneficiary (thus preserving the rollover opportunity) and your trust as contingent beneficiary. After your death, your spouse would have the option to disclaim some or all of his or her interest in your retirement plan, allowing it to flow to the bypass trust. Ultimately, however, no strategy involving a trust is completely simple or risk-free.

I. Estate as Beneficiary

In cases in which an estate is named beneficiary of a retirement plan, private letter rulings have closely paralleled those in which a trust has been named beneficiary. If the participant's spouse is the sole beneficiary of the estate, and no one has the authority to restrict the spouse's access to the estate, several IRS private letter rulings have permitted the spouse to take a distribution of the plan assets and roll them over into an IRA in the spouse's name.

 Think twice before naming your estate as beneficiary. Although many people name their estate as beneficiary of their retirement plan or IRA, there is little advantage to doing so and some significant disadvantages. For example, because your estate is not a designated beneficiary, you are deemed to have no designated beneficiary for required distribution purposes. As a result, distributions could be accelerated after your death unless your spouse is the sole beneficiary of your estate and is permitted to roll over the plan assets. Relying on such an option for your spouse is risky business, however, given that the strategy has thin support from only a few IRS private letter rulings. Whatever it is you want to accomplish by naming your estate as beneficiary of your retirement plan can almost certainly be achieved through another less risky strategy.

J. Annuities

If your retirement plan benefits are to be paid in the form of an annuity, whether to you or to your beneficiary, the required distribution rules must still be satisfied.

1. Start Date

If you die before your RBD, the date by which payments to your beneficiary must begin (the "start date") depends on whether or not your beneficiary is your spouse.

If you have named a non-spouse beneficiary, the start date is December 31 of the year after your death.

If your beneficiary is your spouse, however, the start date is the later of December 31 of the year after your death or December 31 of the year you would have turned 70½.

If you had already started receiving your annuity payments and died before your RBD, payments still must satisfy the required distribution rules described below as of the start date. (If payments had begun under an irrevocable annuity, see Section 3, below.)

2. Form of Payment

In order to satisfy required distribution rules, payments must be in a particular form, although the form varies with the type and terms of the annuity. (See Chapter 6 for more information about types of annuities.) After your death, your beneficiary must take his or her first payment by one of the start dates described above. That payment, however, can be a normal payment.

For example, if your beneficiary intends to take monthly payments over his or her life expectancy, the first monthly payment can be paid in December of the year after your death and monthly thereafter. Your beneficiary need not take the full annual amount in December of that first year.

3. Irrevocable Annuity

If you had already begun receiving payments under an irrevocable annuity at the time of your death, your beneficiary must continue to receive payments with no break in the distribution schedule.

K. Divorce or Separation

If you were divorced or separated at some time during your life, part of your qualified plan, qualified annuity or TDA may be payable to an "alternate payee" (such as a spouse, former spouse or child) under the terms of a QDRO—a court-approved divorce or maintenance agreement. (See Chapter 2, Section C.4, for more information about QDROs.)

If the alternate payee's entire share has not yet been paid at the time of your death, then the alternate payee's distribution options are determined by whether or not the alternate payee's interest was held in a separate account or aggregated with the rest of your benefit.

1. Separate Account

If an alternate payee's share is segregated or separately accounted for (see Chapter 6 for more information about separate accounts), then the life expectancy rule applies to that share, and the alternate payee may take distributions over his or her own life expectancy, beginning no later than December 31 of the year after your death. Remember, though, the plan itself could require application of the five-year rule, in which case the alternate payee's share must be distributed by December 31 of the year containing the fifth anniversary of your death.

a. Spouse or Former Spouse Alternate Payee

A spouse or former spouse alternate payee has all the rights and privileges of a surviving spouse beneficiary as long as the alternate payee's share is in a separate account. The life expectancy rule would apply unless it is prohibited under the plan. Distributions may be made over the ex-spouse's

life expectancy, and must begin by the later of December 31 of the year following the death of the participant or December 31 of the year the participant would have turned 70½.

And if the plan permits, the spouse or former spouse alternate payee may roll over his or her share distribution into a retirement plan or IRA in his or her own name.

QDRO spouses. Although a surviving spouse is not permitted to roll over a retirement plan distribution into another qualified plan, a spouse or former spouse receiving a distribution under a QDRO is not subject to the same restriction. As long as the plan itself permits, the law allows a spouse alternate payee to roll over the plan benefits into either a qualified plan or an IRA.

b. Death of Alternate Payee

If the alternate payee dies before his or her interest has been completely distributed, the alternate payee's beneficiary will be treated as the designated beneficiary of the alternate payee's portion for purposes of the life expectancy rule and the five-year rule.

EXAMPLE: Your former wife is entitled to one-half of your retirement plan benefits under the terms of a QDRO.

Your former wife has named her brother as beneficiary of her share of the retirement plan. Your wife died when you were age 60, before she had received any portion of your retirement plan. You die a year later at the age of 62. Your beneficiary may take distribution of his or her share of the account over his or her own life expectancy. At the same time, your wife's brother can receive your wife's portion over his own life expectancy.

2. No Separate Account

If the plan administrator has not maintained a separate account for the alternate payee of your retirement plan, the beneficiary designation on the plan will determine how distributions will be made after your death. Specifically, the multiple beneficiary rules, described in Section G, above, will apply. The distribution would then be divided among the alternate payee and the beneficiaries in proportion to their interests.

EXAMPLE: Your former husband is entitled to one-half of your retirement plan benefits under the terms of a QDRO. You have named your father as beneficiary of the other half. Your former husband's share has not been segregated or separately accounted for. You die an untimely death at the age of 56. Under the terms of the plan, your beneficiary will use the life expectancy rule. Because the interests of your father and your former husband are aggregated in one account, your father, as beneficiary, is the one whose life expectancy must be used to determine required distributions. Each distribution will be split equally between your former husband and your father.

L. Reporting Distributions

Each year the custodian or trustee of a plan or IRA from which distributions are required to be taken must report to the IRS and to the beneficiary the amount of the required distribution. The custodian or trustee will determine the amount based on the account balance and the life expectancy of the designated beneficiary.

Part II: Old Rules

Because the old rules are optional for 2001 distributions and mandatory for 2000 distributions, we are including them in this book. But as we have mentioned previously, it is almost certainly to your advantage to begin using the new rules as soon as you can. However, if you are taking required distributions from a qualified plan that has not been modified or amended to permit use of the new rules, you will be stuck with the old rules. (Remember, this restriction does not apply to IRAs. If you have an IRA and you must take distributions for 2001, you can begin using the new rules immediately.)

A. Five-Year Rule and Exception

If you die before your RBD, which for most people is April 1 of the year after they turn 70½, then a law known as the "five-year rule" applies automatically. (See Chapter 6 for information about determining your RBD.) The law is designed to ensure that your retirement plan assets are completely distributed within a reasonably short time (five years) so that the government can collect the income taxes you had been deferring.

As usual, this seemingly simple law comes with its complement of exceptions. You'll find a variety of options for surviving spouses, different payout requirements for different beneficiaries and the occasional odd twist to accommodate a divorce

agreement or an annuity that is already in pay status. But first the basic rule.

1. Five-Year Rule

It seems straightforward enough. If you die before your RBD, all of your retirement plan assets must be distributed within five years unless the exception is available to your beneficiary—and the exception usually will be available. (See Section 2, below.) But if your beneficiary is stuck with the five-year rule, he or she actually has a little more than five years to withdraw the assets. This is because the official deadline is December 31 of the fifth year after your death. So, if you die on March 3 in the year 2000, your retirement plan need not be completely distributed until December 31, 2005—five years and almost ten months later.

 A spouse has other options. If your spouse is your beneficiary, he or she has some additional options—including a rollover—which, if elected, will allow him or her to defer total distribution of your retirement account beyond the five-year period. The rollover option is available only to a spouse beneficiary. (See Sections B and H, below.)

a. Required Beginning Date

The five-year rule applies only if you die before your RBD. Once you pass that milestone, a different set of rules will apply and you can forget about the five-year rule (and you should be reading Chapter 8). But note, it is your RBD that counts—not the year you turn 70½. For example, if your RBD is April 1, 2001 but you die on March 15, 2001, the five-year rule will apply even though you have already passed age 70½, even if you have already taken a distribution for your first distribution year. Technically, you have not begun required distributions until you pass your RBD.

> EXAMPLE: You turned 70½ in June 2000, which makes your RBD April 1, 2001. On December 30, 2000 you withdrew $6,000 from your IRA, which was the amount of your first required distribution. But then you died on March 15, 2001, before reaching your RBD. Because you died before your RBD, the five-year rule will apply even though you had already withdrawn an amount that would have satisfied your first required distribution.

b. Beneficiaries

The entity or individual named as beneficiary of your retirement plan at the time of your death is irrelevant in determining whether or not the five-year rule applies. Maybe you didn't even name a beneficiary. The only determining factor is whether you die before your RBD. If you do, the five-year rule applies. It's as simple as that. The beneficiary is important, however, for determining whether the exception to the five-year rule is available or whether one

of the special options for a spouse beneficiary may be used. (See Section 2, below, for information about the exception to the five-year rule, and Section B for information about a spouse's special options.)

c. Distributing the Account

The five-year rule mandates that all assets be distributed from your retirement plan by December 31 of the fifth year after your death, but it places no restriction on the form of payment. For example, your beneficiary could receive the entire amount as a lump sum in the month after your death, monthly installments spread over the five-year period or perhaps nothing at all until the December 31 deadline in the fifth year.

Any of these approaches would be acceptable to the IRS, but the retirement plan itself might have more stringent distribution requirements. Although the law sets a deadline for final distribution, the plan terms govern how payments will be made. Some plans allow beneficiaries to receive installment payments or to leave the funds in the plan until the five-year period is up. If the plan requires immediate distribution of the entire account, however, then that's what your beneficiary will be stuck with.

2. Exception to the Five-Year Rule

An exception to the five-year rule, which will allow your beneficiary to spread distributions over more than five years, is available only if all of the following conditions are met:

- you have named a designated beneficiary for your plan (see Chapter 6)
- the plan itself permits the exception, and
- you elect before your death to have the exception apply, or your beneficiary makes the election on or before December 31 of the year after your death.

The election to use the exception to the five-year rule must be delivered in writing to the trustee or custodian of the plan. Once made, the election becomes irrevocable and your designated beneficiary must spread distributions over a period that is no longer than his or her life expectancy. A minimum payment would be required every year, beginning in the year after your death. Your beneficiary may take a larger payment in any given year, but must take at least the minimum.

Your beneficiary computes the minimum annual payment in much the same way you would have calculated lifetime required distributions if you had survived until your RBD. (See Chapter 6 for more information about required lifetime distributions.) The difference is that your beneficiary must use his or her own single life expectancy. (You were permitted to use the joint life expectancy of you and your beneficiary.) If your beneficiary is not your spouse, the beneficiary may not recalculate his or her life expectancy but instead must reduce it by one each year. If your spouse is your beneficiary, however, you may recalculate his or her life expectancy each year. (See Section B, below.)

Here is the procedure for computing the minimum payment.

Step 1: Determine the Account Balance

Your beneficiary must use your retirement plan account balance as of December 31 of the year of your death to compute the first required payment.

Step 2: Determine the Beneficiary's Life Expectancy

Using his or her age in the year after your death, your beneficiary looks up the appropriate life expectancy factor in Table I. (See Appendix B.)

Step 3: Calculate the Required Payment

To determine the first required payment, your beneficiary divides the account balance by his or her life expectancy (Step 1 divided by Step 2).

EXAMPLE: You died on March 15, 2000, before reaching your RBD. Your son is the beneficiary of your retirement plan, and he turns 48 in 2001. Your account was valued at $100,000 on December 31, 2000. The plan permits the exception to the five-year rule.

Step 1: Determine Account Balance

To compute the first payment, your son must use the account balance as of December 31, 2000, the year of your death. That amount is $100,000.

Step 2: Determine the Beneficiary's Life Expectancy

Your son will be age 48 on his birthday in the year after your death (2001). His single life expectancy at age 48 (from Table I in Appendix B) is 34.9 years.

Step 3: Calculate the Required Payment

Your son's first required distribution is $100,000 divided by 34.9 (Step 1 divided by Step 2), or $2,865. Your son must withdraw at least that amount by December 31, 2001.

For the year 2002, your son will use the December 31, 2001 balance of your retirement account and divide it by his new life expectancy, which is 33.9 years (34.9 – 1).

3. Effect of the Retirement Plan's Rules

As is the case with many qualified plan rules, the law provides a framework for required distributions within which retirement plans may operate. Nonetheless, the plan's own rules can be and usually are more restrictive. In that case, the plan's rules will govern.

a. Optional Provisions

In the best of all worlds (from the taxpayer's perspective), plans would allow beneficiaries to choose between the five-year rule and the exception to the five-year rule. And if a beneficiary chose the five-year rule, the beneficiary would be able to choose how the assets were distributed over that five-year period.

Unfortunately, plan administrators don't always put taxpayers' needs first. In fact, some plans offer no options at all to beneficiaries, but simply mandate distribution of the entire plan in the year of death. At the other extreme, some plans might distribute nothing at all until the end of the fifth year.

Furthermore, many plans have different policies for different beneficiaries. For example, the terms of a plan might require that non-spouse beneficiaries receive a distribution of the entire plan immediately following the participant's death (without the five-year grace period), but give a spouse beneficiary the option to elect the exception to the five-year rule.

If a plan does permit the exception to the five-year rule, it may specify that the election must be made by the participant, the beneficiary or either one.

b. Default Provisions

If the plan is resolutely silent on distributions after the death of the plan participant, certain default provisions kick in by law. If the beneficiary is not a spouse, the five-year rule applies by default, and the account must be distributed by the end of the fifth year. The non-spouse beneficiary may not elect the exception to the five year rule unless the plan permits it. If a spouse is beneficiary, the exception to the five-year rule is the default. That rule gives the spouse plenty of flexibility because plans usually permit beneficiaries to accelerate distributions as well, if they choose to do so.

B. Spouse Beneficiary

If the beneficiary of your retirement plan is your spouse, the five-year rule or its exception would still apply; but your spouse has some additional options.

 The rules are different if your spouse is one of several beneficiaries. If your spouse is not the sole beneficiary of your retirement plan but is only one of several beneficiaries, some of the additional options described below are not available. See Sections E and F, below,

1. Additional Deferral

If the plan permits the exception to the five-year rule and your spouse elects the exception, then your spouse must begin receiving payments by December 31 of the year after your death or December 31 of the year you would have been 70½, whichever date is later. What's more, if the plan is silent, this additional deferral applies by default, taking precedence even over the five-year rule.

EXAMPLE: Ed was born on March 15, 1930 and died June 1, 1995 at the age of 65. Ed's spouse Bertha is beneficiary of his retirement account and she elects to use the exception to the five-year rule, as permitted under the terms of Ed's retirement plan. Bertha may defer distributions from the plan until December 31, 2000, the year Ed would have been 70½. At that time she may begin taking annual distributions based on her remaining life expectancy (or more quickly, if she prefers).

Your spouse can wait. Your spouse may defer distributions after your death until you would have been 70½ even if your spouse has already turned 70½.

2. Recalculation

If your spouse chooses the exception to the five-year rule so that distributions will be spread over his or her life expectancy, your spouse may also choose whether or not to recalculate the life expectancy factor. (Recalculation is explained in Chapter 6.) If your spouse chooses to recalculate, he or she would use Table I each year to determine the new life expectancy factor, instead of simply reducing the factor by one (if not recalculating).

EXAMPLE: As in the previous example, assume Ed died in 1995. Bertha elects the exception to the five-year rule and also plans to recalculate her life expectancy. She must take her first distribution by December 31, 2000, the year Ed would have turned 70½. The balance in Ed's IRA on December 31, 1999 was $115,000. Bertha turns 75 in the year 2000, and her life expectancy at that time is 12.5 years (from Table I). Her first distribution must be at least $9,200 ($115,000 divided by 12.5).

Bertha takes the distribution for the first year. Meanwhile, her investments inside the IRA continue to grow and the account balance on December 31, 2000 is $112,000. For the second year, because Bertha is recalculating, she must refer again to Table I when computing her required distribution. She will be age 76 in the year 2001 and will have a life expectancy of 11.9. Therefore Bertha's minimum distribution for the second year is $9,412 ($112,000 divided by 11.9).

Your spouse may have another option. A spouse has one other deferral opportunity, which is unrelated to the five-year rule: a rollover option. (See Section H, below, for more information about rollovers.)

3. Death of Spouse Beneficiary

If a spouse beneficiary dies after the participant has already died, but before beginning required distributions under the exception to the five-year rule, then the following rules apply:

- In general, the five-year rule and the exception to the five-year rule will apply to the spouse's beneficiary as though the spouse had been the original participant. Specifically, the spouse's date of death and the age of the spouse's beneficiary will determine how required distributions are computed under the exception to the five-year rule. (If the spouse remarries and names his or her new spouse as beneficiary, however, the new spouse will be treated as a non-spouse beneficiary. See the next bullet point.) Note: The five-year rule will apply even if the spouse was part age 70½ so long as the spouse had not yet begun required distributions.

EXAMPLE: You died in 1998 at age 65. Your wife is the sole beneficiary of your retirement plan account and therefore is not required to begin distributions until you would have been age 70½ (in the year 2003). Her sister is the sole beneficiary of her estate. Your wife died in 2001 before beginning required distributions from your retirement account. The five-year rule will apply to distributions to her sister, your spouse's beneficiary. Under the five-year rule, the entire account balance would have to be distributed to her sister no later than December 31, 2006. If the plan permits the exception to the five-year rule and the sister elects to use it, then the sister must begin distributions by December 31, 2002 and take them over her life expectancy.

- If the deceased spouse had remarried and named his or her new spouse as beneficiary, the special additional deferral option, described in Section 1, above, is not available to the new spouse beneficiary. Specifically, the new wife or husband is not permitted to wait until the spouse would have been 70½ to begin required distributions. The new wife or husband is simply treated as a non-spouse and is subject to the rules in the previous bullet point.

EXAMPLE: You died in 1998 at age 65. Your wife is the sole beneficiary of your retirement plan account and therefore is not required to begin distributions until you would have been age 70½ (in the year 2003). Your wife remarried in the year 2000 and named her new husband as beneficiary of her entire estate. She died in the year 2001 before beginning required distributions

from your retirement account. The five-year rule will apply to distributions to her new husband. Under the five-year rule, the entire account balance must be distributed to the new husband no later than December 31, 2006. If the plan permits the exception to the five-year rule and the husband elects to use it, then the husband must begin distributions by December 31, 2002, and take them over his life expectancy. He is not entitled to use the special deferral option of a spouse, however. He may not wait until his spouse (your wife) would have been 70½ to begin distributions.

C. Non-Spouse Beneficiary

As a participant in a retirement plan, or as the spouse of a participant, it is easy to take for granted the special privileges, exceptions and additional distribution options the Tax Code offers. But a non-spouse beneficiary typically must apply the rules in their barest form. And so it is with the five-year rule and the exception to the five-year rule.

 The more beneficiaries you have, the more the rules may change. Different rules might apply if you have named more than one beneficiary of your retirement plan. See Sections E and F, below.

1. Limited Deferral

If a plan allows the exception to the five-year rule, a non-spouse beneficiary must begin distributions no later than December 31 of the year after the participant's death. No additional deferral is permitted. Furthermore, if the plan is silent on post-death distributions, the five-year rule applies by default, and the exception is not even an option.

2. Recalculation

When computing distributions under the exception to the five-year rule (if it is an option), a non-spouse beneficiary may not recalculate his or her own life expectancy. Life expectancy is determined in the first distribution year and reduced by one in all subsequent years.

3. Death of Non-Spouse Beneficiary

If a non-spouse beneficiary dies after the participant has died, but before the retirement plan has been distributed, none of the distribution options change. If distributions are to be made under the five-year rule, the entire account must still be distributed by December 31 of the fifth year after the original participant's death.

Death of a beneficiary. When a primary beneficiary dies after the original participant has died but before all the retirement plan assets have been distributed, where does the remainder go? The answer depends on the laws of your state. Most likely, if the primary beneficiary left a will, the retirement plan will be distributed according to the terms of the will. In the absence of a will, the assets would be distributed to the heirs of the beneficiary according to state law. Each state has its own set of laws that determine who is entitled to your assets if you happen to die without expressing your wishes in a will or other estate planning document.

If the participant or the beneficiary had elected (and the plan permitted) the exception to the five-year rule, distributions will still be made over the life expectancy of the deceased beneficiary, using the beneficiary's age on his or her birthday in the year after the participant's date of death, whether the beneficiary had died before or after distributions had begun.

EXAMPLE: Sara named her brother, Archie, as beneficiary of her retirement plan. She died in 2000 at the age of 68. After her death, Archie notified the plan administrators that he intended to take distributions over his life expectancy beginning in 2001. He would have turned 55 on March 1, 2001, but he died on February 15, 2001. Nonetheless, distributions will continue to be made to his beneficiary as though he were still alive. Archie's life expectancy at age 55 would have been 28.6 years (from Table I). The life expectancy factor will be reduced by one each year until the entire account is distributed.

The plan might permit the person who is to receive the deceased beneficiary's distributions to elect the exception to the five-year rule. Even if that person elects the exception, the calculation is still based on the deceased beneficiary's life expectancy factor.

D. No Designated Beneficiary

If you have not designated a beneficiary for your retirement account, then payout options at your death are restricted. Recall that a designated beneficiary must usually be a natural person, although it may also be a special type of trust. (See Chapter 6 for more information about designated beneficiaries.) And although you are per-

mitted to name any beneficiary you choose, whether a person or an entity, some privileges are reserved for beneficiaries that qualify as designated beneficiaries.

1. Five-Year Rule

If the beneficiary of your retirement plan is not a designated beneficiary, then if you die before your RBD, the five-year rule applies and the entire account must be distributed by December 31 of the fifth year after your death.

2. No Exception to the Five-Year Rule

If your beneficiary is not a designated beneficiary, the exception to the five-year rule is never an option under any circumstances. All of the assets in the plan must be distributed by December 31 of the fifth year after your death.

Payments can be spread out over the five years. Even if the exception to the five-year rule is not an option for a beneficiary, it is still permissible for the beneficiary to take distributions in installments over the five-year period, if the plan will allow it.

3. Changing Beneficiaries

Be careful about giving any of your beneficiaries the right to change the beneficiary designation on your retirement account after your death. If you do, then for purposes of the five-year rule, you are deemed to have no designated beneficiary, and the exception to the five-year rule will not be an option for your beneficiary. After your death, the beneficiary designation may not be changed, as long as the retirement plan remains in your name. And it must remain in your name, unless your spouse is your beneficiary. A spouse—and only a spouse—may change the beneficiary after first changing title on the account to his or her own name, or rolling over the assets into an IRA in his or her name. (See Section H, below, for more information about spousal rollovers.)

The beneficiary's beneficiary.
Many custodians will allow a non-spouse beneficiary to indicate who should receive the plan assets after the beneficiary's death. But that alone does not constitute a change in beneficiary designation and does not affect the required distribution calculations in any way.

E. Multiple Beneficiaries— Separate Accounts

Multiple beneficiaries of a single IRA or retirement plan can be an administrative headache. Your beneficiaries would probably prefer to have their own separate accounts in order to manage their money as they please. Each beneficiary could also make his or her own decision about whether to use the five-year rule or its exception (if the plan permits). And most important, each beneficiary would be able to use his or her own life expectancy for the exception to the five-year rule, instead of using the life expectancy of the oldest beneficiary, as would be required if there were no separate accounts. (See Section F, below.) So here are some ideas about what to do if you want to name multiple beneficiaries.

If you have several IRAs or retirement plans, each with a different beneficiary, then each plan is treated separately for purposes of the five-year rule and its exception. You are not considered to have multiple beneficiaries.

If you do name multiple beneficiaries of a single plan, however, your plan administrator can segregate each beneficiary's share and treat each as a separate account payable to a different beneficiary. And even if the administrator does not segregate the shares, the administrator may treat the shares as separate accounts if the administrator or custodian sets up separate accounting procedures (under which, for example, investment gains and losses are allocated to beneficiaries on a pro rata basis).

EXAMPLE: You have two IRAs, IRA #1 and IRA #2. Your daughter is beneficiary of IRA #1, and your son is beneficiary of IRA #2. If you die before your RBD, and if the IRAs permit the exception to the five-year rule, your daughter may distribute IRA #1 over her single life expectancy, and your son may distribute IRA #2 over his. If you had only one IRA and named both your son and daughter as beneficiaries, then the entire IRA would have to be distributed over the life of the oldest child. See Section F, below.

If you do want your beneficiaries to be able to use the separate-account rules, the accounts must be separate as of your RBD. And if you die before your RBD, the accounts must be separate as of your date of death.

 The phrase "as of the date of death" has caused much consternation. Cautious lawyers and accountants have advised their clients to make sure their retirement accounts are separated—each with a single beneficiary—long before they die so that there is no doubt the accounts were separate as of the date of death. But many people just don't get around to it and they die with all six of their children named as beneficiaries of a single IRA. More aggressive practitioners have argued to the IRS that the accounts are separate as of the date of death if the beneficiaries simply begin keeping track of

their share of the IRA (including their proportionate share of interest income and capital gains and losses) from the moment the original owner stopped breathing. In a recent private letter ruling (PLR #199931049), the IRS went along with that argument. The issue isn't yet settled, however, so it would be best to plan ahead and separate those accounts.

 Your beneficiaries may be stuck. If you have a single account with multiple beneficiaries, the plan administrator may not cooperate with your desire for separate accounting. As a practical matter, many qualified plan administrators are reluctant to shoulder the burden of separate accounting or to physically split your account during your lifetime. Consequently, the beneficiaries may be stuck with the multiple beneficiary rules described in the next section.

IRA custodians, too, are unlikely to provide a separate accounting for you and each beneficiary when multiple beneficiaries are named on the account. In the case of an IRA, however, there is nothing to prevent you from splitting the account during your lifetime into separate IRAs, one for each beneficiary.

 If you do split your IRA, be careful of the one-rollover-per-year rule. (See Chapter 2, Section E.2, for more information about rollovers.) Generally, you may take any amount of money from an IRA and roll it into one or more IRAs only once during a 12-month period. For example, you may not take 25% of your big IRA and roll it into a new one, and then a few days later take another 25% and roll it into another new IRA. Instead, you should remove 50% initially and roll it to two separate IRAs. Or you could wait 12 months between rollovers.

You can avoid this one-rollover rule by asking the custodian to transfer the funds directly from one IRA to another. There is no limit to the number of direct transfers you can make in one year.

F. Multiple Beneficiaries— One Account

The rules change significantly if you name more than one person as beneficiary of a single retirement account and if there is no separate accounting. In fact, all of your planning efforts might go right down the tubes if you're not careful. When a group (even a group of two) inherits one retirement plan, the beneficiaries are no longer free to use their own life expectancies or make their own decisions regarding the five-year rule or its exception. Even a spouse may lose some special privileges if you name both your spouse and a child as primary beneficiaries on a single account.

When you name multiple beneficiaries, for purposes of the five-year rule and its exception all beneficiaries are treated as non-spouse beneficiaries, even if one of them is your spouse. As a result, the most

restrictive rules—those that produce the worst result—will apply to all beneficiaries. For example, if you name your spouse and your children, they must choose from the options available to your children because children have fewer options than spouses.

 When your spouse is one of two or more beneficiaries. Your spouse (and only your spouse) may roll over his or her portion of your plan into an IRA in the spouse's own name and avoid the problem described above. The above rule applies only to a spouse who does not choose the rollover option. See Section H, below, for information about spousal rollovers.

1. Five-Year Rule

Once you name multiple beneficiaries on a single account, the five-year rule becomes the default, kicking in when the plan is silent or when the plan offers the exception to the five-year rule only to a spouse beneficiary. If the plan provides that the five-year rule applies to non-spouse beneficiaries, but the exception is available for a spouse, the spouse is nonetheless prohibited from using the exception if the spouse is one of multiple beneficiaries.

2. Exception to the Five-Year Rule

The exception to the five-year rule is still available when there are multiple beneficiaries on an account, as long as the plan permits the exception. But which beneficiary's life is the measuring life? May the beneficiaries use a joint life? Or must each use his or her own life expectancy?

The least favorable option is the one your beneficiaries must use. The account must be distributed over the single life expectancy of the oldest beneficiary. This will yield the largest distribution and deplete the account most rapidly—exactly what Congress wants. The oldest beneficiary's life expectancy is determined as of his or her age in the first distribution year —the year after your death. Once the distribution amount is calculated and withdrawn, it is divided among the beneficiaries in proportion to their interest in the account.

EXAMPLE: You name your mother and your three children as equal beneficiaries of your retirement plan. You die in 2000. Under the terms of the plan, your beneficiaries are permitted to use the exception to the five-year rule when distributing your retirement account. Because your mother is the oldest beneficiary, the account must be distributed over her life expectancy. She will turn 85 in 2001, the first distribution year. Her life expectancy at that time will be 6.9 years (from Table I). To compute the first distribution, you divide the December 31, 2000 account balance by 6.9. That amount will then be divided equally among your mother and your three children. Each will get a fourth. And because your beneficiaries cannot recalculate, the divisor will drop by one each year and the account will be completely distributed in just seven years.

3. Splitting Accounts

In all likelihood, your beneficiaries will find it most convenient to separate their respective shares of your retirement account in order to have autonomy over investment decisions and to simplify accounting and other record-keeping. As long as the plan itself permits the separation, the law won't stop them. But they will have to carefully comply with the required distribution rules both while they are in the process of splitting the account and after the shares have been separated. Splitting the account *after* your death does not change the fact that the accounts were not separate *at the time* of your death. Thus, even though the shares might eventually be separated for the convenience of the beneficiaries, the separate shares are treated as one account for purposes of computing required distributions.

EXAMPLE: You have only one IRA and you name your three children, Tanya, Durf and Trina, as equal beneficiaries. You die at age 68 when Tanya is 40, Durf is 30 and Trina is 22. Because the children cannot agree on investment strategies, they find it most convenient to split the IRA into three equal IRAs—all in your name—so they can manage their respective shares. All three are taking distributions under the exception to the five-year rule. Because the three of them were named beneficiaries of your single account at the time of your death, all three must use Tanya's (the oldest child's) life expectancy when computing required distributions from their respective shares, even after they have split the account.

a.   Transfer

When separating each beneficiary's share into a separate account, assets must be transferred directly from the trustee or custodian of the original single plan account to the trustee or custodian of each separate account. The beneficiary must not have control of the funds at any time. If the beneficiary is deemed to have control, the IRS will consider the assets fully distributed and fully taxable in the current year.

Furthermore, in the case of non-spouse beneficiaries, the account must remain in the name of the deceased (see Section b,

below), so it cannot be transferred to one or more of the beneficiaries' existing retirement plans or even into a new retirement account in a beneficiary's name. If a spouse is one of the beneficiaries, however, the spouse can roll over his or her share to either an existing or a new IRA in the spouse's name. (See Section H, below.)

b.   Name on Account

When transferring a portion of the plan assets to a new account, the IRS requires that the new account also be in the original participant's name. But financial institutions generally do not like to maintain accounts, let alone set up new ones, in the name of a deceased person. To accommodate both the IRS requirements and their own internal accounting procedures, most custodians construct account titles that identify both the original participant (now deceased) and the beneficiary who is to receive distributions.

> **EXAMPLE:** Joe Corpus died leaving a substantial IRA, in equal shares, to his three children, Dan, Irwin and Bruce. The children want to split the IRA into three separate IRAs so that each can manage his own investments. The IRA custodian set up three new IRA accounts in Joe's name and transferred a third of Joe's original IRA into each one. The title on Dan's account reads: "Joe Corpus, Deceased, for the benefit of (or FBO) Dan Corpus." The other

two accounts are titled "Joe Corpus, Deceased, FBO Irwin Corpus" and "Joe Corpus, Deceased, FBO Bruce Corpus."

⚠ **A dead person can't own property.** Pinpointing what it means to leave an account in the name of a deceased person has stymied many taxpayers since the required distribution regulations were first published. Should the participant and the beneficiary both be named on the account? And whose tax ID number or Social Security number should be used? Most custodians would prefer to use the beneficiary's ID number, and the IRS appears to be going along quietly, but without making a firm pronouncement.

HE DECIDED TO TAKE IT WITH HIM.

The IRS has issued what is called a "revenue procedure" outlining a set of reporting requirements that IRA custodians must adhere to after an IRA participant dies. The custodian must file IRS Form 5498 (see Appendix A) for each beneficiary. The form reports the name of the original owner, the name of the beneficiary, the beneficiary's tax ID or Social Security number and the value of the beneficiary's share of the IRA as of the end of the year. With this information, the IRS can trace the source of the IRA for income tax purposes, and determine who is liable for the deferred tax. The form must be filed every year until the account is depleted.

⚠ **Remember that the beneficiary can't roll over the plan unless he or she is a spouse.** Some beneficiaries and, unfortunately, even some custodians are under the mistaken impression that a beneficiary may roll over a deceased participant's retirement plan into an IRA in the beneficiary's own name. This option is available only to a spouse beneficiary. (See Section H, below, for more information about spousal rollovers.) Non-spouse beneficiaries are never permitted to roll over retirement plan assets into a new or existing IRA in their own names.

c. Measuring Life

Again, even though an account might be split for administrative convenience, it is treated as one account for required distribution purposes. Consequently, if the beneficiaries plan to use the exception to the five-year rule, the entire account must be distributed over the life expectancy of the oldest beneficiary (or more rapidly if they choose).

> **EXAMPLE:** Betty died in 2000 at the age of 69 having named her sister, Marilyn, and her sister's three children as equal beneficiaries of her IRA. The custodian split Betty's IRA into four equal IRAs, one for each beneficiary, but left Betty's name on all the new accounts. The beneficiaries can and do choose to use the exception to the five-year rule. Marilyn turned 61 in 2001, the first distribution year under the exception to the five-year rule. Her life expectancy in 2001 is 23.3 years (from Table I). Although Marilyn's children are all in their thirties and have much longer life expectancies, they must all use Marilyn's shorter life expectancy of 23.3 years when computing required distributions.

d. Choosing the Distribution Option

The effect of naming multiple beneficiaries of one retirement plan account is to limit the deferral period to the life expectancy of the oldest beneficiary. As long as the plan permits, however, there is nothing to prevent one beneficiary from accelerating distributions of his or her share while the remaining beneficiaries use the exception to the five-year rule. The remaining beneficiaries' deferral period would be limited to the life expectancy of the oldest, even if the oldest had already withdrawn some or all of his or her share.

> **EXAMPLE:** Mary, Paul and Peter inherited an IRA from their father, Jake, who died in 2001. Mary, the oldest child, wants to take her share and use it to buy a house. The boys don't need the money right now and want to take their portions out slowly, spreading distributions over as many years as possible. Mary may take her share outright and the boys may spread the distribution of their shares over Mary's life expectancy beginning no later than December 31, 2000.

4. When a Spouse Is One of the Beneficiaries

If your spouse is one of several (or even just two) beneficiaries of your retirement account, your spouse loses the option to defer distributions until you would have been 70½. Instead, distributions under the exception to the five-year rule must begin on December 31 of the year after your death. A spouse beneficiary could still roll over his or her share of the retirement account into an IRA in his or her own name, however. See Section H, below, for more information on rollovers.

5. Designated and Non-Designated Beneficiaries

If any beneficiary of a retirement plan account fails to qualify as a designated beneficiary, the account is deemed to have no designated beneficiary, even if one or more of the other beneficiaries on the account do qualify. If the account is deemed to have no designated beneficiary, the exception to the five-year rule is not available. Instead, the assets must be distributed under the five-year rule. Many a charitably inclined taxpayer, wanting to leave a portion of his or her retirement plan to charity and a portion to a spouse or child, has been blindsided by this unfavorable application of the rules.

EXAMPLE: Paul named his son and the American Cancer Society as equal beneficiaries of his IRA. Paul died in 2001. Because the American Cancer Society is not a natural person or a qualified trust, it is not considered a designated beneficiary. Therefore, the IRA is deemed to have no designated beneficiary, even though Paul's son would have qualified had he been the sole beneficiary. As a result, the entire account must be distributed by December 31, 2006, with half going to Paul's son and half to the American Cancer Society.

The solution to this problem is for Paul to split the IRAs into two separate IRAs before his death, naming the charity as beneficiary of one IRA and his son as beneficiary of the other.

G. Trust Beneficiary

Generally, a beneficiary must be a "natural person" to qualify as a designated beneficiary and be eligible for the exception to the five-year year rule. There is one exception: a trust that meets certain stringent requirements. As explained in Chapter 6, if the trust satisfies all of those requirements, then the beneficiaries of the trust will be treated as designated beneficiaries for purposes of the exception to the five-year rule. In other words, the trustee or custodian of the retirement plan may "look through" the trust to find the designated beneficiary whose life expectancy can be used under the exception to the five-year rule.

1. Non-Spouse Beneficiary of Trust

If you do name a trust as beneficiary and it meets the requirements of a designated beneficiary, distributions under the five-year rule or the exception to the five-year rule will be computed as though there were no trust in place—as though the beneficiary of the trust had been named beneficiary of the retirement plan. Therefore, if the beneficiary of the trust is not your spouse, the five-year rule would apply. If the plan permits, the beneficiary may use the exception to the five-year rule to spread required distributions over the beneficiary's life expectancy beginning in the year after your death. In any case, all distributions would go into the trust and become subject to the terms of the trust, which may or may not call for an immediate distribution to the beneficiary.

2. Spouse Beneficiary of Trust

Similarly, if your spouse is beneficiary of the trust, your spouse will be treated as the designated beneficiary for purposes of the five-year rule and the exception to the five-year rule. If your spouse is permitted to elect the exception to the five-year rule, he or she will also have the option to delay distributions until you would have been 70½. In that case, your spouse would take distributions over his or her life expectancy and, if the plan permits, choose whether or not to recalculate his or her life expectancy.

 Remember the special rules for a spouse! Upon the death of the participant, a spouse beneficiary may have additional options unrelated to the five-year rule. The option to roll over the plan assets is an important one. Some of those options might be available to a spouse even if a trust is the beneficiary of a retirement plan. (See Section H, below, for more information about rollovers.)

3. Multiple Beneficiaries of Trust

If a trust has multiple beneficiaries and meets the criteria for looking through the trust for a designated beneficiary, then for purposes of applying the exception to the five-year rule, the multiple beneficiary rules described in Section F, above, will apply as though the individuals themselves were named beneficiaries of the retirement plan.

 Why name a trust as a beneficiary? You must jump through a raft of hoops to name a trust as beneficiary of a retirement plan and to feel confident that you have accomplished what you intended. Sometimes you never do achieve a high level of confidence. So with all the risk and uncertainty, why would anyone bother? Although people name trusts as beneficiaries for all kinds of reasons—sometimes to maintain more control over the distribution of assets, sometimes because Aunt Bessie suggested it—one reason is to fund a "bypass" trust. The use of trusts in estate planning to minimize death taxes and other costs is complex, but here's a brief summary of what it means to use a retirement plan to fund a bypass trust.

The law allows each individual to leave a certain amount, called an "exclusion amount," to his or her heirs free of death taxes. (The exclusion amount is scheduled to increase incrementally from $675,000 in 2000 to $1,000,000 by the year 2006.) In addition, an individual may leave an unlimited amount to a spouse. If an individual leaves everything outright to a spouse, however, some or all of the individual's exclusion amount could be wasted.

For example, assume a husband and wife have a combined net worth of $1 million. The husband dies in January 2001 and leaves everything to his wife, never using his $675,000 exclusion amount. Although there will be no death taxes upon the husband's death, when the wife dies, she can only leave her own exclusion amount tax free to the children. The remainder will be subject to death taxes. So, if the wife dies in December 2001 and the estate is still worth $1,000,000, she leaves $675,000 tax free to the children, but the remaining $325,000 is subject to death taxes. If the husband had given his $675,000 to the children when he died instead of to his spouse, the entire estate could have passed to the children tax free.

Many people choose not to give large amounts to their children outright because they don't want to risk leaving a spouse strapped for cash. That's where the bypass trust concept comes in. When the husband dies, he can direct his exclusion amount to a trust which is accessible to the wife during her lifetime and which flows to the children upon her death. Technically, the assets in the trust do not belong to the wife, so when she dies, she can give additional amounts equal to the exclusion to the children—all of it tax free.

Now, what role does the IRA or retirement plan play in all of this? For many people, a retirement plan is their most substantial asset, and a bypass trust couldn't be fully funded unless the plan assets were used. In other words, many people don't have enough assets outside the plan to put the exclusion amount into a bypass trust. But the law won't allow a trust to "own" a retirement plan, which means it is not possible to simply transfer the plan into the trust. To fund the trust, a person would have to name the trust as beneficiary so that after-death distributions from the plan would be directed into the trust every year until the trust is fully funded. The spouse could then have access to the funds once they have been distributed from the retirement plan to the trust.

H. Rollovers

One of the most awful feelings in the world has to be driving in a foreign country without knowing the traffic rules. It's impossible to shake the notion that you're about to be blindsided at any moment. Navigating the Tax Code can produce similar feelings. For example, suppose you have been stewing over an unusual tax problem. While browsing through your collection of tax books, you stumble across a law that applies to your particular situation. If you are like most people who browse through tax books, you will immediately begin to wonder if there are other laws buried in the Code that also apply but which you haven't stumbled on yet. It's bad enough to think you might run afoul of the law, but even worse to think about missing out on some big tax break.

The required distribution rules are a case in point. Section 401(a)(9) of the Tax Code deals with required distributions. It tells us that when a participant in a retirement plan or IRA dies before his or her RBD, the five-year rule or its exception will apply to the beneficiary.

But it just so happens that if a spouse is the beneficiary of the plan, the spouse has another quite valuable option: to treat the deceased person's retirement plan or IRA as the spouse's own. And yet this option is nowhere to be found in Section 401(a)(9). It's in a completely separate section of the Tax Code. Fortunately, you have now found it. Here's how it works.

1. Spouse Beneficiary

Only a spouse may elect to treat a deceased person's retirement plan or IRA as the spouse's own. The election can be made in one of three ways:

- The spouse can simply fail to take a required distribution under the five-year rule, the exception to the five-year rule or the additional deferral.

EXAMPLE: Your wife died in the year 2000 at age 63. You were the sole beneficiary of her IRA. At the end of the fifth year after your wife's death, you still had not taken any distributions that would have been required under the five-year rule or its exception. Furthermore, you did not take a distribution in the year 2007 when your wife would have been 70½. Therefore, by missing all of the deadlines for taking a distribution from your wife's account, it is deemed to be your own account on December 31, 2007.

- The spouse can contribute additional amounts of the spouse's own to the account of the deceased.
- The spouse can roll over the deceased person's retirement plan into an IRA in the spouse's name. This method is the cleanest because there is a clear record of what happened and when.

Once the account becomes the spouse's own, it belongs to the spouse in every way—as though he or she were the original owner. Required distributions will be based on the spouse's RBD, and neither the five-year rule nor the exception to the five-year rule is relevant anymore unless the spouse dies before his or her own RBD.

EXAMPLE: Grace died in 2001 at the age of 69. Her husband, George, was the beneficiary of her retirement plan, and he turned 64 on February 14, 2001. At the end of 2001, George rolls over Grace's retirement plan into an IRA in his own name.

George will not need to begin required distributions until his own RBD, which is April 1 of the year after he turns 70½, or April 1, 2008. If he dies before that date, the five-year rule or its exception will apply as though the IRA assets had always belonged only to him.

⚠ The rollover may be to an IRA only. A spouse may not roll over a deceased person's retirement plan into a qualified plan in the spouse's name; the rollover can only be to a new or an existing IRA of the spouse's own.

If a surviving spouse rolls over a deceased participant's retirement plan into a new IRA, the spouse may name a new beneficiary of his or her own choosing.

EXAMPLE: Your husband is the primary beneficiary of your retirement plan, and your brother will inherit the plan if your husband dies before you do. You die in 2001. Your husband decides to roll over your retirement plan into an IRA in his own name. He completes the rollover in December 2001 and names his sister as primary beneficiary. His action is completely legal under the rollover rules. Once he rolls over

your retirement plan, the assets are his. His sister will receive the IRA assets. Your brother will not.

Your spouse may roll over your retirement plan and name a new beneficiary after you die, even if your spouse has passed his or her RBD at the time of the rollover. Your spouse's RBD for purposes of the new IRA is December 31 of the year after the rollover, and required distributions must begin at that time.

EXAMPLE: You died in 2001 at the age of 69. Your wife turned 72 in 2001 and so was past her RBD. In December 2001, she rolled over your retirement plan into an IRA in her name, and designated the children as beneficiaries. Your wife must take her first required distribution by December 31, 2002.

a.   Commingling

Although a surviving spouse is permitted to roll over a participant's retirement plan into either a new or an existing IRA in the spouse's name, it usually isn't a good idea to combine the deceased person's retirement plan with a spouse's preexisting IRA, for several reasons:

- If the spouse anticipates using the existing IRA as a conduit to transfer his or her own retirement plan assets into a qualified plan at a later date, the strategy won't work once the assets have been commingled with assets of a contributory IRA. (See Chapter 1, Section B.1, for more information about contributory IRAs.)

EXAMPLE: Rick died while still employed at The Music Company. Rick had participated in the company's 401(k) plan and had named his wife Lucy as beneficiary. Lucy works for The Comedy Club, which also has a 401(k) plan. In addition, Lucy has an IRA to which she has been making $2,000 contributions every year. When Rick died, Lucy instructed The Music Company to distribute Rick's 401(k) plan assets to her existing IRA. Once Rick's 401(k) plan assets have been mixed with Lucy's IRA assets, Lucy cannot roll over any portion of the IRA assets into her own 401(k) plan at The Comedy Club.

On the other hand, if Lucy had established a brand new IRA and instructed The Music Company to transfer Rick's 401(k) assets to the new IRA, Lucy would be able to roll over the assets from the new IRA into her own 401(k) plan, if the plan allowed it and if Lucy had not made any additional contribution to the new IRA other than Rick's 401(k) assets.

- If the assets are rolled into a new IRA, the spouse may name new beneficiaries and base required distributions on the lives of those beneficiaries. But if the assets are commingled with an existing IRA, the beneficiary designation on the existing plan could affect required distributions if the spouse has already passed his or her RBD.

EXAMPLE: Ginger died at age 67, having named her husband Ted as beneficiary of her IRA. Ted was 75 when Ginger died. Ted has a small IRA of his own and his older brother is the designated beneficiary of that IRA. But Ted would like his children to be the beneficiaries of Ginger's IRA. Ted would also like to use a joint life expectancy with his oldest child to compute required distributions from Ginger's IRA. If Ted combines Ginger's IRA with his own existing IRA, he must use a joint life expectancy with his brother to compute required distributions for the entire combined account, because his brother is the beneficiary with the shortest life expectancy. If he rolls Ginger's IRA into a new IRA in his own name, he can name his children as beneficiaries and use the oldest child's life to compute required distributions from the new IRA. He would also continue to take distributions from his other IRA using his and his brother's joint life expectancy.

⚠ The income tax regulations state clearly that if you roll an IRA that names an older beneficiary into an IRA that names a younger beneficiary, you must continue to perform separate distribution calculations for each part. On the other hand, most practitioners believe that if you roll an IRA that names a younger beneficiary into an IRA that names an older beneficiary, you must use the life expectancy of the older beneficiary to compute required distributions from both parts. (But note: The regulations do not specifically state this.) However, in a recent private letter ruling, the IRS permitted a taxpayer who had commingled IRAs in this latter way to make separate calculations for each part. It is noteworthy that the taxpayer claimed he had kept separate records of gains and losses for each part from the moment the IRAs were commingled. It was this separate accounting that led to the favorable ruling.

b. Timing of Rollover

Some of the required distribution deadlines for a surviving spouse are crystal clear. For example, if your surviving spouse is using the five-year rule, a final distribution must be made by December 31 of the fifth year after your death. And if your spouse chooses the exception to the five-year rule, distributions must begin by December 31 of the year after your death or December 31 of the year you would have turned age 70½, whichever is later. The timing of one extremely critical step in the process remains murky, however. By what date must a spouse elect to treat a deceased participant's retirement plan as the spouse's own IRA?

The regulations help only a little. They indicate that a spouse can make a deceased participant's account his or her own by failing to take a timely distribution of the participant's own required distribution. By inference, then, one could argue that the spouse can wait until the participant would have been 70½.

EXAMPLE: You died in 1998 at age 64. Your wife turned 60 on January 18, 1998. Your wife leaves your IRA in your name, but in the year 2004, when you would have turned 70½, your wife takes no distributions from your retirement account. By failing to do so, your wife has made the account her own, and she must take her first required distribution by her own RBD, which is April 1 of the year after she turns 70½ or April 1, 2009.

But now, suppose in the above example, you were 69 and your wife was 68 when you died. Can your wife wait five years (as permitted by the five-year rule) and then roll it over—even though both of you will have passed age 70½ in the meantime? The advantage of waiting is several more years of tax-deferred growth in the IRA before a distribution would be required.

> EXAMPLE: Rafael dies in 2001 at age 69, leaving his IRA to his wife, Alicia, who turns 68 on March 1, 2001. If Alicia immediately rolls over Rafael's IRA into an IRA in her name, she must begin distributions on or before her own RBD, which is April 1, 2004. But if she leaves the account in Rafael's name until the five-year period is up and rolls over the IRA in 2006, she would not have to begin distributions until the year 2007, the year following the rollover.

This approach seems consistent with the wording of the regulations. The regulations indicate a spouse can make a deceased person's retirement plan his or her own simply by failing to take the deceased person's timely distribution under the five-year rule or the exception to the five-year rule. As long as the spouse takes a distribution at the end of the five-year period, the spouse will not have failed to take a required distribution. Only at the end of the five years would a distribution be required. Failure to take the distribution at that time would make the account the spouse's own.

Although several IRS private letter rulings support this interpretation of the regulations, the strategy does not have an unequivocal stamp of approval. Consequently, you must weigh the advantage of a few more years of tax deferral against the risk that the IRS will frown on your approach and slap you with a penalty for failing to take a required distribution.

 Delay rarely helps. In most cases, there is little to be gained by delaying a spousal rollover of a deceased person's account. Waiting until the fifth year after death will not extend the deferral period, unless both spouses pass (or would have passed) the 70½ mark during the five years.

2. Non-Spouse Beneficiary

When sorting out the rollover rules, it is critical to pay attention to restrictions and follow procedures to the letter, because the penalties for improper rollovers can be costly. Most important, a non-spouse beneficiary is never permitted to roll over a deceased person's retirement plan. Ever. If the beneficiary attempts to do so, the entire rollover could be considered a taxable distribution and an excess contribution to an IRA—and it would be subject to penalties. Even if the excess contribution is corrected, the retirement plan assets cannot be redeposited into the deceased participant's account. Consequently, the beneficiary will owe income tax on the entire amount, whether or not penalties are assessed as well.

A non-spouse beneficiary really has only one option: to leave the retirement account in the name of the deceased participant until the account is completely distributed under the five-year rule or the exception to the five-year rule.

3. Trust Beneficiary

Recall that a trust is often named beneficiary of a retirement plan in order to fund a bypass trust. (See the Planning Note at the end of Section G, above.) But sometimes the surviving spouse discovers after the participant dies that the retirement plan assets are not needed to fund the trust after all. In that case, the surviving spouse might prefer to roll over the assets into his or her own IRA, name a new beneficiary and begin a new schedule of required distributions. Is that permissible if a trust is the beneficiary? Does it make a difference if the spouse is the beneficiary of the trust?

a. Who Can Roll Over Distributions?

The issue is not whether you can "look through" the trust for the designated beneficiary. Looking through the trust relates only to whether or not you are permitted to use a joint life expectancy when computing required distributions.

Instead, this issue relates to which beneficiaries are permitted to roll over retirement plan distributions, and which are not. The law says that only a spouse may roll over distributions—and only if

the spouse acquires the IRA directly from and by reason of the death of the participant.

Now, suppose a trust is named beneficiary of the retirement plan and the spouse is the beneficiary of the trust. Presumably, distributions from the plan go into the trust and then the trust makes distributions from the trust to the spouse. In that case, doesn't the spouse actually acquire the plan assets from the trust, and not directly from the participant? If so, the rollover opportunity is blown.

But taxpayers have argued in numerous private letter rulings that if the provisions of the trust mandate distribution of the plan assets to the spouse, then for all intents and purposes, the assets do pass directly from the deceased participant to the spouse. Similarly, if the spouse has complete control over the assets of the trust, and can distribute all of the assets without interference from any third party, then again the assets arguably pass directly to the spouse from the deceased. The taxpayers have claimed that in both cases, the spouse should be able to roll over the assets into the spouse's own IRA.

b. IRS Position

Happily, the IRS seems to be going along with these arguments. The law does not specifically allow either of these rollover strategies, but the IRS has established a pattern of approving such actions in a number of its private letter rulings.

⚠️ **When naming a trust as beneficiary of a retirement plan.** Be sure to distinguish between transactions we know to be permitted under the law and those we hope and believe the IRS will approve. For example, we know that if a spouse is the beneficiary of a retirement plan, he or she may roll over the retirement plan assets. However, the success of any variation on this beneficiary designation in preserving a spouse's rollover option simply cannot be guaranteed. Consequently, if you name a trust as beneficiary of your retirement plan with the expectation that your spouse can fall back on a rollover, you are taking a risk—in spite of the fact that you have a fistful of consistent private letter rulings to bolster your position.

If you plan to pursue this approach, you may want to do some research of your own. If so, you will need access to a law library to review some of the IRS private letter rulings, or PLRs. Here are some of the favorable ones to start with: PLRs 9633043, 9623056, 9611057, 9608036. In each of these PLRs, a trust was named beneficiary and the spouse was the beneficiary of the trust. Upon the participant's death, the plan assets were distributed to the trust, and from the trust to the spouse, and finally to an IRA in the spouse's name.

c. How to Name a Trust as Beneficiary

If you plan to move forward with the strategy of naming a trust as beneficiary of your retirement plan, you must be careful with the mechanics. In its simplest form, the strategy works as follows: You name a trust as beneficiary of your retirement plan and your spouse as beneficiary of the trust. Upon your death, the retirement plan assets are distributed to the trust. Under the terms of the trust, the assets are then distributed to your spouse, who rolls them over into an IRA in his or her own name.

There are many more complicated variations on this theme. For example, the spouse could be the designated beneficiary (thus preserving the rollover opportunity), while a trust is named contingent beneficiary in case the spouse disclaims, or renounces, his or her interest (thus preserving the potential use of the IRA in funding a bypass trust). Ultimately, no strategy involving a trust is completely simple or risk-free, so proceed with caution.

4. Estate as Beneficiary

In cases in which an estate is named beneficiary of a retirement plan, private letter rulings have closely paralleled those in which a trust has been named beneficiary. If the participant's spouse is the sole beneficiary of the estate, and no one has the authority to restrict the spouse's access to the estate, several IRS private letter rulings have permitted the spouse to take a distribution of the plan assets and roll them over into an IRA in the spouse's name.

Don't name your estate as beneficiary of your retirement plan or IRA. There is little advantage to naming your estate as beneficiary, and some significant disadvantages. For example, because your estate is not a designated beneficiary, you are deemed to have no designated beneficiary for purposes of computing lifetime or after-death distributions. As a result, distributions could be accelerated unless your spouse is the sole beneficiary of your estate and is permitted to roll over the plan assets. Relying on such an option for your spouse is risky business, however, given that the strategy has thin support from only a few IRS private letter rulings. Whatever it is you want to accomplish by naming your estate as beneficiary of your retirement plan can almost certainly be achieved through another less risky strategy.

I. Annuities

If your retirement plan benefits are to be paid in the form of an annuity, whether to you or to your beneficiary, the required distribution rules must still be satisfied.

1. Start Date

If you die before your RBD, the date by which payments to your beneficiary must begin (the "start date") depends on whether or not your beneficiary is your spouse. If you have named a non-spouse beneficiary, the start date is December 31 of the year after your death. If your beneficiary is your spouse, however, the start date is the later of December 31 of the year after your death or December 31 of the year you would have turned 70½.

If you had already started receiving your annuity payments and died before your RBD, payments still must satisfy the required distribution rules described below as of the start date. (If payments had begun under an irrevocable annuity, see Section 3, below.)

2. Form of Payment

In order to satisfy required distribution rules, payments must be in a particular form, although the form varies with the type and terms of the annuity. (See Chapter 6 for more information about types of annuities.) If the annuity has no term certain or a term certain less than or equal to 20 years, your beneficiary must take his or her first payment by December 31 of the year after your death. That payment, however, can be a normal payment. For example, if your beneficiary intends to take monthly payments over his or her life expectancy, the first monthly payment can be paid in December of the year after your death and monthly thereafter. Your beneficiary need not take the full annual amount in December of that first year.

On the other hand, if the annuity has no life component, or if it is a life annuity with a term certain greater than 20 years, then again the first distribution must be made by December 31 of the year after your death, but it must be the full annual amount, even if your beneficiary elects to receive payments on a monthly basis in the future.

3. Irrevocable Annuity

If you had already begun receiving payments under an irrevocable annuity at the time of your death, your beneficiary must continue to receive payments with no break in the distribution schedule.

J. Divorce or Separation

If you were divorced or separated at some time during your life, part of your qualified plan, qualified annuity or TDA may be payable to an "alternate payee" (such as a spouse, former spouse or child) under the terms of a QDRO—a court-approved divorce or maintenance agreement. (See Chapter 2, Section C.4, for more information about QDROs.)

If the alternate payee's entire share has not yet been paid at the time of your death, then the alternate payee's distribution options are determined by whether or not the payee's interest was held in a separate account or aggregated with the rest of your benefit.

1. Separate Account

If an alternate payee's share is segregated or separately accounted for (see Chapter 6 for more information about separate accounts), then the five-year rule applies to that share. Furthermore, if the plan allows you to elect the exception to the five-year rule for post-death distributions, that election option passes to the alternate payee. Under the exception to the five-year rule, the alternate payee may take distributions over his or her own life expectancy, beginning no later than December 31 of the year after your death.

a. Spouse or Former Spouse Alternate Payee

A spouse or former spouse alternate payee has all the rights and privileges of a surviving spouse beneficiary, as long as the alternate payee's share is in a separate account. The five-year rule would apply unless the exception is permitted under the plan. If the exception is permitted, the spouse or former spouse alternate payee may decide whether or not to elect it. If the alternate payee chooses the exception, distributions may be made over his or her life expectancy and must begin by the later of December 31 of the year following the death of the participant or December

31 of the year the participant would have turned 70½.

A spouse or former spouse alternate payee may also choose whether or not to recalculate his or her life expectancy, provided the plan offers the option. And if the plan permits, the spouse or former spouse alternate payee may roll over any distribution into a retirement plan or IRA in his or her own name. (See Section 3, below.)

b. Death of Alternate Payee

If the alternate payee dies before his or her interest has been completely distributed, the alternate payee's beneficiary will be treated as the designated beneficiary of the alternate payee's portion for purposes of the five-year rule and the exception to the five-year rule.

> EXAMPLE: Your former wife is entitled to one-half of your retirement plan benefits under the terms of a QDRO. Your former wife has named her brother as beneficiary of her share of the retirement plan. Your wife died when you were age 60, before she had received any portion of your retirement plan. You die a year later at the age of 62. Under the terms of the plan, your beneficiary may elect the exception to the five-year rule and take distribution of his or her share of the account over his or her own life expectancy. At the same time, your

wife's brother can elect to receive your wife's portion over his life expectancy.

2. No Separate Account

If the plan administrator has not maintained a separate account for the alternate payee of your retirement plan, the beneficiary designation on the plan will determine how distributions will be made after your death. Specifically, the multiple beneficiary rules, described in Section F, above, will apply. The distribution would then be divided among the alternate payee and the beneficiaries in proportion to their interests.

> EXAMPLE: Your former husband is entitled to one-half of your retirement plan benefits under the terms of a QDRO. You have named your father as beneficiary of the other half. Your former husband's share has not been segregated or separately accounted for. You die an untimely death at the age of 56. Under the terms of the plan, your beneficiary may elect the exception to the five-year rule. Because the interests of your father and your former husband are aggregated in one account, your father, as beneficiary, is the one who may choose whether or not to elect the exception to the five-year rule, and distributions must be made over his life expectancy. Each distribution will be split equally

between your former husband and your father.

Even if a spouse or former spouse's share is not in a separate account, he or she may roll over any distribution of his or her interest. (See Section 3, just below.)

3. Rollover

A non-spouse alternate payee is never permitted to roll over a distribution from your retirement plan. A spouse or former spouse alternate payee is entitled to the same benefits as a surviving spouse. Therefore, if a spouse or former spouse alternate payee receives a QDRO distribution, he or she may roll over that distribution into a retirement plan or IRA in his or her own name.

 QDRO rules gives a former spouse more options than a surviving spouse. Although a surviving spouse is not permitted to roll over a retirement plan distribution into another qualified plan, a spouse or former spouse receiving a distribution under a QDRO is not subject to the same restriction. As long as the plan itself permits, the law allows a former spouse alternate payee to roll over the plan benefits into either a qualified plan or an IRA.

Key Tax Code and Regulations Sections

§ 401(a)(9)
Required Distributions From Qualified Plans

§ 1.401(a)(9)
Required Distribution Regulations

§ 402(c)
Rollovers From Qualified Plans

§ 408
Individual Retirement Accounts

§ 1.408-8, A-5
Election by Spouse to Treat Decedent's IRA as Own

Rev. Proc. 89-52
After-Death IRA Reporting Requirements

Chapter 8

Distributions to Your Beneficiary If You Die After Age 70¹/₂

Who Should Read Chapter 8?

➡ Read this chapter if you want to know what happens to your own retirement plan after you die or if you inherit a retirement plan or IRA from someone who died after reaching age 70½ and who had already begun mandatory distributions from the plan or IRA. This chapter describes how the remainder of the account must be distributed.

*E*ven though you are required to start taking money out of your retirement account on your required beginning date (RBD), the account might not be empty when you die. It might even be quite large, especially if you had been withdrawing only the minimum required amount each year—or if you die soon after your RBD. So what happens to the left-overs? The answer to that question is the subject of this chapter.

As we have explained previously in this book, the IRS in January 2001 issued new regulations simplifying and liberalizing the required distribution rules. To allow tax-payers to take advantage of the beneficial changes, the IRS has made the new rules optional for 2001. Some taxpayers might still be required to use the old rules, how-ever, and for that reason, this chapter con-sists of two parts. Part I contains the new rules, and Part II contains the old rules. As you read this chapter, please keep the fol-lowing in mind:

- It bears repeating: The new rules are more favorable, so you will want to start using them as soon as possible.
- If you have an IRA, you can start us-ing the new rules immediately for 2001 distributions.
- If you have a qualified plan, you can use the new rules for 2001 distribu-tions only if the plan has been modi-fied (amended) to incorporate the new rules. To find out whether your plan has been modified, contact the plan administrator.
- If you are still dealing with distribu-tions that you took in 2000 for any type of plan or IRA, then you must use the old rules.
- If you inherited an IRA in 2000 or later, you can use the new rules for distributions that you receive in 2001 and beyond.
- If you inherited a qualified plan in 2000 or later, you can use the new rules for distributions that you re-ceive in 2001 and beyond only if the plan has been modified.
- If you inherited an IRA or other re-tirement plan before 2000, it is not yet clear whether you can switch to the new rules. To be safe, you should continue to use the old rules until the IRS clarifies this issue.
- As you read through Parts I and II, be careful that you don't lose track of which part you are reading. Some of the differences are subtle, but sig-nificant.

Helpful Terms

Annuity. A contract, sold by an insurance company, that promises to make monthly, quarterly, semiannual or annual payments for life or for a specified period of time.

Beneficiary. The person or entity entitled to receive the benefits from insurance or from trust property, such as a retirement plan or IRA.

Deferral Period. The number of years over which distributions from a retirement plan or IRA can be spread.

Distribution. A payout of property (such as shares of stock) or cash from a retirement plan or IRA to the participant or a beneficiary.

Estate. All property that a person owns.

Primary Beneficiary. A person or entity entitled to receive benefits from a retirement plan or IRA upon the death of the original participant.

Recalculated Life Expectancy. Life expectancy that is revised each year according to statistically accurate measures of mortality.

Term Certain. A fixed, identifiable period, such as a specific number of years. For example, a retirement plan that is distributable over a term certain of 20 years must be completely liquidated after 20 years.

Part I: New Rules

A. Administrative Details

Although the rules for computing required distributions after your death might vary depending on who your beneficiary is, the following administrative procedures apply almost across the board.

1. Name on the Account

Unless your beneficiary is your spouse, your retirement account must remain in your name until the account is entirely depleted. If a beneficiary other than your spouse attempts to change the name on the retirement plan account to his or her own name, the action could be a deemed distribution of the entire account. Worse, if the beneficiary attempts to roll over your account into the beneficiary's own IRA, not only will it be a deemed distribution, but penalties for contributing more to an IRA than is allowed may be assessed as well.

Despite the above rule, the trustee or custodian might want to re-title the account to show that you have died. This is permissible as long as the custodian complies with certain procedures for titling the account and reporting distributions. (See Chapter 7 for more information about titling accounts.)

A special rule allows your spouse to treat your retirement plan account as his or her own. See Section B.3, below, to learn how this can be done.

2. Timing of Distributions

Once you pass your RBD, distributions from your account must continue, even after your death. There can be no hiatus in distributions. If you failed to take some or all of your required distribution in the year of your death, your beneficiary must take the remainder before the end of the year. Then your beneficiary must continue to take distributions in all subsequent years until the account is depleted.

The only exception to this rule occurs if your spouse elects to treat the account as his or her own. In that case, required distributions from the account (after the spouse makes it his or her own) will be determined as if the spouse had been the original owner of the account. (See Section B, below, for more about this strategy.)

3. Designated Beneficiary

Recall that you can name any person or organization you choose as the beneficiary of your retirement plan or IRA. When determining how your retirement assets should be distributed after your death, however, only designated beneficiaries are taken into account. (See Chapter 6 for more information about designated beneficiaries.) If one or more of your beneficiaries is not a designated beneficiary, you are deemed to have no designated beneficiary.

a. Deadline for Determining Designated Beneficiary

For purposes of computing post-death required distributions, your designated beneficiary is determined as of December 31 of the year after your death. That doesn't mean someone else can name a new beneficiary of your retirement plan after you die. In fact, no new beneficiaries can be added. Therefore, it is important that you carefully consider and then formally select a beneficiary before you die (using the plan's "designation of beneficiary" form). Not only will that beneficiary receive the assets of your plan, but his or her life expectancy will determine how quickly assets must be distributed after your death.

b. Changing Beneficiaries Before the Deadline

The IRS extended the deadline for determining beneficiaries specifically to give those beneficiaries an opportunity to do some post-mortem planning—to make administration of the retirement plan easier or to "clean up" a disadvantageous situation you left behind. For example, suppose you name your spouse as primary beneficiary and your daughter as contingent beneficiaries. After your death, your spouse might decide she has no need for the assets in your retirement plan. She might disclaim (renounce) her interest in those assets. If she does, the plan assets would go to your daughter, and her life would determine how your retirement plan assets are ultimately distributed.

4. Reporting Distributions

Each year the custodian or trustee of a plan or IRA from which distributions are required to be taken must report to the IRS and to the beneficiary the amount of the required distribution. The custodian or trustee will determine the amount based on the account balance and the life expectancy of the designated beneficiary.

B. Spouse Beneficiary

If your spouse is the sole beneficiary of your retirement account as of December 31 of the year after your death, he or she must take distributions under the rules described in this section.

1. Year of Death

The minimum required distribution for the year of your death will be computed in exactly the same way you would have computed it if you had lived to the end of the year. If you did not take a distribution of the required amount before your death, your spouse beneficiary must do so on your behalf by December 31 of the year of your death. In other words, your spouse would use the uniform table and find the ADP for your age on your birthday in the year of your death. Then your spouse would divide the account balance as of December 31 of the previous year by the ADP for the current year.

If your spouse is more than ten years younger than you are, and if you had been using Table II (joint life expectancy table) to compute lifetime distributions, your spouse would use Table II to find the ADP in the year of your death, as well.

⚠️ **Spouse must take required distribution for year of death.** A spouse beneficiary has the option to treat a deceased participant's retirement plan as the spouse's own. Nonetheless, if you die after your RBD, your spouse must take your required distribution for the year of your death (if you had not already done so) before your spouse can make the account his or her own. Once the account is in the spouse's name, all the required distribution rules apply as though the spouse were the original owner. (See Section 3, below, to learn what happens when the account is placed in the name of a surviving spouse.)

2. Second Year and Beyond

Beginning in the second year (and assuming your spouse does not roll over the account into an IRA in her own name), your spouse will use her own age and Table 1 (single life expectancy table) to look up her ADP each year.

EXAMPLE: Richard died on October 14, 2003, at the age of 75. Richard's wife, Pat, was the sole beneficiary of his IRA. She was 74 in 2003. Richard had been computing required distributions using the uniform table (Table III). Richard withdrew his required distribution for 2003 before he died.

To compute the required distribution for 2004, Pat uses Table I to find her ADP for her age in 2004. Pat turned 75 in 2004, so her ADP from Table I is 12.5. Pat will divide the December 31, 2003, balance of Richard's IRA by 12.5 to determine the required distribution for 2004.

In 2005, Pat turns 76. Her ADP (from Table I) is 11.9. Pat will divide the December 31, 2004, balance of Richard's IRA by 11.9 to determine the required distribution for 2005.

3. Rollover

When you die, your spouse may choose to leave your retirement plan in your name, applying all the distribution rules described above until the account has been completely liquidated.

But if your spouse is the sole beneficiary of your qualified plan or IRA on December 31 of the year after your death, she has another option, which is usually more favorable. She can roll over the plan assets into an IRA of her own. (Note that this option is only available to a spouse beneficiary.)

If your plan is a qualified plan, a rollover to an IRA is the only way to convert the plan to the spouse's own.

But if the retirement plan is an IRA, your spouse has several ways to make the IRA her own. She can do so by:

- rolling over the assets into a new or pre-existing IRA in the spouse's own name (see Section a, below)
- failing to take your post-death required distribution at the proper time (see Section b, below), or
- contributing additional amounts of the spouse's own to your retirement account.

a. Convert to Spouse's IRA By Rollover

Most spouses choose the rollover method because it is convenient and because it leaves a clear trail. Once the rollover is complete, the account belongs to your spouse in every way. Not only can your spouse name a new beneficiary, but your spouse's RBD will determine when future required distributions must begin.

⚠ Rollovers must be into an IRA. A surviving spouse may roll over a participant's retirement plan or IRA only into an IRA in the spouse's name—not into a qualified plan.

If your surviving spouse is not 70½ or older when he or she rolls over your retirement plan or IRA, required distributions may be discontinued until your spouse reaches his or her RBD. Then on your spouse's RBD, your spouse must begin required distributions anew, using the uniform table to determine ADP—or using Table II if your spouse has since married someone else and if the new spouse is more than ten years younger.

⚠ Don't forget to take distribution in the year of death. As mentioned in Section 1, above, if you had not withdrawn your required distribution before your death and if your spouse wants to roll over the account into his or her own name, your spouse must withdraw the required amount for the year of your death before he or she can roll over the account.

After you die, your spouse may roll over your retirement plan or IRA even if your spouse has passed his or her own RBD. In this case, however, there can be no hiatus in required distributions. If your spouse rolls over your IRA in the year of your death, she must take a distribution on your behalf (if you had not done so). The following year, she must take a distribution on her own behalf (because it is not her IRA and she is past her RBD).

EXAMPLE: Richard died on October 14, 2003, at the age of 75. Richard's wife, Pat, was the sole beneficiary of his IRA. She was 74 when Richard died. Richard had already withdrawn the required distribution for 2003.

On December 19, 2003, Pat opened an IRA in her own name and rolled over Richard's IRA into her new account. She named her daughter Tash as beneficiary of the new account. To determine her required distribution for 2004, Pat will use the December 31, 2003, IRA balance. She will divide that balance by the ADP for her age 75 (from the uniform table—Table III), which is 21.8.

b. Convert to Spouse's IRA by Failing to Take a Required Distribution

If you die after your RBD, and if your spouse fails to take a required distribution on your behalf in any year after the year of your death, your spouse is deemed to have made an election to treat your IRA as his or her own. (Remember that because you are past your required beginning date, your spouse must take your required distribution for the year of your death if you had not already done so.) The IRA becomes the spouse's own on December 31 of the year of the failure, and the spouse will not be required to take a distribution until his or her own RBD.

If your spouse has passed her RBD, then she must take a distribution in the year she makes the IRA her own. The distribution will be based on your spouse's age in that year, and the ADP will be determined from the uniform table. If your spouse has remarried by that time to someone who is more than ten years younger than she, the ADP will be determined from Table II, using the surviving spouse's and her new husband's ages.

c. Timing of Rollover

The income tax regulations give your spouse no deadline for converting or rolling over your retirement account to his or her own IRA after your death. Your spouse should be able to make the election at any time—even years after your death—as long as he or she continues to take timely required distributions on your behalf for as long as the account remains in your name.

As a practical matter, if a spouse is past age 59½ and intends to roll over a participant's retirement plan into the spouse's own IRA, there is nothing to be gained from waiting. If the spouse needs money, the spouse can take it freely from his or her own IRA even after rolling it over, because there is no penalty for taking distributions after age 59½.

If the spouse is younger than age 59½, however, free use of the IRA funds could be dicey. Recall that one of the exceptions to the early distribution tax is a distribution to a beneficiary after the death of the original participant. (See Chapter 3 for more information on the early distribution tax.) But that particular exception is not available to a spouse after the spouse rolls over the deceased person's plan into an IRA in the spouse's name. Once it is rolled over, it is the spouse's IRA. Because the spouse is still alive, the after-death exception does not apply. Thus, the spouse must generally postpone distributions until age 59½ to avoid the early distribution tax.

Consequently, if the spouse is younger than age 59½ and needs to use the retirement plan money to live on, the spouse might be better off leaving the plan in the name of the deceased so that the after-death exception can be used. The one disadvantage of this approach is that, according to at least one IRS private letter ruling, once a spouse invokes the after-death exception to the early distribution tax, the spouse forever forfeits the right to roll over the account into an IRA in the spouse's own name.

4. Death of Spouse Beneficiary

When your spouse dies, assuming your spouse did not roll over your retirement plan into an IRA of his or her own, the spouse's beneficiary must continue to take distributions according to the rules discussed in this section.

a. Year of Spouse's Death

The spouse's beneficiary must take a distribution in the year of the spouse's death. The beneficiary will use Table I to find the ADP that corresponds to the spouse's age on his or her birthday in the year of death, and then the beneficiary will divide the account balance as of December 31 of the year before the spouse's death by the ADP for the year of death.

b. Second Year and Beyond

For subsequent years, the ADP is reduced by one each year. The account balance for the previous December 31 is divided by the ADP for the current year to determine the required distribution. This calculation method continues until the account is completely distributed, regardless of whether or not the spouse's beneficiary survives until the account is empty.

> EXAMPLE: Pierre was born on January 10, 1932 and turned 70½ in 2002. Pierre's wife, Zoe, was his designated beneficiary as of his RBD. She turned 68 in 2002. To compute his required distribution for 2002, Pierre used an ADP of 26.2, which he found in the uniform table next to his age of 70.

2002 Distribution:
Pierre's December 31, 2001, IRA account balance was $100,000. Thus, Pierre's first required distribution (for 2002) was $3,817 ($100,000 divided by 26.2).

2003 Distribution:
Pierre died in 2003 before taking his required distribution. Zoe found Pierre's ADP of 25.3 (for age 71) from the uniform table (Table III in Appendix B). The IRA account balance on December 31, 2002 was $106,000. The required distribution for 2003, the year of Pierre's death, was $4,190 ($106,000 divided by 25.3).

2004 Distribution:
Zoe decides not to roll over Pierre's IRA into an IRA in her own name. The required distribution for 2004 is based on Zoe's single life expectancy. Therefore, she will use Table I. Zoe turned 70 in 2004. The ADP for age 70 is 16. The December 31, 2003, IRA balance was $111,000. Therefore, the 2004 required distribution is $6,938 ($111,000 divided by 16).

2005 Distribution:
Zoe died in 2005 before taking her required distribution. Her beneficiaries will again use Table I to find Zoe's ADP for 2005, the year of her death. The ADP for Zoe's age that year, which was 71, is 15.3. The December 31, 2004, balance of the IRA was $115,000. The required distribution is $7,516 ($115,000 divided by 15.3).

2006 Distribution:
For the year after Zoe's death and beyond, Zoe's beneficiaries must simply reduce the ADP for the previous year by one. Therefore, the ADP for 2006 is 14.3 (15.3 − 1). The December 31, 2005, balance of the IRA was $120,000. The required distribution is $8,392 ($120,000 divided by 14.3).

C. Non-Spouse Beneficiary

If the beneficiary of your retirement plan or IRA is not your spouse, distributions after your death are computed according to the rules described in this section.

> ⚠ **If there is more than one beneficiary.** The rules in this section only apply only if there is one beneficiary named on the account. If there is more than one beneficiary, a different set of rules applies. See Sections E and F, below, for more about the multiple beneficiary rules.

1. Year of Death

In the year of your death, if you had not yet taken your required distribution for the year, your beneficiary must do so before the end of the year. Your beneficiary will use the uniform table (Table III in Appendix B) one last time, looking up the ADP for your age on your birthday in the year of your death. If you had already taken your required distribution, your beneficiary need not take another distribution in the year of your death.

2. Second Year and Beyond

Beginning in the year after your death, required distributions are calculated using the beneficiary's single life expectancy in the year following your death. That number will be reduced by one each subsequent year.

EXAMPLE: You turned 70½ in 1996 and began taking required distributions from your IRA at that time. Your designated beneficiary was your daughter, Prudence, who turned 45 in 1996. You had been using the uniform table (Table III, Appendix B).

You died in the year 2006 after having taken your required distribution for the year. Beginning in 2007, the year after your death, Prudence must take a distribution based on her own single life expectancy, determined as of her birthday in the year after your death. Prudence turned 50 in 2007, and her single life expectancy, or ADP (from Table I), was 33.1. To determine the required distribution for 2007, Prudence divides the December 31, 2006, IRA balance by 33.1.

In 2008, Prudence will reduce the ADP by 1 and divide the December 31 2007 balance by 32.1 (33.1 − 1). In future years, the ADP will be reduced by one until the entire IRA is depleted.

3. Death of Non-Spouse Beneficiary

If your non-spouse beneficiary dies after you do but before the account is completely empty, the computation method for required distributions will not change at the beneficiary's death. Distributions will be made to the beneficiary's beneficiary according to the schedule established at your death, using the original beneficiary's life expectancy as the ADP in the year after your death and reducing the ADP by one each subsequent year. Bear in mind, however, that beneficiaries are always permitted to take more than the minimum required distribution.

4. Rollover

A non-spouse beneficiary is never permitted to roll over a deceased participant's retirement plan or IRA. Furthermore, the consequences are the same whether or not the deceased had passed his or her RBD at the time of death. Any rollover attempt will be deemed a distribution, and if the assets are actually deposited into an IRA in the beneficiary's name, the deposit will be considered an excess contribution to an IRA and will be subject to penalties if not withdrawn in timely fashion.

D. No Designated Beneficiary

If you did not name a beneficiary of your retirement plan or if the beneficiary does not qualify as a designated beneficiary, then distributions are based on your own single life expectancy in the year of your death, reduced by one for each subsequent year until the account is depleted.

> EXAMPLE: You turned 70½ in 2002. You named your estate as beneficiary and never got around to changing the designation before your death.
>
> You died in the year 2006 before taking your required distribution for the year. Your beneficiary (that is, the beneficiary of your estate) must use the uniform table (Table III in Appendix B) and your age in 2006 to compute the required distribution for 2006. The ADP for age 74 is 22.7.

For 2007, your beneficiary must find your single life expectancy (from Table I) for your age in 2006 (the year of your death) and reduce it by one. Your single life expectancy for age 74 is 13.2. Therefore, the ADP for the 2007 required distribution is 12.2 (13.2 − 1). In the future, the ADP will be reduced by one each year.

E. Multiple Beneficiaries, Separate Accounts

If you have several IRAs or retirement plans, each with a single beneficiary, then each plan is treated separately for purposes of the required distribution rules. You are not considered to have multiple beneficiaries.

Therefore, a spouse beneficiary to an IRA or plan would use the rules described in Section B, above. A non-spouse beneficiary to an IRA or plan would use the rules described in Section C, above.

F. Multiple Beneficiaries, One Account

If you name more than one designated beneficiary of a single retirement account, then you have multiple beneficiaries for that account, and required distributions after your death will be computed as though the beneficiary with the shortest life expectancy was your sole beneficiary.

For example, if you name your mother and your children as equal beneficiaries of your IRA, distributions are computed after your death as though your mother was your sole beneficiary. But once calculated and withdrawn, the distribution will be divided equally among the beneficiaries.

Segregating accounts probably won't help. You may recall that if you die before your RBD, a plan administrator can separate a single account for multiple beneficiaries, allowing each beneficiary to use his or her own life expectancy to compute his or her own distributions. This strategy does not work when you die after your RBD, however. Even if the accounts are physically separated for convenience, they will be treated as one account for purposes of computing required distributions. (See Section 3, below.)

1. Determining the Designated Beneficiary

As is the case if you die before your RBD, the date for determining whether or not there are multiple beneficiaries named on your retirement account is December 31 of the year following your death. If you had named more than one beneficiary as of your date of death, your beneficiaries still have time to make some changes. For example, one or more beneficiaries might disclaim an interest. Or perhaps the interests of one or more beneficiaries can be distributed by December 31 of the year after your death. (See Section A.2, above, for more information about changes that can be made after your death.) But it will be the beneficiary or beneficiaries that remain on the account as of December 31 of the year after your death that will determine how required distributions must be computed.

2. Computing the Required Distribution

If there are multiple beneficiaries named on your retirement account as of December 31 of the year after your death, distributions must be spread over the life expectancy of the oldest beneficiary. In other words, the ADP is determined as though the oldest beneficiary were the sole beneficiary. Once the distribution is calculated, each beneficiary will receive his or her proportionate share.

> EXAMPLE: You have only one IRA, and you name your three children, Tanya, Durf and Trina, as equal beneficiaries. You die in 2002 at age 74 after having taken your required distribution for the year. As of December 31, 2003, your children were all still named equal beneficiaries of the account. In 2003 Tanya is 40, Durf is 30 and Trina is 22. Because Tanya is the oldest, distributions must be spread over her single life expectancy in the year after your death, reduced

by one each subsequent year. In 2003, the ADP for Tanya's age 40 (from Table 1) is 42.5. Each child will receive one-third of the distribution. In the future, the ADP will be reduced by one each year.

3. Splitting Accounts

The rules for splitting accounts are different depending on whether you die before or after your RBD. You may recall from Chapter 7 that if you die before your RBD and there are multiple beneficiaries on your account, the beneficiaries generally have until December 31 of the year after your death to split the account. They can then usually take distributions of their respective shares over their own life expectancies.

But a strict reading of the IRS Regulations indicates that if you die after your RBD and before splitting the account, the multiple beneficiary rules described in this Section F will apply. In other words, your beneficiaries will have to calculate their distributions using the life expectancy of the oldest beneficiary.

Beneficiaries are still permitted to split the account (for investment autonomy, for example). If they do, they would compute the required distribution as if there were one account. Each beneficiary would then take a proportionate share from his or her own account.

If the beneficiaries do split the account, they will have to carefully comply with the required distribution rules both while they are in the process of splitting the account and after the shares have been separated. (See sections a through c, below.)

a. Transfer

When a beneficiary's share of a plan is transferred to a separate account, the beneficiary must not take possession of the assets at any time before they reach the new account. Instead, the assets must pass directly from one custodian or trustee to another.

b. Name on Account

Even if a beneficiary's share is diverted to a separate account after your death, the new account must bear your name. The account may not be retitled in the name of the beneficiary. (See Chapter 7 for more on how to title accounts.)

c. Choosing a Distribution Option

Any beneficiary may choose to accelerate distribution of his or her share, but no beneficiary can extend the period of time over which the remaining amount must be distributed. In other words, a beneficiary can choose to take more money out of the account than is required, but not less.

Thus, even if the beneficiary with the shortest life expectancy distributes his or her entire share, the remaining beneficiaries must continue to take distributions over that beneficiary's life expectancy—not

over a longer period. Of course, they could accelerate distribution of their own shares, if they choose.

4. Special Rules When a Spouse is a Beneficiary

If you name your spouse as one of several beneficiaries, the multiple beneficiary rules still apply, and the spouse is no longer eligible for special treatment, such as rolling over the account into an IRA in his or her own name.

G. Trust Beneficiary

If you name a trust as beneficiary of your retirement plan or IRA and if that trust meets certain requirements (see Chapter 6 for a discussion of those requirements), then you are permitted to "look through" the trust to find the beneficiary of the trust. The beneficiary can then be treated as a designated beneficiary for purposes of computing required distributions.

All distributions would go into the trust and become subject to the terms of the trust.

1. Non-Spouse Beneficiary of Trust

A non-spouse beneficiary of the trust will use the required distribution rules described in Section C, above. This means the beneficiary may spread required distributions over his or her life expectancy. The beneficiary would find the ADP (from Table 1) corresponding to his or her age in the year after your death. The ADP would then be reduced by one each subsequent year.

2. Spouse Beneficiary of Trust

If your spouse is sole beneficiary of the trust, your spouse will be treated as the designated beneficiary for purposes computing post-death distributions. That means your spouse can take distributions over his or her single life expectancy beginning on December 31 of the year after your death and looking up the ADP for his or her age each year in Table I.

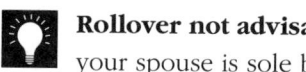 **Rollover not advisable.** Even if your spouse is sole beneficiary of the trust, the IRS regulations state that he or she cannot roll over the retirement plan assets into an IRA in the spouse's own name. (See Section B.3, above, for more information about spousal rollovers.) Some private letter rulings suggest a rollover is still possible in certain circumstances (see Section 4, below), but it's not something you should count on.

3. Multiple Beneficiaries of Trust

If a trust has multiple beneficiaries, then for purposes post-death required distributions, the multiple beneficiary rules described in Section F, above, will apply as though the individuals themselves were named beneficiaries of the retirement plan.

4. Trust Beneficiary and Spousal Rollovers

Recall that a trust—called a bypass trust—is often named the beneficiary of a retirement plan in order to minimize estate taxes. This method usually works in the following way: The plan participant names a trust as the beneficiary of the plan and names his or her spouse as the beneficiary of the trust. When the participant dies, distributions from the plan go into the trust, and then the trust makes distributions to the spouse.

But sometimes the surviving spouse discovers after the participant dies that the retirement plan assets are not needed to fund the trust after all. In that case, the surviving spouse might prefer to get rid of the trust and roll over the assets into his or her own IRA, name his or her own beneficiary and begin a new schedule of required distributions.

The legality of this sort of rollover is in question. This is because the law says that only a spouse beneficiary may roll over assets. Generally, a trust beneficiary may not roll over assets.

But taxpayers have argued that if the spouse is the sole beneficiary of the trust, then for all intents and purposes, the assets do pass directly from the deceased plan participant to the spouse—and thus the rollover complies with the intent, if not the letter, of the law. Similarly, if the spouse has complete control over the assets of the trust and can distribute all of the assets without interference from any third party, then again the assets arguably pass directly from the deceased to the spouse—and thus the rollover is essentially within the law.

Despite the lack of explicit legal approval of these rollover strategies, the IRS in the past established a pattern of approving such actions in a number of its private letter rulings.

In regulations issued in January 2001, however, the IRS changed its position. Those regulations state specifically that a spouse cannot make a deceased participant's IRA her own if a trust is named primary beneficiary of the IRA— even if the spouse is sole beneficiary of the trust.

Some practitioners believe, however, that if the spouse has the power to distribute all the assets of the trust, he or she could distribute the IRA assets to the trust and then distribute the assets from the trust to the spouse. Having done so, the spouse could then roll over the assets into an IRA of his or her own. Although this strategy is not specifically sanctioned by the IRS, some practitioners believe it will pass muster, even under the new regulations.

We believe you should proceed with caution. If you name a trust as beneficiary of your retirement plan with the expectation that your spouse can fall back on a rollover, you are taking a risk.

If you plan to pursue this approach, you may want to do some research of your own. If so, you will need access to a law library to review some of the IRS private letter rulings, or PLRs. Here are some of the favorable ones to start with: PLRs 9633043, 9623056, 9611057 and 9608036. In each of these PLRs, a trust was named beneficiary and the spouse was the beneficiary of the trust. Upon the participant's death, the plan assets were distributed to the trust, and then from the trust to the spouse, and finally to an IRA in the spouse's name. Bear in mind, however, that all of these PLRs were issued before the new regulations.

As an alternative to taking this risk, consider naming your spouse as primary beneficiary (thus preserving the rollover opportunity) and your trust as contingent beneficiary. After your death, your spouse would have the option to disclaim some or all of his or her interest in your retirement plan, allowing it to flow to the bypass trust. Ultimately, however, no strategy involving a trust is completely simple or risk-free.

H. Estate as Beneficiary

The IRS has frequently allowed a spouse to roll over the assets of a retirement plan into an IRA in the spouse's own name when an estate is named beneficiary of the plan and when the spouse is the sole beneficiary of the estate. But the strategy is not sanctioned by the Tax Code or by Tax Regulations, so it remains risky.

Trust versus estate. When you name your estate as beneficiary of your retirement plan, the beneficiaries of your estate may have a more compelling need for a rollover than if you had named a trust as beneficiary. If an estate is named beneficiary, then the plan assets must be distributed over the original participant's life expectancy in the year of death, reduced by one each subsequent year. This is true even if a spouse or child is beneficiary of the estate. There is no "look through" rule for an estate as there is for certain qualified trusts. Consequently, if a participant was elderly at death, the plan might have to be entirely distributed in a short time. But if the spouse, as beneficiary of the estate, is permitted to roll over the assets, the income tax burden can be deferred and quite possibly mitigated, because amounts can be distributed in smaller chunks over the spouse's life ex-

pectancy (or the joint life expectancy of the spouse and his or her beneficiary).

I. Annuities

If you die on or after your RBD and if you had been receiving your retirement benefits as an annuity, the form of the annuity determines how the remaining benefits will be paid to your beneficiary. (See Chapter 6 for more information about types of annuities.)

For example, the annuity might have been a joint and survivor annuity that must continue to pay your beneficiary the same benefits you were receiving. Or the annuity might have been a term certain annuity; if you survive only part of the term, your beneficiary receives payments for the remainder of the term.

J. Divorce or Separation

If you were divorced or separated during your lifetime, some or all of your retirement plan might be distributable to an "alternate payee" such as a spouse, former spouse or child, under the terms of a QDRO—a court-approved divorce or maintenance agreement. (See Chapter 2, Section C.4, for more information about QDROs.)

In such cases, some portion of each distribution during your lifetime was payable to the alternate payee (unless, of course, the alternate payee's share was distributed outright). That doesn't change when you die.

If you die after your RBD, payments from your account will continue to be computed using your beneficiary's ADP in the year after death, reduced by one each subsequent year. If an alternate payee has been receiving a portion of each distribution, the alternate payee is entitled to his or her share of post-death distributions, as well.

> EXAMPLE: On December 31 of the year after your death, the designated beneficiary of your retirement plan was your sister. Under the terms of a QDRO, your former spouse is entitled to half of your retirement plan, and you have been giving your former spouse 50% of each distribution. You died in 2002 after taking your required distribution for the year. In 2003, your sister will take a distribution from your retirement plan using the ADP (from Table I) for her age in 2003. Half of the distribution will go to your sister and half to your former spouse.
>
> In 2004 and beyond, your sister will reduce the previous year's ADP by one when computing required distributions. Half of all distributions must go to your former spouse.

If the alternate payee is a non-spouse, he or she may never roll over a distribution from your retirement plan. However, a spouse or former spouse with an interest in your retirement plan under the terms of a QDRO has all the rights of a surviving spouse beneficiary. When you die, your former spouse may roll over any distribution he or she receives from your plan into an IRA or a retirement plan in his or her own name, provided the former spouse first takes a required distribution on your behalf in the year of your death. If your former spouse has not yet reached his or her RBD, future required distributions may be deferred until that time.

Additional rollover option. A surviving spouse may roll over a participant's distribution only into an IRA. If there is a QDRO in place, however, a spouse or former spouse alternate payee has the additional option of rolling over the distribution into a qualified plan in the spouse's own name.

Part II: Old Rules

A. Administrative Details

The rules for computing required distributions after your death could be different for each beneficiary. The following administrative procedures apply almost across the board, however.

1. Name on the Account

Unless your beneficiary is your spouse, your retirement account must remain in your name until the account is entirely depleted. The trustee or custodian might want to retitle the account to show that you have died, which is permissible as long as the custodian complies with certain procedures—such as keeping your name somewhere on the account. (See Chapter 7 for more information about retitling accounts.) But if a beneficiary other than your spouse attempts to change the name on the retirement plan account to his or her own name, the action could be deemed a distribution of the entire account. Worse, if the beneficiary attempts to roll over your account into the beneficiary's own IRA, not only will it be a deemed distribution, but penalties for contributing more to an IRA than is allowed may be assessed as well.

A special rule allows your spouse to treat your retirement plan account as his or her own. See Section H, below, to learn how this can be done.

2. Timing of Distributions

Because distributions must continue as rapidly after your death as before, there can be no hiatus in distributions from your account. If you failed to take some or all of your minimum required distribution before your death, the remainder must be distributed before the end of the year. Your beneficiary must continue to take distributions in all subsequent years until the account is depleted. The only excep-

tion to this occurs if your spouse elects to treat the account as his or her own. In that case, required distributions from the account will be determined as if the spouse had been the original owner of the account. (See Section H, below, for more about this strategy.)

3. Beneficiaries

Whichever beneficiary's life expectancy you were using to compute required distributions immediately before your death is the same beneficiary's life expectancy that must be used to compute distributions after your death.

⚠ Changing beneficiaries. If you changed beneficiaries after your RBD and your new beneficiary was not a designated beneficiary or had a shorter life expectancy than the previous designated beneficiary, you may have been required to alter your method of computing minimum distributions. (See Chapter 6 for more information.)

EXAMPLE: On your RBD you named your sister Donna, who was age 65, as beneficiary of your IRA. Five years later, you decided to disinherit Donna and name your brother Jim as beneficiary of your IRA. Jim is five years older than Donna, so after changing the beneficiary designation, you were required to use the joint life expectancy of you and Jim, instead of you and Donna. You died two years later while Jim was still your beneficiary. Post-death distributions must use Jim's life expectancy, not Donna's.

B. Spouse Beneficiary

If your spouse is your beneficiary and you were using a joint life expectancy to compute distributions during your lifetime, then the minimum required distribution for the year of your death will be computed in exactly the same way you would have computed it if you had lived to the end of the year. If you did not take a distribution of the required amount before your death, your spouse beneficiary must do so on your behalf by December 31 of the year of your death. (Note: These rules may not apply if your spouse elects to make the account his or her own. See Section H, below.)

If you made an election on your RBD not to recalculate either your life expectancy or your spouse's, the required distribution calculation established during your lifetime remains unchanged until the account is empty. If your life expectancy was being recalculated, however, the computation method will change beginning in the year after your death.

⚠ **A spouse beneficiary can treat a deceased participant's retirement plan as the spouse's own.** Once the account is in the spouse's name, all the required distribution rules apply as though the spouse were the original owner. The following rules apply only for those years (and partial years) the account remains in the deceased participant's name. See Section H, below, to learn what happens when the account is placed in the name of a surviving spouse.

1. Participant and Spouse Recalculating

If you elected to recalculate, that means you chose to use a statistically accurate estimate of your life expectancy each year. During your lifetime, you looked up a new joint life factor in the IRS tables each year (Table II, Appendix B). Beginning in the year after your death, the statistically accurate estimate of your own life expectancy is zero. Your spouse beneficiary is then left with only his or her own single life expectancy for computing future required distributions.

Your life expectancy doesn't become zero until the year after your death. In the year you die, your required distribution is computed as though you survived the entire year.

EXAMPLE: Taro was born on January 10, 1929 and turned 70½ in 1999. Taro's wife, Midori, was his designated beneficiary as of his RBD. She turned 68 in 1999. Their joint life expectancy in 1999 was 21.5 years (from Table II, Appendix B), and Taro elected to recalculate both of their life expectancies.

1999 Distribution: The December 31, 1998 account balance in Taro's IRA was $100,000. Thus, Taro's first required distribution (for 1999) was $4,651 (which is $100,000 divided by 21.5).

2000 Distribution: The following year, Taro used Table II to find the new recalculated joint life expectancy factor for his age, 71, and Midori's age, 69. The new factor was 20.7. The IRA account balance on December 31, 1999 was $106,000. Thus, the required distribution for 2000 was $5,121 ($106,000 divided by 20.7).

2001 Distribution: Taro died in 2001. The required distribution for 2001 is computed in the same way it was computed in 2000, as though Taro had lived through 2001. The new life expectancy factor for ages 72 and 70 (from Table II) is 19.8. The December 31, 2000 IRA balance was $111,000.

Therefore, the 2001 required distribution is $5,606 ($111,000 divided by 19.8).

2002 Distribution: For the year 2002, Taro's recalculated life expectancy is zero, which leaves only Midori's single recalculated life expectancy. Midori must use Table I to find her life expectancy for her current age of 71. That number is 15.3. The IRA account balance on December 31, 2001 was $117,000. The required distribution for the year 2002 is $7,647 ($117,000 divided by 15.3).

In future years, Midori will continue to use Table I to find her single recalculated life expectancy based on her current age.

If your spouse beneficiary dies before you do, his or her life goes to zero and all future distributions until your death must be based on your own single recalculated life expectancy. Then when you die, your life expectancy also goes to zero, and the entire retirement account will have to be distributed the following year.

2. Participant and Spouse Not Recalculating

If you made an election on or before your RBD not to recalculate either your life expectancy or your spouse's, that means you chose to use a "term certain" for distribution of your entire account. In that case, nothing changes when you die. The method for computing required distributions after your death is exactly the same as during your lifetime. Each year the joint life expectancy factor from the previous year is reduced by one, and the account balance is divided by the new factor to arrive at the current required distribution. (See Chapter 6 for more information about how to compute required distributions.)

EXAMPLE: Jerry was born on January 10, 1929 and turned 70½ in 1999. Jerry's wife, Donna, was his designated beneficiary as of his RBD. She turned 68 in 1999. Their joint life expectancy in 1999 was 21.5 years (from Table II, Appendix B), and Jerry elected not to recalculate either of their life expectancies.

1999 Distribution: The December 31, 1998 account balance in Jerry's IRA was $100,000. Thus, Jerry's first required distribution (for 1999) was $4,651 (which is $100,000 divided by 21.5).

2000 Distribution: The following year, Jerry reduced the joint life expectancy factor by one, because neither his life nor Donna's was being recalculated. The new life expectancy was 20.5. The IRA account balance on December 31, 1999 was $106,000, and the required distribution for 2000 was $5,171 ($106,000 divided by 20.5).

2001 Distribution: Jerry died in 2001. The required distribution for 2001 is computed in the same way as in previ-

ous years. The life expectancy factor for 2001 is 19.5 (which is 20.5 - 1). The December 31, 2000 IRA balance was $111,000. Therefore, the 2001 required distribution is $5,692 ($111,000 divided by 19.5).

Required distributions for all future years will be computed in the same way until the account has been completely exhausted.

3. One Spouse Recalculating, the Other Not

It is possible that you elected to recalculate your own life expectancy and not your spouse's, or vice versa. If your life was being recalculated and your spouse's was not, then your life goes to zero in the year after your death and your spouse would compute future distributions based on his or her remaining single life expectancy, reduced by one for each year that has passed since your first distribution year.

EXAMPLE: You turned 70½ in 1996 and began taking required distributions from your IRA at that time over the joint life expectancy of you and your spouse. Your spouse was 68 in 1996. You elected to recalculate your life expectancy but not your spouse's.

You died in the year 2000 after having taken your required distribution for the year. Because you were recalculating, your life expectancy goes to zero in the year 2001. Your spouse must take a distribution based on your spouse's own single life expectancy, determined as of your first distribution year (1996) and reduced by one each year since. In 1996, your spouse's life expectancy (from Table I) was 17.6. In 2001, your spouse's remaining life expectancy is 12.6 (17.6 - 5). For future years, your spouse's life expectancy will be reduced by one until the entire IRA is depleted.

If you had elected to recalculate your spouse's life expectancy, but not your own, your death will have no effect on the calculation method.

If your spouse beneficiary is the first to die and his or her life was being recalculated, then his or her life expectancy goes to zero and you are left with your own single life expectancy for computing distributions until your death. After your death, distributions would continue for your remaining non-recalculated life expectancy. On the other hand, if your spouse was the first to die and was not recalculating (and you were), the computation method would not change after his or her death. At your subsequent death, however, your life expectancy would go to zero and distributions would continue over your spouse's remaining non-recalculated life expectancy.

4. Death of Spouse Beneficiary

If you never look past your own death, it might be difficult to see how critical a recalculation decision can be. But now let's see what happens if your spouse dies after you do.

a. Participant and Spouse Recalculating

If you elected to recalculate both your life expectancy and your spouse's, upon your death your life expectancy goes to zero and your spouse is left with his or her single life expectancy. That means all future distributions must be computed using your spouse's single recalculated life expectancy, which has the effect of accelerating distributions.

When your spouse subsequently dies, however, his or her life expectancy also goes to zero. As a result, the entire remaining account would have to be distributed to your spouse's beneficiaries in the year after your spouse's death. (This could be avoided if your spouse rolled over the plan assets into an IRA in his or her own name. See Section H, below.)

EXAMPLE: Ramesh was born on January 10, 1927 and began taking distributions from his IRA in 1997. His wife, Rekha, was the designated beneficiary of the IRA, and Ramesh had elected to recalculate both of their life expectancies. Ramesh died in 1999.

1999 Distribution: The required distribution for 1999 was computed in the same way it was computed in 1998, as though Ramesh had lived through 1999. The joint life expectancy of Ramesh and Rekha at ages 72 and 70 (from Table II) was 19.8. The December 31, 1998 IRA balance was $111,000. Therefore, the 1999 required distribution was $5,606 ($111,000 divided by 19.8).

2000 Distribution: For the year 2000, Ramesh's recalculated life expectancy is zero, which leaves only Rekha's single recalculated life expectancy. Rekha must use Table I to find the life expectancy factor for her current age of 71. That number is 15.3. The IRA account balance on December 31, 1999 was $117,000. The required distribution for the year 2000 is $7,647 ($117,000 divided by 15.3).

2001 Distribution: Rekha dies in 2001. The required distribution for the year 2001 will be computed as though Rekha had survived the year. Thus, her recalculated life expectancy for age 72 (from Table I) is 14.6. The December 31, 2000 IRA balance is $121,000. The required distribution for the year 2001 is $8,288.

2002 Distribution: Rekha's life expectancy is zero in the year following her death. Consequently, there is no remaining term over which to spread

required distributions, and the entire account must be distributed to her beneficiaries by December 31, 2002. This result could have been avoided if Rekha had rolled over the account into her own name and designated new beneficiaries before she died.

b. Participant and Spouse Not Recalculating

If you elect not to recalculate either your life expectancy or your spouse's, the term certain you establish on your RBD remains unchanged until the entire account is distributed, regardless of whether or not either of you survives the term.

EXAMPLE: Pierre was born on January 10, 1929 and turned 70½ in 1999. Pierre's wife, Zoe, was his designated beneficiary as of his RBD. She turned 68 in 1999. Their joint life expectancy in 1999 was 21.5 years (from Table II, Appendix B), and Pierre elected not to recalculate either of their life expectancies.

1999 Distribution: Pierre's December 31, 1998 IRA account balance was $100,000. Thus, Pierre's first required distribution (for 1999) was $4,651 ($100,000 divided by 21.5).

2000 Distribution: The following year, Pierre reduced the joint life expectancy by one, given that neither his nor Zoe's life was being recalculated. The new joint life expectancy factor was 20.5. The IRA account balance on December 31, 1999 was $106,000. The required distribution for 2000 was $5,171 ($106,000 divided by 20.5).

2001 Distribution: Pierre died in 2001. The required distribution for 2001 is computed the same way the prior two distributions were calculated. The life expectancy factor for 2001 is 19.5 (which is 20.5 - 1). The December 31, 2000 IRA balance was $111,000. Therefore, the 2001 required distribution is $5,692 ($111,000 divided by 19.5).

2002 Distribution: Zoe died in the year 2002. All future required distribution will go to Zoe's beneficiaries. The required distribution for 2002 is computed in the same way all previous years were calculated. The life expectancy factor for the year 2002 is 18.5. The December 31, 2001 balance of the IRA was $115,000. The required distribution is $6,216 ($115,000 divided by 18.5).

Required distributions for all subsequent years will be computed in the same manner until the account is empty.

c. One Spouse Recalculating, the Other Not

Upon the death of a recalculating spouse, his or her life expectancy will go to zero, but the term certain for the nonrecalculating spouse can be used until the term expires, even after the death of the nonre-calculating spouse. For example, if you are recalculating but your spouse is not, upon your death, your life expectancy goes to zero, but your spouse may continue to take distributions over his or her remaining term certain. The term certain is based on your spouse's life expectancy in your first distribution year, reduced by one for each year that has passed. Upon your spouse's death, your spouse's beneficiaries continue to reduce the spouse's term-certain life expectancy by one each year until the entire account is depleted.

Similarly, if you are not recalculating but your spouse is, upon your death, the calculation method does not change. (Because you did not elect to recalculate, your life expectancy does not go to zero.) Upon your spouse's death, his or her life expectancy will go to zero, but the spouse's beneficiaries may continue to use your remaining term certain.

C. Non-Spouse Beneficiary

If the beneficiary of your retirement plan or IRA is not your spouse, the only recalculation election you could have made on your RBD was for yourself, because the life expectancy of a non-spouse beneficiary may never be recalculated. If you elected to recalculate, required distributions after your death will increase, because your life expectancy will be reduced to zero. An unusual exception to this acceleration phenomenon occurs when you name a beneficiary who is more than ten years younger than you are. In that case, required distributions after your death might actually be reduced. (See Section 2, below.)

1. Beneficiary No More Than Ten Years Younger

If your non-spouse beneficiary is no more than ten years younger than you are, required distributions after your death are straightforward. Because you were not permitted to recalculate your beneficiary's life expectancy, only the recalculation choice you made for yourself might affect the required distribution calculation after your death.

a. Participant Recalculating

If you elected to recalculate your life expectancy, the required distribution for the year of your death is computed in the same way you had been computing it during your lifetime. In the year following your death, however, your life expectancy goes to zero. Your beneficiary must continue taking required distributions based on his or her own remaining term certain, determined as of your first distribution year, which is most likely the year you turned 70½.

> EXAMPLE: You turned 70½ in 1996 and began taking required distributions

from your IRA at that time. Your designated beneficiary was your non-marital partner, Cait, who turned 63 in 1996. You were using a joint life expectancy when computing required distributions and had been recalculating your own life expectancy.

You died in the year 2000 after having taken your required distribution for the year. Your life expectancy for the year 2001 is zero, so Cait must continue distributions from the IRA using only her remaining life expectancy. Her life expectancy in 1996 at age 63 was 21.6 years. Because her life expectancy cannot be recalculated, it will be reduced by one each year. In the year 2001, her remaining life expectancy is 16.6 (which is 21.6 - 5). That is the period over which the remaining IRA balance must be distributed.

b. Participant Not Recalculating

If you elected not to recalculate your life expectancy, calculations after your death do not change. During your lifetime, you reduced your joint life expectancy factor by one each year. After your death, the factor will continue to be reduced by one until the entire account is distributed.

c. Death of Non-Spouse Beneficiary

Whether or not you were recalculating your life expectancy, your non-spouse beneficiary's death, after your own, has no effect on the computation of required distributions. The factor used to compute the required distribution in the year after your death will be reduced by one each year until the account is liquidated. If your beneficiary dies in the meantime, nothing changes—except that the distributions are paid to your beneficiary's beneficiary.

Bear in mind that beneficiaries may accelerate distributions, but the computation of the minimum required distribution remains fixed.

2. Beneficiary More Than Ten Years Younger

If your designated beneficiary is not your spouse and also is more than ten years younger than you are, the post-death rules are complicated by the fact that lifetime distributions were based on the MDIB rule. (See Chapter 6 for more information about the MDIB rule.)

If you name a beneficiary who is more than ten years younger than you are, during your lifetime you must compute required distributions in two ways. First you must use what is known as the regular method and refer to Table I (single) or II (joint) (both in Appendix B) to find a life expectancy factor. Then you must use the MDIB rule, which means taking the life expectancy factor from Table III (Appendix B). Whichever method yields the smallest life expectancy factor is the one you must

use to compute required distributions as described in Chapter 6. As a practical matter, you can ignore the regular method during your lifetime because the MDIB table will always yield a smaller factor.

The MDIB rule applies only to lifetime distributions, however. Consequently, beginning in the year after your death, required distributions are calculated using the regular method—as though it had been used from the start. The MDIB rule (and the use of Table III) simply disappears. Just how this works in practice is described below.

a. Participant Recalculating

In the year of your death, the required distribution is computed the same way you computed it during your lifetime, which means the MDIB table must be used in the year of death. The following year, however, the MDIB rule no longer applies and the required distribution calculation reverts to the regular method.

Under the regular method, the decision about whether or not to recalculate your life expectancy, which you made on your RBD, is quite relevant. The election had no effect during your lifetime because you were using the MDIB table, but once you die, the election becomes important.

If you made no election at all on your RBD, you are deemed to have made a recalculation election by default. In that case, your life expectancy goes to zero in the year after your death, and your beneficiary is left with his or her own remaining life expectancy, determined as of the year of your first required distribution (usually the year you turned 70½) and reduced by one for each year that has passed.

EXAMPLE: You turned 70½ in 1996 and began taking required distributions from your IRA at that time. Your designated beneficiary was your daughter, Prudence, who turned 45 in 1996. You were using a joint life expectancy when computing required distributions and had been using the MDIB table (Table III, Appendix B). Furthermore, on your RBD, you made no election at all with regard to recalculation, which by default constitutes an election to recalculate your life expectancy.

You died in the year 2000 after having taken your required distribution for the year. Beginning in 2001, the year after your death, the MDIB rule no longer applies. Therefore, because you were recalculating your life expectancy, in 2001 your life expectancy goes to zero. Prudence must take a distribution based on her own single life expectancy, determined as of your first distribution year and reduced by one for each year since. In 1996, your first distribution year, Prudence was 45 and her single life expectancy (from Table I) was 37.7. In 2001, her remaining life expectancy is 32.7 (37.7 - 5). In future years, Prudence's life expectancy will be reduced by one until the entire IRA is depleted.

b. Participant Not Recalculating

If you make an election not to recalculate your life expectancy, and also name a beneficiary who is more than ten years younger, your election has no effect until your death because you are required to use the MDIB table before then. But beginning in the year after your death, the MDIB rule no longer applies and the required distribution calculation reverts to the regular method. To arrive at a life expectancy factor for the year after your death, your beneficiary looks up your joint life expectancy (because you weren't recalculating) for your first distribution year (using Table II, Appendix B) and reduces the number by one for each year that has passed.

EXAMPLE: You were born on June 1, 1926. You turned 70½ in 1996 and began taking required distributions from your IRA at that time. Your designated beneficiary was your son, Mack, who turned 45 in 1996. You were using a joint life expectancy when computing required distributions and had been using the MDIB table (Table III, Appendix B). Furthermore, on your RBD, you made an election not to recalculate your life expectancy.

You died in the year 2000 after having taken your required distribution for the year. Beginning in 2001, the year after your death, the MDIB rule no longer applies. Because you had made a non-recalculation election, Mack must look up his and your joint life expectancy for 1996, your first distribution year, and then reduce the number by one for each year that has passed. Your joint life expectancy in 1996, when you were 70 and Mack was 45, was 38.3 (Table II, Appendix B). Because you elected not to recalculate your life expectancy, but to use a term certain, Mack may continue to use your joint life expectancy (from 1996) reduced by one each year. Therefore, in 2001, the joint life expectancy factor Mack must use to compute the required distribution is 33.3 (38.3 - 5). In the future, that number will be reduced by one each year until the entire IRA is depleted.

Recalculating may not make sense!
If you name a beneficiary who is more than ten years younger than you are, you have everything to gain and nothing to lose by not recalculating your life expectancy. The reason is simple. During your lifetime, you are required to use the MDIB tables. Consequently, your election has no effect on lifetime distributions. But after your death, your beneficiary must use the regular method to compute required distributions, and under the regular method, your recalculation election is quite relevant. If you had been recalculating, your life expectancy becomes zero after your death, which means your beneficiary may use

only his or her single life expectancy when computing future required distributions. If you had chosen not to recalculate your life expectancy, however, your beneficiary could continue to use a joint life expectancy after your death, as illustrated in the above examples.

c. Death of Non-Spouse Beneficiary

If your non-spouse beneficiary who is more than ten years younger than you are dies after you do but before the account is completely depleted, the computation method for required distributions will not change at the beneficiary's death. Distributions will be made to the beneficiary's beneficiary according to the schedule established at your death. Bear in mind, however, that your beneficiary is always permitted to take more than the minimum required distribution.

D. No Designated Beneficiary

If you did not name a beneficiary of your retirement plan or if the beneficiary does not qualify as a designated beneficiary, then your lifetime distributions are based on your own single life expectancy. (See Chapter 6.) After you die, distributions might or might not be accelerated, depending on whether you elected to recalculate your life expectancy.

1. Participant Recalculating

If you elected to recalculate your life expectancy (or simply failed to make any election), your life expectancy goes to zero in the year after your death. If you did not name a designated beneficiary, the entire account must be distributed to your non-designated beneficiary or to your heirs according to the laws of your state in the year after your death. As a result, a chunk of the distribution will immediately be lost to income taxes.

EXAMPLE: You turned 70½ in 1996 and began taking required distributions from your IRA at that time. You were single and named your estate as beneficiary of your IRA. Consequently, you were deemed to have no designated beneficiary, and were required to use your own single life expectancy for computing required distributions. Furthermore, on your RBD, you made no election at all with regard to recalculation, which by default constitutes an election to recalculate your life expectancy.

You died in the year 2000 after having taken your required distribution for the year. Your life expectancy goes to zero in the year 2001, and the entire IRA must be distributed to your estate by December 31, 2001.

2. Participant Not Recalculating

If you made an election not to recalculate your life expectancy, after your death your beneficiary may continue to use your remaining term certain when distributing the balance of the account, even if your beneficiary is not a designated beneficiary.

EXAMPLE: You turned 70½ in 1996, and before beginning required distributions from your IRA, you made an election not to recalculate your life expectancy. Because you named your estate as beneficiary, you were deemed to have no designated beneficiary for purposes of computing required distributions, and had to use your own single life expectancy.

You died in the year 2000 after having taken your required distribution for the year. Because you had not been recalculating your life expectancy, your beneficiary (that is, the beneficiary of your estate) will continue to compute distributions just as you were. Your life expectancy in 1996, when you were age 70, was 16 years. You had been reducing that factor by one each year. For the year 2000, the life expectancy factor on which you based your required distribution was 12 (16 - 4). In 2001, your beneficiary will use a life expectancy factor of 11. For future years, your beneficiary will continue to reduce the factor by one until the entire account is distributed.

E. Multiple Beneficiaries— Separate Accounts

Naming multiple beneficiaries on a single retirement account or IRA generally causes more administrative problems than it solves, especially after the original participant dies. Most beneficiaries would prefer that their shares were in separate accounts. Then after your death, each would be able to make his or her own investment and distribution decisions and also would not be restricted by the life expectancy limitations of an older beneficiary.

There are several ways to set up separate accounts or separate shares of your retirement plan, each with a different beneficiary. (See Chapter 7 for more on splitting accounts during your lifetime.) But this separation must have occurred before your RBD. If it did, the required distribution rules will be applied to each account separately. Even if one or more of your plans named several beneficiaries, but the plan administrator segregated each beneficiary's share or prepared a separate accounting for each beneficiary from and after your RBD, then each share may be treated as a separate account for purposes of computing required distributions. In such cases, all the rules described in the previous sections of this chapter will apply separately to each share or account.

Bear in mind that if the accounts were not separate at the time of your RBD, then after your death, even if the accounts are physically separated for convenience, they will be treated as one account for purposes of computing required distributions.

F. Multiple Beneficiaries— One Account

As you may recall, if you name more than one designated beneficiary of a single retirement account, your lifetime required distribution calculations are based on the joint life expectancy of you and the beneficiary with the shortest life expectancy. And required distributions after your death will be computed as though that beneficiary—the one with the shortest life expectancy—was your sole beneficiary.

For example, if you name your mother and your children as equal beneficiaries of your IRA, then during your lifetime you base required distributions on the joint life expectancy of you and your mother, given that she has the shortest life expectancy. After your death, distributions are computed as though your mother was your sole beneficiary. But once calculated and withdrawn, the distribution will be divided equally among the beneficiaries.

1. Splitting Accounts

Whether you die before or after your RBD, the rules for separating multiple beneficiaries' shares into separate accounts after your death are exactly the same. (See Chapter 7 for detailed information about splitting accounts.) Even if your beneficiaries choose to split the account, all future required distributions are computed as though the beneficiaries' shares had remained aggregated in one account. But then each beneficiary's proportionate share of the distribution is withdrawn from his or her account.

a. Transfer vs. Rollover

When a beneficiary's share of your plan is transferred to a separate account, the beneficiary must not take possession of the assets at any time before they reach the new account. Instead the assets must pass directly from one custodian or trustee to another.

b. Name on Account

Even if a beneficiary's share is diverted to a separate account after your death, the new account must bear your name. The account may not be retitled in the name of the beneficiary. (There is a special exception if the beneficiary is a spouse of the original participant. See Section H, below.)

⚠️ **The account must remain in the deceased participant's name.** A literal interpretation of the law would require that a deceased participant's name remain on the retirement account if the beneficiary is a non-spouse. The purpose of this requirement is to help the IRS ensure that a non-spouse beneficiary does not roll over the retirement account into an IRA or qualified plan of the beneficiary's own. As a practical matter, though, IRA custodians and plan trustees are coping with this requirement in different ways—and as their legal departments see fit. Consequently, you may find that your particular custodian or trustee has its own solution to the account title problem. If you confirm that the custodian or trustee is familiar with the IRS titling requirement and that the custodian or trustee is nonetheless confident that its peculiar method will pass muster with the IRS, you have probably done all you can do. See Chapter 7 for more on how to title accounts.

c. Measuring Life Expectancy

Distributions after your death must be computed using the joint life expectancy of you and the beneficiary with the shortest life expectancy, whether or not the beneficiaries choose to separate their respective shares.

d. Choosing a Distribution Option

Any beneficiary may choose to accelerate distribution of his or her share, but the period of time over which the remaining amount is required to be distributed may not be extended. Thus, even if the beneficiary with the shortest life expectancy distributes his or her entire share, the remaining beneficiaries must continue to take distributions over that beneficiary's life expectancy—not over a longer period. Of course, they can accelerate distribution of their shares, if they choose.

2. Special Rules When a Spouse Is a Beneficiary

If you name your spouse as one of several beneficiaries, both the multiple beneficiary and the MDIB rules apply during your lifetime. For example, if your spouse is the oldest beneficiary, you are permitted to use the joint life expectancy of you and your spouse to compute required distributions. But if your spouse is more than ten years younger than you, the MDIB rule also applies, because the special exception to the MDIB rule for a spouse is not available when you name multiple beneficiaries. After your death, however, the MDIB rule no longer applies. Therefore, distributions are computed according to the regular method and are subject to any recalculation election you made for yourself or your spouse.

A spouse can opt for a rollover. Even though a spouse may be one of several beneficiaries named on a retirement account, the spouse may choose to take a distribution of his or her share and roll it over into an IRA in the spouse's own name. Only a spouse has this option. (See Section H, below, for more information about this strategy.)

G. Trust Beneficiary

If you name a trust as beneficiary of your retirement plan or IRA and that trust meets certain requirements (see Chapter 6), then you are permitted to "look through" the trust to find the beneficiaries of the trust. Those beneficiaries can then be treated as designated beneficiaries for purposes of computing required distributions during your lifetime. In other words, you can use a joint life expectancy, thereby extending the period over which the retirement plan must be distributed. If the trust did not meet the requirements of a designated beneficiary, you would be stuck with your own single life expectancy when computing the minimum required amounts.

If the trust qualifies as a designated beneficiary, after your death the rules for computing required distributions apply as though the beneficiary of the trust was your designated beneficiary. All post-death distributions go into the trust, however, and become subject to the terms of the trust, rather than going directly to the beneficiary of the trust.

H. Rollovers

The rollover rules that apply to your beneficiary are much the same whether you die before or after your RBD. (See Chapter 7 for information about a beneficiary's rollover options if you die before your RBD.)

1. Spouse as Beneficiary

When you die, your spouse may choose to leave your retirement plan or IRA in your name, applying all the rules described in the previous sections of this chapter to the account until it has been completely liquidated.

Your spouse has another option, too, which is usually more favorable: Your spouse can elect to treat the account as his or her own. If your plan is a qualified plan or a TDA, your spouse can make that election by rolling the plan assets into an IRA. If your plan is an IRA, your spouse has several options for making it his or her own, including the following:

- failing to take your post-death required distribution at the proper time
- contributing additional amounts of his or her own to your IRA, or
- rolling the assets over into an IRA in his or her own name.

The rollover option is probably the best one because it leaves an unambiguous trail showing exactly what happened and when.

a. Convert to Spouse's IRA by Rollover

Most spouses choose the rollover method. Once the rollover is complete, the account belongs to your spouse in every way. Not only can your spouse name a new beneficiary, but your spouse's RBD will determine when future required distributions must begin.

Rollovers have their limits. A surviving spouse may roll over a participant's retirement plan or IRA only into an IRA in the spouse's name—not into a qualified plan.

If your surviving spouse is not 70½ or older in the year after rolling over your retirement plan or IRA, required distributions may be discontinued until your spouse reaches his or her RBD. Then on your spouse's RBD, your spouse must begin required distributions anew and must choose whether or not to recalculate his or her life expectancy. Note that your spouse is not bound by any recalculation election you made when the account was in your name.

A required distribution cannot be rolled over even after death. If you had not withdrawn your required distribution before your death and your spouse wants to roll over the account into his or her own name, the required amount must be withdrawn before the rollover can be completed. If you had taken your required distribution in the year of your death but your spouse waits until the year after your death to roll over the account, your spouse must again take a required distribution on your behalf—using your computation method—before rolling over the account.

EXAMPLE: Sonny died on October 14, 1999 at the age of 75. Sonny's youthful wife, Sheryl, was the sole beneficiary of his IRA. She was 43 when Sonny died. Sonny had been computing required distributions based on his and Sheryl's joint life expectancy and had elected to recalculate both lives. He had already withdrawn the required distribution for 1999 by the time he died.

Sheryl wanted to roll over Sonny's IRA into an IRA in her own name in February 2000. First, she had to take a required distribution for the year 2000 using the calculation method Sonny had been using. Because Sonny's recalculated life expectancy is zero in the year after his death, Sheryl had to use only her own recalculated life expectancy to compute the required amount. She was 43 when Sonny died, so in the year 2000, she was 44 and her life expectancy (from Table I) was 38.7 years. To compute the required distribution for the year 2000, she should divide the December 31, 1999 account balance by 38.7.

Beginning in the year 2001 after a rollover, Sheryl can suspend required distributions until she reaches her own RBD (April 1 of the year after turning 70½). At that time, distributions will be based on her own beneficiary designation and recalculation election.

After you die, your spouse may roll over your retirement plan or IRA even if he or she has passed his or her own RBD, which can be a huge advantage if your spouse wishes to extend the deferral period. Once the retirement plan is rolled over, the spouse may name a young beneficiary, such as a child, to spread distributions over a longer period.

EXAMPLE: Richard died on October 14, 1999 at the age of 75. Richard's wife, Pat, was the sole beneficiary of his IRA. She was 74 when Richard died. Richard had been computing required distributions based on his and Pat's joint life expectancy and had elected to recalculate both lives. Richard had already withdrawn the required distribution for 1999, based on their joint life expectancy (for ages 75 and 74) of 16.9 years (from Table II, Appendix B).

On December 19, 1999, Pat opened an IRA in her own name and rolled over Richard's IRA into her new account. She named her daughter Tash as beneficiary of the new account and elected not to recalculate her life expectancy. Pat's required distribution for the year 2000 will be based on the joint life expectancy of Pat and Tash. Because Tash is more than ten years younger than Pat, Pat must use the MDIB table (Table III, Appendix B). The life expectancy factor she should use for the year 2000, based on her age of 75 and a beneficiary more than ten years younger, is 21.8.

b. Convert to Spouse's IRA by Failing to Take a Required Distribution

If you die after your RBD, and your spouse fails to take a required distribution on your behalf in the year of your death, your spouse is deemed to have made an election to treat your account as his or her own. The retirement plan becomes the spouse's own on December 31 of the year of your death, and the spouse will not be required to take a distribution on his or her own behalf until the spouse's own RBD. If the spouse has passed his or her RBD, then the spouse is required to take a distribution in the year after the account becomes the spouse's own.

This method of converting your IRA to your spouse's IRA is different from a rollover. In a rollover, the spouse transfers the assets in your IRA to another IRA in the spouse's name. In the above case, however, the assets remain in the same IRA, but the account is deemed to be the spouse's. The significance of this distinction is that, in the case of a rollover, a distribution is required on behalf of the deceased owner in the year of death. When the account is simply deemed converted, though, no such distribution takes place. Whether or not a penalty should apply for failing to take a required distribution from the account when it is still deemed to be yours has yet to be resolved by the IRS.

EXAMPLE: Fred died in 2001 at the age of 75. Fred's wife, Ethel, was the beneficiary of his IRA and was only 65 when Fred died. Ethel wants to make Fred's account her own so that she can defer future required distributions until her own RBD. She intends to make the account her own by discontinuing Fred's required distributions. Fred had not withdrawn his required distribution for 2001 and Ethel did not take a distribution in 2001, either. Therefore, Fred's IRA became Ethel's on December 31, 2001. Ethel will not have to take any required distribution from the converted IRA until her own RBD. But will the IRS assess a penalty for failing to take Fred's 2001 distribution before the IRA was converted to Ethel's IRA? Had Ethel taken a distribution on Fred's behalf, the IRA would not automatically become hers, because she would have taken a required distribution.

Can the IRS have it both ways? In at least one recent private letter ruling, the IRS said that the beneficiary should not be assessed a required distribution penalty in this situation. If this ruling were to become IRS policy, a surviving spouse would have a new planning opportunity—the option to leave a deceased's required distribution in the IRA for an extra year and gain additional tax deferral. But one private letter ruling does not a policy make. Until the IRS provides clear guidance, the threat of a

50% penalty (for failing to take a required distribution) will be a strong deterrent to experimenting with this strategy.

c. Commingling

Although a spouse is permitted to roll over a deceased person's retirement plan or IRA into an existing IRA of the spouse's own, it is generally not a good idea, for the reasons described in Chapter 7. Commingling would preclude any future rollover to a qualified plan belonging to the spouse. It might also force a spouse to use a disadvantageous distribution method on the combined assets when the beneficiaries of the commingled accounts are different.

d. Timing of Rollover

The tax regulations do not give your spouse a clear deadline for converting your retirement account to his or her own account after your death. We can draw some inferences, however, from the portion of the regulations that describes how your spouse can make the account his or her own. Recall that one method is for your spouse to roll over the account into his or her own name. Another is for your spouse simply to fail to take a timely required distribution on your behalf after your death.

Logic suggests that your spouse should be able to make the election at any time—even years after your death—as long as your spouse continues to take timely required distributions on your behalf for as long as the account remains in your name. In support of this viewpoint, IRS private letter rulings have allowed rollovers in the year of death, the year after and even two years after. No private letter rulings have yet disallowed a rollover because it occurred too many years after the participant's death.

As a practical matter, if a spouse is past age 59½ and intends to roll over a participant's retirement plan, there is nothing to be gained from waiting. If the spouse needs money, the spouse can take it freely from the IRA even after rolling it over, because there is no penalty for taking distributions after age 59½.

If the spouse is younger than age 59½, however, free use of the IRA funds could be dicey. Recall that one of the exceptions to the early distribution tax is a distribution to a beneficiary after the death of the original participant. (See Chapter 3 for more information on the early distribution tax.) But that particular exception is not available to a spouse after the spouse rolls over the deceased person's plan into an IRA in the spouse's name. Once it is rolled over, it is the spouse's IRA, and, because the spouse is still alive, the after-death exception does not apply. Thus, the spouse must generally postpone distributions until age 59½ to avoid the early distribution tax.

Consequently, if the spouse is younger than age 59½ and needs to use the retirement plan money to live on, the spouse might be better off leaving the plan in the name of the deceased so that the after-death exception can be used. The one disadvantage of this approach is that, according to at least one IRS private letter ruling, once a spouse invokes the after-death exception to the early distribution tax, the spouse forever forfeits the right to roll over the account into an IRA in the spouse's own name.

2. Non-Spouse as Beneficiary

A non-spouse beneficiary is never permitted to roll over a deceased person's retirement plan or IRA. Furthermore, the consequences are the same whether or not the deceased had passed his or her RBD at the time of death. Any rollover attempt will be a deemed distribution, and if the assets are actually deposited into an IRA in the beneficiary's name, the deposit will be considered an excess contribution to an IRA and subject to penalties if not withdrawn in a timely fashion.

The required distribution rules for a non-spouse beneficiary are easy to remember. The beneficiary simply leaves the retirement account in the name of the deceased and continues to take distributions using the method already established by the deceased (subject only to changes due to recalculation elections or the lifetime use of the MDIB table).

3. Trust as Beneficiary

If a trust is named beneficiary of a retirement plan or IRA, the rollover issues are precisely the same whether the participant dies before or after his or her RBD. (See Chapter 7 for a detailed discussion of these issues.)

4. Estate as Beneficiary

The IRS has frequently allowed a spouse to roll over the assets of a retirement plan into an IRA in the spouse's own name when an estate is named beneficiary of the plan and the spouse is the sole beneficiary of the estate. But the strategy is not sanctioned by the Tax Code or the Tax Regulations, so it remains risky.

IRS rulings save the day. It is quite charitable of the IRS to permit such rollovers. Because an estate does not qualify as a designated beneficiary, a participant is required to use his or her own single life expectancy when computing required distributions. This is true even if the spouse is beneficiary of the estate. There is no "look-through" rule for an estate as there is for certain qualified trusts. Consequently, if a participant names his or her estate and uses a recalculated life expectancy factor, then in the year after death, the factor goes to zero and the entire account must be distributed.

But if the spouse, as beneficiary of the estate, is permitted to roll over the assets, the income tax can be deferred and quite possibly reduced, because amounts can be distributed in smaller chunks over the spouse's life expectancy (or the joint life expectancy of the spouse and his or her beneficiary).

I. Annuities

If you die on or after your RBD and you had been receiving your retirement benefits as an annuity, the form of the annuity determines how the remaining benefit will be paid to your beneficiary. (See Chapter 6 for more information about types of annuities.) For example, the annuity might have been a joint and survivor annuity that must continue to pay your beneficiary the same benefits you were receiving. Or the annuity might have been a term certain annuity; if you survive only part of the term, your beneficiary receives payments for the remainder of the term.

If you began receiving an irrevocable annuity before your RBD, the start date of the annuity is treated as your RBD for purposes of identifying your designated beneficiary and determining if payments satisfy the required distribution rules. After your death, payments continue in accordance with the form of payment you established when you purchased the annuity.

J. Divorce or Separation

If you were divorced or separated during your lifetime, some or all of your retirement plan might be distributable to an "alternate payee" such as a spouse, former spouse or child, under the terms of a QDRO—a court-approved divorce or maintenance agreement. (See Chapter 2, Section C.4 for more information about QDROs.)

If so, then unless the alternate payee's share was distributed outright to the alternate payee, some portion of each distribution during your lifetime was payable to the alternate payee. That doesn't change when you die.

If you die after your RBD, payments from your account will continue to be computed using the method you elected on your RBD. If an alternate payee has been receiving a portion of each distribution, the alternate payee is entitled to his or her share of post-death distributions, as well.

EXAMPLE: On your RBD, you had designated your sister as the beneficiary of your retirement plan and elected not to recalculate your own life expectancy. Under the terms of a QDRO, your former spouse is entitled to half of your retirement plan, and you have been giving your former spouse 50% of each distribution. You die at the age of 72. After your death, distributions will continue to be based on the joint life expectancy of you and your sister, reduced by one each year until the account is emptied. Half of each distribution will go to your sister and half to your former spouse.

If the alternate payee is a non-spouse, he or she may never roll over a distribution from your retirement plan. However, a spouse or former spouse with an interest in your retirement plan under the terms of a QDRO has all the rights of a surviving spouse beneficiary. Thus, when you die, your former spouse may roll over any distribution he or she receives from your plan into an IRA or a retirement plan in his or her own name, provided the former spouse first takes a required distribution on your behalf for all years the account remains in your name, including the rollover year. If your former spouse has not yet reached his or her RBD, future required distributions may be deferred until that time.

A former spouse has special privileges. A surviving spouse can roll over a participant's distribution only into an IRA. A spouse or former spouse alternate, however, has the additional option of rolling over the distribution into a qualified plan in the spouse's or former spouse's own name—provided there is a QDRO in place.

Key Tax Code and Regulations Sections, IRS Pronouncements

§ 401(a)(9)
Required Distributions From Qualified Plans

§ 1.401(a)(9)
Required Distribution Regulations

§ 402(c)
Rollovers From Qualified Plans

§ 408
Individual Retirement Accounts

§ 1.408-8, A-5
Election by Spouse to Treat Decedent's IRA as Own

Rev. Proc. 89-52
After-Death IRA Reporting Requirements

Ann. 95-99
Employee Plans Examination Guidelines

Chapter 9

Roth IRAs

Who Should Read Chapter 9

➡️ Read this chapter if you have a Roth IRA, if you are considering opening one or if you would like to convert a traditional IRA to a Roth IRA.

*I*n its eternal quest for the most effective way to encourage people to save for retirement, Congress is now dangling before us one of the biggest sugarcoated carrots we've ever seen. It's called a Roth IRA, brought to us by the Taxpayer Relief Act of 1997. This new retirement plan is named after Senator William Roth, who vigorously supported the measure.

Congress designed the Roth IRA to be much like a traditional IRA, but with a few attractive modifications. When the modifications began to fill pages rather than paragraphs, the new creature was given its own section in the Tax Code—Section 408A. The new section begins with the statement that all the traditional IRA rules apply to Roth IRAs except as noted. This chapter focuses on the exceptions, with special attention to the unusual treatment of distributions.

The lure of the Roth IRA is powerful. Although contributions are not deductible (meaning they are made with after-tax dollars), all distributions, including the earnings on contributions, are potentially tax free—as will be explained in Section A, below.

Unfortunately, Roth IRAs don't work for everyone. Here's a summary of the key differences between traditional IRAs and Roth IRAs:

- You may make a contribution to a traditional IRA no matter how high your income is, as long as you have earned income (income from employment) and are under age 70½. But in the case of a Roth IRA, you may not make any contribution if your income exceeds a certain level. That level is $160,000 if you are married filing a joint return, $110,000 if you are single and $10,000 if you are married and filing a separate return from your spouse.

- No contribution to a traditional IRA is permitted after age 70½. However, you may continue to make contributions to a Roth IRA after age 70½, as long as you have earned income and your adjusted gross income doesn't exceed the limits described above.

- A contribution to a traditional IRA is always deductible if neither you nor your spouse is covered by a qualified plan. If even one of you is covered by a plan, the deduction is phased out as your income increases. On the other hand, no contribution to a Roth IRA is ever deductible, whether or not you are covered by another plan.

- Earnings that accumulate inside a traditional IRA are always subject to income tax when withdrawn. But earnings in a Roth IRA can be com-

Helpful Terms

Adjusted Gross Income (AGI). Total taxable income reduced by certain expenses such as qualified plan contributions, IRA contributions and alimony payments.

After-Tax Dollars. The amount of income left after all income taxes have been withheld or paid.

Beneficiary. The person or entity entitled to receive the benefits from insurance or from trust property, such as a retirement plan or IRA.

Deferral Period. The number of years over which distributions from a retirement plan or IRA can be spread.

Distribution. A payout of property (such as shares of stock) or cash from a retirement plan or IRA to the participant or a beneficiary.

Earned Income. Income received for providing goods or services. Earned income might be wages or salary or net profit from a business.

Nondeductible Contribution. A contribution to a retirement plan or IRA that may not be used as a business expense or an adjustment to offset taxable income on an income tax return.

Traditional IRA. Any contributory or rollover IRA that is not a Roth IRA or a SIMPLE IRA.

---

pletely tax free when distributed if certain requirements are satisfied. (See Section A, below.)

- If you have a traditional IRA, you must begin required distributions on or before your required beginning date—your RBD. If you have a Roth IRA, you are not required to withdraw any amount during your lifetime. (See Section D, below.)

The contrast between traditional IRAs and Roth IRAs is most stark in the treatment of distributions. The differences turn up not only in the ordinary income tax rules, but also in the application of the early distribution tax and the required distribution rules.

A. Taxation of Distributions

The income tax rules for traditional IRAs are straightforward. Generally, distributions are taxed as ordinary income unless they are rolled over into another retirement plan or IRA. If you made nondeductible (after-tax) contributions to your traditional IRA over the years, those amounts are not subject to tax when distributed. That's the good news. The bad news is that those after-tax contributions are deemed to come out pro rata—not all at once. In other words, the nondeductible portion of a traditional IRA comes out only as a part of each distribution you ever take from the IRA. Consequently, only a percentage of each distribution is tax free. (See Chapter 2, Section B.2, for more information about calculating the nontaxable portion of a distribution from a traditional IRA.)

The basic rule for Roth IRAs is similar: the taxable portion of any distribution must be included on your income tax return, and it will be taxed as ordinary income unless you roll it over. But that's where the similarity ends.

The key to squeezing the maximum benefit from a Roth IRA is to be aware of which distributions are taxable and which are not. Maintaining that vigilance is not difficult; you must simply view your Roth IRA as the sum of two distinct parts. One part consists of the contributions you have made. The second part consists of the earnings on those contributions, such as interest earned on bond investments or gains from stock sales.

1. Distribution of Nondeductible Contributions

The portion of your Roth IRA that consists of your contributions is never subject to income tax when it comes out. Never.

Even if you take it out the day after you put it in. That's because all contributions you made were nondeductible, which means you have already paid tax on the money. You don't have to pay tax a second time when you take it out. Fair is fair.

Furthermore, any distribution you take from a Roth IRA is presumed to be a return of your contributions until you have withdrawn all contributions you made to it over the years (or to all Roth IRAs, if you have more than one). In other words, all contributions are recovered before earnings are recovered. This simple rule gives the Roth IRA an advantage over a traditional IRA. It means you may retrieve your contributions whenever you want without incurring any income tax. In this way, the contributions can serve as an emergency fund.

EXAMPLE: Dain began making contributions to a Roth IRA in 1998, contributing $2,000 every year. By the end of the year 2001, the Roth IRA had grown to $11,000. Of that amount, $8,000 was from Dain's annual contributions and $3,000 was from investment returns. In 2002, Dain had an auto accident and totaled his car. Dain needed to purchase a new car but didn't have any resources other than his Roth IRA. In 2002, he withdrew $8,000 from his Roth IRA. The $8,000 is not subject to tax because Dain's distribution is deemed to be a return of his contributions.

2. Distribution of Investment Returns

When you contribute to an IRA, you ordinarily use the contributed funds to purchase investments that will earn money for you. For example, you might invest in bonds or CDs to generate interest. Or you might buy stock, hoping the price will shoot up so you can make a bundle on a later sale. As long as those earnings—the interest and the stock proceeds—stay inside the IRA, they are not taxed. But what happens when they come out? In the case of a traditional IRA, all of the earnings are subject to ordinary income tax. The advantage of the Roth IRA is that when you distribute earnings, they are tax free—even though they have never been taxed before—as long as the distribution is considered a "qualified" distribution.

a. Qualified Distributions

It will pay you handsomely to nail down the tax free advantage a Roth IRA offers.

All you have to do is follow a few simple rules. First, don't take a distribution of your investment returns for five years. A distribution within five calendar years of when you first establish a Roth IRA can never be a qualified distribution.

⚠ If you die before the five years are up. If you die before satisfying the five-year holding period, your beneficiary must wait until you would have satisfied it, or the distribution will not be qualified.

So, counting the year of your first contribution as year one, you will satisfy the five-year requirement if you wait until the sixth year before withdrawing any earnings.

EXAMPLE: Jessica opened a Roth IRA in June 1999 and made a $2,000 contribution in each of the years 1999 through 2002. At the end of 2002, her account was worth $15,000, of which $8,000 was from contributions and $7,000 was from investment earnings. In June 2003, Jessica withdrew $10,000 to pay for a trip to China. Of that amount, $8,000 is deemed to be from contributions and will not be subject to income tax. The remaining $2,000 is deemed to come from earnings. Because the distribution did not satisfy the five-year holding requirement, the $2,000 will be subject to income tax. (It might also be subject to an early distribution penalty. See Section B, below).

Although you are permitted to make a contribution to a Roth IRA after the end of the year (until April 15), the five-year holding period for a qualified distribution begins on the first day of the calendar year to which your very first contribution relates, which might be an earlier year than the one during which the contribution was actually made.

EXAMPLE: Soren wanted to set up a Roth IRA and make a contribution for 1998. He finally got around to doing so in February 1999, well before the April 15, 1999 deadline. Because the contribution is for 1998, Soren will count 1998 as year one when computing the five-year holding period, even though he didn't actually make the contribution until 1999.

Simply satisfying the five-year requirement will not automatically make a distribution "qualified." It must also be at least one of the following:

- a distribution you take after reaching age 59½
- a distribution you take after becoming disabled
- a distribution to your beneficiary or your estate after your death, or
- a distribution you take to purchase a first home (up to a lifetime withdrawal limit of $10,000).

If your distribution satisfies the five-year requirement and falls into one of the above categories, it will be qualified and thus entirely tax free.

 Remember, contributions are never subject to income tax when they come out of a Roth IRA. So even if they are part of a nonqualified distribution, they are tax free. Only the earnings will be taxed if they are part of a nonqualified distribution.

EXAMPLE: Lara began making contributions to a Roth IRA in 1998. By June 2000, she had accumulated $6,500. Of that amount, $6,000 was from contributions she made in the years 1998, 1999 and 2000. The remaining $500 was from earnings on her investments. In December 2000, Lara withdrew $6,200 from the IRA. The distribution is a nonqualified distribution because it occurred within five years of her initial contribution. Only $200 is subject to tax, however, because her contributions, which total $6,000, are deemed to come out first—they are never subject to tax.

 Municipal bonds offer another form of tax free investment. Typically, when you purchase municipal bonds, all of the interest you earn on the bonds is tax free. As an investment vehicle, a Roth IRA has two distinct advantages over a municipal bond. First, inside a Roth IRA, money can be invested in stocks and other diverse investments that are likely to yield a greater return over the long term than do municipal bonds. Second, although the interest on municipal bonds is tax free, you must be diligent about reinvesting the interest or you will soon have taxable income. For example, if you invest $10,000 in a municipal bond that pays 5% interest, you receive $500 of tax free interest during the year. But if you place that interest in a regular interest-bearing account or another investment that generates taxable income, the earnings on the $500 will be taxable. To ensure that all future earnings are tax free, you must reinvest in more municipal bonds, which might be difficult with only $500 of cash. Municipal bonds are rarely sold in increments of $500.

In contrast, all distributions from a Roth IRA are potentially tax free, whether you invest in stocks, corporate bonds or CDs. Thus, not only can you invest in a variety of securities, but also you won't have the same reinvestment concerns you would have if municipal bonds were your only investment option. For example, if you invest in a CD that generates $500 of interest income, you could reinvest in stocks, bonds or another CD.

b. Nonqualified Distributions

Any distribution from a Roth IRA that does not satisfy the requirements of a qualified distribution is automatically nonqualified. Nonqualified distributions are treated very much like traditional IRA distributions. The contributions you made will come out tax free, but the earnings are taxable. There is one critical difference, however: as mentioned above, the contributions you make to the Roth IRA (which were made with after-tax dollars) are presumed to come out first—before any earnings. This means if you must take a nonqualified distribution, some or all of it will escape income tax, as long as you have not previously withdrawn all of your contributions.

EXAMPLE: JJ has contributed $2,000 to a Roth IRA in each of the years 1998, 1999 and 2000. By June 2000, he had accumulated $7,000, of which $6,000 was from contributions and $1,000 was from earnings. In December, JJ withdrew $6,000 from his IRA. Although the distribution was nonqualified, the $6,000 was nontaxable because it was all attributable to his contributions. In April 2001, JJ contributed another $2,000 to his Roth IRA. By December, he had a total of $3,200 in the IRA. Only $2,000 was attributable to contributions because he had already withdrawn all contributions for prior years. The remaining $1,200 represented earnings. JJ decided to withdraw $3,000. The entire distribution is nonqualified, but the $2,000 attributable to contributions would be tax free. Only $1,000 of the distribution is attributable to earnings, and that portion will be subject to income tax.

3. Conversions and Rollovers

When you have a Roth IRA, your rollover opportunities are limited. You can roll over assets from a Roth IRA to another Roth IRA, or if you qualify, you can roll over—or convert—assets from a traditional IRA or a SEP IRA or SIMPLE IRA to a Roth IRA. No other rollovers or conversions involving Roth IRAs are permitted. For example, you may never roll over assets from a Roth IRA to a traditional IRA. (The rollover can go in only one direction—from a traditional IRA to a Roth IRA.) Also, you are not permitted to roll over a Roth IRA to a qualified plan or vice versa.

⚠ **SEP IRAs.** This section applies to SEP IRAs in exactly the same way. In other words, a SEP IRA can be converted to a Roth IRA.

⚠ **SIMPLE IRAs.** You can also convert a SIMPLE IRA to a Roth IRA, but only after two years from the date you first established a SIMPLE IRA. Before the two years have expired, the SIMPLE IRA is ineligible for conversion.

You can also convert your traditional IRA to a Roth IRA without rolling it over. You can simply instruct your custodian to change the title on the account to show that it is now a Roth IRA. Although the funds aren't technically moved from one account to another, you are deemed to have rolled over the assets from a traditional IRA to a Roth IRA. Whether you convert your traditional IRA by changing title or by rolling it over, the law identifies the assets as "converted" amounts, meaning they were once in a traditional IRA but are now in a Roth IRA. As explained in the paragraphs below, some special rules apply to converted amounts.

a. Rollover From Roth IRA

If you take a distribution from a Roth IRA with the intention of rolling it over, you may roll it over only to another Roth IRA. This is logical when you think about it. Distributions from Roth IRAs are all potentially tax free, whereas most, if not all, distributions from a traditional IRA or a qualified plan are taxable. If you were allowed to mix plans indiscriminately, the IRS would have a hard time tracking the source of the various distributions to determine which funds are taxable.

Except for the fact that you may only roll a Roth IRA to another Roth IRA, all the rules governing rollovers between IRAs apply to rollovers between Roth IRAs. (See Chapter 2, Section E, for more about IRA rollovers.) Among the most important of those rules are the following:

- Once you take a distribution from a Roth IRA, you have only 60 days to complete the rollover to another Roth IRA.
- You are permitted only one Roth-to-Roth rollover per year.

- Rollover distributions between IRAs are not subject to income tax withholding.

b. Rollover to Roth IRA

There are only two possible sources of a rollover to a Roth IRA. The rollover may come from another Roth IRA, or it may come from a traditional IRA. A Roth IRA may be rolled into another Roth IRA without any restrictions other than those that apply to rollovers between traditional IRAs, as described in the previous section. A rollover from a traditional IRA is called a conversion and is more complex.

c. Conversion to Roth IRA

If you want to convert assets from a traditional IRA to a Roth IRA, you must be eligible and you must face the consequences. First the consequences.

i. Consequences

If you determine that you are eligible to convert your traditional IRA to a Roth IRA (see Section ii, below), and if you elect to do so, you must pay the piper. Specifically, the entire amount of the conversion will be subject to income tax at ordinary rates. Congress wasn't about to wipe out all of those deferred taxes with one stroke of the pen. Once you've ponied up the money and converted the assets, however, all future distributions of the converted amounts will be free of income tax. Fur-

thermore, distributions of future earnings on converted amounts will be tax free as long as those distributions satisfy the five-year holding period and are qualified. (See Section 2.a, above, for information about qualified distributions.)

> EXAMPLE: In 1999, you convert your $20,000 traditional IRA to a Roth IRA. On your tax return for 1999, you include the $20,000 and pay tax on it. By 2005, your Roth IRA has grown to $35,000, and you withdraw $30,000 to throw yourself a 65th birthday party. The entire $30,000 distribution is tax free because you are over age 59½ and you have satisfied the five-year holding period.

Can you find non-IRA sources to pay the tax? The conversion of a traditional IRA to a Roth IRA can be a real boon to young investors who can pay the tax from non-IRA funds. These folks have years of tax free compounding ahead of them. However, if the tax is paid out of IRA funds, the advantage of the conversion declines and may even disappear altogether.

As a practical matter, it may be difficult for people with sizable traditional IRAs to convert the entire account to a Roth IRA unless they have large amounts of cash outside the IRA. Imagine paying regular income tax on a $100,000 IRA. In 2000, at the top federal income tax bracket, for example, you would have to come up with about $40,000. One way around this problem would be to convert the traditional IRA to a Roth IRA in bits and pieces over a number of years to keep the tax at a manageable level. Nothing in the law prevents you from converting part of your traditional IRA instead of the whole thing. Furthermore, there is no time limit on conversion. In fact, many people won't be able to qualify at all until retirement, when they no longer have a salary. As long as the law doesn't change, you can simply wait and convert some or all of your traditional IRA when you do qualify.

For older IRA participants, converting a traditional IRA to a Roth IRA is not necessarily the correct decision. If you must include a large IRA in income, some or all of it could easily be taxed at the maximum tax rate, and you might not recover from that financial outlay (through tax free compounded growth) before your death. If your primary concern is passing wealth to your beneficiaries, however, a conversion could save estate taxes and also give your beneficiaries an opportunity for additional tax free growth after your death.

The decision to convert or not to convert a traditional IRA to a Roth IRA can involve some complex calculations. You must factor in age, health, income and estate tax rates and investment returns. If you are young, healthy and able to pay the taxes with money outside the IRA, the rollover is likely to pay off for you.

If you are younger than 59½ and you elect to use some of the converted IRA to pay the tax, the portion that goes to taxes could be subject to the early distribution tax. (See Section B.2.b, below.)

ii. Eligibility

Even if it makes sense for you to convert a traditional IRA to a Roth IRA, you must determine whether you are eligible to do so. You are not eligible if either of the following is true:

- If your modified adjusted gross income (modified AGI) exceeds $100,000, you may not convert a traditional IRA to a Roth IRA. This income cap applies whether you are married or single.

  When calculating your modified AGI, you make the following adjustments to your regular AGI:

  1. exclude the converted amount from income

  2. add back income from U.S. savings bonds used for higher education expenses

  3. add back employer-paid adoption expenses

  4. add back excluded foreign earned income and payments received for foreign housing

  5. add back any deduction claimed for a regular IRA contribution, and

  6. add back the deduction for educational loan interest.

Remember, modified AGI is used only to determine if you qualify to convert. It is not used to compute your tax liability.

> **EXAMPLE:** Tyson's modified AGI for the year 2000 is $90,000. He has accumulated $25,000 in a traditional IRA and would like to convert it to a Roth IRA before the end of the year. Because Tyson's modified AGI (not including the $25,000 in his IRA) is under $100,000, he qualifies to convert his traditional IRA to a Roth IRA. On his tax return for the year 2000, he will report income of $115,000 (which is $90,000 plus $25,000).

 Note the income threshold for a conversion. To convert a traditional IRA to a Roth IRA, the income threshold is more restrictive than to make annual contributions to a Roth IRA. You may set up and contribute some amount to a Roth IRA as long as you have earnings from employment and your modified AGI does not exceed $160,000 (if you are filing a joint return) or $110,000 (if you are single). The conversion threshold, however, is only $100,000.

Another part of the Roth IRA law, which does not take effect until the year 2005, will also allow you to exclude from your modified AGI distributions you are required to take from your traditional IRA because you have passed age 70½. (See Chapter 5 for a summary of the required distribution rules.) But the required distribution may be excluded only for purposes of computing whether or not you qualify to convert your traditional IRA to a Roth IRA. You must still pay tax on it. And again, this benefit is not available until the year 2005.

> **EXAMPLE:** Nolan's income for the year 2007 includes $80,000 from interest and dividends and $30,000 in required distributions he must withdraw from his traditional IRA. Nolan plans to convert another $20,000 of his traditional IRA to a Roth IRA. Although the total income he must report on his tax return is $130,000 (which is $80,000 + $30,000 + 20,000), he still qualifies to convert the $20,000 from his traditional IRA because his income is under $100,000 when he excludes the required distribution and the converted amount.

 You are not permitted to roll over or convert a required distribution. Therefore, in the above example, Nolan's $30,000 required distribution must be placed in a regular account, not an IRA account of any kind. The $20,000 conversion amount must be an additional distribution from his traditional IRA—over and above the required amount of $30,000.

- You cannot convert any portion of a traditional IRA to a Roth IRA if you are a married person using the "married filing separate" status on your tax return (instead of "married filing joint"). Any person using the married filing separate status is automatically ineligible to convert a traditional IRA to a Roth IRA.

 Filing separately doesn't quite leave you out of the Roth IRA boon.
Although an individual who is married and filing a separate return may not convert a traditional IRA to a Roth IRA, he or she may still establish a Roth IRA—but only if his or her modified AGI does not exceed $10,000.

iii. Related Rules

If you decide to proceed with the conversion of a traditional IRA to a Roth IRA, you will find that Congress has built in a little tax relief for you.

- If you converted a traditional IRA into a Roth IRA before January 1, 1999, you were permitted to spread the income tax hit over four years, by including only 25% of the converted amount on your tax return in the years 1998 through 2001. To qualify for this tax relief, you must have elected to use the four-year spread by the due date for filing your 1998 tax return (or the extended due date if you requested and were granted an extension of time for filing your tax return).

If you made the election, beware of taking distributions from the account before the four years are up. If you do, you will lose some of the benefits of the deferral. Specifically, you will have to include in income not only the regular installment for the year but also the amount of the distribution—to the extent it is less than or equal to the remaining deferred amount.

EXAMPLE: Angie has $10,000 in a traditional IRA. Angie converts the IRA into a Roth IRA in 1998 and elects the four-year spread. As a result of the conversion, $2,500 is to be included in income each year for the next four years. She reports $2,500 for tax year 1998. At the beginning of 1999, the value of the account is $11,000 and Angie makes a withdrawal of $1,000, which she will use to celebrate her sixtieth birthday. For the 1999 tax year, Angie must include $3,500 as income on her tax return—the $2,500 regular installment under the four-year rule, plus the extra $1,000. In the year 2000 she will include the usual $2,500. But in 2001 she will be required to include only the remaining $1,500.

If you happen to die before paying all the tax, any remaining deferred amounts will be included on your final income tax return for the year of your death—unless your spouse is your beneficiary. In that case, your spouse may continue the four-year deferral, reporting the income in installments on his or her tax return for the remainder of the four years, just as you would have if you had survived.

- If you convert a traditional IRA to a Roth IRA, the conversion is ignored for purposes of the "one rollover per year" rule. (See Chapter 2, Section E.2, for more information about this rule.)

- Even if you are younger than 59½ when you convert a traditional IRA to a Roth IRA, the distribution will not be subject to the early distribution tax, as long as the entire taxable amount is rolled over. (Beware of using part of the rollover to pay income tax, though. See Section B.2.b, below.)

- For income tax purposes, distributions of converted amounts are treated like distributions of nondeductible contributions. The converted portion will not be subject to income tax when it is distributed in future years, but the earnings will be subject to tax unless they are part of a qualified distribution. (See Section A.2.a for the definition of a qualified distribution.)

4. Correcting Errors: Recharacterizing

If you convert a traditional IRA to a Roth IRA during the year and discover at the end of the year that your modified AGI was too high, you won't be in serious trouble. The law allows you to transfer the funds back out of the Roth IRA and into the same or even a different traditional IRA before the due date of your tax return (or the extended due date, if you request and receive an extension of time for filing your return). This is called a recharacterization. The proper approach is to have the custodian of the Roth IRA transfer the errant funds plus any investment earnings on those funds directly to the custodian of the traditional IRA. If this is all done in timely fashion, there will be no income tax or penalties.

If you recharacterize a converted amount—meaning you undo a conversion from a traditional IRA to a Roth IRA by putting the money back into a traditional IRA—you may not reconvert those funds to a Roth IRA until the following tax year or until 30 days have passed, if that period of time is longer. For example, if you recharacterize in June, you must wait until the next January to reconvert. If you recharacterize on December 31, you can reconvert on January 30 of the next year.

Roth IRA waiting periods. The waiting period for reconverting was added to the Roth IRA laws somewhat belatedly to quash a tax-saving maneuver that was spreading like wildfire. Smart taxpayers were converting and recharacterizing several times during a year to take advantage of dips in the market. When the market dips, the value of an IRA drops—and so does the tax cost of conversion.

> EXAMPLE: You converted your $100,000 traditional IRA to a Roth IRA in June. By November, the value of the assets had declined to $75,000. So under the old rules, you would be able to recharacterize the Roth IRA to a traditional IRA (transfer the assets back) and then reconvert before the end of the year. You would then pay tax on $75,000 instead.

B. Early Distribution Tax

Understanding how the early distribution tax applies to Roth IRAs is complicated by the fact that there are two types of distributions (qualified and nonqualified) and a special set of rules for converted amounts. (Early distribution tax rules for traditional IRAs and other retirement plans are discussed in Chapter 3.)

1. Qualified Distributions

Qualified distributions from Roth IRAs are not subject to the early distribution tax. It's as simple as that. This rule, too, has some logic to it. The early distribution tax applies only to distributions that are included in income—those that are required to be reported on your tax return. Because all qualified distributions from Roth IRAs are tax free, they are all exempt from the early distribution tax.

2. Nonqualified Distributions

Nonqualified distributions from Roth IRAs are treated in most respects like distributions from traditional IRAs. Any portion of the distribution that is required to be included on your income tax return is subject to the early distribution tax, unless the distribution qualifies for an exception. The exceptions for nonqualified distributions from Roth IRAs are the same as those for traditional IRA distributions. (See Chapter 3 for a detailed description of all the exceptions to the early distribution tax.) The key exceptions to the early distribution tax include distributions:

- after you reach age 59½
- because of your death or disability
- that are substantially equal periodic payments
- for certain medical expenses
- for certain health insurance

- for higher education expenses, or
- for a first home purchase (limited to $10,000).

a. Distributions of Nondeductible Contributions

Bear in mind that all of your nondeductible contributions to a Roth IRA will come out before any earnings. Because the contributions are nondeductible, they are not subject to tax when distributed, even if they are part of a nonqualified distribution. And because they are tax free and not includible on your income tax return, they automatically escape the early distribution tax. Any earnings that are distributed as part of a nonqualified distribution are subject to the early distribution tax, unless an exception applies.

Again, for planning purposes, this means you can take your contributions out of a Roth IRA at any time, and they will be subject neither to income tax nor to the early distribution tax.

> EXAMPLE: In 1998, you established a Roth IRA. You contributed $2,000 in 1998, 1999 and 2000. By November of the year 2001, the account had grown to $6,600. Finding yourself a little strapped for cash, you withdraw $4,000 from the account in late November. Because the distribution is less than your total contributions of $6,000, the $4,000 will not be subject to either income tax or the early distribution tax.

b. Distribution of Converted Amounts

A special rule exempts converted amounts from the early distribution tax in the year of the conversion, as long as the entire amount of the conversion goes into the Roth IRA. There are two ways to get caught by an early distribution tax when you convert a traditional IRA to a Roth IRA. You might use some of the converted amount to pay the income tax you owe on the conversion, or you might withdraw the converted amount too soon. But remember, the early distribution tax would never apply if you were older than 59½ at the time of the distribution (or if another exception, described in Chapter 3, applies).

i. Paying Income Tax With Converted Amounts

If you qualify to convert a traditional IRA to a Roth IRA (see Section A.3.b, above), the amount actually deposited into the Roth IRA will not be subject to an early distribution tax. Even though it is included on your tax return and you pay income tax on the converted amount, you are spared the early distribution tax if you roll over everything. But if you use some of the money from the traditional IRA to pay the income tax liability instead of rolling it over, the portion used for taxes will be subject to the early distribution tax—unless you are older than 59½ or another exception applies. (See Chapter 3 for more information about the early distribution tax and exceptions to the tax.)

ii. Withdrawing Converted Amounts Too Soon

Even though converted amounts in a Roth IRA are after-tax amounts (because you paid tax in the year of conversion), if you withdraw any converted dollars within five years, that portion of the distribution will be treated as though it is taxable—but only for purposes of determining the early distribution tax. (Recall that the early distribution tax generally does not apply to amounts that are excluded from your income for tax purposes. This is an exception to that rule.)

> EXAMPLE: You have a traditional IRA to which you have been making $2,000 deductible contributions each year. By the time you are 50, the account has grown to $15,000. You convert the IRA to a Roth IRA, paying tax on the entire $15,000. The following year, you withdraw $10,000 to bail your son out of jail. Because you are younger than 59½ and you withdrew the $10,000 within five years of converting your traditional IRA to a Roth IRA, you must pay an early distribution tax of $1,000 ($10,000 x 10%). You will not owe regular income tax on the $10,000.

The portion of a distribution that is subject to the early distribution tax is limited to the amount that you included in your taxable income and reported on your tax return in the year of conversion.

> EXAMPLE: You have a traditional IRA to which you have made deductible contributions of $4,000 and nondeductible (after-tax) contributions of $6,000. By the time you are 51, the account has grown to $17,000. You convert the IRA to a Roth IRA, paying tax on $11,000. (You don't have to pay tax on the $6,000 of nondeductible contributions.) The next year, when you are 52, you withdraw $17,000 to help your daughter start a new business. You must pay an early distribution tax on the $11,000, because that is the amount that was included on your income tax return in the year of conversion. The early distribution tax is $1,100 ($11,000 x 10%).

How the earnings are treated. The earnings on converted amounts are treated exactly the same as earnings on contributory amounts. Only qualified distributions of earnings escape the early distribution tax, unless another early distribution tax exception applies.

C. Ordering of Distributions

You might think you should be able to pick and choose which amounts come out of your Roth IRA first. For example, if you take a distribution before the five-year holding period is up, you would want to take your contributions first, because they are not subject to tax or penalties. Or if you converted one of your traditional IRAs six years ago and another two years ago, you would want to take a distribution from the one that was converted six years ago, because those converted amounts satisfy the five-year holding period and would not be subject to an early distribution tax.

Sadly, you cannot pick and choose the origin of each distribution you take. But serendipitously, the ordering rules you are required to use are quite favorable. Distributions are deemed to come out in the following order:

- Regular Roth IRA contributions are distributed first.
- Next are converted amounts, starting with the amounts first converted. If you converted a traditional IRA containing both taxable and nontaxable amounts (for example, if you had made deductible and nondeductible contributions), the taxable portion is deemed to come out first.
- Earnings come out last.

The benefits can be dramatic. For example, if you take a distribution before the five-year holding period is up or if you fail to satisfy the other requirements of a qualified distribution, the withdrawal still won't be subject to the early distribution tax as long as you have taken less than the total amount of all contributions you have made to all your Roth IRAs. Note that for purposes of these ordering rules, all Roth IRAs are considered a single Roth IRA.

EXAMPLE: You have two traditional IRAs: IRA #1 and IRA #2. In 1998, you convert IRA #1, then valued at $10,000, to a Roth IRA. In 2002, you convert IRA #2, valued at $20,000, to a Roth IRA. You also have a separate contributory Roth IRA, which you established in 1998 and to which you have been making annual contributions of $2,000. By 2006, the contributory Roth IRA has grown to $15,000—$8,000 of contributions and $7,000 of earnings. In November 2006, on your 40th birthday, you withdraw $25,000 to pay for your trip to India. The source of the distribution is deemed to be:

- $8,000 from Roth IRA contributions
- $10,000 from the oldest converted amount (IRA #1)
- $7,000 from the next oldest converted amount (IRA #2).

The $8,000 of contributions are not subject to either income tax or the early distribution tax because they are all from nondeductible after-tax contributions. The $10,000 deemed to be from IRA #1 is also not subject to either income tax (which you already paid in the year of conversion) or the early distribution tax (because the conversion occurred more than five years before). The remaining $7,000 will not be subject to income tax, because it was converted from a traditional IRA and you already paid tax on it in 2002. However, it will be subject to an early distribution tax of $700 (10% of $7,000), because it was distributed within five years of the conversion and you are under age 59½.

D. Required Distributions

The required distribution rules—those that will eventually force you to start taking money out of your retirement plan or your traditional IRA—have a broad reach. (See Chapter 5 for a summary of the required distribution rules.) They apply to IRAs, qualified plans, plans that behave like qualified plans and even some nonqualified plans. But as broad as that reach is, a significant exception has been carved out for Roth IRAs.

1. During Your Lifetime

During your lifetime, you are not required to take distributions from a Roth IRA. Ever. In fact, you could die without ever having removed a cent. This rule, which allows Roth IRA participants to accumulate a tax-favored nest egg and then simply pass it on to another generation, seems to conflict with the government's long-standing policy to ensure that tax-favored retirement plans primarily benefit the original participant.

But there is a logical, if cynical, explanation. Because the Roth IRA was structured

to allow all qualified distributions to be tax free, the government has no real incentive to force distributions. There are no deferred taxes to collect. So much for public policy.

2. After Your Death, Before Your RBD

Once you die, the distribution rules for Roth IRAs again merge with those for traditional IRAs. All of the post-death required distribution rules apply to Roth IRAs in the same way they apply to traditional IRAs. Thus, if you die before your RBD, the life expectancy rule or the five-year rule will apply. Those rules, as well as other required distribution rules that kick in if you die before your RBD, are explained in Chapter 7.

3. After Your Death, After Your RBD

If you have a traditional IRA, you must begin required distributions when you reach your required beginning date or RBD. If you die after your RBD, a special set of distribution rules applies. (See Chapter 8.) But because you are not required to take distributions from a Roth IRA during your lifetime, you have no RBD for that purpose. Consequently, it is irrelevant whether you die before or after your RBD (or the date that would be your RBD for traditional IRA purposes). Instead, the life expectancy rule or the five-year rule (explained in Chapter 7) will apply to Roth IRA distributions, regardless of when you die.

 Roth IRAs can be a boon to your beneficiaries. Although the post-death required distribution rules for traditional IRAs are essentially the same as those for Roth IRAs, the planning implications could be quite different. Because distributions to beneficiaries from a Roth IRA are not subject to income tax, beneficiaries have access to 100% of the funds when the IRA participant dies (unless some of it must be used to pay death taxes). For this reason, there will undoubtedly be a real temptation for beneficiaries to take distribution of their shares immediately upon the participant's death. Free money. But because assets inside the Roth IRA could continue to grow tax free, it is usually to the beneficiary's advantage to defer distributions for as long as possible.

Key Tax Code and Regulations Sections

§ 72(t)
Early Distribution Tax and Exceptions

§ 72(t)(2)(F)
First Home-Purchase Exception to Early Distribution Tax

§ 401(a)(9)
Required Distributions From Qualified Plans

§ 1.401(a)(9)
Required Distribution Regulations

§ 408A
Roth IRAs

§ 1.408A
Roth IRA Regulations

Appendix A

IRS Forms, Notices and Schedules

Form **4972**

Tax on Lump-Sum Distributions

(From Qualified Retirement Plans of Plan Participants Born Before 1936)

► Attach to Form 1040 or Form 1041.   ► See instructions.

Department of the Treasury
Internal Revenue Service (99)

OMB No. 1545-0193

2000

Attachment
Sequence No. **28**

Name of recipient of distribution

Identifying number

Part I	**Complete this part to see if you qualify to use Form 4972**		Yes	No
1	Was this a distribution of a plan participant's entire balance from all of an employer's qualified plans of one kind (pension, profit-sharing, or stock bonus)? If "No," **do not** use this form	1		
2	Did you roll over any part of the distribution? If "Yes," **do not** use this form	2		
3	Was this distribution paid to you as a beneficiary of a plan participant who was born before 1936? . . .	3		
4	Were you **(a)** a plan participant who received this distribution, **(b)** born before 1936, **and (c)** a participant in the plan for at least 5 years before the year of the distribution?	4		
	If you answered "No" to both questions 3 **and** 4, **do not** use this form.			
5a	Did you use Form 4972 after 1986 for a previous distribution from your own plan? If "Yes," **do not** use this form for a 2000 distribution from your own plan	5a		
b	If you are receiving this distribution as a beneficiary of a plan participant who died, did you use Form 4972 for a previous distribution received for that plan participant after 1986? If "Yes," **do not** use the form for this distribution	5b		

Part II	**Complete this part to choose the 20% capital gain election** (see instructions)		
6	Capital gain part from box 3 of Form 1099-R	6	
7	Multiply line 6 by 20% (.20) . . . . ►	7	
	If you also choose to use Part III, go to line 8. Otherwise, include the amount from line 7 in the total on Form 1040, line 40, or Form 1041, Schedule G, line 1b, whichever applies.		

Part III	**Complete this part to choose the 10-year tax option** (see instructions)			
8	Ordinary income from Form 1099-R, box 2a minus box 3. If you did not complete Part II, enter the taxable amount from box 2a of Form 1099-R	8		
9	Death benefit exclusion for a beneficiary of a plan participant who died before August 21, 1996	9		
10	Total taxable amount. Subtract line 9 from line 8	10		
11	Current actuarial value of annuity (from Form 1099-R, box 8). If none, enter -0-	11		
12	Adjusted total taxable amount. Add lines 10 and 11. If this amount is $70,000 or more, **skip** lines 13 through 16, enter this amount on line 17, and go to line 18	12		
13	Multiply line 12 by 50% (.50), but **do not** enter more than $10,000 .	13			
14	Subtract $20,000 from line 12. If line 12 is $20,000 or less, enter -0-	14			
15	Multiply line 14 by 20% (.20)	15			
16	Minimum distribution allowance. Subtract line 15 from line 13	16		
17	Subtract line 16 from line 12	17		
18	Federal estate tax attributable to lump-sum distribution	18		
19	Subtract line 18 from line 17. If line 11 is zero, **skip** lines 20 through 22 and go to line 23 . .	19		
20	Divide line 11 by line 12 and enter the result as a decimal (rounded to at least four places)	20	.	
21	Multiply line 16 by the decimal on line 20	21		
22	Subtract line 21 from line 11	22		
23	Multiply line 19 by 10% (.10)	23		
24	Tax on amount on line 23. Use the Tax Rate Schedule in the instructions	24		
25	Multiply line 24 by ten (10). If line 11 is zero, **skip** lines 26 through 28, enter this amount on line 29, and go to line 30	25		
26	Multiply line 22 by 10% (.10)	26		
27	Tax on amount on line 26. Use the Tax Rate Schedule in the instructions	27		
28	Multiply line 27 by ten (10) . . . . ►	28		
29	Subtract line 28 from line 25. (Multiple recipients, see instructions.) . . . . ►	29		
30	**Tax on lump-sum distribution.** Add lines 7 and 29. Also include this amount in the total on Form 1040, line 40, or Form 1041, Schedule G, line 1b, whichever applies . . . . . ►	30		

For Paperwork Reduction Act Notice, see instructions.

Cat. No. 13187U

Form **4972** (2000)

General Instructions

Section references are to the Internal Revenue Code.

Purpose of Form

Use Form 4972 to figure the tax on a qualified lump-sum distribution (defined below) you received in 2000 using the 20% capital gain election, the 10-year tax option, or both. These are special formulas used to figure a separate tax on the distribution.

You pay the tax **only once,** for the year you receive the distribution, not over the next 10 years. The separate tax is added to the regular tax figured on your other income. Using these special formulas may result in a **smaller** tax than you would pay if you reported the taxable amount of the distribution as ordinary income.

Related Publications

Pub. 575, Pension and Annuity Income

Pub. 721, Tax Guide to U.S. Civil Service Retirement Benefits

Pub. 939, General Rule for Pensions and Annuities

What Is a Qualified Lump-Sum Distribution?

It is the distribution or payment in 1 tax year of a plan participant's entire balance from all of the employer's qualified plans of one kind (for example, pension, profit-sharing, or stock bonus plans) in which the participant had funds. The participant's entire balance does not include deductible voluntary employee contributions or certain forfeited amounts. The participant **must** have been born before 1936.

Distributions upon death of the participant. If you received a qualifying distribution as a beneficiary after the plan participant's death, the participant must have been born before 1936 for you to use this form for that distribution.

Distributions to alternate payees. If you are the spouse or former spouse of a plan participant who was born before 1936 and you received a qualified lump-sum distribution as an alternate payee under a qualified domestic relations order, you can use Form 4972 to make the 20% capital gain election and use the 10-year tax option to figure your tax on the distribution.

See **How To Report the Distribution** on this page.

Distributions That Do Not Qualify for the 20% Capital Gain Election or the 10-Year Tax Option

The following distributions are not qualified lump-sum distributions and **do not** qualify for the 20% capital gain election or the 10-year tax option.

1. Any distribution that is partially rolled over to another qualified plan or an IRA.

2. Any distribution if an earlier election to use either the 5- or 10-year tax option had been made after 1986 for the same plan participant.

3. U.S. Retirement Plan Bonds distributed with the lump sum.

4. Any distribution made during the first 5 tax years that the participant was in the plan, unless it was paid because the participant died.

5. The current actuarial value of any annuity contract included in the lump sum (the payer's statement should show this amount, which you use only to figure tax on the ordinary income part of the distribution).

6. Any distribution to a 5% owner that is subject to penalties under section 72(m)(5)(A).

7. A distribution from an IRA.

8. A distribution from a tax-sheltered annuity (section 403(b) plan).

9. A distribution of the redemption proceeds of bonds rolled over tax free to a qualified pension plan, etc., from a qualified bond purchase plan.

10. A distribution from a qualified plan if the participant or his or her surviving spouse previously received an eligible rollover distribution from the same plan (or another plan of the employer that must be combined with that plan for the lump-sum distribution rules) and the previous distribution was rolled over tax free to another qualified plan or an IRA.

11. A corrective distribution of excess deferrals, excess contributions, excess aggregate contributions, or excess annual additions.

12. A lump-sum credit or payment from the Federal Civil Service Retirement System (or the Federal Employees Retirement System).

How To Report the Distribution

If you qualify to use Form 4972, attach it to Form 1040 (individuals) or Form 1041 (estates or trusts). The payer should have given you a Form 1099-R or other statement that shows the separate amounts to use in completing the form. The following choices are available.

20% capital gain election. If there is an amount in Form 1099-R, box 3, you can use Part II of Form 4972 to apply a 20% tax rate to the capital gain portion. See **Capital Gain Election** on this page.

10-year tax option. You can use Part III to figure your tax on the lump-sum distribution using the 10-year tax option whether or not you make the 20% capital gain election.

Where to report. Report amounts from your Form 1099-R either directly on your tax return (Form 1040 or 1041) or on Form 4972.

• If you do **not** use **any** part of Form 4972, report the entire amount from Form 1099-R, box 1 (Gross distribution), on Form 1040, line 16a, and the taxable amount on line 16b (or on Form 1041, line 8). If your pension or annuity is fully taxable, enter the amount from Form 1099-R, box 2a (Taxable amount), on Form 1040, line 16b; **do not** make an entry on line 16a.

• If you do **not** use Part III of Form 4972, but you do use Part II, report only the ordinary income portion of the distribution on Form 1040, lines 16a and 16b (or on Form 1041, line 8). The ordinary income portion is the amount in Form 1099-R, box 2a, minus the amount in box 3 of that form.

• If you use Part III of Form 4972, do not include any part of the distribution on Form 1040, lines 16a and 16b (or on Form 1041, line 8).

The entries in other boxes on Form 1099-R may also apply in completing Form 4972.

• Box 6 (Net unrealized appreciation in employer's securities). See **Net unrealized appreciation (NUA)** on page 3.

• Box 8 (Other). Current actuarial value of an annuity.

If applicable, get the amount of Federal estate tax paid attributable to the taxable part of the lump-sum distribution from the administrator of the deceased's estate.

How Often You May Use Form 4972

After 1986, you may use Form 4972 only once for each plan participant. If you receive more than one lump-sum distribution for the same plan participant in 1 tax year, you must treat all those distributions the same way. Combine them on a single Form 4972.

If you make an election as a beneficiary of a deceased participant, it does not affect any election you can make for qualified lump-sum distributions from your own plan. You can also make an election as the beneficiary of more than one qualifying person.

Example. Your mother and father died and each was born before 1936. Each had a qualified plan of which you are the beneficiary. You also received a qualified lump-sum distribution from your own plan and you were born before 1936. You may make an election for each of the distributions: one for yourself, one as your mother's beneficiary, and one as your father's. It does not matter if the distributions all occur in the same year or in different years. File a separate Form 4972 for each participant's distribution.

Note: *An earlier election on Form 4972 or Form 5544 for a distribution before 1987 does not prevent you from making an election for a distribution after 1986 for the same plan participant, provided the participant was under age 59½ at the time of the pre-1987 distribution.*

When You May File Form 4972

You can file Form 4972 with either an original or amended return. Generally, you have 3 years from the later of the due date of your tax return or the date you filed your return to choose to use any part of Form 4972.

Capital Gain Election

If the distribution includes a capital gain, you can **(a)** make the 20% capital gain election in Part II of Form 4972 or **(b)** treat the capital gain as ordinary income.

Only the taxable amount of distributions resulting from pre-1974 participation qualifies for capital gain treatment. The capital gain amount should be shown in Form 1099-R, box 3. If there is an amount in Form 1099-R, box 6 (net unrealized appreciation (NUA)), part of it may also qualify for capital gain treatment. Use the NUA Worksheet on page 3 to figure the capital gain part of NUA if you make the election to include NUA in your taxable income.

Form 4972 (2000)

You may report the ordinary income portion of the distribution on Form 1040, line 16b (or Form 1041, line 8) or you may figure the tax using the 10-year tax option. The ordinary income portion is the difference between Form 1099-R, box 3, and Form 1099-R, box 2a.

Net unrealized appreciation (NUA). Normally, the NUA in employer securities received as part of a lump-sum distribution is not taxable until the securities are sold. However, you can elect to include NUA in taxable income in the year received.

The total amount to report as NUA should be shown in Form 1099-R, box 6. Part of the amount in box 6 will qualify for capital gain treatment if there is an amount in Form 1099-R, box 3. To figure the total amount subject to capital gain treatment including the NUA, complete the NUA Worksheet on this page.

Specific Instructions

Name of recipient of distribution and identifying number. At the top of Form 4972, fill in the name and identifying number of the recipient of the distribution.

If you received more than one qualified distribution in 2000 for the same plan participant, add them and figure the tax on the total amount. If you received qualified distributions in 2000 for more than one participant, file a separate Form 4972 for the distributions of each participant.

If you and your spouse are filing a joint return and each has received a lump-sum distribution, complete and file a separate Form 4972 for each spouse's election, combine the tax, and include the combined tax in the total on Form 1040, line 40.

If you are filing for a trust that shared the distribution only with other trusts, figure the tax on the total lump sum first. The trusts then share the tax in the same proportion that they shared the distribution.

Multiple recipients of a lump-sum distribution. If you shared in a lump-sum distribution from a qualified retirement plan when not all recipients were trusts (a percentage will be shown in Form 1099-R, boxes 8 and/or 9a), figure your tax on Form 4972 as follows.

Step 1. Complete Form 4972, Parts I and II. If you make the 20% capital gain election in Part II and also elect to include NUA in taxable income, see **Net unrealized appreciation (NUA)** on this page to determine the amount of NUA that qualifies for capital gain treatment.

Step 2. Use this step **only if you do not elect to include NUA** in your taxable income or if you do not have NUA. If you elect to include NUA in taxable income, skip Step 2 and go to Step 3. (Box numbers used below are all from Form 1099-R.)

1. If you are not making the capital gain election, divide the amount in box 2a by your percentage of distribution in box 9a. Enter this amount on Form 4972, line 8.

2. If you are making the capital gain election, subtract the amount in box 3 from the amount in box 2a. Divide the result by your percentage of distribution in box 9a. Enter the result on Form 4972, line 8.

3. Divide the amount in box 8 by the percentage in box 8. Enter the result on Form 4972, line 11.

Step 3. Use this step **only if you elect to include NUA** in your taxable income.

1. If you are not making the capital gain election, add the amount in box 2a to the amount in box 6. Divide the result by your percentage of distribution in box 9a. Enter the result on Form 4972, line 8.

2. If you are making the capital gain election, subtract the amount in box 3 from the amount in box 2a. Add to the result the amount from line F of your NUA Worksheet. Then divide the total by your percentage of distribution in box 9a. Enter the result on Form 4972, line 8.

3. Divide the amount in box 8 by the percentage in box 8. Enter the result on Form 4972, line 11.

Step 4. Complete Form 4972 through line 28.

Step 5. Complete the following worksheet to figure the entry for line 29:

A. Subtract line 28 from line 25 .	_____
B. Enter your percentage of distribution from Form 1099-R, box 9a.	_____
C. Multiply line A by line B. Enter here and on line 29. Also, write "MRD" on the dotted line next to the entry space.	_____

NUA Worksheet (keep for your records)

A. Enter the amount from Form 1099-R, box 3 . . . . **A.** _____

B. Enter the amount from Form 1099-R, box 2a . . . . **B.** _____

C. Divide line A by line B and enter the result as a decimal (rounded to at least three places) . . . . **C.** _____

D. Enter the amount from Form 1099-R, box 6 . . . . **D.** _____

E. Capital gain portion of NUA. Multiply line C by line D . . . . . **E.** _____

F. Ordinary income portion of NUA. Subtract line E from line D . . . **F.** _____

G. Total capital gain portion of distribution. Add lines A and E. Enter here and on Form 4972, line 6. On the dotted line next to line 6, write "NUA" and the amount from line E above. . . . . **G.** _____

Death Benefit Worksheet (keep for your records)

A. Enter the amount from Form 1099-R, box 3, or, if you are including NUA in taxable income, the amount from line G of the NUA Worksheet **A.** _____

B. Enter the amount from Form 1099-R, box 2a, plus, if you are including NUA in taxable income, the amount from Form 1099-R, box 6 . . . **B.** _____

C. Divide line A by line B and enter the result as a decimal (rounded to at least three places) . . . . **C.** _____

D. Enter your share of the death benefit exclusion* . . . . **D.** _____

E. Multiply line D by line C . . . . **E.** _____

F. Subtract line E from line A. Enter here and on Form 4972, line 6 . . **F.** _____

*Applies only for participants who died before August 21, 1996. If there are multiple recipients of the distribution, the $5,000 maximum death benefit exclusion must be allocated among the recipients in the same proportion that they share the distribution.

Part II

See **Capital Gain Election** on page 2 before completing Part II.

Line 6. Leave this line blank if your distribution does not include a capital gain amount **or** you are not making the 20% capital gain election, and go to Part III.

Generally, enter on line 6 the amount from Form 1099-R, box 3. However, if you elect to include NUA in your taxable income, use the NUA Worksheet on this page to figure the amount to enter. If you are taking a **death benefit exclusion** (for a participant who died before August 21, 1996), use the Death Benefit Worksheet on this page to figure the amount to enter on line 6. The remaining allowable death benefit exclusion should be entered on line 9 if you choose the 10-year tax option. See the instructions for line 9.

If any Federal estate tax was paid on the lump-sum distribution, you must decrease the capital gain amount by the amount of estate tax applicable to it. To figure the amount, multiply the total Federal estate tax paid on the lump-sum distribution by the decimal from line C of the Death Benefit Worksheet. The result is the portion of the Federal estate tax applicable to the capital gain amount. Then use that result to reduce the amount in Form 1099-R, box 3, if you don't take the death benefit exclusion, or reduce line F of the Death Benefit Worksheet if you do. Enter the remaining capital gain on line 6. If you elected to include NUA in taxable income, subtract the portion of Federal estate tax applicable to the capital gain amount from the amount on line G of the NUA Worksheet. Enter the result on line 6. Enter the remainder of the Federal estate tax on line 18.

Note: If you take the death benefit exclusion *and* Federal estate tax was paid on the capital gain amount, the capital gain amount must be reduced by both the procedures on page 3 to figure the correct entry for line 6.

Part III

Line 8. If the payer of the distribution left box 2a (Taxable amount) of Form 1099-R blank, you must first figure the taxable amount. For details on how to do this, see Pub. 575.

If you **made the 20% capital gain election,** enter only the ordinary income from Form 1099-R on this line. To figure this amount, subtract Form 1099-R, box 3, from Form 1099-R, box 2a. Enter the result on line 8. Add to that result the amount from line F of the NUA Worksheet if you included NUA capital gain in the 20% capital gain election.

If you **did not make the 20% capital gain election** and did not elect to include NUA in taxable income, enter the amount from Form 1099-R, box 2a. If you did not make the 20% capital gain election but did elect to include NUA in your taxable income, add the amount from Form 1099-R, box 2a, to the amount from Form 1099-R, box 6. Enter the total on line 8. On the dotted line next to line 8, write "NUA" and the amount of NUA included.

Note: Community property laws do not apply in figuring tax on the amount you report on line 8.

Line 9. If you received the distribution because of the plan participant's death and the participant died before August 21, 1996, you may be able to exclude up to $5,000 of the lump sum from your gross income. If there are multiple recipients of the distribution not all of whom are trusts, enter on line 9 the full remaining allowable death benefit exclusion (after the amount taken against the capital gain portion of the distribution by all recipients—see the instructions for line 6) without allocation among the recipients. (The exclusion is in effect allocated among the recipients through the computation under

Multiple recipients of a lump-sum distribution on page 3.) This exclusion applies to the beneficiaries or estates of common-law employees, self-employed individuals, and shareholder-employees who owned more than 2% of the stock of an S corporation. Pub. 575 gives more information about the death benefit exclusion.

Enter the death benefit exclusion on line 9. But see the instructions for line 6 if you made a capital gain election.

Line 18. A beneficiary who receives a lump-sum distribution because of a plan participant's death must reduce the taxable part of the distribution by any Federal estate tax paid on the lump-sum distribution. Do this by entering on line 18 the Federal estate tax attributable to the lump-sum distribution. Also see the instructions for line 6.

Lines 24 and 27. Use the following tax rate schedule to complete lines 24 and 27.

Tax Rate Schedule

If the amount on line 23 or 26 is:		Enter on line 24 or 27:	
Over	But not over—		Of the amount over—
$ 0	$1,190	- - - - - 11%	$ 0
1,190	2,270	$130.90 + 12%	1,190
2,270	4,530	260.50 + 14%	2,270
4,530	6,690	576.90 + 15%	4,530
6,690	9,170	900.90 + 16%	6,690
9,170	11,440	1,297.70 + 18%	9,170
11,440	13,710	1,706.30 + 20%	11,440
13,710	17,160	2,160.30 + 23%	13,710
17,160	22,880	2,953.80 + 26%	17,160
22,880	28,600	4,441.00 + 30%	22,880
28,600	34,320	6,157.00 + 34%	28,600
34,320	42,300	8,101.80 + 38%	34,320
42,300	57,190	11,134.20 + 42%	42,300
57,190	85,790	17,388.00 + 48%	57,190
85,790	- - - - -	31,116.00 + 50%	85,790

Paperwork Reduction Act Notice. We ask for the information on this form to carry out the Internal Revenue laws of the United States. You are required to give us the information. We need it to ensure that you are complying with these laws and to allow us to figure and collect the right amount of tax.

You are not required to provide the information requested on a form that is subject to the Paperwork Reduction Act unless the form displays a valid OMB control number. Books or records relating to a form or its instructions must be retained as long as their contents may become material in the administration of any Internal Revenue law. Generally, tax returns and return information are confidential, as required by section 6103.

The time needed to complete this form will vary depending on individual circumstances. The estimated average time is:

Recordkeeping	52 min.
Learning about the law or the form	20 min.
Preparing the form . . .	1 hr., 11 min.
Copying, assembling, and sending the form to the IRS	20 min.

If you have comments concerning the accuracy of these time estimates or suggestions for making this form simpler, we would be happy to hear from you. See the instructions for the tax return with which this form is filed.

Tax Rate Schedule for 1986

If the amount on line 30 or 33 is:		Enter on line 31 or 34:			
Over—	But not over—	Amount		Plus percentage	Of the amount over—
$0	$1,190	- - - - - -		11%	$0
1,190	2,270	$130.90	+	12%	1,190
2,270	4,530	260.50	+	14%	2,270
4,530	6,690	576.90	+	15%	4,530
6,690	9,170	900.90	+	16%	6,690
9,170	11,440	1,297.70	+	18%	9,170
11,440	13,710	1,706.30	+	20%	11,440
13,710	17,160	2,160.30	+	23%	13,710
17,160	22,880	2,953.80	+	26%	17,160
22,880	28,600	4,441.00	+	30%	22,880
28,600	34,320	6,157.00	+	34%	28,600
34,320	42,300	8,101.80	+	38%	34,320
42,300	57,190	11,134.20	+	42%	42,300
57,190	85,790	17,388.00	+	48%	57,190
85,790	- - - - -	31,116.00	+	50%	85,790

Form **5329**

Department of the Treasury
Internal Revenue Service

**Additional Taxes Attributable to IRAs,
Other Qualified Retirement Plans, Annuities,
Modified Endowment Contracts, and MSAs**
(Under Sections 72, 530, 4973, and 4974 of the Internal Revenue Code)
▶ Attach to Form 1040.   ▶ See separate instructions.

OMB No. 1545-0203

2000

Attachment
Sequence No. **29**

Name of individual subject to additional tax. (If married filing jointly, see page 2 of the instructions.) | **Your social security number**

**Fill in Your Address Only
If You Are Filing This
Form by Itself and Not
With Your Tax Return**

Home address (number and street), or P.O. box if mail is not delivered to your home | Apt. no.

City, town or post office, state, and ZIP code | If this is an amended return, check here ▶ ☐

If you **only** owe the 10% tax on early distributions, you may be able to report this tax directly on Form 1040 without filing Form 5329. See **Who Must File** on page 1 of the instructions.

Part I   **Tax on Early Distributions**

Complete this part if a taxable distribution was made from your qualified retirement plan (including an IRA other than an education IRA), annuity contract, or modified endowment contract before you reached age 59½. If you received a Form 1099-R that incorrectly indicates an early distribution (with no known exception to the additional tax) or you received a Roth IRA distribution, you also may have to complete this part. See page 2 of the instructions.
Note: *You must include the taxable amount of the distribution on Form 1040, line 15b or 16b.*

1	Early distributions included in gross income. For Roth IRA distributions, see page 2 of the instructions	**1**	
2	Early distributions not subject to additional tax. Enter the appropriate exception number from page 2 of the instructions: _____	**2**	
3	Amount subject to additional tax. Subtract line 2 from line 1	**3**	
4	**Tax due.** Enter 10% (.10) of line 3. Also include this amount on Form 1040, line 54 . . .	**4**	
	Caution: *If any part of the amount on line 3 was a distribution from a SIMPLE retirement plan, you may have to include 25% of that amount on line 4 instead of 10%. See page 3 of the instructions.*		

Part II   **Tax on Certain Taxable Distributions From Education (Ed) IRAs**

Complete this part if you had a taxable amount on Form 8606, line 30.
Note: *You must include the taxable amount of the distribution on Form 1040, line 15b.*

5	Taxable distributions from your Ed IRAs, from Form 8606, line 30	**5**	
6	Taxable distributions not subject to additional tax. See page 3 of the instructions	**6**	
7	Amount subject to additional tax. Subtract line 6 from line 5	**7**	
8	**Tax due.** Enter 10% (.10) of line 7. Also include this amount on Form 1040, line 54	**8**	

Part III   **Tax on Excess Contributions to Traditional IRAs**

Complete this part if you contributed more to your traditional IRAs for 2000 than is allowable or you had an excess contribution on line 16 of your 1999 Form 5329.

9	Enter your excess contributions from line 16 of your 1999 Form 5329. If zero, go to line 15 . .		**9**	
10	If your traditional IRA contributions for 2000 are less than your maximum allowable contribution, see page 3. Otherwise, enter -0- .	**10**		
11	Taxable 2000 distributions from your traditional IRAs	**11**		
12	2000 withdrawals of prior year excess contributions included on line 9. See page 3	**12**		
13	Add lines 10, 11, and 12		**13**	
14	Prior year excess contributions. Subtract line 13 from line 9. If zero or less, enter -0-		**14**	
15	Excess contributions for 2000. See page 3. Do not include this amount on Form 1040, line 23		**15**	
16	Total excess contributions. Add lines 14 and 15		**16**	
17	**Tax due.** Enter 6% (.06) of the **smaller** of line 16 **or** the value of your traditional IRAs on December 31, 2000 (including contributions for 2000 made in 2001). Also include this amount on Form 1040, line 54 . .		**17**	

For Paperwork Reduction Act Notice, see page 4 of separate instructions.   Cat. No. 13329Q   Form **5329** (2000)

Form 5329 (2000)   Page **2**

Part IV   Tax on Excess Contributions to Roth IRAs

Complete this part if you contributed more to your Roth IRAs for 2000 than is allowable or you had an excess contribution on line 24 of your 1999 Form 5329.

18	Enter your excess contributions from line 24 of your 1999 Form 5329. If zero, go to line 23 . .	18	
19	If your Roth IRA contributions for 2000 are less than your maximum allowable contribution, see page 3. Otherwise, enter -0-	19	
20	2000 distributions from your Roth IRAs, from Form 8606, line 17 . .	20	
21	Add lines 19 and 20	21	
22	Prior year excess contributions. Subtract line 21 from line 18. If zero or less, enter -0- . . .	22	
23	Excess contributions for 2000. See page 3	23	
24	Total excess contributions. Add lines 22 and 23	24	
25	**Tax due.** Enter 6% (.06) of the **smaller** of line 24 **or** the value of your Roth IRAs on December 31, 2000 (including contributions for 2000 made in 2001). Also include this amount on Form 1040, line 54 . . .	25	

Part V   Tax on Excess Contributions to Education (Ed) IRAs

Complete this part if the contributions to your Ed IRAs in 2000 were more than is allowable or you had an excess contribution on line 32 of your 1999 Form 5329.

26	Enter the excess contributions from line 32 of your 1999 Form 5329. If zero, go to line 31 . .	26	
27	If the contributions to your Ed IRAs in 2000 were less than the maximum allowable contribution, see page 3. Otherwise, enter -0- . .	27	
28	2000 distributions from your Ed IRAs, from Form 8606, line 28 . .	28	
29	Add lines 27 and 28	29	
30	Prior year excess contributions. Subtract line 29 from line 26. If zero or less, enter -0- . . .	30	
31	Excess contributions for 2000. See page 4	31	
32	Total excess contributions. Add lines 30 and 31	32	
33	**Tax due.** Enter 6% (.06) of the **smaller** of line 32 **or** the value of your Ed IRAs on December 31, 2000. Also include this amount on Form 1040, line 54	33	

Part VI   Tax on Excess Contributions to Medical Savings Accounts (MSAs)

Complete this part if you or your employer contributed more to your MSAs in 2000 than is allowable or you had an excess contribution on line 40 of your 1999 Form 5329.

34	Enter the excess contributions from line 40 of your 1999 Form 5329. If zero, go to line 39 . .	34	
35	If the contributions to your MSAs for 2000 are less than the maximum allowable contribution, see page 4. Otherwise, enter -0-	35	
36	Taxable 2000 distributions from your MSAs, from Form 8853, line 8	36	
37	Add lines 35 and 36	37	
38	Prior year excess contributions. Subtract line 37 from line 34. If zero or less, enter -0- . . .	38	
39	Excess contributions for 2000. See page 4. Do not include this amount on Form 1040, line 25	39	
40	Total excess contributions. Add lines 38 and 39	40	
41	**Tax due.** Enter 6% (.06) of the **smaller** of line 40 **or** the value of your MSAs on December 31, 2000. Also include this amount on Form 1040, line 54	41	

Part VII   Tax on Excess Accumulation in Qualified Retirement Plans

Complete this part if you did not receive the minimum required distribution from your qualified retirement plan (including an IRA other than an Ed IRA or Roth IRA).

42	Minimum required distribution. See page 4	42	
43	Amount actually distributed to you	43	
44	Subtract line 43 from line 42. If zero or less, enter -0-	44	
45	**Tax due.** Enter 50% (.50) of line 44. Also include this amount on Form 1040, line 54	45	

Signature. Complete **only** if you are filing this form by itself and not with your tax return.

Please Sign Here	Under penalties of perjury, I declare that I have examined this form, including accompanying schedules and statements, and to the best of my knowledge and belief, it is true, correct, and complete. Declaration of preparer (other than taxpayer) is based on all information of which preparer has any knowledge.		
	▶ Your signature	▶ Date	

Paid Preparer's Use Only	Preparer's signature ▶	Date	Check if self-employed ☐	Preparer's SSN or PTIN
	Firm's name (or yours if self-employed), address, and ZIP code ▶		EIN	
			Phone no. ( )	

Form **5329** (2000)

2000

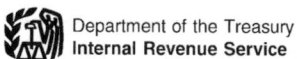 Department of the Treasury
Internal Revenue Service

Instructions for Form 5329

Additional Taxes Attributable to IRAs, Other Qualified Retirement Plans, Annuities, Modified Endowment Contracts, and MSAs

Section references are to the Internal Revenue Code unless otherwise noted.

General Instructions

Purpose of Form

Use Form 5329 to report any additional taxes on individual retirement arrangements (IRAs), annuities, other qualified retirement plans, modified endowment contracts, or medical savings accounts (MSAs).

Who Must File

You **must** file Form 5329 if any of the following apply.

● You received a distribution from a qualified retirement plan that is subject to the tax on early distributions, but distribution code 1 is not shown in box 7 of **Form 1099-R,** Distributions From Pensions, Annuities, Retirement or Profit-Sharing Plans, IRAs, Insurance Contracts, etc.

Note: *You **do not** have to file Form 5329 if distribution code 1 is correctly shown in box 7 of Form 1099-R. Instead, see the instructions for Form 1040, line 54, for how to report the 10% tax directly on Form 1040, line 54.*

● You meet an exception to the tax on early distributions, but the correct distribution code for the exception is not shown in box 7 of Form 1099-R.

● You received distributions from education (Ed) IRAs in excess of your qualified higher education expenses.

● Your contributions for 2000 to your traditional IRAs, Roth IRAs, Ed IRAs, or MSAs are more than is allowable or you had an excess contribution on line 16, 24, 32, or 40 of your 1999 Form 5329.

● You did not receive the minimum required distribution from your qualified retirement plan.

TIP *If you rolled over part or all of a distribution from a qualified retirement plan, the part rolled over is not subject to the tax on early distributions. See the instructions for Form 1040, lines 15a and 15b or lines 16a and 16b, or Form 1040A, lines 11a and 11b or 12a and 12b, for how to report the rollover.*

When and Where To File

File Form 5329 with your 2000 Form 1040 by the due date, including extensions, of your Form 1040.

If you do not have to file a 2000 income tax return, complete and file Form 5329 by itself at the time and place you would be required to file Form 1040. Be sure to include your address on page 1 and your signature and date on page 2. Enclose, but do not attach, a check or money order payable to the "**United States Treasury**" for any taxes due. Write your social security number and "2000 Form 5329" on the check or money order.

Filing for Previous Tax Years

If you are filing Form 5329 for a previous year, you must use that year's version of the form. For example, if you are paying a tax for 1999, you must use the 1999 Form 5329 to report the tax. If you have other changes, file Form 5329 for that year with **Form 1040X,** Amended U.S. Individual Income Tax Return. If you do not have any other changes for the previous year, file Form 5329 by itself. See **When and Where To File** above.

Definitions

Qualified Retirement Plan

A qualified retirement plan includes:

● A qualified pension, profit-sharing, or stock bonus plan (including a 401(k) plan),

● A tax-sheltered annuity contract,

● A qualified annuity plan, and

● An individual retirement account or annuity.

Note: *Ed IRAs and MSAs are not qualified retirement plans.*

Traditional IRAs

A traditional IRA is any IRA, including a simplified employee pension (SEP) IRA, other than a SIMPLE IRA, Roth IRA, or Ed IRA.

SEP IRAs. A SEP includes a salary reduction SEP.

Early Distribution

Generally, any distribution from your traditional IRA, Roth IRA, or other qualified retirement plan, annuity, or modified endowment contract before you reach age 59½ is an early distribution. See **Part I—Tax on Early Distributions** on page 2 for details.

Rollover

A rollover is a tax-free distribution of assets from one qualified retirement plan that is reinvested in another plan or the same plan. Generally, you must complete the rollover within 60 days following the distribution. Any taxable amount not rolled over must be included in income and may be subject to the tax on early distributions. See **Pub. 590,** Individual Retirement Arrangements (IRAs), for details.

Note: *If you instruct the trustee of your plan to transfer funds directly to another plan, the transfer is **not** considered a rollover. Do not include the amount transferred in income or deduct the amount transferred as a contribution. A transfer from a qualified employee plan to an IRA, however, is considered a rollover.*

Compensation

Compensation includes wages, salaries, professional fees, and other pay you receive for services you perform. It also includes sales commissions, commissions on insurance premiums, pay based on a percentage of profits, tips, and bonuses. It includes net earnings from self-employment but only for a trade or business in which your personal services are a material income-producing factor.

For IRAs, treat all taxable alimony received under a decree of divorce or separate maintenance as compensation.

Compensation does not include any amounts received as a pension or annuity and does not include any amount received as deferred compensation.

Taxable compensation is your compensation that is included in gross income reduced by any deductions on Form 1040, lines 27 and 29, but not by any loss from self-employment.

Additional Information

See Pub. 590 and **Pub. 575,** Pension and Annuity Income.

Specific Instructions

Joint returns. If both you and your spouse are required to file Form 5329, complete a separate form for each of you. Include the combined tax on Form 1040, line 54.

Amended return. If you are filing an amended 2000 Form 5329, check the box at the top of page 1 of the form. **Do not** use the 2000 Form 5329 to amend your return for any other year. Instead, see **Filing for Previous Tax Years** on page 1.

Part I—Tax on Early Distributions

In general, if you receive an early distribution (including an involuntary cashout) from a traditional IRA, Roth IRA, or other qualified retirement plan, or a modified endowment contract, the taxable part of the distribution is subject to an additional 10% tax.

The tax on early distributions does **not** apply to:
- 2000 IRA contributions withdrawn during the year;
- 1999 excess contributions withdrawn in 2000 by the due date (including extensions) of your 1999 tax return;
- Excess IRA contributions for years before 1999 withdrawn in 2000 and 1999 excess contributions withdrawn after the due date (including extensions) of your 1999 tax return if **(a)** no deduction was allowable (without regard to the modified adjusted gross income (AGI) limitation) nor taken for the excess contributions and **(b)** your total IRA contributions for the tax year for which the excess contributions were made were not more than $2,250 for tax years before 1997 or $2,000 for tax years after 1996 (if your total contributions for the year included employer contributions to a SEP, increase that amount by the smaller of the employer contributions or $30,000);
- Distributions from a traditional or SIMPLE IRA that were converted to a Roth IRA;
- Distributions of excess contributions from a qualified cash or deferred arrangement;
- Distributions of excess aggregate contributions to meet nondiscrimination requirements for employee contributions and matching employer contributions;
- Distributions of excess deferrals; and
- Amounts distributed from unfunded deferred compensation plans of tax-exempt or state and local government employers.

See the instructions for line 2 on this page for other distributions that are not subject to the tax.

Line 1

Enter the taxable amount of early distributions you received from:

- A qualified retirement plan, including traditional IRAs and Roth IRAs (and income earned on excess contributions to your traditional IRAs and Roth IRAs), or
- A modified endowment contract entered into after June 20, 1988.

Exception for Roth IRA Distributions

If you received an early distribution from a Roth IRA, include on line 1 the amount from your 2000 Form 8606, line 19, reduced by the amount, if any, allocable to the amount on your 1998, 1999, or 2000 Form 8606, line 15. The amount on line 19 is allocable (in the order shown) to the amounts on the lines listed below (to the extent a distribution from line 20 of your 1998 Form 8606 or line 19 of your 1999 Form 8606 was not allocable to the amount below.) See **Are Distributions From My Roth IRA Taxable?** in Pub. 590 for details.

- Your 1998 Form 8606, line 16.
- Your 1998 Form 8606, line 15.
- Your 1999 Form 8606, line 16.
- Your 1999 Form 8606, line 15.
- Your 2000 Form 8606, line 16.
- Your 2000 Form 8606, line 15.
- Your 2000 Form 8606, line 26.

Example. You converted $20,000 from a traditional IRA to a Roth IRA in 1998 and converted $10,000 in 1999. Your 1998 Form 8606 had $5,000 on line 15 and $15,000 on line 16 and your 1999 Form 8606 had $3,000 on line 15 and $7,000 on line 16. You made Roth IRA contributions of $2,000 for 1998 and 1999. You did not make any Roth IRA conversions or contributions for 2000 or 2001 or take any Roth IRA distributions in 1998 or 1999. On July 9, 2000, at age 58, you took a $33,000 distribution from your Roth IRA. The first $4,000 of the distribution is allocated to your two $2,000 Roth IRA contributions, and $29,000 is shown on your 2000 Form 8606, line 19. Next, $15,000 of the $29,000 is allocated first to your 1998 Form 8606, line 16, then $5,000 to your 1998 Form 8606, line 15, and $7,000 to your 1999 Form 8606, line 16. The remaining $2,000 is allocated to the $3,000 on your 1999 Form 8606, line 15. Your amount subject to tax on early distributions to enter on line 1 is $22,000 ($29,000 minus the sum of $5,000 and $2,000). If you take a Roth IRA distribution in 2001, the first $1,000 will be allocated to the $1,000 remaining from your 1999 Form 8606, line 15, and will not be subject to the tax on early distributions.

Certain prohibited transactions, such as borrowing from your IRA or pledging your IRA assets as security for a loan, are considered to be taxable distributions and may also cause you to owe the tax on early distributions. See Pub. 590 for details.

Line 2

The 10% additional tax does not apply to the distributions described below. Enter on line 2 the amount that can be excluded. In the space provided, enter the applicable exception number (01-11).

No.	Exception
01	Distribution due to separation from service in or after the year of reaching age 55 (applies only to qualified employee plans).
02	Distribution made as part of a series of substantially equal periodic payments (made at least annually) for your life (or life expectancy) or the joint lives (or joint life expectancies) of you and your designated beneficiary (if from a qualified employee plan, payments must begin after separation from service).
03	Distribution due to total and permanent disability.
04	Distribution due to death (does not apply to modified endowment contracts).
05	Distribution to the extent you have deductible medical expenses that can be claimed on line 4 of Schedule A (Form 1040) (does not apply to annuity or modified endowment contracts).
06	Distributions made to an alternate payee under a qualified domestic relations order (applies only to qualified employee plans).
07	Distributions made to unemployed individuals for health insurance premiums (applies only to IRAs).
08	Distributions made for higher education expenses (applies only to IRAs).
09	Distributions made for purchase of a first home, up to $10,000 (applies only to IRAs).
10	Distributions due to an IRS levy of the qualified plan.
11	Other (see instructions below).

Other. The following exceptions also apply.
- A distribution was incorrectly indicated as an early distribution by a code **1** or **S** in box 7 of Form 1099-R. Include on line 2 the amount you received when you were age 59½ or older.
- Any distributions from a plan maintained by an employer if:
  1. You separated from service by March 1, 1986;
  2. As of March 1, 1986, your entire interest was in pay status under a written election that provides a specific schedule for distribution of your entire interest; and
  3. The distribution is actually being made under the written election.
- Distributions that are dividends paid with respect to stock described in section 404(k).
- Distributions from annuity contracts to the extent that the distributions are

allocable to the investment in the contract before August 14, 1982.

For additional exceptions that apply to annuities, see Pub. 575.

Line 4

If any amount on line 3 was a distribution from a SIMPLE retirement plan received within 2 years from the date you first participated in the plan, you must multiply that amount by 25% instead of 10%. These distributions are included in boxes 1 and 2a of Form 1099-R and are designated with code **S** in box 7.

Part II—Tax on Certain Taxable Distributions From Education (Ed) IRAs

Line 6

The 10% additional tax does not apply to distributions that are:

- Due to the death or disability of the beneficiary;
- Made on account of a tax-free scholarship, allowance, or payment described in section 25A(g)(2); or
- Taxable solely because you elected to waive any exclusion you may be entitled to for your 2000 qualified higher education expenses. (This election was made by checking the "Yes" box on line 29 of Form 8606.)
- Excess contributions to an Ed IRA that are distributed to you by the due date of your return (including extensions). The distribution must include earnings on the excess contributions.

Enter on line 6 the total amount that can be excluded from the 10% additional tax.

Part III—Tax on Excess Contributions to Traditional IRAs

If you contributed more to your traditional IRA for 2000 than is allowable or you had an excess contribution from prior years on line 16 of your 1999 Form 5329, you may owe this tax. But you may be able to avoid the tax on any 2000 excess contributions. See the instructions for line 15.

Line 10

If you contributed less to your traditional IRA for 2000 than your contribution limit, enter the difference.

If you are not married filing jointly, your **contribution limit** is the **smaller** of $2,000 or your taxable compensation (see page 1). If you are married filing jointly, your contribution limit is generally $2,000. But if the combined taxable compensation for you and your spouse is less than $4,000, see **How Much Can Be Contributed?** in Pub. 590 for special rules.

Also include on line 9a or 9b of the IRA Deduction Worksheet in the instructions for Form 1040, line 23, the **smaller** of **(a)**

Form 5329, line 10, or **(b)** the excess, if any, of Form 5329, line 9, over the sum of Form 5329, lines 11 and 12.

Line 11

Enter on line 11 any withdrawals from your IRA in 2000 that are included in your income. Do not include any withdrawn contributions that will be reported on line 12.

Line 12

Enter any excess contributions to your IRA for 1976 through 1998 that you withdrew in 2000. Also include any 1999 excess contributions that you withdrew after the due date (including extensions) of your 1999 income tax return if:

- You did not claim a deduction for the excess and no deduction was allowable (without regard to the modified AGI limitation) and
- The total contributions to your IRA for the tax year for which the excess contributions were made were not more than $2,250 for tax years before 1997 or $2,000 for tax years after 1996. (If the total contributions for the year included employer contributions to a SEP, increase that amount by the smaller of the amount of the employer contributions or $30,000.)

Line 15

Enter the excess of your contributions to traditional IRAs for 2000 over your contribution limit (unless you properly withdraw the excess contributions—see below). See the instructions for line 10 to figure your contribution limit.

Any amount you contribute to a traditional IRA for the year in which you reach age 70½ or a later year is an excess contribution (that is, your contribution limit is zero). Do not include rollover contributions in figuring your excess contributions.

You may withdraw some or all of your excess contributions for 2000 and they will not be treated as excess contributions **if:**

- You make the withdrawal by the due date, including extensions, of your 2000 tax return,
- You do not claim a deduction for the amount of the withdrawn contribution, and
- You withdraw any income earned on the contribution and report the earnings on Form 1040 for the year in which you made the contribution. Also, if you had not reached age 59½ at the time of the withdrawal, include the earnings as an early distribution on line 1 of Form 5329 for the year in which you report the earnings.

Part IV—Tax on Excess Contributions to Roth IRAs

If you contributed more to your Roth IRA for 2000 than is allowable or you had an excess contribution on line 24 of your 1999 Form 5329, you may owe this tax. But you may be able to avoid the tax on

any 2000 excess contributions. See the instructions for line 23.

Line 19

If you contributed less to your Roth IRA for 2000 than your contribution limit for Roth IRAs, enter the difference. Your contribution limit for Roth IRAs is generally your contribution limit for traditional IRAs (see the instructions for line 10) reduced by the amount you contributed to traditional IRAs. But your contribution limit for Roth IRAs may be further reduced or eliminated if your modified AGI for Roth IRA purposes is over:

- $150,000 if married filing jointly,
- $0 if married filing separately and you lived with your spouse at any time in 2000, or
- $95,000 for any other taxpayer.

See Pub. 590 for details.

Line 23

Enter the amount you contributed to Roth IRAs for 2000 in excess of your contribution limit for Roth IRAs (see the instructions for line 19). Do not include rollovers. Any amounts converted from a traditional IRA or SIMPLE IRA to a Roth IRA are excess contributions if your modified AGI for Roth IRA purposes is over $100,000 or your filing status is married filing separately and you lived with your spouse at any time in 2000. See "Recharacterizations" in the Instructions for Form 8606, and Pub. 590, for details.

You may withdraw some or all of your excess contributions for 2000 and they will not be treated as excess contributions or taxed as distributions **if:**

- You make the withdrawal by the due date, including extensions, of your 2000 tax return and
- You withdraw any income earned on the withdrawn contribution and report the earnings on Form 1040 for the year in which you made the contribution. Also, if you had not reached age 59½ at the time of the withdrawal, include the earnings as an early distribution on line 1 of Form 5329 for the year in which you report the earnings.

Part V—Tax on Excess Contributions to Ed IRAs

If the contributions to your Ed IRAs for 2000 were more than is allowable or an excess contribution is shown on line 32 of your 1999 Form 5329, you may owe this tax. But you may be able to avoid the tax on any 2000 excess contributions. See the instructions for line 31.

Line 27

Enter the excess, if any, of the maximum amount that may be contributed to your Ed IRAs for 2000 over the amount actually contributed in 2000. See the instructions for line 31 to figure the maximum amount that may be contributed.

Line 31

Enter the excess of the contributions to your Ed IRAs in 2000 (not including rollovers) over your contribution limit for Ed IRAs. Your contribution limit is the **smaller** of $500 or the sum of the maximum amounts allowed to be contributed by the contributor(s) to your Ed IRA(s). The maximum contribution a person may make to an Ed IRA may be limited based on the person's modified AGI. See Pub. 590 for details.

Also, all amounts contributed to an Ed IRA are excess contributions if any amount is contributed to a qualified state tuition program for the same beneficiary (except for contributions to a qualified state tuition program made from a distribution from the beneficiary's Ed IRA).

You may withdraw some or all of the excess contributions for 2000 and they will not be treated as excess contributions or taxed as distributions **if:**

• You make the withdrawal by the due date, including extensions, of your 2000 tax return (or by the date your return would be due if you were required to file a return) and

• You also withdraw any income earned on the withdrawn contribution and include the earnings in gross income for 2000.

Part VI—Tax on Excess Contributions to Medical Savings Accounts (MSAs)

If you or your employer contributed more to your MSA for 2000 than is allowable or an excess contribution from prior years is shown on line 39 of your 1999 Form 5329, you may owe this tax. But you may be able to avoid the tax on any 2000 excess contributions. See the instructions for line 39.

Line 35

If the contribution limit for your MSA (the **smaller** of line 3 or line 4 of Form 8853) is greater than the contributions to your MSA for 2000, enter the difference on line 35. Also include on line 5 of your 2000 Form 8853 the **smaller** of:

• Form 5329, line 35, or

• The excess, if any, of Form 5329, line 34, over Form 5329, line 36.

Line 39

Enter the excess of your contributions to your MSA for 2000 (from Form 8853, line 2) over your contribution limit (the smaller of line 3 or line 4 of Form 8853). However, you may withdraw some or all of the

excess contributions for 2000 and they will not be treated as excess contributions or taxed as a distribution **if:**

• You make the withdrawal by the due date, including extensions, of your 2000 tax return and

• You withdraw any income earned on the withdrawn contribution and include the earnings in gross income for the year in which you receive the withdrawn contribution and earnings.

Include the withdrawn contribution and related earnings on Form 8853, lines 6a and 6b.

Also include on line 39 any excess contributions your employer made. See Form 8853 for details.

Part VII—Tax on Excess Accumulation in Qualified Retirement Plans

You owe this tax if you do not receive the minimum required distribution from your qualified retirement plan (including an IRA or an eligible deferred compensation plan under section 457 but not an Ed IRA or a Roth IRA). The additional tax is 50% of the excess accumulation (the difference between the amount that was required to be distributed and the amount that was actually distributed).

Required Distributions

IRA (other than an Ed IRA or a Roth IRA). You must start receiving distributions from your IRA by April 1 of the year following the year in which you reach age 70½. At that time, you may receive your entire interest in the IRA or begin receiving periodic distributions over your life expectancy or over the joint life expectancy of you and your designated beneficiary (or over a shorter period).

If you choose to receive periodic distributions, you must receive a minimum required distribution each year. Figure the minimum required distribution by dividing the account balance of the IRA on December 31 of the year preceding the distribution by the applicable life expectancy. For applicable life expectancies, you must use the expected return multiples from the tables in Pub. 590 or **Pub. 939,** General Rule for Pensions and Annuities.

Under an alternative method, if you have more than one IRA, you may take the minimum distribution from any one or more of the individual IRAs.

For more details on the minimum distribution rules (including examples), see Pub. 590.

Qualified pension, profit-sharing, stock bonus, or section 457 deferred compensation plan. In general, you must begin receiving distributions from your plan no later than April 1 following the **later** of (a) the year in which you reach age 70½ or (b) the year in which you retire.

Exception. If you owned more than 5% of the employer maintaining the plan, you must begin receiving distributions no later than April 1 of the year following the year in which you reach age 70½, regardless of when you retire.

Your plan administrator figures the amount that must be distributed each year.

Note: *The IRS may waive this tax if you can show that any shortfall in the amount of withdrawals was due to reasonable error and you are taking appropriate steps to remedy the shortfall. If you believe you qualify for this relief, file Form 5329, pay the tax, and attach a letter of explanation. If the IRS waives the tax, we will send you a refund.*

Paperwork Reduction Act Notice. We ask for the information on this form to carry out the Internal Revenue laws of the United States. You are required to give us the information. We need it to ensure that you are complying with these laws and to allow us to figure and collect the right amount of tax.

You are not required to provide the information requested on a form that is subject to the Paperwork Reduction Act unless the form displays a valid OMB control number. Books or records relating to a form or its instructions must be retained as long as their contents may become material in the administration of any Internal Revenue law. Generally, tax returns and return information are confidential, as required by section 6103.

The time needed to complete and file this form will vary depending on individual circumstances. The estimated average time is: **Recordkeeping,** 2 hr., 5 min.; **Learning about the law or the form,** 33 min.; **Preparing the form,** 2 hr., 7 min.; **Copying, assembling, and sending the form to the IRS,** 14 min.

If you have comments concerning the accuracy of these time estimates or suggestions for making this form simpler, we would be happy to hear from you. You can write to the Tax Forms Committee, Western Area Distribution Center, Rancho Cordova, CA 95743-0001. **Do not** send the form to this address. Instead, see **When and Where To File** on page 1.

Form **5330** (Rev. August 1998) Department of the Treasury Internal Revenue Service	**Return of Excise Taxes Related to Employee Benefit Plans** (Under sections 4971, 4972, 4973(a)(3), 4975, 4976, 4977, 4978, 4978A, 4978B, 4979, 4979A, and 4980 of the Internal Revenue Code)	OMB No. 1545-0575

Filer tax year beginning _____ , _____ and ending _____ , _____

A Name of filer (see instructions on page 3)

Number, street, and room or suite no. (If a P.O. box, see page 3 of the instructions)

City or town, state, and ZIP code

C Name and address of plan sponsor

D Name of plan

B Check applicable box and see instructions.

☐ Employer identification number (EIN)
☐ Social security number (SSN)

Filer's identification number ▶

E Plan sponsor's EIN

F Plan year ending

G Plan number

H Check here if this is an amended return . . . . ▶ ☐

Part I   Summary of Taxes Due

		FOR IRS USE ONLY		
1	Section 4972 tax on nondeductible contributions to qualified plans (from line 13l) . . .	161	**1**	
2	Section 4973(a)(3) tax on excess contributions to section 403(b)(7)(A) custodial accounts (from line 22)	164	**2**	
3	Section 4976 tax on disqualified benefits (from line 23)	200	**3**	
4a	Section 4978 and 4978A tax on certain ESOP dispositions (from line 24a)	209	**4a**	
b	Section 4978B tax on certain ESOP dispositions (from line 24b)	202	**4b**	
5	Section 4979A tax on certain prohibited allocations of qualified ESOP securities (from line 25) . .	203	**5**	
6	Section 4975 tax on prohibited transactions (from line 26c)	159	**6**	
7	Section 4971 tax on failure to meet minimum funding standards (from line 31)	163	**7**	
8	Section 4977 tax on excess fringe benefits (from line 32d)	201	**8**	
9	Section 4979 tax on excess contributions to certain plans (from line 33b)	205	**9**	
10	Section 4980 tax on reversion of qualified plan assets to an employer (from line 36) . .	204	**10**	
11	Section 4971(f) tax on failure to pay liquidity shortfall (from line 41)	226	**11**	
12a	**Total tax.** Add lines 1 through 11 (see instructions)		**12a**	
b	Enter amount of tax paid with Form 5558 or any other tax paid prior to filing this return . . .		**12b**	
c	**Total tax due.** Subtract line 12b from line 12a. Attach check or money order for full amount payable to "United States Treasury." Write your name, identification number, and "Form 5330, Section(s) _____ " on it . . . . ▶		**12c**	

Please Sign Here

Under penalties of perjury, I declare that I have examined this return, including accompanying schedules and statements, and to the best of my knowledge and belief, it is true, correct, and complete. Declaration of preparer (other than taxpayer) is based on all information of which preparer has any knowledge.

▶ Your signature   ▶ ( ) Telephone number   ▶ Date

Paid Preparer's Use Only

Preparer's signature ▶   Date

Firm's name (or yours if self-employed) and address ▶

For Privacy Act and Paperwork Reduction Act Notice, see page 6 of the instructions.   Cat. No. 11870M   Form **5330** (Rev. 8-98)

Form 5330 (Rev. 8-98)   Page **2**

DUE DATE: Taxes listed on this page are due on the last day of the 7th month after the end of the tax year of the filer.

Part II   Tax on Nondeductible Employer Contributions to Qualified Plans (Section 4972)

13a Total contributions for your tax year to your qualified (under section 401(a), 403(a), or 408(k), or 408(p)) plan . . . .

b Amount allowable as a deduction under section 404 . . . .

c Subtract line 13b from line 13a . . . .

d Enter amount of any prior year nondeductible contributions made for years beginning after 12/31/86 . . . .

e Amount of any prior year nondeductible contributions for years beginning after 12/31/86 returned to you in this tax year or any prior tax year . . .

f Subtract line 13e from line 13d . . . .

g Amount of line 13f carried forward and deductible in this tax year . . . .

h Subtract line 13g from line 13f . . . .

i Tentative taxable excess contributions. Add lines 13c and 13h . . . .

j Nondeductible section 4972(c)(6) contributions exempt from excise tax . . . .

k Taxable excess contributions. Subtract line 13j from line 13i . . . .

l Multiply line 13k by 10%. Enter here and on line 1 . . . . ▶

Part III   Tax on Excess Contributions to Section 403(b)(7)(A) Custodial Accounts (Section 4973(a)(3))

14 Total amount contributed for current year less rollovers (see instructions) . . . .

15 Amount excludable from gross income under section 403(b) (see instructions) . . . .

16 Current year excess contributions (line 14 less line 15, but not less than zero) . . . .

17 Prior year excess contributions not previously eliminated. If zero, go to line 21 . . . .

18 Contribution credit (if line 15 is more than line 14, enter the excess; otherwise, enter -0-) . . . .

19 Total of all prior years' distributions out of the account included in your gross income under section 72(e) and not previously used to reduce excess contributions . . . .

20 Adjusted prior years' excess contributions (line 17 less the total of lines 18 and 19) . . . . . .

21 Taxable excess contributions (line 16 plus line 20) . . . .

22 **Excess contributions tax.** Enter the lesser of 6% of line 21 or 6% of the value of your account as of the last day of the year. Enter here and on line 2 . . . . ▶

Part IV   Tax on Disqualified Benefits (Section 4976)

23 If your welfare benefit fund has provided a disqualified benefit during your taxable year, enter the amount of the disqualified benefit here and on line 3 (see instructions) . . . . ▶

Part V   Tax on Certain ESOP Dispositions (Sections 4978, 4978A, and 4978B)

24a Enter your section 4978 or 4978A tax on dispositions of employer securities by employee stock ownership plans and certain worker-owned cooperatives here and on line 4a (see instructions) ▶

Check the box to indicate whether the tax applies as a result of the application of

☐ Section 664(g)   ☐ Section 4978A   ☐ Section 1042

b Enter your section 4978B tax on dispositions of employer securities to which section 133 applied here and on line 4b . . . . ▶

Part VI   Tax on Certain Prohibited Allocations of Qualified ESOP Securities (Section 4979A)

25 Enter 50% of the prohibited allocation or the allocation described in section 664(g)(5)(A), here and on line 5 (see instructions) . . . . ▶

Form 5330 (Rev. 8-98)   Page **3**

DUE DATE: Section 4975 taxes are due on the last day of the 7th month after the end of the tax year of the filer.

Part VII   Tax on Prohibited Transactions (Section 4975)

26a Is the excise tax a result of a prohibited transaction that was (check one or more):

☐ discrete   ☐ other than discrete (a lease or a loan)

b Transaction number	**(a)** Date of transaction (see instructions)	**(b)** Description of prohibited transaction	**(c)** Amount involved in prohibited transaction (see instructions)	**(d)** Initial tax on prohibited transaction (multiply each transaction in column (c) by the appropriate rate (see instructions))
(i)				
(ii)				
(iii)				
(iv)				

26c Add amounts in column (d). Enter here and on line 6 . . . . ▶

27 Have you corrected **all** of the prohibited transactions that you are reporting on this return? (See instructions) . . . . ☐ Yes ☐ No
If "Yes," complete Part IX. If "No," complete Part IX and see instructions.

Part VIII   Schedule of Other Participating Disqualified Persons (See instructions)

28	**(a)** Name and address of disqualified person	**(b)** Transaction number from Part VII	**(c)** Employer identification number or social security number
(i)			
(ii)			
(iii)			
(iv)			

Part IX   Description of Correction (See line 27 instructions.)

29 **(a)** Transaction number from Part VII	**(b)** Nature of correction	**(c)** Date of correction
(i)		
(ii)		
(iii)		
(iv)		

Form 5330 (Rev. 8-98)   Page **4**

DUE DATE: See **When To File** for taxes due under sections 4971, 4977, 4979, 4980, and 4971(f).

Part X   Tax on Failure To Meet Minimum Funding Standards (Section 4971)

30 Accumulated funding deficiency in the plan's minimum funding standard account (see instructions)
31 Multiply line 30 by tax rate (see instructions for applicable tax rates). Enter here and on line 7 . ▶

Part XI   Tax on Excess Fringe Benefits (Section 4977)

32a Did you make an election to be taxed under section 4977? . . . . . . ☐ Yes ☐ No
   b If "Yes," enter the calendar year in which the excess fringe benefits were paid ▶
   c If line 32a is "Yes," enter the excess fringe benefits on this line (see instructions) . . . . . .

   d Enter 30% of line 32c on this line and on line 8 . . . . ▶

Part XII   Tax on Excess Contributions to Certain Plans (Section 4979)

33a Enter the amount of any excess contributions under a cash or deferred arrangement that is part of
   a plan qualified under section 401(a), 403(a), 403(b), 408(k), 501(c)(18) or excess aggregate
   contributions described in section 401(m) . . . .

   b Multiply line 33a by 10%. Enter here and on line 9 . . . . ▶

Part XIII   Tax on Reversion of Qualified Plan Assets to an Employer (Section 4980)

34 Date reversion occurred ▶ month ____ day ____ year____
35a Employer reversion amount _____ **b** Excise tax rate _____ %
36 Multiply line 35a by line 35b and enter the amount here and on line 10 (see instructions) . . ▶
37 Explain below why you qualify for a rate other than 50%:

Part XIV   Tax on Failure to Correct Liquidity Shortfall (Section 4971(f))

		1st Quarter	2nd Quarter	3rd Quarter	4th Quarter	Total
38	Amount of shortfall . . .					
39	Amount corrected					
40	Net shortfall amount . . .					
41	Multiply line 40 (total column) by 10%. Enter here and on line 11. . . . . ▶					

Instructions for Form 5330

(Revised August 1998)

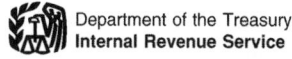

Department of the Treasury
Internal Revenue Service

Return of Excise Taxes
Related to Employee Benefit Plans

Section references are to the Internal Revenue Code unless otherwise noted.

General Instructions

Changes To Note

• The example for the first tier prohibited transaction excise tax has been revised. The Small Business Job Protection Act of 1996 increased the first tier prohibited transactions excise tax from 5% to 10% for prohibited transactions occurring after August 20, 1996 while the Taxpayer Relief Act of 1997 increased the first tier prohibited transactions excise tax from 10% to 15% for prohibited transactions occurring after August 5, 1997.

• The Health Insurance Portability and Accountability Act and The Taxpayer Relief Act of 1997 amended section 4975(e) to include medical savings accounts described in section 220(d) and educational individual retirement accounts described in section 530.

• The Taxpayer Relief Act of 1997 amended section 4978 to include certain dispositions to which section 664(g) applies.

• The Taxpayer Relief Act of 1997 amended section 4979A to include allocations described in section 664(g)(5)(A).

• The instructions clarify that generally the filing of a Form 5330 affects the statute of limitations only with respect to the type of excise tax(es) actually reported on the form even though one Form 5330 may be used for other excise taxes with the same filing due date. See the instructions for **When To File** on page 2.

Purpose of Form

File Form 5330 to report the tax on: **(a)** a minimum funding deficiency (section 4971); **(b)** nondeductible contributions to qualified plans (section 4972); **(c)** excess contributions to a section 403(b)(7)(A) custodial account (section 4973(a)(3)); **(d)** a prohibited transaction (section 4975); **(e)** a disqualified benefit provided by funded welfare plans (section 4976); **(f)** excess fringe benefits (section 4977); **(g)** certain ESOP dispositions (sections 4978, 4978A, and 4978B); **(h)** excess contributions to plans with cash or deferred arrangements (section 4979); **(i)** certain prohibited allocations of qualified securities by an ESOP (section 4979A); **(j)** reversions of qualified plan assets to employers (section 4980); and **(k)** a failure to pay liquidity shortfall (section 4971(f)).

Who Must File

A Form 5330 must be filed by:

1. Any employer who is liable for the tax under section 4971 for failure to meet the minimum funding standards under section 412 (liability for tax in the case of an employer who is a party to a collective bargaining agreement, see section 413(b)(6));

2. Any employer who is liable for the tax under section 4971(f) for a failure to meet the liquidity requirement of section 412(m)(5);

3. Any employer who is liable for the tax under section 4972 for nondeductible contributions to qualified plans;

4. Any individual who is liable for the tax under section 4973(a)(3) because an excess contribution to a section 403(b)(7)(A) custodial account was made for them and that excess has not been eliminated as specified in sections 4973(c)(2)(A) and (B);

5. Any disqualified person who is liable for the tax under section 4975 for participating in a prohibited transaction (other than a fiduciary acting only as such, or an individual (or his or her beneficiary) who engages in a prohibited transaction with respect to his or her individual retirement account) for each tax year or part of a tax year in the "taxable period" applicable to such prohibited transaction;

6. Any employer who is liable for the tax under section 4976 for maintaining a funded welfare benefit plan that provides a disqualified benefit during any tax year;

7. Any employer who pays excess fringe benefits and has elected to be taxed under section 4977 on such payments;

8. Any employer or worker-owned cooperative (as defined in section 1042(c)(2)) that maintains an ESOP that disposes of the qualified securities (as defined in section 1042(a)(1)) or section 133 securities within the specified 3-year period. See the instructions for Part V for details on the excise tax under sections 4978, 4978A, and 4978B;

9. Any employer who is liable for the tax under section 4979 on excess contributions to plans with a cash or deferred arrangement, etc.;

10. Any employer or worker-owned cooperative that made the written statement described in section 664(g)(1)(E) or 1042(b)(3)(B) and made an allocation prohibited under section 409(n) of qualified securities of an ESOP taxable under section 4979A; or

11. Any employer who receives an employer reversion from a deferred compensation plan that is taxable under section 4980.

A Form 5330 and tax payment is required:

• For each year that you fail to meet the minimum funding standards under section 412 or contribute an excess amount to your 403(b)(7)(A) custodial account,

• For each year that any of the items in 3 or 5 through 10 above apply,

• For a reversion of plan assets from a qualified plan that is taxable under section 4980, or

• For each year (or part of a year) in the "taxable period" applicable to a prohibited transaction. See the instructions for Part VII, line 26b, column (c), for a definition of taxable period.

Definitions

Plan.— For purposes of prohibited transactions (section 4975), the term "plan" means **any** of the following:

• A trust described in section 401(a) that forms part of a plan;

• A plan described in section 403(a), and that trust or plan is exempt from tax under section 501(a);

• An individual retirement account described in section 408(a);

• An individual retirement annuity described in section 408(b);

• A medical savings account described in section 220(d);

• An educational individual retirement account described in section 530;

• A trust described in section 501(c)(22).

Note: *If the Internal Revenue Service determined at any time that your plan was a "plan" as defined above, it will always remain subject to the excise tax on prohibited transactions (section 4975). This also applies to the tax on minimum funding deficiencies (section 4971).*

Section 4979 applies to plans described in sections 401(a), 403(a), 403(b), 408(k), or 501(c)(18).

Plan sponsor.— The term "plan sponsor" means:

1. The employer, for an employee benefit plan that a single employer establishes or maintains;

2. The employee organization in the case of a plan of an employee organization; or

3. The association, committee, joint board of trustees, or other similar group of representatives of the parties who

Cat. No. 11871X

establish or maintain the plan, if the plan is established or maintained jointly by one or more employers and one or more employee organizations, or by two or more employers.

Disqualified person.— A "disqualified person" is any person who is:

1. A fiduciary;

2. A person providing services to the plan;

3. An employer, any of whose employees are covered by the plan;

4. An employee organization, any of whose members are covered by the plan;

5. Any direct or indirect owner of 50% or more of **(a)** the combined voting power of all classes of stock entitled to vote, or the total value of shares of all classes of stock of a corporation, **(b)** the capital interest or the profits interest of a partnership, or **(c)** the beneficial interest of a trust or unincorporated enterprise, which is an employer or an employee organization described in **3** or **4;**

6. A member of the family of any individual described in **1, 2, 3,** or **5** (member of a family is the spouse, ancestor, lineal descendant, and any spouse of a lineal descendant);

7. A corporation, partnership, or trust or estate of which (or in which) any direct or indirect owner holds 50% or more of the interest described in **5(a), (b),** or **(c).** For purposes of **(c),** the beneficial interest of the trust or estate is owned directly or indirectly, or held by persons described in **1** through **5;**

8. An officer, director (or an individual having powers or responsibilities similar to those of officers or directors), a 10% or more shareholder or highly compensated employee (earning 10% or more of the yearly wages of an employer) of a person described in **3, 4, 5,** or **7;**

9. A 10% or more (in capital or profits) partner or joint venturer of a person described in **3, 4, 5,** or **7;** or

10. Any disqualified person, as described in **1** through **9** above, who is a disqualified person with respect to any plan to which a section 501(c)(22) trust applies, is permitted to make payments under section 4223 of ERISA.

Prohibited transaction.— A "prohibited transaction" is any direct or indirect:

1. Sale or exchange, or leasing of any property between a plan and a disqualified person; or a transfer of real or personal property by a disqualified person to a plan where the property is subject to a mortgage or similar lien placed on the property by the disqualified person within 10 years prior to the transfer, or the property transferred is subject to a mortgage or similar lien which the plan assumes;

2. Lending of money or other extension of credit between a plan and a disqualified person;

3. Furnishing of goods, services, or facilities between a plan and a disqualified person;

4. Transfer to, or use by or for the benefit of, a disqualified person of income or assets of a plan;

5. Act by a disqualified person who is a fiduciary whereby he or she deals with the income or assets of a plan in his or her own interest or account; or

6. Receipt of any consideration for his or her own personal account by any disqualified person who is a fiduciary from any party dealing with the plan connected with a transaction involving the income or assets of the plan.

Exemptions.— See sections 4975(d) and 4975(f)(6)(B)(ii) for specific exemptions to prohibited transactions.

Also, see section 4975(c)(2) for certain other transactions or classes of transactions that have been exempted.

When To File

Use one Form 5330 to report excise taxes with the same filing due date. For example, all of the excise taxes on pages 2 and 3 of the form have the same filing due dates. One Form 5330 may be filed to report one or more of these taxes. However, if the taxes are from separate plans, file separate forms for each plan. Also file a separate Form 5330 to report taxes with different filing due dates. Generally, the filing of a Form 5330 starts the statute of limitations running only with respect to the particular excise tax(es) reported on that 5330. However, statutes of limitations with respect to the prohibited transaction excise tax(es) are based on the filing of the applicable Form 5500.

1. For taxes due under sections 4972, 4973(a)(3), 4975, 4976, 4978, 4978A, 4978B, and 4979A, file Form 5330 by the last day of the 7th month after the end of the tax year of the employer or other person who must file this return.

2. For tax due under section 4971 and 4971(f), file Form 5330 by the later of the last day of the 7th month after the end of the employer's tax year or 8½ months after the last day of the plan year that ends with or within the filer's tax year.

3. For tax due under section 4977, file Form 5330 by the last day of the 7th month after the end of the calendar year in which the excess fringe benefits were paid to your employees.

4. For tax due under section 4979, file Form 5330 by the last day of the 15th month after the close of the plan year to which the excess contributions or excess aggregate contributions relate.

5. For tax due under section 4980, file Form 5330 no later than the last day of the month following the month in which the reversion occurred.

Extension.— File **Form 5558,** Application of Extension of Time to File Certain Employee Plan Returns, to request an extension of time to file. If approved, you may be granted an extension of up to 6 months.

Caution: Form 5558 does not extend the time to pay your taxes. See the instructions for Form 5558.

Where To File

File your return at the applicable IRS address listed below.

If the taxpayer is located in	Use the following Internal Revenue Service Center address
Connecticut, Delaware, District of Columbia, Foreign Address, Maine, Maryland, Massachusetts, New Hampshire, New Jersey, New York, Pennsylvania, Puerto Rico, Rhode Island, Vermont, Virginia	Holtsville, NY 00501
Alabama, Alaska, Arkansas, California, Florida, Georgia, Hawaii, Idaho, Louisiana, Mississippi, Nevada, North Carolina, Oregon, South Carolina, Tennessee, Washington	Atlanta, GA 39901
Arizona, Colorado, Illinois, Indiana, Iowa, Kansas, Kentucky, Michigan, Minnesota, Missouri, Montana, Nebraska, New Mexico, North Dakota, Ohio, Oklahoma, South Dakota, Texas, Utah, West Virginia, Wisconsin	Memphis, TN 37501

Interest and Penalties

Interest.— Interest is charged on taxes not paid by the due date even if an extension of time to file is granted. Interest is also charged on penalties imposed for failure to file, negligence, fraud, gross valuation overstatements, and substantial understatements of tax from the due date (including extensions) to the date of payment. The interest charge is figured at a rate determined under section 6621 as amended by Public Law 105-206.

Penalty for late filing of return.— If you do not file a return by the due date, including extensions, you may have to pay a penalty of 5% of the unpaid tax for each month or part of a month the return is late, up to a maximum of 25% of the unpaid tax. The minimum penalty for a return that is more than 60 days late is the smaller of the tax due or $100. The penalty will not be imposed if you can show that the failure to file on time was due to reasonable cause. If you file late, you must attach a statement to Form 5330 explaining the reasonable cause.

Penalty for late payment of tax.— If you do not pay the tax when due, you may have to pay a penalty of ½ of 1% of the unpaid tax for each month or part of a month the tax is not paid, up to a maximum of 25% of the unpaid tax. The penalty will not be imposed if you can show that the failure to pay on time was due to reasonable cause.

Note: Interest and penalties will be billed separately after the return is filed.

Claim for Refund or Credit/Amended Return

File an amended Form 5330 for any of the following:

- To claim a refund of overpaid taxes reportable on Form 5330;
- For a credit for overpaid taxes; or
- To report additional taxes due within the same tax year of the filer if those taxes have the same due date as those previously reported. Check the "Amended Return" box in item H on page 1 of the return and report the correct amount of taxes in Parts II through XIV, as appropriate, and on lines 1 through 12a of Part I. See instructions for lines 12a through 12c.

Note: *If you file an amended return to claim a refund or credit, the claim must state in detail the reasons for claiming the refund. In order for us to promptly consider your claim, you must explain why you are filing the claim and provide the appropriate supporting evidence. See Regulations section 301.6402-2 for more details.*

Specific Instructions

Filer tax year.— Enter the tax year of the employer, entity, or individual on whom the tax is imposed.

Item A.—Name and address of filer.— Enter the name and address of the employer, individual, or other entity who is liable for the tax.

Include the suite, room, or other unit numbers after the street number. If the Post Office does not deliver mail to the street address and you have a P.O. box, show the box number instead of the street address.

Item B.—Filer's identification number.— The identification number of an individual (other than a sole proprietor with an employer identification number) is his or her social security number. The identification number of all others is their employer identification number.

Item C.—Name and address of plan sponsor.— The term "plan sponsor" means:

1. The employer, for an employee benefit plan that a single employer established or maintains;
2. The employee organization in the case of a plan of an employee organization; or
3. The association, committee, joint board of trustees, or other similar group of representatives of the parties who establish or maintain the plan, if the plan is established or maintained jointly by one or more employers and one or more employee organizations, or by two or more employers.

Include the suite, room, or other unit numbers after the street number. If the Post Office does not deliver mail to the street address and you have a P.O. box, show the box number instead of the street address.

Item D.—Name of plan.— Enter the formal name of the plan, group insurance arrangement, or enough information to identify the plan. This should be the same name indicated on the Form 5500 series return/report filed for the plan.

Item E.—Plan sponsor's EIN.— Enter the nine-digit employer identification number (EIN) assigned to the plan sponsor. This should be the same number used to file the Form 5500 series return/report.

Item F.—Plan year ending.— Plan year means the calendar or fiscal year on which the records of the plan are kept. Enter four digits in year-month order. This number assists the IRS in properly identifying the plan and time period for which Form 5330 is being filed. For example, a plan year ended March 31, 1996 should be shown as 9603.

Item G.—Plan number.— Enter the three-digit number that the employer or plan administrator assigned to the plan.

Item H.— If this is an amended return, check the box.

Filer's signature.— Please sign and date the form. Also enter a daytime phone number where you can be reached.

Preparer's signature.— Anyone who prepares your return and does not charge you should not sign your return. For example, a regular full-time employee or your business partner who prepares the return should not sign.

Generally, anyone who is paid to prepare a return must sign it and fill in the Paid Preparer's Use Only area.

The paid preparer must complete the required preparer information and—

- Sign the return by hand, in the space provided for the preparer's signature (signature stamps and labels are not acceptable).
- Give a copy of the return to the filer.

Part I

Lines 12a through 12c.— If you are filing an amended Form 5330 and you paid tax with your original return and those taxes have the same due date as those previously reported, check the box in item H and enter the tax reported on your original return in the entry space for line 12b. If you file Form 5330 for a claim for refund or credit, show the amount of overreported tax in parentheses on line 12c. Otherwise, show the amount of additional tax due on line 12c and include the payment with the amended Form 5330.

Part II (Section 4972)

Tax on Nondeductible Employer Contributions to Qualified Plans

Section 4972 imposes an excise tax on employers who make nondeductible contributions to their qualified plans. A "qualified plan" for purposes of this tax means any plan qualified under section 401(a), any annuity plan qualified under section 403(a), and any simplified employee pension plan qualified under section 408(k) or 408(p). The term "qualified plan" does not include certain governmental plans and certain plans maintained by tax-exempt organizations.

The nondeductible contributions are computed as of the end of the employer's tax year. The current year nondeductible contributions are equal to the amount contributed during the employer's tax year over the amount of contributions allowable as a deduction under section 404. In addition, prior year nondeductible contributions (for tax years beginning after December 31, 1986) continue to be subject to this tax annually until eliminated by either distributions to the employer of the amount of nondeductible contributions, or a carryforward deduction in years after the nondeductible contributions are made.

Note: *Although pre-1987 nondeductible contributions are not subject to this excise tax, they are taken into account to determine the extent to which post-1986 contributions are deductible. See section 4972 and* **Pub. 560,** *Retirement Plans for Small Business, for more details.*

Part III (Section 4973(a)(3))

Tax on Excess Contributions to Section 403(b)(7)(A) Custodial Accounts

Line 14.— Reduce total current year contributions by any rollover contributions described in sections 403(b)(8) or 408(d)(3)(A)(iii).

Line 15.— The amount excludable for your tax year is the **smaller** of the exclusion allowance or the annual employer contribution limitation. Figure the amount to enter on line 15 according to the following steps:

Step 1. Multiply the compensation received during the tax year from your employer that was included in gross income by 20%.

Step 2. Multiply the amount in step 1 by the number of years of service as of the end of the tax year for the tax year you are computing this exclusion allowance.

Step 3. Add all of the amounts contributed by your employer in previous years that were not included in your gross income.

Step 4. Subtract step 3 from step 2.

Step 5. Enter the smaller of $30,000 (see the note below), or 25% of the compensation you received during the tax year.

Step 6. Enter the smaller of step 4 or step 5 on line 15, Part III of Form 5330.

Note: *The $30,000 limitation in effect under section 415(c)(1)(A) is subject to changes in the cost-of-living as described in section 415(d). Currently, the dollar limit for a calendar year as adjusted annually for cost-of-living increases is published during the fourth quarter of the prior calendar year in the Internal Revenue Bulletin.*

If you are an employee of an educational institution, hospital, or home health service agency, you may elect

Page 3

alternative limitations under section 415(c)(4)(A), (B), or (C).

Part IV (Section 4976)

Tax on Disqualified Benefits for Funded Welfare Plans

Section 4976 imposes an excise tax on employers who maintain a funded welfare benefit plan that provides a disqualified benefit during any tax year. The tax is 100% of the disqualified benefit.

Generally, a "disqualified benefit" is any of the following:

• Any post-retirement medical benefit or life insurance benefit provided for a key employee unless the benefit is provided from a separate account established for the key employee under section 419A(d);

• Any post-retirement medical or life insurance benefit unless the plan meets the nondiscrimination requirements of section 505(b) for those benefits; or

• Any portion of the fund that reverts to the benefit of the employer.

Part V (Sections 4978, 4978A and 4978B)

Tax on Certain ESOP Dispositions

Caution: *Section 4978A does not apply to the estate of a person who died after December 19, 1989.*

Line 24a.— Report the section 4978 or section 4978A tax on line 24a. Check the box on line 24a to show which tax you are reporting.

Section 4978 imposes an excise tax on dispositions of securities acquired in a sale to which section 1042 applied or in a qualified gratuitous transfer to which section 664(g) applied, if the dispositions take place within 3 years after the date of the acquisition of the qualified securities (as defined in section 1042(c)(1) or a section 664(g) transfer). The tax is 10% of the amount realized on the disposition of the qualified securities if an ESOP or eligible worker-owned cooperative (as defined in section 1042(c)(2)) disposes of the qualified securities within the 3-year period described above, and either of the following applies:

• The total number of shares held by that plan or cooperative after the disposition is less than the total number of employer securities held immediately after the sale, or

• Except to the extent provided in regulations, the value of qualified securities held by the plan or cooperative after the disposition is less than 30% of the total value of all employer securities as of the disposition (60% of the total value of all employer securities in the case of any qualified employer securities acquired in a qualified gratuitous transfer to which section 664(g) applied).

See section 4978(b)(2) for the limitation on the amount of tax.

The section 4978 tax must be paid by the employer or the eligible worker-owned cooperative that made the written statement described in section 1042(b)(3)(B) on dispositions that occurred during their tax year.

The section 4978 tax does not apply to a distribution of qualified securities or sale of such securities if any of the following occurs:

• The death of the employee;

• The retirement of the employee after the employee has reached age 59½;

• The disability of the employee (within the meaning of section 72(m)(7)); or

• The separation of the employee from service for any period that results in a 1-year break in service (as defined in section 411(a)(6)(A)).

For purposes of section 4978, an exchange of qualified securities in a reorganization described in section 368(a)(1) for stock of another corporation will not be treated as a disposition.

Section 4978A imposes a tax on certain transactions involving qualified employer securities. Qualified employer securities for purposes of this tax are defined in section 2057(d).

Section 4978A taxes any disposition of qualified employer securities acquired on or before December 20, 1989, if the disposition of the qualified securities takes place within 3 years after the date the ESOP or eligible worker-owned cooperative acquired the qualified securities.

The section 4978A tax also applies to dispositions of qualified securities that occur after the 3-year period if the qualified securities were not allocated to participants' accounts or the proceeds from the disposition were not allocated to the participants' accounts.

The tax under section 4978A is 30% of the amount realized on the disposition or 30% of the amount repaid on the loan, whichever applies.

Line 24b.— Section 4978B imposes a tax on certain dispositions of section 133 securities held by an employee stock ownership plan (ESOP). This tax is 10% of the amount realized on section 133 securities that are **(1)** disposed of within 3 years of the date the securities were acquired, or **(2)** disposed of before the securities were allocated to participants' accounts and the proceeds of the disposition are not allocated to the accounts of the participants. For exceptions, see section 4978B.

This tax must be paid by the employer.

Part VI (Section 4979A)

Tax on Certain Prohibited Allocations of Qualified ESOP Securities

Section 4979A.— Report on lines 25 and 5 the section 4979A tax on the prohibited allocation of qualified securities by any ESOP or eligible worker-owned cooperative or an allocation described in

section 664(g)(5)(A). The tax is 50% of the prohibited allocation.

Part VII (Section 4975)

Tax on Prohibited Transactions

Note: *Section 141.4975-13 of the Temporary Excise Tax Regulations states that, until permanent regulations are written under section 4975(f), the definitions of "amount involved" and "correction" found in section 53.4941(e)-1 of the Foundation Excise Tax Regulations will apply.*

Line 26a.— Check the box that best characterizes the prohibited transaction for which an excise tax is being paid. A prohibited transaction is discrete unless it is of an ongoing nature. Transactions involving the use of money (loans, etc.) or other property (rent, etc.) are of an ongoing nature and will be treated as a new prohibited transaction on the first day of each succeeding tax year or part of a tax year that is within the **taxable period**.

Line 26b, Column (a).— List all prohibited transactions that took place in connection with a particular plan during the current tax year. Also list all prohibited transactions that took place in prior years unless either the transaction was corrected in a prior tax year or the section 4975(a) tax was assessed in the prior tax year. A disqualified person who engages in a prohibited transaction must file a separate Form 5330 to report the excise tax due under section 4975 for each tax year.

Line 26b, Column (c)—Amount Involved in Prohibited Transaction.— The "amount involved" in a prohibited transaction means the greater of the amount of money and the fair market value of the other property given, or the amount of money and the fair market value of the other property received. However, for services described in sections 4975(d)(2) and (10), the "amount involved" only applies to excess compensation. Fair market value must be determined as of the date on which the prohibited transaction occurs. If the use of money or other property is involved, the amount involved is the greater of the amount paid for the use or the fair market value of the use for the period for which the money or other property is used. In addition, transactions involving the use of money or other property will be treated as giving rise to a prohibited transaction occurring on the date of the actual transaction plus a new prohibited transaction on the first day of each succeeding tax year or portion of a succeeding tax year which is within the "taxable period." The **taxable period** is the period of time beginning with the date of the prohibited transaction and ending with the earliest of: **(a)** the date correction is completed, **(b)** the date of the mailing of a notice of deficiency, or **(c)** the date on which the tax under section 4975(a) is assessed. See the instruction for line 27 for the definition of "correction."

Example for 1996

PART VII—Tax on Prohibited Transactions (section 4975)

b Transaction number	(a) Date of transaction (see instructions)	(b) Description of prohibited transaction	(c) Amount involved in prohibited transaction (see instructions)	(d) Initial tax on prohibited transaction (multiply each transaction in column (c) by the appropriate rate (see instructions))
(i)	7-1-96	Loan	$6,000	$300
(ii)				
(iii)				
26c Add amounts in column (d). Enter here and on line 6 . . . . ▶				$300

Example for 1997

PART VII—Tax on Prohibited Transactions (section 4975)

b Transaction number	(a) Date of transaction (see instructions)	(b) Description of prohibited transaction	(c) Amount involved in prohibited transaction (see instructions)	(d) Initial tax on prohibited transaction (multiply each transaction in column (c) by the appropriate rate (see instructions))
(i)	7-1-96	Loan	$6,000	$300
(ii)	1-1-97	Loan	12,000	1200
(iii)				
26c Add amounts in column (d). Enter here and on line 6 . . . . ▶				$1500

The following example of a prohibited transaction does not cover all types of prohibited transactions. For more examples, see Regulations section 53.4941(e)-1(b)(4).

Example: A disqualified person borrows money from a plan in a prohibited transaction under section 4975. The fair market value of the use of the money and the actual interest on the loan is $1,000 per month. The loan was made on July 1, 1996, and repaid on December 31, 1997 (date of correction). The disqualified person's taxable year is the calendar year. On July 31, 1998, the disqualified person files a delinquent Form 5330 for the 1996 plan year and a timely Form 5330 for the 1997 plan year. No Notice of Deficiency with respect to the tax imposed by section 4975(a) has been mailed to the disqualified person and no assessment of such tax has been made before the time the disqualified person filed the Forms 5330.

When a loan is a prohibited transaction, the loan is treated as giving rise to a prohibited transaction on the date the transaction occurs, and an additional prohibited transaction on the first day of each succeeding taxable year (or portion of a taxable year) within the taxable period that begins on the date the loan occurs. Each prohibited transaction has its own separate taxable period which begins on the date the prohibited transaction occurred or is deemed to occur and ends on the date of the correction. The taxable period that begins on the date the loan occurs runs from July 1, 1996 (date of loan) through December 31, 1997 (date of correction). Therefore, in this example, there are two prohibited transactions, the first occurring on July 1, 1996, and the second occurring on January 1, 1997. **Section 4975(a) imposes an excise tax on the amount involved for each taxable year or part thereof in the taxable period of each**

prohibited transaction. The excise tax rate was increased from 5% to 10% for prohibited transactions occurring after August 20, 1996, and increased from 10% to 15% for prohibited transactions occurring after August 5, 1997.

The amount involved to be reported on the Form 5330 filed for 1996 is $6,000 (6 months X $1,000). The amount of tax due is $300 ($6,000 X 5%). (Any interest and penalties imposed for the delinquent filing of the Form 5330 for 1996 will be billed separately to the disqualified person.)

The taxable period for the second prohibited transaction runs from January 1, 1997, through December 31, 1997 (date of correction). Because there are two prohibited transactions with taxable periods running during 1997, the section 4975(a) tax is due for the 1997 taxable year for both prohibited transactions. The excise tax to be reported on the Form 5330 filed for 1997 would include both the prohibited transaction of July 1, 1996, with an amount involved of $6,000, resulting in a tax due of $300 ($6,000 X 5%) and the second prohibited transaction of January 1, 1997, with an amount involved of $12,000 (12 months X $1,000), resulting in a tax due of $1,200 ($12,000 X 10%). Complete line 26 of the Forms 5330 as shown.

Line 27.— To avoid liability for additional taxes and penalties under section 4975, and in some cases further initial taxes, a correction of the prohibited transaction must be made within the taxable period. The term "correction" is defined as undoing the prohibited transaction to the extent possible, but in any case placing the plan in a financial position not worse than that in which it would be if the disqualified person were acting under the highest fiduciary standards.

If the "No" box is checked on line 27, there has not been a correction of ALL of the prohibited transactions by the end of

the tax year for which this Form 5330 is being filed. Please attach a statement indicating when correction has been or will be made. Also, complete line 29, Part IX, for each prohibited transaction that has been corrected, if any, giving the following information: **(a)** the number of the transaction from Part VII; **(b)** the nature of the correction; and **(c)** the date of the correction.

Part VIII

Schedule of Other Participating Disqualified Persons

If more than one disqualified person participated in the same prohibited transaction, list on this schedule the name, address, and the social security number or employer identification number of each disqualified person, other than the disqualified person who files this return.

Part X (Section 4971(a))

Tax on Failure To Meet Minimum Funding Standards

Line 30.— If your plan has an accumulated funding deficiency as defined in section 412(a) (section 418B if this is a multiemployer plan in reorganization), complete line 30.
Line 31.— Multiply line 30 by the applicable tax rate shown below and enter the result on line 31.

● 10% for plans (other than multiemployer plans).

● 5% for all multiemployer plans.

Note: *Except in the case of a multiemployer plan, all members of a controlled group are jointly and severally liable for this tax. A "controlled group" in this case means a controlled group of corporations (section 414(b)), a group of trades or businesses under common control (section 414(c)), an affiliated service group (section 414(m)), and any*

Page 5

other group treated as a single employer under section 414(o).

Note: *To avoid liability for additional taxes and penalties under section 4971, the accumulated funding deficiency must be corrected.*

Part XI (Section 4977)

Tax on Excess Fringe Benefits

Line 32.— If you made an election to be taxed under section 4977 to continue your nontaxable fringe benefit policy that was in existence on or after January 1, 1984, check the "Yes" box on line 32a and complete lines 32b through 32d.

Line 32c.— The excess fringe benefits are figured by subtracting 1% of the aggregate compensation paid by you to your employees during the calendar year that was includable in their gross income from the aggregate value of the nontaxable fringe benefits under sections 132(a)(1) and 132(a)(2).

Part XII (Section 4979)

Tax on Excess Contributions to Plans With a Cash or Deferred Arrangement

Section 4979.— Any employer who maintains a plan described in section 401(a), 403(a), 403(b), 408(k), or 501(c)(18) may be subject to an excise tax on the excess aggregate contributions made on behalf of highly compensated employees. The employer may also be subject to an excise tax on the excess contributions to a cash or deferred arrangement connected with the plan.

The tax is on the excess contributions and the excess aggregate contributions made to or on behalf of the highly compensated employees (as defined in section 414(q)).

For years beginning *before* January 1, 1997, generally, a highly compensated employee is an employee who, at any time during the year or the preceding year:

1. Was a 5-percent owner,

2. Received more than $100,000 (for 1996) in annual compensation from the employer,

3. Received more than $66,000 (for 1996) in annual compensation from the employer and was in the top-paid group of employees during the same year, or

4. Was an officer of the employer who received compensation in excess of $60,000 (for 1996).

For years beginning *after* December 31, 1996, generally, a highly compensated employee is an employee who:

1. Was a 5-percent owner at any time during the year or the preceding year, or,

2. For the preceding year had compensation from the employer in

excess of a dollar amount for the year ($80,000 for 1997 and 1998) and, if the employer so elects, was in the top-paid group for the preceding year.

An employee is in the top-paid group for any year if the employee is in the group consisting of the top 20 percent of the employees of the employer when ranked on the basis of compensation paid. An employee (who is not a 5-percent owner) who has compensation in excess of $80,000 is not a highly compensated employee if the employer elects the top-paid group limitation and the employee is not a member of the top-paid group.

The "excess contributions" subject to the section 4979 excise tax are equal to the amount by which employer contributions actually paid over to the trust exceed the employer contributions that could have been made without violating the special nondiscrimination requirements of section 401(k)(3).

The "excess aggregate contributions" subject to the section 4979 excise tax are equal to the amount by which the aggregate matching contributions of the employer and the employee contributions (and any qualified nonelective contribution or elective contribution taken into account in computing the contribution percentage under section 401(m)) actually made on behalf of the highly compensated employees for each plan year exceed the maximum amount of the contributions permitted in the contribution percentage computation under section 401(m)(2)(A).

However, there is no excise tax liability if the excess contributions or the excess aggregate contributions and any income earned on the excess contributions are distributed (or, if forfeitable, forfeited) to the participants for whom the excess contributions were made within 2½ months after the end of the plan year.

Part XIII (Section 4980)

Tax on Reversion of Qualified Plan Assets to an Employer

Section 4980.— Include on lines 36 and 10 the section 4980 tax on employer reversions from a qualified plan. The reversion excise tax is either 50% or 20%. The excise tax rate is 50% if the employer **(1)** does not establish or maintain a qualified replacement plan following the plan termination, or **(2)** provide certain pro-rata benefit increases in connection with the plan termination. See section 4980(d)(1)(A) or (B) for more information.

If you owe the section 4980 tax, enter the date of the reversion on line 34 and the reversion amount and applicable excise tax rate on line 35. If you use a tax percentage other than 50%, explain on line 37 why you qualify to use a rate other than 50%.

Part XIV (Section 4971(f))

Tax on Failure to Correct Liquidity Shortfall

Section 4971(f).— If your plan has a liquidity shortfall for which an excise tax under 4971(f) is imposed for any quarter of the plan year, complete lines 38 through 41.

Line 38.— Include on line 38 the amount of the liquidity shortfall(s) for each quarter of the plan year.

Line 39.— Include on line 39 the amount of any contributions made to the plan by the due date of the required quarterly installment(s) which partially "corrected" the liquidity shortfall(s) reported on line 38.

Line 40.— Include on line 40 the net amount of the liquidity shortfall (subtract line 39 from line 38).

Recordkeeping	18 hr., 39 min.
Learning about the law or the form	8hr., 50 min.
Preparing and sending the form to the IRS	9hr., 32min.

2828   ☐ VOID   ☐ CORRECTED

TRUSTEE'S or ISSUER'S name, street address, city, state, and ZIP code	1 IRA contributions (other than amounts in boxes 2, 3, and 7–10) $	OMB No. 1545-0747	
	2 Rollover contributions $	**2000** Form **5498**	**IRA Contribution Information**
TRUSTEE'S or ISSUER'S Federal identification no.	PARTICIPANT'S social security number	3 Roth conversion amount $	**Copy A**
PARTICIPANT'S name		4 Fair market value of account $	5 Life insurance cost included in box 1 $	**For Internal Revenue Service Center** File with Form 1096.
Street address (including apt. no.)		6 IRA ☐ SEP ☐ SIMPLE ☐ Roth IRA ☐ Rechar. ☐ Ed IRA ☐	For Privacy Act and Paperwork Reduction Act
City, state, and ZIP code		7 SEP contributions $	8 SIMPLE contributions $	Notice, see the **2000 General Instructions for**
Account number (optional)		9 Roth IRA contributions $	10 Ed IRA contributions $	**Forms 1099, 1098, 5498, and W-2G.**

Form **5498**   Cat. No. 50010C   Department of the Treasury - Internal Revenue Service

Do NOT Cut or Separate Forms on This Page   —   Do NOT Cut or Separate Forms on This Page

Form **8606**	**Nondeductible IRAs**	OMB No. 1545-1007
Department of the Treasury Internal Revenue Service (99)	▶ See separate instructions. ▶ Attach to Form 1040, Form 1040A, or Form 1040NR.	**2000** Attachment Sequence No. **48**

Name. If married, file a separate form for each spouse required to file Form 8606. See page 3 of the instructions.   **Your social security number**

Fill in Your Address Only if You Are Filing This Form by Itself and Not With Your Tax Return ▷

Home address (number and street, or P.O. box if mail is not delivered to your home)   Apt. no.

City, town or post office, state, and ZIP code

Part I   Traditional and SIMPLE IRAs

Complete Part I if:
- You made nondeductible contributions to a traditional IRA for 2000,
- You received distributions from a traditional or SIMPLE IRA in 2000 **and** you made nondeductible contributions to a traditional IRA in 2000 or an earlier year, **or**
- You converted part, but not all, of your traditional or SIMPLE IRAs to Roth IRAs in 2000 **and** you made nondeductible contributions to a traditional IRA in 2000 or an earlier year. See the instructions for lines 8, 11, and 15 for special computations.

1	Enter your nondeductible contributions to traditional IRAs for 2000, including those made for 2000 from January 1, 2001, through April 16, 2001. See page 3 of the instructions	1	
2	Enter your total basis in traditional IRAs for 1999 and earlier years. See page 3 of the instructions .	2	
3	Add lines 1 and 2	3	

Did you receive any distributions from traditional or SIMPLE IRAs or make a Roth IRA conversion in 2000? — **No** ——▶ Enter the amount from line 3 on line 12. Do not complete the rest of Part I.

— **Yes** ——▶ Go to line 4.

4	Enter only those contributions included on line 1 that were made from January 1, 2001, through April 16, 2001. See page 3 of the instructions	4	
5	Subtract line 4 from line 3	5	
6	Enter the value of **all** your traditional and SIMPLE IRAs as of December 31, 2000, plus any outstanding rollovers. See page 4 of the instructions	6	
7	Enter your total distributions from traditional and SIMPLE IRAs in 2000. **Do not** include rollovers or Roth IRA conversions. See page 4 of the instructions	7	
8	Add lines 6 and 7. (But if you converted any amount from traditional or SIMPLE IRAs to Roth IRAs in 2000, see page 4 of the instructions for the amount to enter.) . .	8	
9	Divide line 5 by line 8 and enter the result as a decimal (rounded to at least 3 places). **Do not** enter more than "1.000"	9	× .
10	Multiply line 7 by line 9. This is the amount of your nontaxable distributions for 2000	10	
11	Subtract line 10 from line 5. (But if you converted any amount from traditional or SIMPLE IRAs to Roth IRAs in 2000, see page 4 of the instructions for the amount to enter.) This is your basis in traditional IRAs as of December 31, 2000.	11	
12	Add lines 4 and 11. This is your **total basis in traditional IRAs for 2000 and earlier years** . . .	12	
13	**Taxable distributions from traditional and SIMPLE IRAs.** Subtract line 10 from line 7. Also include this amount on Form 1040, line 15b; Form 1040A, line 11b; or Form 1040NR, line 16b	13	

Part II   2000 Conversions From Traditional or SIMPLE IRAs to Roth IRAs

Caution: *If your modified adjusted gross income is over $100,000 **or** you are married filing separately and you lived with your spouse at any time in 2000, you* **cannot** *convert any amount from traditional or SIMPLE IRAs to Roth IRAs for 2000. If you erroneously made a conversion, you must recharacterize (correct) the conversion. See page 4 of the instructions for details.*

14a	Enter the total amount you converted from traditional and SIMPLE IRAs to Roth IRAs in 2000 . .	14a	
b	Enter the portion of the amount on line 14a that you **recharacterized** back to a traditional or SIMPLE IRA. **Do not** include earnings or reduce the amount recharacterized by any loss that occurred in the Roth IRA. See page 5 of the instructions	14b	
c	Subtract line 14b from line 14a. This is the net amount you converted to Roth IRAs in 2000 . . .	14c	
15	Enter your basis in the amount on line 14c from traditional IRAs. See page 6 of the instructions . .	15	
16	**Taxable amount of conversions.** Subtract line 15 from line 14c. Also include this amount on Form 1040, line 15b; Form 1040A, line 11b; or Form 1040NR, line 16b	16	

For Paperwork Reduction Act Notice, see page 8.   Cat. No. 63966F   Form **8606** (2000)

Form 8606 (2000)   Page **2**

Part III — Distributions From Roth IRAs

Complete Part III **only** if you received a Roth IRA distribution in 2000 or you recharacterized 2000 contributions to or from a Roth IRA.

(TIP) Be sure to keep copies of all Forms 1099-R, 5498, and 8606 for all years. You will need amounts from these forms if you take a nonqualified distribution (see page 2 of the instructions) from a Roth IRA in future years.

17	Enter your total distributions from Roth IRAs in 2000. **Do not** include rollovers	17
18a	Enter your basis in Roth IRA contributions for **1998** and **1999**. See page 6 of the instructions	18a
b	Enter your contributions to Roth IRAs for 2000, including those made for 2000 from January 1, 2001, through April 16, 2001. **Do not** include rollovers or amounts converted from traditional or SIMPLE IRAs	18b
c	Recharacterizations of 2000 contributions to or from Roth IRAs. See page 6 of the instructions	18c
d	Combine lines 18a through 18c	18d
19	Subtract line 18d from line 17. If zero or less, enter -0- and **do not** complete the rest of Part III	19

Note: If you converted amounts from traditional IRAs to Roth IRAs in **1998** and elected to report the taxable portion over 4 years, go to line 20a; otherwise, skip to line 21.

20a	Enter the amount from your **1998** Form 8606, line 16	20a
b	Enter the amount from line 5 of the worksheet on page 6 of the instructions	20b
c	Enter the amount from line 8 of the worksheet on page 6 of the instructions ▶	20c
d	Add lines 20b and 20c	20d
e	Subtract line 20d from line 20a. If zero or less, enter -0-	20e
21	Enter the **smaller** of line 19 or line 20e. If line 20e is blank, enter -0- ▶	21
22	Subtract line 21 from line 19. If zero, skip lines 23 through 26 and go to line 27	22
23	Enter your basis in Roth IRA conversions for **1998** and **1999**. See page 7 of the instructions	23
24	Enter the amount, if any, from line 14c of this form	24
25	Add lines 23 and 24	25
26	Subtract line 25 from line 19. If zero or less, enter -0- ▶	26
27	**Taxable distributions from Roth IRAs.** Add lines 20c, 21, and 26. Also include this amount in the total on Form 1040, line 15b; Form 1040A, line 11b; or Form 1040NR, line 16b	27

Note: You may be subject to an additional 10% tax. See page 7 of the instructions for details.

Part IV — Distributions From Education (Ed) IRAs

Caution: For 2000, you can receive up to $500 of contributions to Ed IRAs. See page 7 of the instructions if the contributions to your Ed IRAs were over $500.

28	Enter the total distributions from your Ed IRAs in 2000. **Do not** include rollovers	28
29	Do you elect to waive the exclusion from income for Ed IRA distributions? If you check "No" and exclude from income any portion of an Ed IRA distribution, no Hope or lifetime learning credit can be claimed for your 2000 qualified higher education expenses.	29
	☐ **Yes.** Enter -0-.	
	☐ **No.** Enter your qualified higher education expenses for 2000.	
30	**Taxable amount.** Is line 28 equal to or less than line 29?	30
	☐ **Yes.** Enter -0-; none of your Ed IRA distributions are taxable for 2000. Be sure to keep a copy of this form for your records so you can figure your basis in your Ed IRAs. You may need to know your basis in future years. See page 7 of the instructions.	
	☐ **No.** See the worksheet on page 7 of the instructions for the amount to enter. Also include this amount in the total on Form 1040, line 15b; Form 1040A, line 11b; or Form 1040NR, line 16b. See page 8 of the instructions to find out if you owe an additional 10% tax.	

Sign Here Only if You Are Filing This Form by Itself and Not With Your Tax Return

Under penalties of perjury, I declare that I have examined this form, including accompanying attachments, and to the best of my knowledge and belief, it is true, correct, and complete.

▶ _____   ▶ _____
Your signature   Date

Form **8606** (2000)

20**00**

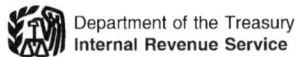

Department of the Treasury
Internal Revenue Service

Instructions for Form 8606

Nondeductible IRAs

Section references are to the Internal Revenue Code unless otherwise noted.

General Instructions

Purpose of Form

Use Form 8606 to report:
- Nondeductible contributions to traditional IRAs,
- Distributions from traditional or SIMPLE IRAs, if you have ever made nondeductible contributions to traditional IRAs,
- Distributions from Roth IRAs,
- Distributions from education (Ed) IRAs,
- Conversions from traditional or SIMPLE IRAs to Roth IRAs, and
- Recharacterizations of Roth IRA conversions or contributions to or from a Roth IRA.

Additional information. See **Pub. 590,** Individual Retirement Arrangements (IRAs), and Regulations section 1.408A for more details.

 If you received distributions from a traditional or SIMPLE IRA in 2000 and you have never made nondeductible contributions to traditional IRAs, do not report the distributions on Form 8606. Instead, see the instructions for Form 1040, lines 15a and 15b; Form 1040A, lines 11a and 11b; or Form 1040NR, lines 16a and 16b. Also, to find out if any of your contributions to traditional IRAs are deductible, see the instructions for Form 1040, line 23; Form 1040A, line 16; or Form 1040NR, line 24.

Who Must File

File Form 8606 if any of the following apply.
- You made nondeductible contributions to a traditional IRA for 2000.
- You received distributions from a traditional or SIMPLE IRA in 2000 **and** you have ever made nondeductible contributions to a traditional IRA.

- You converted an amount from a traditional or SIMPLE IRA to a Roth IRA in 2000 (even if you later recharacterized the conversion).
- You received distributions from a Roth IRA in 2000.
- You recharacterized a 2000 Roth IRA contribution as a traditional IRA contribution, or vice versa.
- You are the beneficiary of an Ed IRA **and** you received distributions from an Ed IRA in 2000.

TIP *You are **not** required to file Form 8606 solely to report contributions to Roth IRAs. But see **What Records Must I Keep?** on page 3.*

1998 Roth IRA Conversions

If you converted a traditional IRA to a Roth IRA in 1998 and are reporting the taxable portion of the conversion over 4 years, the 2000 taxable portion generally is the same amount as you reported on your 1998 Form 8606, line 17. However, if you received a Roth IRA distribution in 1998 or 1999, the 2000 taxable portion cannot exceed one-half of the amount from your 1998 Form 8606, line 16, reduced by the sum of line 22 of that Form 8606 and line 21 of your 1999 Form 8606.

How To Report

Report the 2000 taxable portion of your 1998 Roth IRA conversion as follows.
- If you did not receive a Roth IRA distribution in 2000, include the 2000 taxable portion on Form 1040, line 15b; Form 1040A, line 11b; or Form 1040NR, line 16b. **Do not** file Form 8606 unless you are otherwise required to do so.
- If you received a Roth IRA distribution in 2000, complete lines 17 through 19 of Form 8606. If line 19 is zero, **do not** complete the rest of Part III and include the 2000 taxable portion on Form 1040, line 15b; Form 1040A, line 11b; or Form 1040NR,

line 16b. If line 19 is more than zero, complete the rest of Part III. The 2000 taxable portion will be figured on line 20c and included in the total on line 27. Include the total from line 27 on Form 1040, line 15b; Form 1040A, line 11b; or Form 1040NR, line 16b.

Death of Roth IRA owner. If the owner of the Roth IRA died in 2000, the entire amount not taxed in 1998 and 1999 generally must be reported on the decedent's final tax return. However, a surviving spouse who acquires the entire interest in all of the decedent's Roth IRAs may elect to continue to report the taxable amount over the remaining 2 tax years. To make the election, attach a statement to the surviving spouse's timely filed 2000 tax return (and to the decedent's final return, if a joint return is not filed). Include the following items on the election statement.
- A statement that the surviving spouse elects to continue to report the taxable portion from the decedent's 1998 Roth IRA conversion over the remaining 2 tax years.
- The names and social security numbers (SSNs) of the surviving spouse and the decedent.
- The total taxable amount of the decedent's 1998 Roth IRA conversion from the decedent's 1998 Form 8606, line 16.
- The amounts, if any, reported on the decedent's 1998 Form 8606, line 22, and 1999 Form 8606, line 21.

The surviving spouse must report as a taxable IRA distribution for 2000 the same amount as the decedent would have reported, and in the same manner, on the surviving spouse's tax return. See Pub. 590 for details.

When and Where To File

File Form 8606 with your 2000 Form 1040, 1040A, or 1040NR. If you are not required to file an income tax return but are required to file Form 8606, sign Form 8606 and send it to the Internal Revenue Service at the

Cat. No. 25399E

same time and place you would otherwise file Form 1040, 1040A, or 1040NR.

Definitions

Traditional IRAs

A traditional IRA is an individual retirement account or an individual retirement annuity. It includes a SEP IRA but does not include a SIMPLE IRA, Ed IRA, or Roth IRA.

Contributions. An overall contribution limit applies to traditional IRAs and Roth IRAs. See page 3. Contributions to a traditional IRA may be fully deductible, partially deductible, or completely nondeductible.

Basis. Your basis in traditional IRAs is the total of all your nondeductible contributions to traditional IRAs minus the total of all your nontaxable distributions. Keep track of your basis to figure the nontaxable part of your future distributions.

SEP IRAs. A simplified employee pension (SEP) is an employer-sponsored plan under which an employer can make contributions to traditional IRAs for its employees.

SIMPLE IRAs

If your employer has a SIMPLE IRA retirement plan, you or your employer may make contributions to your SIMPLE IRA. Your participation in a SIMPLE IRA plan does not prevent you from making contributions to a traditional or Roth IRA. SIMPLE IRA distributions are reported like traditional IRA distributions.

Education (Ed) IRAs

An Ed IRA is not a qualified retirement plan, but is a trust or custodial account created exclusively for paying the qualified higher education expenses of a designated beneficiary. See Pub. 590 for details on Ed IRAs.

Roth IRAs

A Roth IRA is similar to a traditional IRA but has the following features.

● Contributions are never deductible.

● Contributions can be made after the owner reaches age 70½.

● No minimum distributions are required during the owner's lifetime.

● Qualified distributions are not includible in income.

Generally, a **qualified distribution** is any distribution made:

● On or after age 59½,

● Upon death,

● Due to disability, or

● For qualified first-time homebuyer expenses.

However, any distribution made during the 5-year period beginning with the first year for which you made a Roth IRA contribution or conversion is **not** a qualified distribution, and may be taxable. A nonqualified distribution is any distribution that does not meet the conditions of a qualified distribution. Because 1998 was the first year for which Roth IRA contributions or conversions could be made, **all** Roth IRA distributions prior to 2003 are nonqualified distributions.

Contributions. You can contribute to a Roth IRA only if your 2000 modified adjusted gross income (AGI) for Roth IRA purposes is less than:

● $10,000 if married filing separately and you lived with your spouse at any time in 2000;

● $160,000 if married filing jointly; or

● $110,000 if single, head of household, or qualifying widow(er), or if married filing separately and you did not live with your spouse at any time in 2000.

Use the **Maximum Roth IRA Contribution Worksheet** below to figure the maximum amount you can contribute to a Roth IRA for 2000.

 If you contributed more than your maximum amount to a Roth IRA, see **Recharacterizations** *on page 4.*

Modified AGI for Roth IRA purposes. Refigure your AGI from Form 1040, line 33; Form 1040A, line 19; or Form 1040NR, line 33; by:

1. Subtracting any amount due to Roth IRA conversions included on Form 1040, line 15b; Form 1040A, line 11b; or Form 1040NR, line 16b; and

2. Adding the following:

● IRA deduction from Form 1040, line 23; Form 1040A, line 16; or Form 1040NR, line 24;

● Student loan interest deduction from Form 1040, line 24; Form 1040A, line 17; or Form 1040NR, line 25;

● Exclusion of interest from **Form 8815,** Exclusion of Interest From Series EE and I U.S. Savings Bonds Issued After 1989;

● Exclusion of employer-provided adoption benefits from **Form 8839,** Qualified Adoption Expenses;

● Foreign earned income exclusion from **Form 2555,** Foreign Earned

Maximum Roth IRA Contribution Worksheet (keep for your records)

> ⚠ **CAUTION** *If married filing jointly and the combined taxable compensation for you and your spouse is less than $4,000,* **do not** *use this worksheet. Instead, see Pub. 590 for special rules.*

1 If married filing jointly enter $2,000. All others, enter the **smaller** of $2,000 or your taxable compensation (defined on page 3) . . .	**1** _____
2 Enter your total contributions to traditional IRAs for 2000 . . .	**2** _____
3 Subtract line 2 from line 1	**3** _____
4 Enter: $160,000 if married filing jointly; $10,000 if married filing separately and you lived with your spouse at any time in 2000. All other filers, enter $110,000	**4** _____
5 Enter your modified AGI for Roth IRA purposes (see above)	**5** _____
6 Subtract line 5 from line 4. If zero or less, **stop here;** you may not contribute to a Roth IRA for 2000. See **Recharacterizations** on page 4 if you made Roth IRA contributions for 2000	**6** _____
7 If line 4 above is $110,000, enter $15,000; otherwise, enter $10,000. If line 6 is more than or equal to line 7, skip lines 8 and 9 and enter the amount from line 3 on line 10	**7** _____
8 Divide line 6 by line 7 and enter the result as a decimal (rounded to at least 3 places). Do not enter more than "1.000"	**8** _____
9 Multiply line 1 by line 8. If the result is not a multiple of $10, round it up to the next multiple of $10 (for example, round $490.30 to $500). Enter the result, but not less than $200	**9** _____
10 Maximum 2000 Roth IRA Contribution. Enter the **smaller** of line 3 or line 9. See **Recharacterizations** on page 4 if you contributed more than this amount to Roth IRAs for 2000	**10** _____

Page 2

Income, or **Form 2555-EZ,** Foreign Earned Income Exclusion; and

• Foreign housing exclusion or deduction from Form 2555.

 When figuring modified AGI for Roth IRA purposes, you may have to refigure items based on modified AGI, such as taxable social security benefits and passive activity losses allowed under the special allowance for rental real estate activities. See **Can I Contribute to a Roth IRA** *in Pub. 590 for details.*

Distributions. See the instructions for Part III beginning on page 6.

Overall Contribution Limit for Traditional and Roth IRAs

If you are **not** married filing jointly, your limit on contributions to traditional and Roth IRAs is the **smaller** of $2,000 or your taxable compensation (see below). If you are married filing jointly, your contribution limit is generally $2,000 (and your spouse's contribution limit is $2,000 as well). But if the combined taxable compensation of both you and your spouse is less than $4,000, see Pub. 590 for special rules. This limit does not apply to employer contributions to a SEP or SIMPLE IRA.

 The amount you may contribute to a Roth IRA may also be limited by your modified AGI (see **Roth IRAs** *on page 2).*

Taxable compensation includes the following.

• Wages, salaries, tips, etc.

• Self-employment income. If you are self-employed (a sole proprietor or a partner), taxable compensation is your net earnings from your trade or business (provided your personal services are a material income-producing factor) reduced by your deduction for contributions made on your behalf to retirement plans and the deduction allowed for one-half of your self-employment tax.

• Alimony and separate maintenance.

See Pub. 590 for details.

Note: *Rollovers and Roth IRA conversions* **do not** *affect your contribution limit.*

Amending Form 8606

After you file your return, you may change a nondeductible contribution to a traditional IRA to a deductible contribution or vice versa. You also may be able to make a recharacterization (see page 4). If necessary, complete a new Form 8606 showing the revised information and file it with **Form 1040X,** Amended U.S. Individual Income Tax Return.

Penalty for Not Filing

If you are required to file Form 8606 for 2000 but do not do so, you must pay a $50 penalty, unless you can show reasonable cause.

Penalty for Overstatement

If you overstate your nondeductible contributions, you must pay a $100 penalty, unless you can show reasonable cause.

What Records Must I Keep?

To verify the nontaxable part of distributions from your IRAs, including Roth IRAs and Ed IRAs, keep a copy of the following forms and records until all distributions are made from your IRAs.

• Page 1 of Forms 1040 (or Forms 1040A, 1040NR, or 1040-T) filed for each year you made a nondeductible contribution to a traditional IRA.

• Forms 8606 and any supporting statements and worksheets for all applicable years.

• Forms 5498 or similar statements you received each year showing contributions you made to a traditional IRA, Roth IRA, or Ed IRA.

• Forms 5498 or similar statements you received showing the value of your traditional IRAs and Ed IRAs for each year you received a distribution.

• Forms 1099-R or W-2P you received for each year you received a distribution.

Note: *Forms 1040-T and W-2P are forms used in prior years.*

Specific Instructions

Name and social security number (SSN). If you file a joint return, enter only the name and SSN of the spouse whose IRA information is being reported on Form 8606.

Part I—Traditional and SIMPLE IRAs

Line 1

If you used the **IRA Deduction Worksheet** in the Form 1040 or 1040A instructions, subtract line 10 of the worksheet (line 8 of the Form 1040A worksheet) (or the amount you chose to deduct on Form 1040, line 23, or Form 1040A, line 16, if less) from the **smaller** of line 8 or line 9 of the worksheet (line 6 or line 7 of the Form 1040A worksheet). Enter the result on line 1 of Form 8606. You cannot deduct the amount included on line 1.

If you used the **Worksheet for Reduced IRA Deduction** in Pub. 590, enter on line 1 of Form 8606 any nondeductible contributions from the appropriate lines of that worksheet.

If you did not have any deductible contributions, you may make nondeductible contributions up to your contribution limit. Enter on line 1 of Form 8606 your nondeductible contributions.

Do not include on line 1 contributions that were returned to you with the related earnings (or less any loss). See the instructions for line 7.

Line 2

If this is the first year you are required to file Form 8606, enter zero. Otherwise, use the chart below to find the amount to enter on line 2.

IF the last Form 8606 you filed was for . . .	THEN enter on line 2 . . .
A year after 1992	The amount from line 12 of that Form 8606
A year after 1988 and before 1993	The amount from line 14 of that Form 8606
1988	The total of the amounts on lines 7 and 16 of that Form 8606
1987	The total of the amounts on lines 4 and 13 of that Form 8606

Line 4

If you made contributions for 2000 in 2000 and 2001 and you have both deductible and nondeductible contributions, you may choose to treat the contributions made in 2000 first as nondeductible contributions and then as deductible contributions, or vice versa. But the amount on line 1 minus the amount on line 4 cannot be more than the contributions you actually made in 2000.

Example. You made contributions of $1,000 in 2000 and $1,000 in 2001, of which $1,500 are deductible and $500 are nondeductible. You choose $500 of your contribution in 2000 to be nondeductible. You enter the $500 on line 1, but not line 4, and it becomes part of your basis for 2000.

Although the contributions for 2000 that you made from January 1, 2001, through April 16, 2001, to traditional IRAs can be treated as nondeductible, they are not included in figuring the nontaxable part of any distributions you received in 2000.

Line 6

Enter the total value of **all** your traditional IRAs and SIMPLE IRAs as of December 31, 2000, **plus** any outstanding rollovers. You should receive a statement by January 31, 2001, showing the value of each IRA on December 31, 2000. However, if you recharacterized any amounts, enter on line 6 the total value taking into account all recharacterizations, including recharacterizations made after December 31, 2000.

For line 6, a **rollover** is a tax-free distribution from one traditional or SIMPLE IRA that is contributed to another traditional or SIMPLE IRA. The rollover must be completed within 60 days of receiving the distribution from the first IRA. An **outstanding rollover** is any amount distributed from one traditional or SIMPLE IRA within 60 days before the end of 2000 (from November 2 through December 31) that was rolled over to another traditional or SIMPLE IRA after December 31, 2000, but within the 60-day rollover period.

Line 7

! *If you received a distribution in 2000 from a traditional or SIMPLE IRA and you also made contributions for 2000 to a traditional IRA that may not be fully deductible because of the income limits, you must make a special computation before completing this form. For details, including how to*

complete Form 8606, see **Are Distributions Taxable?** in Chapter 1 of Pub. 590.

Do not include any of the following amounts on line 7.

1. Distributions from a traditional or SIMPLE IRA in 2000 that you converted to a Roth IRA.

2. Distributions you received from a traditional or SIMPLE IRA in 2000 and rolled over to another traditional or SIMPLE IRA by December 31, 2000.

3. Outstanding rollovers included on line 6.

4. Contributions you do not deduct that were distributed (returned to you) with the related earnings (or less any loss) by the due date of your tax return, including extensions. You may **not** deduct any loss that occurred. Include any related earnings in income for the year in which you made the contribution. For contributions made in 2000, report the total amount withdrawn on line 15a and any earnings on line 15b if filing Form 1040; lines 11a and 11b if filing Form 1040A; or lines 16a and 16b if filing Form 1040NR. Also, see Form 5329 if you were under age 59½ at the time of the distribution. Withdrawn contributions are treated as if they were never contributed for purposes of figuring basis and therefore are not reported on Form 8606.

5. If your contributions to traditional IRAs for 2000 were $2,000 or less, any portion of those contributions not allowable as a deduction (without regard to the modified adjusted gross income limitation), and that you did not deduct, that were returned to you after the due date of your return, including extensions.

Line 8

If you converted part or all of your traditional or SIMPLE IRAs to Roth IRAs in 2000, complete lines 14a through 14c before completing line 8. Then enter the total of lines 6, 7, and 14c on line 8.

Line 11

If you converted part or all of your traditional or SIMPLE IRAs to Roth IRAs in 2000, multiply line 9 by line 14c and add the result to the amount on line 10. Then subtract that total from line 5 and enter the result on line 11.

Part II—2000 Conversions From Traditional or SIMPLE IRAs to Roth IRAs

Limit on number of conversions. If you converted an amount from a traditional or SIMPLE IRA to a Roth IRA in 2000 and then recharacterized the amount back to a traditional or SIMPLE IRA, you may not reconvert that amount until the **later** of January 1, 2001, or 30 days after the rechracterization. See Pub. 590 and Regulations section 1.408A-5 for details.

  *You may not convert any amount from your traditional IRAs to Roth IRAs in 2000 if **(a)** your modified AGI for Roth IRA purposes (see page 2) is more than $100,000 **or (b)** your filing status is married filing separately and you lived with your spouse at any time in 2000. If you erroneously made a conversion, you must recharacterize the converted amount.*

Recharacterizations

Generally, you may recharacterize (correct) an IRA contribution or Roth IRA conversion by making a trustee-to-trustee transfer from one IRA to another type of IRA. Trustee-to-trustee transfers are made directly between financial institutions or within the same financial institution. You generally must make the transfer by the due date of your return (including extensions) and reflect it on your return. However, if you timely filed your return without making the transfer, you still may make the transfer within 6 months of the due date of your return, excluding extensions. If necessary, file an amended return reflecting the transfer. Write "Filed pursuant to section 301.9100-2" on the amended return and file it at the same place you filed the original return.

There are three types of recharacterizations.

1. You converted an amount from a traditional or SIMPLE IRA to a Roth IRA and later recharacterize part or all of it back to a traditional or SIMPLE IRA.

2. You made a contribution to a traditional IRA and later recharacterize part or all of it to a Roth IRA.

3. You made a contribution to a Roth IRA and later recharacterize part or all of it to a traditional IRA.

Any recharacterized conversion will be treated as though it had not occurred. Any recharacterized contributions will be treated as having been contributed to the second IRA and not the first IRA. You cannot take a deduction for a contribution to a traditional IRA if the amount is later recharacterized. The amount transferred **must** include related earnings or be reduced by any loss.

Completion of Form 8606 for Recharacterizations

Traditional IRAs. Complete Part I of Form 8606 to reflect your traditional IRAs after the recharacterization. For example, you convert a traditional IRA to a Roth IRA. Later, you recharacterize the balance from the Roth IRA back to a traditional IRA. Disregard the conversion to the Roth IRA and report the original balances for your traditional IRAs on Part I.

Roth IRAs. If you convert an amount from a traditional or SIMPLE IRA to a Roth IRA and later recharacterize part or all of the amount back to a traditional or SIMPLE IRA, complete Part II as follows.

1. On line 14a, report the amount you originally converted.

2. On line 14b, report the portion of the amount you originally converted that you recharacterized, excluding earnings or any loss.

3. On line 14c, show the net result after any changes. If you recharacterized the entire amount you converted, lines 14a and 14b will be the same and line 14c will be zero.

4. If line 14c is more than zero, complete the rest of Part II as instructed.

Statement explaining recharacterization. Attach a statement to Form 8606 explaining the recharacterization. For example, for a recharacterized contribution, attach a statement that shows the total amount recharacterized, the original contribution, the earnings or loss, and the amount that is now a deductible traditional IRA contribution, if any.

If you recharacterized contributions to or from a Roth IRA, complete Part III. Enter on line 18b the amount originally contributed to a Roth IRA

and on line 18c the amount recharacterized, excluding earnings or any loss. If you received a distribution from a Roth IRA in 2000, complete the rest of Part III as instructed.

Note: *You may receive a Form 1099-R for each conversion (showing the distribution from the traditional or SIMPLE IRA) and a Form 1099-R for each recharacterization (showing the distribution from the IRA). Or, you may receive one Form 1099-R showing the net results of all your transactions, with instructions on how to enter amounts on Form 8606 and on your tax return. In either case, include the gross distribution from box 1 of all Forms 1099-R on Form 1040, line 15a; Form 1040A, line 11a; or Form 1040NR, line 16a. Also include the gross amount of any distribution reported on Form 8606 even if you did not receive a Form 1099-R before filing your tax return. Because the Forms 1099-R reflect the fair market value at the time of the distribution, the amounts that you enter on this line of your tax return will likely differ from the amounts you enter on lines 14a and 14b of Form 8606. Attach a statement explaining the difference. If you **do not** receive a Form 1099-R before you file your return, use other appropriate records and include the correct amounts on Form 8606 and Form 1040, 1040A, or 1040NR.*

Example. On May 4, 2000, Jodi (who is single) converted $100,000 from a traditional IRA to a Roth IRA. Her basis in the traditional IRA was $10,000. On July 9, 2000, Jodi contributed $2,000 for 2000 to a second Roth IRA.

On March 31, 2001, Jodi determined that her 2000 modified AGI for Roth IRA purposes is $111,000, which is more than the permitted limits for Roth IRA contributions and conversions. Jodi recharacterizes the conversion back to a traditional IRA and recharacterizes the Roth IRA contribution to a traditional IRA.

As of March 31, 2001, the first Roth IRA is worth $109,000 and the second Roth IRA is worth $1,900. Jodi makes a trustee-to-trustee transfer of $109,000 from the first Roth IRA to a traditional IRA to recharacterize the conversion. Jodi also makes a trustee-to-trustee transfer of $1,900 from the second Roth IRA to a traditional IRA (as a

nondeductible contribution) to recharacterize the contribution.

Completion of Form 8606. Jodi enters her nondeductible traditional IRA contribution of $2,000 (not $1,900) on line 1. Her previous traditional IRA basis of $10,000 is reported on line 2. Because Jodi did not receive any other distributions from her traditional IRAs in 2000, she then completes only lines 3 and 12 (entering $12,000) as instructed.

In Part II, Jodi enters $100,000 on line 14a. She also enters $100,000 on line 14b and -0- on line 14c. She does not include the $9,000 of earnings on line 14b (nor would she have reduced the amount entered on line 14b if a loss had occurred).

In Part III, Jodi is only required to complete lines 18b through 18d because she did not receive any Roth IRA distributions in 2000 other than the recharacterizations. Jodi enters $2,000 on line 18b, $2,000 (not $1,900) as a negative amount on line 18c, and -0- on line 18d.

In January 2001, Jodi receives a Form 1099-R for the conversion of $100,000. In January 2002, she will receive two more Forms 1099-R for the recharacterizations showing distributions of $109,000 and $1,900. On her 2000 Form 1040, line 15a, Jodi enters $210,900, the total of all three of the distributions. She enters -0- on line 15b because there is no taxable amount.

Finally, Jodi attaches a statement to her Form 8606 explaining:

• The conversion amount of $100,000 was recharacterized and the amount transferred was $109,000 because there was a $9,000 gain.

• Her previous basis of $10,000 is reported on line 2 of Form 8606.

• A Roth IRA contribution of $2,000 was recharacterized to a traditional IRA and the amount transferred was $1,900 because there was a $100 loss. She also indicates that no amount is deductible.

When Jodi receives the two 2001 Forms 1099-R in January 2002, she does not report them on her 2001 tax return. The Forms 1099-R represent recharacterizations of a conversion and a contribution made for 2000 and were reported on her 2000 tax return.

Lines 14a Through 14c

If in 2000 you converted amounts from a traditional or SIMPLE IRA to a Roth IRA, complete lines 14a through 14c as follows. Enter on line 14a the total of all amounts converted in 2000. Enter on line 14b the portion of any amount on line 14a that you recharacterized in 2000, or in 2001 by the due date of your tax return, including extensions. **Do not** include on line 14b related earnings that were transferred with the recharacterized amount or reduce the amount on line 14b if the amount transferred was less because of a loss that occurred while the amount was in the Roth IRA. See the earlier example for details.

Line 15

If you completed line 9, multiply line 9 by line 14c and enter the result. Otherwise, enter the amount from line 2 (or the amount you would have entered on line 2 if you had completed Part I) plus any contributions included on line 1 that were made before the conversion.

Part III—Distributions From Roth IRAs

Complete Part III to figure the taxable part of your 2000 Roth IRA distributions (or to report recharacterized contributions). Distributions from Roth IRAs are applied in the following order.

1. Roth IRA contributions. These amounts represent a return of your basis (amounts you contributed) and are not taxable upon distribution. This amount is figured on line 18d.

2. Accelerated income inclusion. If, in 1998, you converted amounts from a traditional IRA to a Roth IRA and are reporting the taxable amount over 4 years, the amount you must include in income for 2000 may be more than one-fourth of the taxable amount. The accelerated income is figured on line 21.

3. Amounts converted from traditional or SIMPLE IRAs to Roth IRAs. These amounts represent a return of basis and are not included in gross income upon distribution.

4. Earnings. Any remaining amount is earnings, which are taxable because the distribution is not a qualified distribution (see page 2).

Line 17

Do not include on line 17 distributions that were rolled over to another Roth IRA within 60 days. Also, do not

Worksheet for Lines 20b and 20c

1	Enter the amount from your 1998 Form 8606, line 16	1 _____
2	Enter one-half of line 1 above	2 _____
3	Enter the amount, if any, from your 1998 Form 8606, line 22 . .	3 _____
4	Enter the amount, if any, from your 1999 Form 8606, line 21 . .	4 _____
5	Add lines 2 through 4. Enter here and on Form 8606, line 20b . .	5 _____
6	Subtract line 5 from line 1	6 _____
7	Enter one-half of line 2 above	7 _____
8	Enter the **smaller** of line 6 or line 7 here and on Form 8606, line 20c	8 _____

include excess contributions that were distributed (returned to you) with the related earnings (or less any loss) by the due date of your tax return, including extensions. You may **not** deduct any loss that occurred. Include any related earnings in income for the year in which you made the contribution. For contributions made in 2000, report the total amount withdrawn on line 15a and any earnings on line 15b if filing Form 1040; lines 11a and 11b if filing Form 1040A; or lines 16a and 16b if filing Form 1040NR. Also see Form 5329 if you were under age 59½ at the time of a distribution with related earnings. Withdrawn excess contributions are treated as if they were never contributed for purposes of figuring basis and therefore are not reported on Form 8606.

Line 18a

Figure the amount to enter on line 18a as follows.

1. Figure the excess of your Roth IRA contributions for 1998 (including contributions made in 1999 for 1998), adjusted for any recharacterizations, over the amount of any Roth IRA distributions you made in 1998.

2. Add the amount figured in **1** above and your Roth IRA contributions for 1999 (including contributions made in 2000 for 1999).

3. Figure the excess of the amount figured in **2** above over the amount of any Roth IRA distributions you made in 1999. Enter the result on line 18a. This is your basis in Roth IRA contributions for 1998 and 1999.

If you completed Part III of Form 8606 for 1999, you can find the amount to enter by figuring the excess of line 18d of that Form 8606 over line 17 of that Form 8606. This amount can also be found on line 5 of the **Roth IRA Basis Worksheet** on page 6 of your 1999 Instructions for Form 8606.

Line 18b

Do not include on line 18b excess contributions that were distributed (returned to you) with the related earnings (or less any loss) by the due date of your tax return, including extensions. See the instructions for line 17.

Line 18c

Example of a contribution to a traditional IRA recharacterized to a Roth IRA. On July 9, 2000, Ellen contributed $2,000 to a traditional IRA. On April 10, 2001, she recharacterized the contribution (which was then worth $1,500) to a Roth IRA. Ellen enters -0- on line 18b and $2,000 (not $1,500) on line 18c.

Example of a contribution to a Roth IRA recharacterized to a traditional IRA. On June 14, 2000, Steven contributed $2,000 to a Roth IRA. On March 13, 2001, he recharacterized the contribution (which was then worth $2,500) to a traditional IRA. Steven enters $2,000 on line 18b and $2,000 as a negative amount (not $2,500) on line 18c.

Lines 20b and 20c

Complete the worksheet on this page to figure the amount to enter on lines 20b and 20c. Line 20a shows the total portion of your 1998 Roth IRA conversion that is taxable over 4 years. The amount figured for line 20b is the portion of line 20a that was taxable in 1998 and 1999. The amount figured for line 20c is the portion of line 20a that is taxable for 2000 without regard to any 2000 Roth IRA distribution. Any remaining portion of line 20a is taxed in 2000 on line 21 to the extent of any remaining distribution on line 19.

If the owner of a Roth IRA died in 2000, the entire excess of line 20a over line 20b generally must be included in income in 2000. However, a surviving spouse may be able to elect to continue reporting the taxable

Page 6

income over 4 years. See **1998 Roth IRA Conversions** on page 1 and Pub. 590 for details.

Line 23

Enter the excess, if any, of the sum of the amounts from your 1998 Form 8606, line 14c, and your 1999 Form 8606, line 14c, over the total of the following amounts.

- The amount, if any, of your 1998 Form 8606, line 22.
- The **smaller** of line 23 or line 24 of your 1998 Form 8606.
- The amount, if any, on your 1999 Form 8606, line 21.
- The **smaller** of line 22 or line 25 of your 1999 Form 8606.

This is your basis in Roth IRA conversions for 1998 and 1999.

If you completed all of Part III of Form 8606 for 1999, you can find the amount to enter on line 23 by figuring the excess of line 25 of that Form 8606 over line 22 of that Form 8606. This amount can also be found on line 12 of the **Roth IRA Basis Worksheet** on page 6 of your 1999 Instructions for Form 8606.

Additional 10% Tax

There generally is an additional 10% tax on 2000 distributions from a Roth IRA that are shown on line 19 if you were under 59½ at the time of the distribution. The additional tax is figured in Part I of Form 5329.

Part IV—Distributions From Education (Ed) IRAs

 If the total Ed IRA contributions made in 2000 on behalf of the beneficiary are more than $500 (or more than the total amount allowed to be contributed by all contributors to the account, if less), the excess contributions (plus related earnings) must be distributed by the due date (including extensions) of the beneficiary's tax return (or by April 16, 2001, if the beneficiary is not required to file a return). Otherwise, the beneficiary is subject to the excess contributions penalty. See Pub. 590 and Form 5329 for details, including how to figure the penalty.

Line 28

Enter the total Ed IRA distributions (withdrawals) received in 2000. Do not include amounts rolled over within 60 days (only one rollover is allowed

during any 12-month period). Also, do not include contributions that were distributed with the related earnings (or less any loss) by the due date of the beneficiary's tax return, including extensions (or by April 16, 2001, if the beneficiary is not required to file a tax return). **Do not** deduct any loss that occurred. Report the total amount withdrawn on line 15a and any related earnings on line 15b if filing Form 1040; lines 11a and 11b if filing Form 1040A; or lines 16a and 16b if filing Form 1040NR. Withdrawn contributions are treated as if they were never contributed for purposes of figuring basis and therefore are not reported on Form 8606.

If the beneficiary reaches age 30 or dies, the account balance generally must be distributed to the beneficiary (or to the estate of the beneficiary) within 30 days. However, any balance in an Ed IRA generally may be rolled over to an Ed IRA of a family member under age 30. (The same result generally may be accomplished by changing the beneficiary of the existing Ed IRA.) If a rollover is made from one family member's Ed IRA to another's, attach a statement to the tax return of the beneficiary of the Ed IRA from which the rollover was made. Indicate on the statement the amount and date of the rollover, and the name and SSN of the family member to whose Ed IRA the rollover

Ed IRA Worksheet (keep for your records)

If line 28 is more than line 29 on Form 8606, use this worksheet to figure the amount of taxable distributions you received from Ed IRAs in 2000. Also use this worksheet to figure your year-end basis in each Ed IRA.

 You should complete this worksheet to figure your basis, even if you are not required to complete it. You may need to know your basis to figure the nontaxable part of future distributions.

Complete lines 1 through 17 separately for each of your Ed IRAs.

1. Enter the amount contributed to this Ed IRA in 2000 . . . . . . **1** _____
2. Enter your basis in this Ed IRA as of December 31, 1999. See instructions . . . . **2** _____
3. Add lines 1 and 2 . . . . **3** _____
4. Did you receive any distributions in 2000 from this Ed IRA?
   ☐ **Yes.** Go to line 5.
   ☐ **No.** Enter the amount from line 3 on line 17 and do not complete the rest of this worksheet for this Ed IRA.
5. Enter the total amount of all distributions you received from this Ed IRA in 2000. Do not include rollovers . . . . **5** _____
6. Enter the amount of qualified higher education expenses from Form 8606, line 29, attributable to distributions from this Ed IRA . . . **6** _____
7. Subtract line 6 from line 5 . . . . **7** _____
8. Enter the total value of this Ed IRA as of December 31, 2000, plus any outstanding rollovers. See instructions . . . . **8** _____
9. Add lines 5 and 8 . . . . **9** _____
10. Divide line 3 by line 9 and enter the result as a decimal (rounded to at least 3 places). Do not enter more than "1.000" . . . . . **10** _____
11. Multiply line 5 by line 10. This is the nontaxable portion of your distributions from this Ed IRA . . . . **11** _____
    Note: If line 7 is zero, skip lines 12 through 15, enter -0- on line 16, and go to line 17.
12. Subtract line 11 from line 5 . . . . **12** _____
13. Did you check **Yes** on line 29 of the form?
    ☐ **Yes.** Enter the amount from line 12 on line 16 and go to line 17.
    ☐ **No.** Go to line 14.
14. Divide line 6 by line 5 and enter the result as a decimal (rounded to at least 3 places). Do not enter more than "1.000" . . . . . **14** _____
15. Multiply line 12 by line 14 . . . . **15** _____
16. Subtract line 15 from line 12. This is the amount of **taxable distributions you received from this Ed IRA in 2000.** Enter the result here and include it on line 30 of Form 8606 . . . . . **16** _____
17. Subtract line 11 from line 3. This is your **basis in this Ed IRA as of December 31, 2000** . . . . **17** _____

was contributed. Also, report the amount of the rollover on Form 1040, line 15a; Form 1040A, line 11a; or Form 1040NR, line 16a. See Pub. 590 for details.

Line 29

Qualified higher education expenses include tuition, fees, books, supplies, and equipment required for the attendance of the beneficiary at an eligible educational institution. Education expenses also include the cost of room and board while attending the educational institution, if the student is attending at least half-time. See Pub. 590 for details.

The Hope and lifetime learning credits (education credits) may not be claimed for a student's expenses in the same tax year in which the student takes a tax-free withdrawal from an Ed IRA. To allow the education credits to be claimed for the student's expenses, check "Yes" on line 29. Checking this box indicates you are waiving any exclusion from income of a distribution from an Ed IRA.

Note: *No deduction or credit (for example, a business expense deduction for education expenses on Schedule C or C-EZ (Form 1040) or miscellaneous itemized deduction on Schedule A (Form 1040)) is allowed for any qualified education expenses to the extent the expenses are used in determining the exclusion for an Ed IRA distribution.*

Line 30

Instructions for Ed IRA Worksheet

Line 2. Your basis in each Ed IRA as of December 31, 1999, is the total of all contributions to the Ed IRA in

1998 and 1999, less the nontaxable portion of any distributions you received in 1998 and 1999. This amount can also be found on line 17 of your **Ed IRA Worksheet** for this Ed IRA, on page 7 of the 1999 Instructions for Form 8606.

Line 8. Enter the total value of this Ed IRA as of December 31, 2000, plus any outstanding rollovers contributed to the account after December 31, 1999, but before the end of the 60-day rollover period. You should receive a statement by January 31, 2001, for each Ed IRA showing the value on December 31, 2000.

A **rollover** is a tax-free distribution from one Ed IRA that is contributed to another Ed IRA. The rollover must be completed within 60 days of receiving the distribution from the first Ed IRA. An **outstanding rollover** is any amount distributed from one Ed IRA within 60 days before the end of 2000 (November 2 through December 31) that was rolled over to another Ed IRA after December 31, 2000, but within the 60-day rollover period.

Additional 10% Tax

If you have a taxable amount on line 30, you may be subject to an additional 10% tax. The tax is figured on Form 5329.

Exceptions. The additional tax does not apply to distributions that are:

• Taxable solely because you checked "Yes" on line 29,

• Due to the death or disability of the beneficiary, or

• Made on account of a scholarship, allowance, or payment described in section 25A(g)(2).

See the Instructions for Form 5329 for details.

Paperwork Reduction Act Notice. We ask for the information on this form to carry out the Internal Revenue laws of the United States. You are required to give us the information. We need it to ensure that you are complying with these laws and to allow us to figure and collect the right amount of tax.

You are not required to provide the information requested on a form that is subject to the Paperwork Reduction Act unless the form displays a valid OMB control number. Books or records relating to a form or its instructions must be retained as long as their contents may become material in the administration of any Internal Revenue law. Generally, tax returns and return information are confidential, as required by section 6103.

The time needed to complete and file this form will vary depending on individual circumstances. The estimated average time is: **Recordkeeping,** 53 min.; **Learning about the law or the form,** 2 hr.; **Preparing the form,** 1 hr., 46 min.; **Copying, assembling, and sending the form to the IRS,** 1 hr., 43 min.

If you have comments concerning the accuracy of these time estimates or suggestions for making this form simpler, we would be happy to hear from you. See the instructions for the tax return with which this form is filed.

Notice 89-25, Question and Answer 12

Q-12: In the case of an IRA or individual account plan, what constitutes a series of substantially equal periodic payments for purposes of section 72(t)(2)(A)(iv)?

A-12: Section 72(t)(1) imposes an additional tax of 10 percent on the portion of early distributions from qualified retirement plans (including IRAs) includible in gross income. However, section 72(t)(2)(A)(iv) provides that this tax shall not apply to distributions which are part of a series of substantially equal periodic payments (not less frequently than annually) made for the life (or life expectancy) of the employee or the joint lives (or joint life expectancies) of the employee and beneficiary. Section 72(t)(4) provides that, if the series of periodic payments is subsequently modified within five years of the date of the first payment, or, if later, age 59¹/₂, the exception to the 10 percent tax under section 72(t)(2)(A)(iv) does not apply, and the taxpayer's tax for the year of modification shall be increased by an amount, determined under regulations, which (but for the 72(t)(2)(A)(iv) exception) would have been imposed, plus interest.

Payments will be considered to be substantially equal periodic payments within the meaning of section 72(t)(2)(A)(iv) if they are made according to one of the methods set forth below.

Payments shall be treated as satisfying section 72(t)(2)(A)(iv) if the annual payment is determined using a method that would be acceptable for purposes of calculating the minimum distribution required under section 401(a)(9). For this purpose, the payment may be determined based on the life expectancy of the employee or the joint life and last survivor expectancy of the employee and beneficiary.

Payments will also be treated as substantially equal periodic payments within the meaning of section 72(t)(2)(A)(iv) if the amount to be distributed annually is determined by amortizing the taxpayer's account balance over a number of years equal to the life expectancy of the account owner or the joint life and last survivor expectancy of the account owner and beneficiary (with life expectancies determined in accordance with proposed section 1.401(a)(9)-1 of the regulations) at an interest rate that does not exceed a reasonable interest rate on the date payments commence. For example, a 50 year old individual with a life expectancy of 33.1, having an account balance of $100,000, and assuming an interest rate of 8 percent, could satisfy section 72(t)(2)(A)(iv) by distributing $9,679 annually, derived by amortizing $100,000 over 33.1 years at 8 percent interest.

Notice 89-25, Question and Answer 12 (continued)

Finally, payments will be treated as substantially equal periodic payments if the amount to be distributed annually is determined by dividing the taxpayer's account balance by an annuity factor (the present value of an annuity of $1 per year beginning at the taxpayer's age attained in the first distribution year and continuing for the life of the taxpayer) with such annuity factor derived using a reasonable mortality table and using an interest rate that does not exceed a reasonable interest rate on the date payments commence. If substantially equal monthly payments are being deter-

mined, the taxpayer's account balance would be divided by an annuity factor equal to the present value of an annuity of $1 per month beginning at the taxpayer's age attained in the first distribution year and continuing for the life of the taxpayer. For example, if the annuity factor for a $1 per year annuity for an individual who is 50 years old is 11.109 (assuming an interest rate of 9 percent and using the UP-1984 Mortality Table), an individual with a $100,000 account balance would receive an annual distribution of $9,002 ($100,000/ 11.109 = $9,002).

Table S: Present Worth of Single Life Annuity at 6.0 Percent

Age	Annuity	Age	Annuity	Age	Annuity	Age	Annuity
0	16.1278	28	15.2157	56	11.6505	83	5.1801
1	16.2522	29	15.1484	57	11.4505	84	4.9372
2	16.2395	30	15.0780	58	11.2463	85	4.6961
3	16.2220	31	15.0044	59	11.0387	86	4.4592
4	16.2016	32	14.9274	60	10.8279	87	4.2294
5	16.1787	33	14.8467	61	10.6136	88	4.0070
6	16.1540	34	14.7623	62	10.3951	89	3.7920
7	16.1273	35	14.6737	63	10.1723	90	3.5847
8	16.0988	36	14.5810	64	9.9456	91	3.3882
9	16.0680	37	14.4841	65	9.7151	92	3.2065
10	16.0350	38	14.3824	66	9.4804	93	3.0388
11	15.9997	39	14.2761	67	9.2407	94	2.8827
12	15.9624	40	14.1646	68	8.9967	95	2.7346
13	15.9236	41	14.0475	69	8.7490	96	2.5955
14	15.8844	42	13.9249	70	8.4988	97	2.4666
15	15.8450	43	13.7967	71	8.2473	98	2.3457
16	15.8060	44	13.6628	72	7.9951	99	2.2278
17	15.7669	45	13.5237	73	7.7429	100	2.1130
18	15.7274	46	13.3792	74	7.4898	101	2.0000
19	15.6867	47	13.2298	75	7.2349	102	1.8890
20	15.6441	48	13.0751	76	6.9775	103	1.7790
21	15.5995	49	12.9152	77	6.7177	104	1.6616
22	15.5530	50	12.7497	78	6.4560	105	1.5468
23	15.5041	51	12.5787	79	6.1941	106	1.3994
24	15.4526	52	12.4027	80	5.9340	107	1.2209
25	15.3981	53	12.2219	81	5.6778	108	0.9439
26	15.3407	54	12.0363	82	5.4265	109	0.4717
27	15.2797	55	11.8459				

Table S: Present Worth of Single Life Annuity at 6.2 Percent

Age	Annuity	Age	Annuity	Age	Annuity	Age	Annuity
0	15.6396	28	14.8099	56	11.4290	83	5.1331
1	15.7615	29	14.7474	57	11.2366	84	4.8940
2	15.7505	30	14.6819	58	11.0402	85	4.6567
3	15.7349	31	14.6133	59	10.8403	86	4.4232
4	15.7165	32	14.5415	60	10.6371	87	4.1966
5	15.6959	33	14.4661	61	10.4304	88	3.9772
6	15.6734	34	14.3872	62	10.2195	89	3.7649
7	15.6491	35	14.3042	63	10.0041	90	3.5600
8	15.6231	36	14.2174	64	9.7849	91	3.3659
9	15.5950	37	14.1264	65	9.5617	92	3.1861
10	15.5646	38	14.0308	66	9.3342	93	3.0203
11	15.5322	39	13.9307	67	9.1017	94	2.8658
12	15.4978	40	13.8256	68	8.8648	95	2.7192
13	15.4621	41	13.7151	69	8.6240	96	2.5813
14	15.4259	42	13.5993	70	8.3806	97	2.4537
15	15.3897	43	13.4779	71	8.1357	98	2.3339
16	15.3538	44	13.3510	72	7.8900	99	2.2170
17	15.3180	45	13.2190	73	7.6440	100	2.1033
18	15.2818	46	13.0817	74	7.3970	101	1.9911
19	15.2445	47	12.9396	75	7.1480	102	1.8810
20	15.2054	48	12.7923	76	6.8963	103	1.7719
21	15.1644	49	12.6399	77	6.6421	104	1.6553
22	15.1217	50	12.4819	78	6.3858	105	1.5414
23	15.0767	51	12.3185	79	6.1290	106	1.3949
24	15.0292	52	12.1502	80	5.8738	107	1.2175
25	14.9789	53	11.9771	81	5.6222	108	0.9417
26	14.9258	54	11.7992	82	5.3753	109	0.4708
27	14.8693	55	11.6165				

Table S: Present Worth of Single Life Annuity at 6.4 Percent

Age	Annuity	Age	Annuity	Age	Annuity	Age	Annuity
0	15.1785	28	14.4229	56	11.2145	83	5.0868
1	15.2978	29	14.3648	57	11.0295	84	4.8516
2	15.2884	30	14.3038	58	10.8404	85	4.6178
3	15.2745	31	14.2399	59	10.6479	86	4.3877
4	15.2579	32	14.1729	60	10.4520	87	4.1642
5	15.2392	33	14.1024	61	10.2526	88	3.9477
6	15.2188	34	14.0286	62	10.0488	89	3.7381
7	15.1966	35	13.9508	63	9.8407	90	3.5357
8	15.1728	36	13.8693	64	9.6285	91	3.3438
9	15.1471	37	13.7839	65	9.4124	92	3.1660
10	15.1192	38	13.6940	66	9.1918	93	3.0019
11	15.0893	39	13.5997	67	8.9663	94	2.8490
12	15.0576	40	13.5005	68	8.7361	95	2.7039
13	15.0245	41	13.3962	69	8.5020	96	2.5674
14	14.9911	42	13.2866	70	8.2652	97	2.4410
15	14.9578	43	13.1716	71	8.0267	98	2.3222
16	14.9248	44	13.0512	72	7.7872	99	2.2063
17	14.8918	45	12.9259	73	7.5473	100	2.0935
18	14.8586	46	12.7954	74	7.3061	101	1.9823
19	14.8244	47	12.6601	75	7.0628	102	1.8731
20	14.7885	48	12.5198	76	6.8167	103	1.7649
21	14.7508	49	12.3744	77	6.5679	104	1.6490
22	14.7115	50	12.2236	78	6.3168	105	1.5360
23	14.6700	51	12.0674	79	6.0650	106	1.3905
24	14.6262	52	11.9064	80	5.8147	107	1.2140
25	14.5797	53	11.7405	81	5.5676	108	0.9395
26	14.5305	54	11.5700	82	5.3249	109	0.4699
27	14.4781	55	11.3947				

Table S: Present Worth of Single Life Annuity at 6.6 Percent							
Age	Annuity	Age	Annuity	Age	Annuity	Age	Annuity
0	14.7424	28	14.0537	56	11.0068	83	5.0413
1	14.8592	29	13.9996	57	10.8289	84	4.8097
2	14.8511	30	13.9427	58	10.6468	85	4.5796
3	14.8387	31	13.8831	59	10.4613	86	4.3527
4	14.8238	32	13.8205	60	10.2724	87	4.1324
5	14.8068	33	13.7546	61	10.0798	88	3.9187
6	14.7882	34	13.6854	62	9.8830	89	3.7117
7	14.7679	35	13.6125	63	9.6817	90	3.5117
8	14.7462	36	13.5360	64	9.4764	91	3.3220
9	14.7225	37	13.4556	65	9.2670	92	3.1462
10	14.6968	38	13.3710	66	9.0532	93	2.9838
11	14.6692	39	13.2822	67	8.8342	94	2.8325
12	14.6399	40	13.1886	68	8.6106	95	2.6888
13	14.6093	41	13.0899	69	8.3830	96	2.5536
14	14.5784	42	12.9862	70	8.1525	97	2.4283
15	14.5476	43	12.8772	71	7.9202	98	2.3106
16	14.5172	44	12.7630	72	7.6867	99	2.1958
17	14.4869	45	12.6439	73	7.4526	100	2.0839
18	14.4564	46	12.5198	74	7.2172	101	1.9736
19	14.4249	47	12.3910	75	6.9795	102	1.8652
20	14.3919	48	12.2572	76	6.7388	103	1.7577
21	14.3572	49	12.1184	77	6.4952	104	1.6428
22	14.3210	50	11.9743	78	6.2492	105	1.5306
23	14.2827	51	11.8249	79	6.0023	106	1.3860
24	14.2423	52	11.6708	80	5.7566	107	1.2106
25	14.1992	53	11.5119	81	5.5139	108	0.9373
26	14.1536	54	11.3483	82	5.2754	109	0.4690
27	14.1050	55	11.1800				

Table S: Present Worth of Single Life Annuity at 6.8 Percent

Age	Annuity	Age	Annuity	Age	Annuity	Age	Annuity
0	14.3295	28	13.7011	56	10.8056	83	4.9964
1	14.4438	29	13.6507	57	10.6344	84	4.7686
2	14.4368	30	13.5976	58	10.4591	85	4.5418
3	14.4258	31	13.5419	59	10.2802	86	4.3183
4	14.4123	32	13.4834	60	10.0979	87	4.1009
5	14.3969	33	13.4217	61	9.9120	88	3.8900
6	14.3799	34	13.3569	62	9.7218	89	3.6857
7	14.3614	35	13.2885	63	9.5271	90	3.4880
8	14.3414	36	13.2166	64	9.3283	91	3.3004
9	14.3196	37	13.1410	65	9.1254	92	3.1265
10	14.2959	38	13.0613	66	8.9180	93	2.9659
11	14.2704	39	12.9774	67	8.7054	94	2.8161
12	14.2432	40	12.8890	68	8.4881	95	2.6738
13	14.2148	41	12.7957	69	8.2668	96	2.5399
14	14.1862	42	12.6975	70	8.0424	97	2.4158
15	14.1577	43	12.5942	71	7.8161	98	2.2992
16	14.1296	44	12.4857	72	7.5884	99	2.1853
17	14.1017	45	12.3724	73	7.3600	100	2.0744
18	14.0736	46	12.2543	74	7.1301	101	1.9650
19	14.0447	47	12.1316	75	6.8978	102	1.8574
20	14.0143	48	12.0040	76	6.6623	103	1.7507
21	13.9824	49	11.8715	77	6.4238	104	1.6367
22	13.9489	50	11.7338	78	6.1828	105	1.5253
23	13.9136	51	11.5908	79	5.9406	106	1.3816
24	13.8762	52	11.4432	80	5.6995	107	1.2072
25	13.8363	53	11.2908	81	5.4611	108	0.9352
26	13.7940	54	11.1339	82	5.2268	109	0.4682
27	13.7488	55	10.9722				

Table S: Present Worth of Single Life Annuity at 7.0 Percent							
Age	Annuity	Age	Annuity	Age	Annuity	Age	Annuity
0	13.9381	28	13.3641	56	10.6108	83	4.9523
1	14.0499	29	13.3171	57	10.4459	84	4.7280
2	14.0440	30	13.2676	58	10.2769	85	4.5047
3	14.0341	31	13.2155	59	10.1044	86	4.2843
4	14.0219	32	13.1608	60	9.9286	87	4.0699
5	14.0079	33	13.1030	61	9.7490	88	3.8618
6	13.9924	34	13.0422	62	9.5651	89	3.6599
7	13.9754	35	12.9779	63	9.3767	90	3.4646
8	13.9570	36	12.9103	64	9.1842	91	3.2791
9	13.9369	37	12.8391	65	8.9875	92	3.1071
10	13.9150	38	12.7640	66	8.7863	93	2.9482
11	13.8914	39	12.6848	67	8.5799	94	2.7999
12	13.8661	40	12.6013	68	8.3687	95	2.6590
13	13.8398	41	12.5130	69	8.1533	96	2.5263
14	13.8132	42	12.4198	70	7.9348	97	2.4034
15	13.7868	43	12.3218	71	7.7143	98	2.2878
16	13.7608	44	12.2187	72	7.4923	99	2.1749
17	13.7350	45	12.1110	73	7.2694	100	2.0649
18	13.7092	46	11.9985	74	7.0448	101	1.9564
19	13.6825	47	11.8815	75	6.8177	102	1.8497
20	13.6546	48	11.7597	76	6.5874	103	1.7438
21	13.6250	49	11.6332	77	6.3539	104	1.6305
22	13.5942	50	11.5014	78	6.1176	105	1.5199
23	13.5615	51	11.3646	79	5.8801	106	1.3772
24	13.5269	52	11.2231	80	5.6433	107	1.2039
25	13.4899	53	11.0770	81	5.4092	108	0.9330
26	13.4507	54	10.9263	82	5.1788	109	0.4673
27	13.4086	55	10.7709				

Table S: Present Worth of Single Life Annuity at 7.2 Percent

Age	Annuity	Age	Annuity	Age	Annuity	Age	Annuity
0	13.5666	28	13.0419	56	10.4219	83	4.9089
1	13.6760	29	12.9980	57	10.2631	84	4.6881
2	13.6710	30	12.9517	58	10.1002	85	4.4680
3	13.6622	31	12.9030	59	9.9338	86	4.2508
4	13.6512	32	12.8517	60	9.7640	87	4.0393
5	13.6383	33	12.7975	61	9.5905	88	3.8338
6	13.6241	34	12.7404	62	9.4127	89	3.6345
7	13.6085	35	12.6800	63	9.2303	90	3.4415
8	13.5916	36	12.6164	64	9.0438	91	3.2581
9	13.5730	37	12.5493	65	8.8532	92	3.0879
10	13.5527	38	12.4785	66	8.6579	93	2.9307
11	13.5308	39	12.4037	67	8.4574	94	2.7839
12	13.5073	40	12.3247	68	8.2521	95	2.6444
13	13.4828	41	12.2411	69	8.0425	96	2.5129
14	13.4581	42	12.1527	70	7.8297	97	2.3911
15	13.4335	43	12.0596	71	7.6148	98	2.2765
16	13.4095	44	11.9616	72	7.3982	99	2.1646
17	13.3857	45	11.8591	73	7.1807	100	2.0555
18	13.3618	46	11.7519	74	6.9613	101	1.9479
19	13.3372	47	11.6403	75	6.7393	102	1.8420
20	13.3114	48	11.5240	76	6.5139	103	1.7369
21	13.2842	49	11.4031	77	6.2852	104	1.6245
22	13.2556	50	11.2770	78	6.0536	105	1.5147
23	13.2254	51	11.1460	79	5.8206	106	1.3729
24	13.1933	52	11.0103	80	5.5882	107	1.2005
25	13.1590	53	10.8701	81	5.3582	108	0.9308
26	13.1225	54	10.7254	82	5.1317	109	0.4664
27	13.0834	55	10.5760				

Table S: Present Worth of Single Life Annuity at 7.4 Percent

Age	Annuity	Age	Annuity	Age	Annuity	Age	Annuity
0	13.2136	28	12.7335	56	10.2387	83	4.8661
1	13.3207	29	12.6925	57	10.0858	84	4.6487
2	13.3165	30	12.6492	58	9.9287	85	4.4320
3	13.3086	31	12.6036	59	9.7681	86	4.2177
4	13.2986	32	12.5555	60	9.6041	87	4.0091
5	13.2869	33	12.5047	61	9.4365	88	3.8063
6	13.2739	34	12.4510	62	9.2644	89	3.6094
7	13.2595	35	12.3942	63	9.0879	90	3.4186
8	13.2439	36	12.3343	64	8.9072	91	3.2373
9	13.2267	37	12.2711	65	8.7223	92	3.0690
10	13.2078	38	12.2041	66	8.5327	93	2.9133
11	13.1874	39	12.1335	67	8.3380	94	2.7680
12	13.1655	40	12.0587	68	8.1383	95	2.6298
13	13.1427	41	11.9794	69	7.9343	96	2.4996
14	13.1197	42	11.8956	70	7.7270	97	2.3789
15	13.0968	43	11.8071	71	7.5175	98	2.2654
16	13.0745	44	11.7139	72	7.3062	99	2.1544
17	13.0525	45	11.6163	73	7.0938	100	2.0462
18	13.0305	46	11.5140	74	6.8795	101	1.9394
19	13.0078	47	11.4075	75	6.6624	102	1.8344
20	12.9839	48	11.2965	76	6.4418	103	1.7301
21	12.9587	49	11.1808	77	6.2178	104	1.6184
22	12.9323	50	11.0601	78	5.9908	105	1.5094
23	12.9044	51	10.9345	79	5.7622	106	1.3685
24	12.8746	52	10.8045	80	5.5340	107	1.1972
25	12.8427	53	10.6698	81	5.3080	108	0.9287
26	12.8087	54	10.5308	82	5.0853	109	0.4655
27	12.7722	55	10.3871				

\multicolumn{8}{c}{Table S: Present Worth of Single Life Annuity at 7.6 Percent}

Age	Annuity	Age	Annuity	Age	Annuity	Age	Annuity
0	12.8778	28	12.4382	56	10.0611	83	4.8240
1	12.9827	29	12.3998	57	9.9137	84	4.6100
2	12.9792	30	12.3593	58	9.7622	85	4.3964
3	12.9721	31	12.3166	59	9.6071	86	4.1852
4	12.9631	32	12.2715	60	9.4487	87	3.9793
5	12.9523	33	12.2237	61	9.2866	88	3.7791
6	12.9404	34	12.1733	62	9.1202	89	3.5846
7	12.9271	35	12.1198	63	8.9492	90	3.3961
8	12.9127	36	12.0633	64	8.7740	91	3.2167
9	12.8968	37	12.0036	65	8.5947	92	3.0502
10	12.8792	38	11.9404	66	8.4107	93	2.8962
11	12.8602	39	11.8736	67	8.2214	94	2.7523
12	12.8397	40	11.8028	68	8.0271	95	2.6155
13	12.8184	41	11.7276	69	7.8286	96	2.4865
14	12.7969	42	11.6480	70	7.6266	97	2.3669
15	12.7757	43	11.5639	71	7.4223	98	2.2543
16	12.7549	44	11.4751	72	7.2162	99	2.1443
17	12.7345	45	11.3821	73	7.0088	100	2.0370
18	12.7141	46	11.2845	74	6.7993	101	1.9311
19	12.6932	47	11.1829	75	6.5871	102	1.8268
20	12.6711	48	11.0767	76	6.3712	103	1.7233
21	12.6478	49	10.9660	77	6.1517	104	1.6125
22	12.6233	50	10.8505	78	5.9291	105	1.5042
23	12.5974	51	10.7301	79	5.7048	106	1.3642
24	12.5697	52	10.6052	80	5.4807	107	1.1939
25	12.5401	53	10.4759	81	5.2587	108	0.9265
26	12.5084	54	10.3422	82	5.0397	109	0.4647
27	12.4744	55	10.2040				

Table S: Present Worth of Single Life Annuity at 7.8 Percent

Age	Annuity	Age	Annuity	Age	Annuity	Age	Annuity
0	12.5581	28	12.1552	56	9.8889	83	4.7825
1	12.6608	29	12.1193	57	9.7467	84	4.5718
2	12.6579	30	12.0813	58	9.6005	85	4.3613
3	12.6516	31	12.0412	59	9.4507	86	4.1530
4	12.6434	32	11.9989	60	9.2977	87	3.9499
5	12.6335	33	11.9540	61	9.1409	88	3.7523
6	12.6225	34	11.9065	62	8.9798	89	3.5602
7	12.6103	35	11.8561	63	8.8141	90	3.3738
8	12.5969	36	11.8029	64	8.6443	91	3.1964
9	12.5821	37	11.7465	65	8.4703	92	3.0317
10	12.5658	38	11.6868	66	8.2916	93	2.8792
11	12.5480	39	11.6235	67	8.1076	94	2.7368
12	12.5289	40	11.5564	68	7.9186	95	2.6013
13	12.5089	41	11.4851	69	7.7253	96	2.4735
14	12.4888	42	11.4094	70	7.5285	97	2.3549
15	12.4690	43	11.3294	71	7.3292	98	2.2434
16	12.4497	44	11.2448	72	7.1280	99	2.1343
17	12.4307	45	11.1561	73	6.9255	100	2.0279
18	12.4119	46	11.0630	74	6.7208	101	1.9228
19	12.3925	47	10.9659	75	6.5132	102	1.8193
20	12.3720	48	10.8644	76	6.3018	103	1.7166
21	12.3504	49	10.7584	77	6.0868	104	1.6065
22	12.3277	50	10.6477	78	5.8686	105	1.4990
23	12.3036	51	10.5322	79	5.6484	106	1.3600
24	12.2779	52	10.4123	80	5.4283	107	1.1906
25	12.2504	53	10.2881	81	5.2101	108	0.9244
26	12.2209	54	10.1595	82	4.9948	109	0.4638
27	12.1890	55	10.0265				

Table S: Present Worth of Single Life Annuity at 8.0 Percent

Age	Annuity	Age	Annuity	Age	Annuity	Age	Annuity
0	12.2534	28	11.8839	56	9.7217	83	4.7417
1	12.3540	29	11.8502	57	9.5845	84	4.5342
2	12.3516	30	11.8146	58	9.4434	85	4.3268
3	12.3460	31	11.7769	59	9.2987	86	4.1214
4	12.3385	32	11.7371	60	9.1507	87	3.9210
5	12.3295	33	11.6949	61	8.9991	88	3.7258
6	12.3193	34	11.6502	62	8.8431	89	3.5360
7	12.3080	35	11.6027	63	8.6826	90	3.3518
8	12.2956	36	11.5524	64	8.5179	91	3.1763
9	12.2818	37	11.4992	65	8.3490	92	3.0133
10	12.2666	38	11.4426	66	8.1754	93	2.8624
11	12.2500	39	11.3827	67	7.9965	94	2.7215
12	12.2320	40	11.3191	68	7.8126	95	2.5872
13	12.2133	41	11.2514	69	7.6243	96	2.4606
14	12.1945	42	11.1794	70	7.4325	97	2.3431
15	12.1759	43	11.1033	71	7.2381	98	2.2325
16	12.1580	44	11.0227	72	7.0418	99	2.1243
17	12.1403	45	10.9380	73	6.8439	100	2.0188
18	12.1228	46	10.8491	74	6.6438	101	1.9145
19	12.1048	47	10.7563	75	6.4407	102	1.8119
20	12.0859	48	10.6591	76	6.2338	103	1.7099
21	12.0658	49	10.5577	77	6.0231	104	1.6006
22	12.0448	50	10.4515	78	5.8091	105	1.4939
23	12.0224	51	10.3407	79	5.5930	106	1.3557
24	11.9985	52	10.2256	80	5.3768	107	1.1873
25	11.9728	53	10.1061	81	5.1624	108	0.9223
26	11.9453	54	9.9824	82	4.9506	109	0.4630
27	11.9155	55	9.8543				

Table S: Present Worth of Single Life Annuity at 8.2 Percent							
Age	Annuity	Age	Annuity	Age	Annuity	Age	Annuity
0	11.9627	28	11.6235	56	9.5594	83	4.7015
1	12.0612	29	11.5919	57	9.4270	84	4.4971
2	12.0594	30	11.5585	58	9.2907	85	4.2927
3	12.0543	31	11.5231	59	9.1510	86	4.0901
4	12.0475	32	11.4857	60	9.0079	87	3.8923
5	12.0392	33	11.4459	61	8.8611	88	3.6997
6	12.0298	34	11.4038	62	8.7100	89	3.5121
7	12.0193	35	11.3589	63	8.5544	90	3.3300
8	12.0078	36	11.3114	64	8.3947	91	3.1565
9	11.9949	37	11.2611	65	8.2307	92	2.9952
10	11.9807	38	11.2076	66	8.0621	93	2.8459
11	11.9651	39	11.1508	67	7.8881	94	2.7063
12	11.9483	40	11.0904	68	7.7091	95	2.5733
13	11.9307	41	11.0261	69	7.5256	96	2.4478
14	11.9130	42	10.9576	70	7.3386	97	2.3314
15	11.8957	43	10.8851	71	7.1490	98	2.2218
16	11.8789	44	10.8082	72	6.9573	99	2.1145
17	11.8625	45	10.7274	73	6.7640	100	2.0098
18	11.8462	46	10.6425	74	6.5684	101	1.9063
19	11.8295	47	10.5537	75	6.3697	102	1.8045
20	11.8119	48	10.4607	76	6.1670	103	1.7032
21	11.7933	49	10.3634	77	5.9606	104	1.5947
22	11.7737	50	10.2616	78	5.7506	105	1.4888
23	11.7529	51	10.1552	79	5.5385	106	1.3515
24	11.7307	52	10.0446	80	5.3262	107	1.1840
25	11.7067	53	9.9298	81	5.1154	108	0.9202
26	11.6810	54	9.8107	82	4.9071	109	0.4621
27	11.6531	55	9.6873				

Table S: Present Worth of Single Life Annuity at 8.4 Percent

Age	Annuity	Age	Annuity	Age	Annuity	Age	Annuity
0	11.6851	28	11.3735	56	9.4018	83	4.6619
1	11.7816	29	11.3438	57	9.2741	84	4.4606
2	11.7802	30	11.3124	58	9.1424	85	4.2591
3	11.7757	31	11.2791	59	9.0073	86	4.0593
4	11.7694	32	11.2439	60	8.8688	87	3.8641
5	11.7618	33	11.2064	61	8.7267	88	3.6738
6	11.7531	34	11.1667	62	8.5804	89	3.4885
7	11.7434	35	11.1244	63	8.4296	90	3.3085
8	11.7326	36	11.0795	64	8.2745	91	3.1369
9	11.7207	37	11.0319	65	8.1153	92	2.9773
10	11.7073	38	10.9812	66	7.9514	93	2.8294
11	11.6927	39	10.9273	67	7.7822	94	2.6912
12	11.6768	40	10.8700	68	7.6079	95	2.5595
13	11.6603	41	10.8088	69	7.4292	96	2.4352
14	11.6437	42	10.7436	70	7.2468	97	2.3198
15	11.6274	43	10.6745	71	7.0618	98	2.2111
16	11.6117	44	10.6012	72	6.8746	99	2.1047
17	11.5964	45	10.5240	73	6.6857	100	2.0009
18	11.5813	46	10.4427	74	6.4945	101	1.8982
19	11.5658	47	10.3578	75	6.3000	102	1.7971
20	11.5495	48	10.2687	76	6.1016	103	1.6966
21	11.5321	49	10.1755	77	5.8992	104	1.5889
22	11.5139	50	10.0778	78	5.6932	105	1.4837
23	11.4946	51	9.9756	79	5.4850	106	1.3473
24	11.4738	52	9.8692	80	5.2764	107	1.1808
25	11.4514	53	9.7587	81	5.0691	108	0.9181
26	11.4274	54	9.6441	82	4.8642	109	0.4613
27	11.4013	55	9.5252				

Table S: Present Worth of Single Life Annuity at 8.6 Percent

Age	Annuity	Age	Annuity	Age	Annuity	Age	Annuity
0	11.4198	28	11.1333	56	9.2488	83	4.6229
1	11.5143	29	11.1054	57	9.1254	84	4.4246
2	11.5133	30	11.0759	58	8.9982	85	4.2260
3	11.5093	31	11.0446	59	8.8675	86	4.0289
4	11.5036	32	11.0114	60	8.7335	87	3.8363
5	11.4965	33	10.9760	61	8.5960	88	3.6484
6	11.4885	34	10.9386	62	8.4541	89	3.4653
7	11.4794	35	10.8985	63	8.3078	90	3.2872
8	11.4694	36	10.8561	64	8.1574	91	3.1175
9	11.4582	37	10.8110	65	8.0027	92	2.9595
10	11.4457	38	10.7629	66	7.8434	93	2.8132
11	11.4319	39	10.7118	67	7.6788	94	2.6763
12	11.4170	40	10.6573	68	7.5091	95	2.5459
13	11.4014	41	10.5991	69	7.3349	96	2.4227
14	11.3858	42	10.5371	70	7.1570	97	2.3083
15	11.3705	43	10.4711	71	6.9764	98	2.2006
16	11.3558	44	10.4011	72	6.7936	99	2.0951
17	11.3415	45	10.3274	73	6.6090	100	1.9921
18	11.3274	46	10.2496	74	6.4220	101	1.8902
19	11.3130	47	10.1683	75	6.2316	102	1.7898
20	11.2978	48	10.0829	76	6.0373	103	1.6901
21	11.2816	49	9.9935	77	5.8389	104	1.5831
22	11.2647	50	9.8997	78	5.6368	105	1.4787
23	11.2466	51	9.8015	79	5.4324	106	1.3431
24	11.2273	52	9.6992	80	5.2274	107	1.1775
25	11.2063	53	9.5929	81	5.0236	108	0.9160
26	11.1838	54	9.4825	82	4.8221	109	0.4604
27	11.1594	55	9.3678				

Table S: Present Worth of Single Life Annuity at 8.8 Percent

Age	Annuity	Age	Annuity	Age	Annuity	Age	Annuity
0	11.1660	28	10.9024	56	9.1001	83	4.5844
1	11.2586	29	10.8762	57	8.9809	84	4.3891
2	11.2579	30	10.8484	58	8.8579	85	4.1933
3	11.2543	31	10.8189	59	8.7315	86	3.9989
4	11.2491	32	10.7876	60	8.6018	87	3.8088
5	11.2426	33	10.7542	61	8.4686	88	3.6232
6	11.2351	34	10.7188	62	8.3311	89	3.4423
7	11.2267	35	10.6810	63	8.1892	90	3.2662
8	11.2173	36	10.6408	64	8.0431	91	3.0983
9	11.2068	37	10.5981	65	7.8929	92	2.9420
10	11.1950	38	10.5525	66	7.7379	93	2.7971
11	11.1821	39	10.5039	67	7.5777	94	2.6616
12	11.1680	40	10.4521	68	7.4125	95	2.5324
13	11.1533	41	10.3967	69	7.2426	96	2.4103
14	11.1385	42	10.3376	70	7.0692	97	2.2969
15	11.1242	43	10.2746	71	6.8929	98	2.1901
16	11.1104	44	10.2078	72	6.7143	99	2.0855
17	11.0970	45	10.1372	73	6.5339	100	1.9833
18	11.0839	46	10.0629	74	6.3509	101	1.8822
19	11.0705	47	9.9849	75	6.1646	102	1.7826
20	11.0563	48	9.9031	76	5.9742	103	1.6836
21	11.0413	49	9.8173	77	5.7797	104	1.5774
22	11.0255	50	9.7272	78	5.5814	105	1.4737
23	11.0086	51	9.6328	79	5.3806	106	1.3389
24	10.9905	52	9.5344	80	5.1792	107	1.1743
25	10.9709	53	9.4320	81	4.9789	108	0.9139
26	10.9499	54	9.3255	82	4.7805	109	0.4596
27	10.9269	55	9.2149				

Table S: Present Worth of Single Life Annuity at 9.0 Percent

Age	Annuity	Age	Annuity	Age	Annuity	Age	Annuity
0	10.9229	28	10.6803	56	8.9556	83	4.5466
1	11.0137	29	10.6556	57	8.8404	84	4.3541
2	11.0134	30	10.6294	58	8.7215	85	4.1611
3	11.0101	31	10.6016	59	8.5992	86	3.9693
4	11.0053	32	10.5721	60	8.4736	87	3.7816
5	10.9993	33	10.5406	61	8.3445	88	3.5984
6	10.9924	34	10.5071	62	8.2112	89	3.4195
7	10.9845	35	10.4713	63	8.0735	90	3.2455
8	10.9758	36	10.4332	64	7.9316	91	3.0793
9	10.9659	37	10.3927	65	7.7856	92	2.9247
10	10.9548	38	10.3494	66	7.6350	93	2.7813
11	10.9426	39	10.3033	67	7.4790	94	2.6470
12	10.9293	40	10.2540	68	7.3180	95	2.5190
13	10.9154	41	10.2012	69	7.1524	96	2.3980
14	10.9014	42	10.1449	70	6.9832	97	2.2856
15	10.8879	43	10.0848	71	6.8110	98	2.1797
16	10.8749	44	10.0208	72	6.6365	99	2.0760
17	10.8624	45	9.9534	73	6.4602	100	1.9746
18	10.8502	46	9.8821	74	6.2812	101	1.8743
19	10.8377	47	9.8074	75	6.0988	102	1.7754
20	10.8245	48	9.7289	76	5.9122	103	1.6772
21	10.8104	49	9.6466	77	5.7215	104	1.5717
22	10.7957	50	9.5600	78	5.5269	105	1.4687
23	10.7799	51	9.4692	79	5.3298	106	1.3348
24	10.7630	52	9.3745	80	5.1319	107	1.1711
25	10.7447	53	9.2758	81	4.9348	108	0.9118
26	10.7249	54	9.1732	82	4.7397	109	0.4587
27	10.7034	55	9.0665				

Table S: Present Worth of Single Life Annuity at 9.2 Percent

Age	Annuity	Age	Annuity	Age	Annuity	Age	Annuity
0	10.6900	28	10.4665	56	8.8151	83	4.5093
1	10.7791	29	10.4433	57	8.7038	84	4.3197
2	10.7789	30	10.4186	58	8.5887	85	4.1294
3	10.7761	31	10.3923	59	8.4703	86	3.9401
4	10.7717	32	10.3645	60	8.3487	87	3.7549
5	10.7661	33	10.3347	61	8.2236	88	3.5738
6	10.7597	34	10.3030	62	8.0943	89	3.3971
7	10.7523	35	10.2691	63	7.9606	90	3.2250
8	10.7441	36	10.2330	64	7.8228	91	3.0606
9	10.7348	37	10.1946	65	7.6809	92	2.9075
10	10.7244	38	10.1535	66	7.5344	93	2.7655
11	10.7128	39	10.1096	67	7.3825	94	2.6326
12	10.7002	40	10.0627	68	7.2256	95	2.5057
13	10.6870	41	10.0124	69	7.0642	96	2.3858
14	10.6739	42	9.9586	70	6.8990	97	2.2744
15	10.6611	43	9.9012	71	6.7309	98	2.1695
16	10.6489	44	9.8400	72	6.5604	99	2.0666
17	10.6372	45	9.7754	73	6.3880	100	1.9660
18	10.6257	46	9.7072	74	6.2128	101	1.8664
19	10.6140	47	9.6356	75	6.0342	102	1.7683
20	10.6017	48	9.5602	76	5.8514	103	1.6708
21	10.5886	49	9.4811	77	5.6644	104	1.5660
22	10.5748	50	9.3979	78	5.4734	105	1.4637
23	10.5601	51	9.3105	79	5.2798	106	1.3307
24	10.5442	52	9.2193	80	5.0852	107	1.1679
25	10.5270	53	9.1242	81	4.8914	108	0.9098
26	10.5085	54	9.0253	82	4.6994	109	0.4579
27	10.4882	55	8.9223				

Table S: Present Worth of Single Life Annuity at 9.4 Percent

Age	Annuity	Age	Annuity	Age	Annuity	Age	Annuity
0	10.4667	28	10.2607	56	8.6785	83	4.4725
1	10.5540	29	10.2388	57	8.5709	84	4.2857
2	10.5541	30	10.2154	58	8.4595	85	4.0980
3	10.5515	31	10.1907	59	8.3449	86	3.9113
4	10.5475	32	10.1643	60	8.2270	87	3.7284
5	10.5423	33	10.1361	61	8.1057	88	3.5496
6	10.5363	34	10.1062	62	7.9803	89	3.3749
7	10.5294	35	10.0740	63	7.8505	90	3.2047
8	10.5218	36	10.0398	64	7.7167	91	3.0421
9	10.5130	37	10.0033	65	7.5787	92	2.8905
10	10.5031	38	9.9642	66	7.4361	93	2.7500
11	10.4922	39	9.9225	67	7.2882	94	2.6183
12	10.4803	40	9.8778	68	7.1353	95	2.4926
13	10.4677	41	9.8298	69	6.9778	96	2.3738
14	10.4553	42	9.7784	70	6.8166	97	2.2633
15	10.4432	43	9.7236	71	6.6524	98	2.1593
16	10.4317	44	9.6651	72	6.4858	99	2.0572
17	10.4207	45	9.6032	73	6.3171	100	1.9575
18	10.4100	46	9.5378	74	6.1458	101	1.8587
19	10.3990	47	9.4691	75	5.9709	102	1.7613
20	10.3875	48	9.3967	76	5.7917	103	1.6644
21	10.3752	49	9.3207	77	5.6083	104	1.5603
22	10.3623	50	9.2406	78	5.4208	105	1.4588
23	10.3486	51	9.1565	79	5.2306	106	1.3266
24	10.3337	52	9.0687	80	5.0394	107	1.1647
25	10.3176	53	8.9770	81	4.8487	108	0.9077
26	10.3002	54	8.8815	82	4.6597	109	0.4570
27	10.2811	55	8.7821				

Table S: Present Worth of Single Life Annuity at 9.6 Percent

Age	Annuity	Age	Annuity	Age	Annuity	Age	Annuity
0	10.2523	28	10.0623	56	8.5457	83	4.4363
1	10.3379	29	10.0416	57	8.4415	84	4.2522
2	10.3383	30	10.0196	58	8.3337	85	4.0671
3	10.3360	31	9.9962	59	8.2227	86	3.8829
4	10.3323	32	9.9713	60	8.1085	87	3.7023
5	10.3275	33	9.9446	61	7.9909	88	3.5257
6	10.3219	34	9.9162	62	7.8691	89	3.3530
7	10.3154	35	9.8857	63	7.7431	90	3.1847
8	10.3082	36	9.8532	64	7.6130	91	3.0238
9	10.3000	37	9.8185	65	7.4788	92	2.8738
10	10.2906	38	9.7814	66	7.3400	93	2.7346
11	10.2803	39	9.7417	67	7.1960	94	2.6042
12	10.2689	40	9.6991	68	7.0470	95	2.4796
13	10.2570	41	9.6533	69	6.8933	96	2.3618
14	10.2452	42	9.6042	70	6.7359	97	2.2524
15	10.2337	43	9.5517	71	6.5756	98	2.1492
16	10.2229	44	9.4957	72	6.4127	99	2.0479
17	10.2125	45	9.4364	73	6.2477	100	1.9490
18	10.2025	46	9.3737	74	6.0800	101	1.8509
19	10.1923	47	9.3077	75	5.9087	102	1.7543
20	10.1815	48	9.2382	76	5.7331	103	1.6581
21	10.1700	49	9.1651	77	5.5531	104	1.5548
22	10.1579	50	9.0881	78	5.3691	105	1.4539
23	10.1450	51	9.0071	79	5.1822	106	1.3225
24	10.1311	52	8.9224	80	4.9942	107	1.1616
25	10.1160	53	8.8340	81	4.8067	108	0.9056
26	10.0996	54	8.7418	82	4.6207	109	0.4562
27	10.0816	55	8.6458				

Table S: Present Worth of Single Life Annuity at 9.8 Percent

Age	Annuity	Age	Annuity	Age	Annuity	Age	Annuity
0	10.0464	28	9.8711	56	8.4164	83	4.4006
1	10.1304	29	9.8516	57	8.3157	84	4.2192
2	10.1309	30	9.8307	58	8.2113	85	4.0367
3	10.1289	31	9.8086	59	8.1037	86	3.8549
4	10.1255	32	9.7850	60	7.9930	87	3.6765
5	10.1210	33	9.7597	61	7.8789	88	3.5020
6	10.1158	34	9.7328	62	7.7607	89	3.3314
7	10.1097	35	9.7038	63	7.6383	90	3.1649
8	10.1029	36	9.6730	64	7.5118	91	3.0056
9	10.0951	37	9.6400	65	7.3813	92	2.8572
10	10.0863	38	9.6047	66	7.2462	93	2.7193
11	10.0765	39	9.5668	67	7.1059	94	2.5902
12	10.0657	40	9.5262	68	6.9605	95	2.4668
13	10.0543	41	9.4825	69	6.8106	96	2.3500
14	10.0431	42	9.4356	70	6.6569	97	2.2415
15	10.0322	43	9.3853	71	6.5002	98	2.1392
16	10.0220	44	9.3317	72	6.3410	99	2.0388
17	10.0122	45	9.2749	73	6.1796	100	1.9406
18	10.0028	46	9.2147	74	6.0154	101	1.8433
19	9.9932	47	9.1513	75	5.8476	102	1.7473
20	9.9831	48	9.0845	76	5.6755	103	1.6518
21	9.9724	49	9.0142	77	5.4989	104	1.5492
22	9.9611	50	8.9400	78	5.3183	105	1.4491
23	9.9490	51	8.8620	79	5.1346	106	1.3185
24	9.9359	52	8.7803	80	4.9498	107	1.1585
25	9.9217	53	8.6950	81	4.7653	108	0.9036
26	9.9062	54	8.6060	82	4.5822	109	0.4554
27	9.8893	55	8.5132				

Table S: Present Worth of Single Life Annuity at 10.0 Percent

Age	Annuity	Age	Annuity	Age	Annuity	Age	Annuity
0	9.8484	28	9.6867	56	8.2907	83	4.3654
1	9.9309	29	9.6682	57	8.1931	84	4.1866
2	9.9316	30	9.6485	58	8.0920	85	4.0066
3	9.9298	31	9.6275	59	7.9877	86	3.8272
4	9.9267	32	9.6052	60	7.8804	87	3.6511
5	9.9225	33	9.5812	61	7.7696	88	3.4787
6	9.9176	34	9.5556	62	7.6549	89	3.3100
7	9.9119	35	9.5282	63	7.5359	90	3.1453
8	9.9055	36	9.4988	64	7.4130	91	2.9877
9	9.8981	37	9.4675	65	7.2860	92	2.8407
10	9.8897	38	9.4338	66	7.1544	93	2.7043
11	9.8804	39	9.3977	67	7.0177	94	2.5763
12	9.8701	40	9.3589	68	6.8760	95	2.4540
13	9.8593	41	9.3172	69	6.7297	96	2.3383
14	9.8486	42	9.2723	70	6.5796	97	2.2307
15	9.8383	43	9.2242	71	6.4264	98	2.1292
16	9.8286	44	9.1728	72	6.2707	99	2.0296
17	9.8194	45	9.1183	73	6.1128	100	1.9322
18	9.8106	46	9.0605	74	5.9521	101	1.8357
19	9.8016	47	8.9996	75	5.7877	102	1.7404
20	9.7921	48	8.9354	76	5.6189	103	1.6456
21	9.7820	49	8.8678	77	5.4457	104	1.5437
22	9.7714	50	8.7963	78	5.2683	105	1.4443
23	9.7600	51	8.7211	79	5.0878	106	1.3145
24	9.7478	52	8.6423	80	4.9061	107	1.1553
25	9.7344	53	8.5600	51	4.7246	108	0.9016
26	9.7198	54	8.4740	82	4.5443	109	0.4545
27	9.7038	55	8.3843				

Appendix B

Life Expectancy Tables

Table I: Single Life Expectancies							
Age	Divisor	Age	Divisor	Age	Divisor	Age	Divisor
35	47.3	54	29.5	73	13.9	92	4.4
36	46.4	55	28.6	74	13.2	93	4.1
37	45.4	56	27.7	75	12.5	94	3.9
38	44.4	57	26.8	76	11.9	95	3.7
39	43.5	58	25.9	77	11.2	96	3.4
40	42.5	59	25.0	78	10.6	97	3.2
41	41.5	60	24.2	79	10.0	98	3.0
42	40.6	61	23.3	80	9.5	99	2.8
43	39.6	62	22.5	81	8.9	100	2.7
44	38.7	63	21.6	82	8.4	101	2.5
45	37.7	64	20.8	83	7.9	102	2.3
46	36.8	65	20.0	84	7.4	103	2.1
47	35.9	66	19.2	85	6.9	104	1.9
48	34.9	67	18.4	86	6.5	105	1.8
49	34.0	68	17.6	87	6.1	106	1.6
50	33.1	69	16.8	88	5.7	107	1.4
51	32.2	70	16.0	89	5.3	108	1.3
52	31.3	71	15.3	90	5.0	109	1.1
53	30.4	72	14.6	91	4.7	110	1.0

Table II: Joint Life and Last Survivor Expectancy

AGES	35	36	37	38	39	40	41	42	43	44
35	54.0	53.5	53.0	52.6	52.2	51.8	51.4	51.1	50.8	50.5
36	53.5	53.0	52.5	52.0	51.6	51.2	50.8	50.4	50.1	49.8
37	53.0	52.5	52.0	51.5	51.0	50.6	50.2	49.8	49.5	49.1
38	52.6	52.0	51.5	51.0	50.5	50.0	49.6	49.2	48.8	48.5
39	52.2	51.6	51.0	50.5	50.0	49.5	49.1	48.6	48.2	47.8
40	51.8	51.2	50.6	50.0	49.5	49.0	48.5	48.1	47.6	47.2
41	51.4	50.8	50.2	49.6	49.1	48.5	48.0	47.5	47.1	46.7
42	51.1	50.4	49.8	49.2	48.6	48.1	47.5	47.0	46.6	46.1
43	50.8	50.1	49.5	48.8	48.2	47.6	47.1	46.6	46.0	45.6
44	50.5	49.8	49.1	48.5	47.8	47.2	46.7	46.1	45.6	45.1
45	50.2	49.5	48.8	48.1	47.5	46.9	46.3	45.7	45.1	44.6
46	50.0	49.2	48.5	47.8	47.2	46.5	45.9	45.3	44.7	44.1
47	49.7	49.0	48.3	47.5	46.8	46.2	45.5	44.9	44.3	43.7
48	49.5	48.8	48.0	47.3	46.6	45.9	45.2	44.5	43.9	43.3
49	49.3	48.5	47.8	47.0	46.3	45.6	44.9	44.2	43.6	42.9
50	49.2	48.4	47.6	46.8	46.0	45.3	44.6	43.9	43.2	42.6
51	49.0	48.2	47.4	46.6	45.8	45.1	44.3	43.6	42.9	42.2
52	48.8	48.0	47.2	46.4	45.6	44.8	44.1	43.3	42.6	41.9
53	48.7	47.9	47.0	46.2	45.4	44.6	43.9	43.1	42.4	41.7
54	48.6	47.7	46.9	46.0	45.2	44.4	43.6	42.9	42.1	41.4
55	48.5	47.6	46.7	45.9	45.1	44.2	43.4	42.7	41.9	41.2
56	48.3	47.5	46.6	45.8	44.9	44.1	43.3	42.5	41.7	40.9
57	48.3	47.4	46.5	45.6	44.8	43.9	43.1	42.3	41.5	40.7
58	48.2	47.3	46.4	45.5	44.7	43.8	43.0	42.1	41.3	40.5
59	48.1	47.2	46.3	45.4	44.5	43.7	42.8	42.0	41.2	40.4
60	48.0	47.1	46.2	45.3	44.4	43.6	42.7	41.9	41.0	40.2
61	47.9	47.0	46.1	45.2	44.3	43.5	42.6	41.7	40.9	40.0
62	47.9	47.0	46.0	45.1	44.2	43.4	42.5	41.6	40.8	39.9
63	47.8	46.9	46.0	45.1	44.2	43.3	42.4	41.5	40.6	39.8

Table II: Joint Life and Last Survivor Expectancy (continued)

AGES	35	36	37	38	39	40	41	42	43	44
64	47.8	46.8	45.9	45.0	44.1	43.2	42.3	41.4	40.5	39.7
65	47.7	46.8	45.9	44.9	44.0	43.1	42.2	41.3	40.4	39.6
66	47.7	46.7	45.8	44.9	44.0	43.1	42.2	41.3	40.4	39.5
67	47.6	46.7	45.8	44.8	43.9	43.0	42.1	41.2	40.3	39.4
68	47.6	46.7	45.7	44.8	43.9	42.9	42.0	41.1	40.2	39.3
69	47.6	46.6	45.7	44.8	43.8	42.9	42.0	41.1	40.2	39.3
70	47.5	46.6	45.7	44.7	43.8	42.9	41.9	41.0	40.1	39.2
71	47.5	46.6	45.6	44.7	43.8	42.8	41.9	41.0	40.1	39.1
72	47.5	46.6	45.6	44.7	43.7	42.8	41.9	40.9	40.0	39.1
73	47.5	46.5	45.6	44.6	43.7	42.8	41.8	40.9	40.0	39.0
74	47.5	46.5	45.6	44.6	43.7	42.7	41.8	40.9	39.9	39.0
75	47.4	46.5	45.5	44.6	43.6	42.7	41.8	40.8	39.9	39.0
76	47.4	46.5	45.5	44.6	43.6	42.7	41.7	40.8	39.9	38.9
77	47.4	46.5	45.5	44.6	43.6	42.7	41.7	40.8	39.8	38.9
78	47.4	46.4	45.5	44.5	43.6	42.6	41.7	40.7	39.8	38.9
79	47.4	46.4	45.5	44.5	43.6	42.6	41.7	40.7	39.8	38.9
80	47.4	46.4	45.5	44.5	43.6	42.6	41.7	40.7	39.8	38.8
81	47.4	46.4	45.5	44.5	43.5	42.6	41.6	40.7	39.8	38.8
82	47.4	46.4	45.4	44.5	43.5	42.6	41.6	40.7	39.7	38.8
83	47.4	46.4	45.4	44.5	43.5	42.6	41.6	40.7	39.7	38.8
84	47.4	46.4	45.4	44.5	43.5	42.6	41.6	40.7	39.7	38.8
85	47.4	46.4	45.4	44.5	43.5	42.6	41.6	40.7	39.7	38.8
86	47.3	46.4	45.4	44.5	43.5	42.5	41.6	40.6	39.7	38.8
87	47.3	46.4	45.4	44.5	43.5	42.5	41.6	40.6	39.7	38.7
88	47.3	46.4	45.4	44.5	43.5	42.5	41.6	40.6	39.7	38.7
89	47.3	46.4	45.4	44.4	43.5	42.5	41.6	40.6	39.7	38.7
90	47.3	46.4	45.4	44.4	43.5	42.5	41.6	40.6	39.7	38.7
91	47.3	46.4	45.4	44.4	43.5	42.5	41.6	40.6	39.7	38.7
92	47.3	46.4	45.4	44.4	43.5	42.5	41.6	40.6	39.7	38.7

Table II: Joint Life and Last Survivor Expectancy (continued)

AGES	45	46	47	46	49	50	51	52	53	54
45	44.1	43.6	43.2	42.7	42.3	42.0	41.6	41.3	41.0	40.7
46	43.6	43.1	42.6	42.2	41.8	41.4	41.0	40.6	40.3	40.0
47	43.2	42.6	42.1	41.7	41.2	40.8	40.4	40.0	39.7	39.3
48	42.7	42.2	41.7	41.2	40.7	40.2	39.8	39.4	39.0	38.7
49	42.3	41.8	41.2	40.7	40.2	39.7	39.3	38.8	38.4	38.1
50	42.0	41.4	40.8	40.2	39.7	39.2	38.7	38.3	37.9	37.5
51	41.6	41.0	40.4	39.8	39.3	38.7	38.2	37.8	37.3	36.9
52	41.3	40.6	40.0	39.4	38.8	38.3	37.8	37.3	36.8	36.4
53	41.0	40.3	39.7	39.0	38.4	37.9	37.3	36.8	36.3	35.8
54	40.7	40.0	39.3	38.7	38.1	37.5	36.9	36.4	35.8	35.3
55	40.4	39.7	39.0	38.4	37.7	37.1	36.5	35.9	35.4	34.9
56	40.2	39.5	38.7	38.1	37.4	36.8	36.1	35.6	35.0	34.4
57	40.0	39.2	38.5	37.8	37.1	36.4	35.8	35.2	34.6	34.0
58	39.7	39.0	38.2	37.5	36.8	36.1	35.5	34.8	34.2	33.6
59	39.6	38.8	38.0	37.3	36.6	35.9	35.2	34.5	33.9	33.3
60	39.4	38.6	37.8	37.1	36.3	35.6	34.9	34.2	33.6	32.9
61	39.2	38.4	37.6	36.9	36.1	35.4	34.6	33.9	33.3	32.6
62	39.1	38.3	37.5	36.7	35.9	35.1	34.4	33.7	33.0	32.3
63	38.9	38.1	37.3	36.5	35.7	34.9	34.2	33.5	32.7	32.0
64	38.8	38.0	37.2	36.3	35.5	34.8	34.0	33.2	32.5	31.8
65	38.7	37.9	37.0	36.2	35.4	34.6	33.8	33.0	32.3	31.6
66	38.6	37.8	36.9	36.1	35.2	34.4	33.6	32.9	32.1	31.4
67	38.5	37.7	36.8	36.0	35.1	34.3	33.5	32.7	31.9	31.2
68	38.4	37.6	36.7	35.8	35.0	34.2	33.4	32.5	31.8	31.0
69	38.4	37.5	36.6	35.7	34.9	34.1	33.2	32.4	31.6	30.8
70	38.3	37.4	36.5	35.7	34.8	34.0	33.1	32.3	31.5	30.7
71	38.2	37.3	36.5	35.6	34.7	33.9	33.0	32.2	31.4	30.5
72	38.2	37.3	36.4	35.5	34.6	33.8	32.9	32.1	31.2	30.4
73	38.1	37.2	36.3	35.4	34.6	33.7	32.8	32.0	31.1	30.3

Table II: Joint Life and Last Survivor Expectancy (continued)

AGES	45	46	47	46	49	50	51	52	53	54
74	38.1	37.2	36.3	35.4	34.5	33.6	32.8	31.9	31.1	30.2
75	38.1	37.1	36.2	35.3	34.5	33.6	32.7	31.8	31.0	30.1
76	38.0	37.1	36.2	35.3	34.4	33.5	32.6	31.8	30.9	30.1
77	38.0	37.1	36.2	35.3	34.4	33.5	32.6	31.7	30.8	30.0
78	38.0	37.0	36.1	35.2	34.3	33.4	32.5	31.7	30.8	29.9
79	37.9	37.0	36.1	35.2	34.3	33.4	32.5	31.6	30.7	29.9
80	37.9	37.0	36.1	35.2	34.2	33.4	32.5	31.6	30.7	29.8
81	37.9	37.0	36.0	35.1	34.2	33.3	32.4	31.5	30.7	29.8
82	37.9	36.9	36.0	35.1	34.2	33.3	32.4	31.5	30.6	29.7
83	37.9	36.9	36.0	35.1	34.2	33.3	32.4	31.5	30.6	29.7
84	37.8	36.9	36.0	35.1	34.2	33.2	32.3	31.4	30.6	29.7
85	37.8	36.9	36.0	35.1	34.1	33.2	32.3	31.4	30.5	29.6
86	37.8	36.9	36.0	35.0	34.1	33.2	32.3	31.4	30.5	29.6
87	37.8	36.9	35.9	35.0	34.1	33.2	32.3	31.4	30.5	29.6
88	37.8	36.9	35.9	35.0	34.1	33.2	32.3	31.4	30.5	29.6
89	37.8	36.9	35.9	35.0	34.1	33.2	32.3	31.4	30.5	29.6
90	37.8	36.9	35.9	35.0	34.1	33.2	32.3	31.3	30.5	29.6
91	37.8	36.8	35.9	35.0	34.1	33.2	32.2	31.3	30.4	29.5
92	37.8	36.8	35.9	35.0	34.1	33.2	32.2	31.3	30.4	29.5

Table II: Joint Life and Last Survivor Expectancy (continued)

AGES	55	56	57	58	59	60	61	62	63	64
55	34.4	33.9	33.5	33.1	32.7	32.3	32.0	31.7	31.4	31.1
56	33.9	33.4	33.0	32.5	32.1	31.7	31.4	31.0	30.7	30.4
57	33.5	33.0	32.5	32.0	31.6	31.2	30.8	30.4	30.1	29.8
58	33.1	32.5	32.0	31.5	31.1	30.6	30.2	29.9	29.5	29.2
59	32.7	32.1	31.6	31.1	30.6	30.1	29.7	29.3	28.9	28.6
60	32.3	32.7	31.2	30.6	30.1	29.7	29.2	28.8	28.4	28.0
61	32.0	31.4	30.8	30.2	29.7	29.2	28.7	28.3	27.8	27.4
62	31.7	31.0	30.4	29.9	29.3	28.8	28.3	27.8	27.3	26.9
63	31.4	30.7	30.1	29.5	28.9	28.4	27.8	27.3	26.9	26.4
64	31.1	30.4	29.8	29.2	28.6	28.0	27.4	26.9	26.4	25.9
65	30.9	30.2	29.5	28.9	28.2	27.6	27.1	26.5	26.0	25.5
66	30.6	29.9	29.2	28.6	27.9	27.3	26.7	26.1	25.6	25.1
67	30.4	29.7	29.0	28.3	27.6	27.0	26.4	25.8	25.2	24.7
68	30.2	29.5	28.8	28.1	27.4	26.7	26.1	25.5	24.9	24.3
69	30.1	29.3	28.6	27.8	27.1	26.5	25.8	25.2	24.6	24.0
70	29.9	29.1	28.4	27.6	26.9	26.2	25.6	24.9	24.3	23.7
71	29.7	29.0	28.2	27.5	26.7	26.0	25.3	24.7	24.0	23.4
72	29.6	28.8	28.1	27.3	26.5	25.8	25.1	24.4	23.8	23.1
73	29.5	28.7	27.9	27.1	26.4	25.6	24.9	24.2	23.5	22.9
74	29.4	28.6	27.8	27.0	26.2	25.5	24.7	24.0	23.3	22.7
75	29.3	28.5	27.7	26.9	26.1	25.3	24.6	23.8	23.1	22.4
76	29.2	28.4	27.6	26.8	26.0	25.2	24.4	23.7	23.0	22.3
77	29.1	28.3	27.5	26.7	25.9	25.1	24.3	23.6	22.8	22.1
78	29.1	28.2	27.4	26.6	25.8	25.0	24.2	23.4	22.7	21.9
79	29.0	28.2	27.3	26.5	25.7	24.9	24.1	23.3	22.6	21.8
80	29.0	28.1	27.3	26.4	25.6	24.8	24.0	23.2	22.4	21.7
81	28.9	28.1	27.2	26.4	25.5	24.7	23.9	23.1	22.3	21.6
82	28.9	28.0	27.2	26.3	25.5	24.6	23.8	23.0	22.3	21.5
83	28.6	28.0	27.1	26.3	25.4	24.6	23.8	23.0	22.2	21.4
84	28.8	27.9	27.1	26.2	25.4	24.5	23.7	22.9	22.1	21.3

Table II: Joint Life and Last Survivor Expectancy (continued)

AGES	55	56	57	58	59	60	61	62	63	64
85	28.8	27.9	27.0	26.2	25.3	24.5	23.7	22.8	22.0	21.3
86	28.7	27.9	27.0	26.1	25.3	24.5	23.6	22.8	22.0	21.2
87	28.7	27.8	27.0	26.1	25.3	24.4	23.6	22.8	21.9	21.1
88	28.7	27.8	27.0	26.1	25.2	24.4	23.5	22.7	21.9	21.1
89	28.7	27.8	26.9	26.1	25.2	24.4	23.5	22.7	21.9	21.1
90	28.7	27.8	26.9	26.1	25.2	24.3	23.5	22.7	21.8	21.0
91	28.7	27.8	26.9	26.0	25.2	24.3	23.5	22.6	21.8	21.0
92	28.6	27.8	26.9	26.0	25.2	24.3	23.5	22.6	21.8	21.0
93	28.6	27.8	26.9	26.0	25.1	24.3	23.4	22.6	21.8	20.9
94	28.6	27.7	26.9	26.0	25.1	24.3	23.4	22.6	21.7	20.9
95	28.6	27.7	26.9	26.0	25.1	24.3	23.4	22.6	21.7	20.9
96	28.6	27.7	26.9	26.0	25.1	24.2	23.4	22.6	21.7	20.9
97	28.6	27.7	26.8	26.0	25.1	24.2	23.4	22.5	21.7	20.9
98	28.6	27.7	26.8	26.0	25.1	24.2	23.4	22.5	21.7	20.9
99	28.6	27.7	26.8	26.0	25.1	24.2	23.4	22.5	21.7	20.9
100	28.6	27.7	26.8	26.0	25.1	24.2	23.4	22.5	21.7	20.8
101	28.6	27.7	26.8	25.9	25.1	24.2	23.4	22.5	21.7	20.8
102	28.6	27.7	26.8	25.9	25.1	24.2	23.3	22.5	21.7	20.8
103	28.6	27.7	26.8	25.9	25.1	24.2	23.3	22.5	21.7	20.8
104	28.6	27.7	26.8	25.9	25.1	24.2	23.3	22.5	21.6	20.8
105	28.6	27.7	26.8	25.9	25.1	24.2	23.3	22.5	21.6	20.8
106	28.6	27.7	26.8	25.9	25.1	24.2	23.3	22.5	21.6	20.8
107	28.6	27.7	26.8	25.9	25.1	24.2	23.3	22.5	21.6	20.8
108	28.6	27.7	26.8	25.9	25.1	24.2	23.3	22.5	21.6	20.8
109	28.6	27.7	26.8	25.9	25.1	24.2	23.3	22.5	21.6	20.8
110	28.6	27.7	26.8	25.9	25.1	24.2	23.3	22.5	21.6	20.8
111	28.6	27.7	26.8	25.9	25.0	24.2	23.3	22.5	21.6	20.8
112	28.6	27.7	26.8	25.9	25.0	24.2	23.3	22.5	21.6	20.8
113	28.6	27.7	26.8	25.9	25.0	24.2	23.3	22.5	21.6	20.8
114	28.6	27.7	26.8	25.9	25.0	24.2	23.3	22.5	21.6	20.8
115	28.6	27.7	26.8	25.9	25.0	24.2	23.3	22.5	21.6	20.8

Table II: Joint Life and Last Survivor Expectancy (continued)

AGES	65	66	67	68	69	70	71	72	73	74
65	25.0	24.6	24.2	23.8	23.4	23.1	22.8	22.5	22.2	22.0
66	24.6	24.1	23.7	23.3	22.9	22.5	22.2	21.9	21.6	21.4
67	24.2	23.7	23.2	22.8	22.4	22.0	21.7	21.3	21.0	20.8
68	23.8	23.3	22.8	22.3	21.9	21.5	21.2	20.8	20.5	20.2
69	23.4	22.9	22.4	21.8	21.5	21.1	20.7	20.3	20.0	19.6
70	23.1	22.5	22.0	21.5	21.1	20.6	20.2	19.8	19.4	19.1
71	22.8	22.2	21.7	21.2	20.7	20.2	19.8	19.4	19.0	18.6
72	22.5	21.9	21.3	20.8	20.3	19.8	19.4	18.9	18.5	18.2
73	22.2	21.6	21.0	20.5	20.0	19.4	19.0	18.5	18.1	17.7
74	22.0	21.4	20.8	20.2	19.6	19.1	18.6	18.2	17.7	17.3
75	21.8	21.1	20.5	19.9	19.3	18.8	18.3	17.8	17.3	16.9
76	21.6	20.9	20.3	19.7	19.1	18.5	18.0	17.5	17.0	16.5
77	21.4	20.7	20.1	19.4	18.8	18.3	17.7	17.2	16.7	16.2
78	21.2	20.5	19.9	19.2	18.6	18.0	17.5	16.9	16.4	15.9
79	21.1	20.4	19.7	19.0	18.4	17.8	17.2	16.7	16.1	15.6
80	21.0	20.2	19.5	18.9	18.2	17.6	17.0	16.4	15.9	15.4
81	20.8	20.1	19.4	18.7	18.1	17.4	16.8	16.2	15.7	15.1
82	20.7	20.0	19.3	18.6	17.9	17.3	16.6	16.0	15.5	14.9
83	20.6	19.9	19.2	18.5	17.8	17.1	16.5	15.9	15.3	14.7
84	20.5	19.8	19.1	18.4	17.7	17.0	16.3	15.7	15.1	14.5
85	20.5	19.7	19.0	18.3	17.6	16.9	16.2	15.6	15.0	14.4
86	20.4	19.6	18.9	18.2	17.5	16.8	16.1	15.5	14.8	14.2
87	20.4	19.6	18.8	18.1	17.4	16.7	16.0	15.4	14.7	14.1
88	20.3	19.5	18.8	18.0	17.3	16.8	15.9	15.3	14.6	14.0
89	20.3	19.5	18.7	18.0	17.2	16.5	15.8	15.2	14.5	13.9
90	20.2	19.4	18.7	17.9	17.2	16.5	15.8	15.1	14.5	13.8
91	20.2	19.4	18.6	17.9	17.1	16.4	15.7	15.0	14.4	13.7
92	20.2	19.4	18.6	17.8	17.1	16.4	15.7	15.0	14.3	13.7
93	20.1	19.3	18.6	17.8	17.1	16.3	15.6	14.9	14.3	13.6

Table II: Joint Life and Last Survivor Expectancy (continued)

AGES	65	66	67	68	69	70	71	72	73	74
94	20.1	19.3	18.5	17.8	17.0	16.3	15.6	14.9	14.2	13.8
95	20.1	19.3	18.5	17.8	17.0	16.3	15.6	14.9	14.2	13.5
96	20.1	19.3	18.5	17.7	17.0	16.2	15.5	14.8	14.2	13.5
97	20.1	19.3	18.5	17.7	17.0	16.2	15.5	14.8	14.1	13.5
98	20.1	19.3	18.5	17.7	16.9	16.2	15.5	14.8	14.1	13.4
99	20.0	19.2	18.5	17.7	16.9	16.2	15.5	14.7	14.1	13.4
100	20.0	19.2	18.4	17.7	16.9	16.2	15.4	14.7	14.0	13.4
101	20.0	19.2	18.4	17.7	16.9	16.1	15.4	14.7	14.0	13.3
102	20.0	19.2	18.4	17.6	16.9	16.1	15.4	14.7	14.0	13.3
103	20.0	19.2	18.4	17.6	16.9	16.1	15.4	14.7	14.0	13.3
104	20.0	19.2	18.4	17.6	16.9	16.1	15.4	14.7	14.0	13.3
105	20.0	19.2	18.4	17.6	16.8	16.1	15.4	14.6	13.9	13.3
106	20.0	19.2	18.4	17.6	16.8	16.1	15.3	14.6	13.9	13.3
107	20.0	19.2	18.4	17.6	16.8	16.1	15.3	14.6	13.9	13.2
108	20.0	19.2	18.4	17.6	16.8	16.1	15.3	14.6	13.9	13.2
109	20.0	19.2	18.4	17.6	16.8	16.1	15.3	14.6	13.9	13.2
110	20.0	19.2	18.4	17.6	16.8	16.1	15.3	14.6	13.9	13.2
111	20.0	19.2	18.4	17.6	16.8	16.0	15.3	14.6	13.9	13.2
112	20.0	19.2	18.4	17.6	16.8	16.0	15.3	14.6	13.9	13.2
113	20.0	19.2	18.4	17.6	16.8	16.0	15.3	14.6	13.9	13.2
114	20.0	19.2	18.4	17.6	16.8	16.0	15.3	14.6	13.9	13.2
115	20.0	19.2	18.4	17.6	16.8	16.0	15.3	14.6	13.9	13.2

Table II: Joint Life and Last Survivor Expectancy (continued)									
Ages	**75**	**76**	**77**	**78**	**79**	**80**	**81**	**82**	**83**	**84**
75	16.5	16.1	15.8	15.4	15.1	14.9	14.6	14.4	14.2	14.0
76	16.1	15.7	15.4	15.0	14.7	14.4	14.1	13.9	13.7	13.5
77	15.8	15.4	15.0	14.6	14.3	14.0	13.7	13.4	13.2	13.0
78	15.4	15.0	14.6	14.2	13.9	13.5	13.2	13.0	12.7	12.5
79	15.1	14.7	14.3	13.9	13.5	13.2	12.8	12.5	12.3	12.0
80	14.9	14.4	14.0	13.5	13.2	12.8	12.5	12.2	11.9	11.6
81	14.6	14.1	13.7	13.2	12.8	12.5	12.1	11.8	11.5	11.2
82	14.4	13.9	13.4	13.0	12.5	12.2	11.8	11.5	11.1	10.9
83	14.2	13.7	13.2	12.7	12.3	11.9	11.5	11.1	10.8	10.5
84	14.0	13.5	13.0	12.5	12.0	11.6	11.2	10.9	10.5	10.2
85	13.8	13.3	12.8	12.3	11.8	11.4	11.0	10.6	10.2	9.9
86	13.7	13.1	12.6	12.1	11.6	11.2	10.8	10.4	10.0	9.7
87	13.5	13.0	12.4	11.9	11.4	11.0	10.6	10.1	9.8	9.4
88	13.4	12.8	12.3	11.8	11.3	10.8	10.4	10.0	9.6	9.2
89	13.3	12.7	12.2	11.6	11.1	10.7	10.2	9.8	9.4	9.0
90	13.2	12.6	12.1	11.5	11.0	10.5	10.1	9.6	9.2	8.8
91	13.1	12.5	12.0	11.4	10.9	10.4	9.9	9.5	9.1	8.7
92	13.1	12.5	11.9	11.3	10.8	10.3	9.8	9.4	8.9	8.5
93	13.0	12.4	11.8	11.3	10.7	10.2	9.7	9.3	8.8	8.4
94	12.9	12.3	11.7	11.2	10.6	10.1	9.6	9.2	8.7	8.3
95	12.9	12.3	11.7	11.1	10.6	10.1	9.6	9.1	8.6	8.2
96	12.9	12.2	11.6	11.1	10.5	10.0	9.5	9.0	8.5	8.1
97	12.8	12.2	11.6	11.0	10.5	9.9	9.4	8.9	8.5	8.0
98	12.8	12.2	11.5	11.0	10.4	9.9	9.4	8.9	8.4	8.0
99	12.7	12.1	11.5	10.9	10.4	9.8	9.3	8.8	8.3	7.9
100	12.7	12.1	11.5	10.9	10.3	9.8	9.2	8.7	8.3	7.8
101	12.7	12.1	11.4	10.8	10.3	9.7	9.2	8.7	8.2	7.8
102	12.7	12.0	11.4	10.8	10.2	9.7	9.2	8.7	8.2	7.7
103	12.6	12.0	11.4	10.8	10.2	9.7	9.1	8.6	8.1	7.7

Table II: Joint Life and Last Survivor Expectancy (continued)

Ages	75	76	77	78	79	80	81	82	83	84
104	12.6	12.0	11.4	10.8	10.2	9.6	9.1	8.6	8.1	7.6
105	12.6	12.0	11.3	10.7	10.2	9.6	9.1	8.5	8.0	7.6
106	12.6	11.9	11.3	10.7	10.1	9.6	9.0	8.5	8.0	7.5
107	12.6	11.9	11.3	10.7	10.1	9.6	9.1	8.5	8.0	7.5
108	12.6	11.9	11.3	10.7	10.1	9.5	9.0	8.5	8.0	7.5
109	12.6	11.9	11.3	10.7	10.1	9.5	9.0	8.4	7.9	7.5
110	12.6	11.9	11.3	10.7	10.1	9.5	9.0	8.4	7.9	7.4
111	12.5	11.9	11.3	10.7	10.1	9.5	8.9	8.4	7.9	7.4
112	12.5	11.9	11.3	10.6	10.1	9.5	8.9	8.4	7.9	7.4
113	12.5	11.9	11.2	10.6	10.0	9.5	8.9	8.4	7.9	7.4
114	12.5	11.9	11.2	10.6	10.0	9.5	8.9	8.4	7.9	7.4
115	12.5	11.9	11.2	10.6	10.0	9.5	8.9	8.4	7.9	7.4

Ages	85	86	87	88	89	90	91	92	93	94
Table II: Joint Life and Last Survivor Expectancy (continued)										
85	9.6	9.3	9.1	8.9	8.7	8.5	8.3	8.2	8.0	7.9
86	9.3	9.1	8.8	8.6	8.3	8.2	8.0	7.8	7.7	7.6
87	9.1	8.8	8.5	8.3	8.1	7.9	7.7	7.5	7.4	7.2
88	8.9	8.6	8.3	8.0	7.8	7.6	7.4	7.2	7.1	6.9
89	8.7	8.3	8.1	7.8	7.5	7.3	7.1	6.9	6.8	6.6
90	8.5	8.2	7.9	7.6	7.3	7.1	6.9	6.7	6.5	6.4
91	8.3	8.0	7.7	7.4	7.1	6.9	6.7	6.5	6.3	6.2
92	8.2	7.8	7.5	7.2	6.9	6.7	6.5	6.3	6.1	5.9
93	8.0	7.7	7.4	7.1	6.8	6.5	6.3	6.1	5.9	5.8
94	7.9	7.6	7.2	6.9	6.6	6.4	6.2	5.9	5.8	5.6
95	7.8	7.5	7.1	6.8	6.5	6.3	6.0	5.8	5.6	5.4
96	7.7	7.3	7.0	6.7	6.4	6.1	5.9	5.7	5.5	5.3
97	7.6	7.3	6.9	6.6	6.3	6.0	5.8	5.5	5.3	5.1
98	7.6	7.2	6.8	6.5	6.2	5.9	5.6	5.4	5.2	5.0
99	7.5	7.1	6.7	6.4	6.1	5.8	5.5	5.3	5.1	4.9
100	7.4	7.0	6.6	6.3	6.0	5.7	5.4	5.2	5.0	4.8
101	7.3	6.9	6.6	6.2	5.9	5.8	5.3	5.1	4.9	4.7
102	7.3	6.9	6.5	6.2	5.8	5.5	5.3	5.0	4.8	4.6
103	7.2	6.8	6.4	6.1	5.8	5.5	5.2	4.9	4.7	4.5
104	7.2	6.8	6.4	6.0	5.7	5.4	5.1	4.8	4.6	4.4
105	7.1	6.7	6.3	6.0	5.6	5.3	5.0	4.8	4.5	4.3
106	7.1	6.7	6.3	5.9	5.6	5.3	5.0	4.7	4.5	4.2
107	7.1	6.6	6.2	5.9	5.5	5.2	4.9	4.6	4.4	4.2
108	7.0	6.6	6.2	5.8	5.5	5.2	4.9	4.6	4.3	4.1
109	7.0	6.6	6.2	5.8	5.5	5.1	4.8	4.5	4.3	4.1
110	7.0	6.6	6.2	5.8	5.4	5.1	4.8	4.5	4.3	4.0
111	7.0	6.5	6.1	5.7	5.4	5.1	4.8	4.5	4.2	4.0
112	7.0	6.5	6.1	5.7	5.4	5.0	4.7	4.4	4.2	3.9
113	6.9	6.5	6.1	5.7	5.4	5.0	4.7	4.4	4.2	3.9
114	6.9	6.5	6.1	5.7	5.3	5.0	4.7	4.4	4.1	3.9
115	6.9	6.5	6.1	5.7	5.3	5.0	4.7	4.4	4.1	3.9

Table III: MDIB or Uniform Table

Age	Applicable Divisor	Age	Applicable Divisor	Age	Applicable Divisor
70	26.2	86	13.1	101	5.3
71	25.3	87	12.4	102	5.0
72	24.4	88	11.8	103	4.7
73	23.5	89	11.1	104	4.4
74	22.7	90	10.5	105	4.1
75	21.8	91	9.9	106	3.8
76	20.9	92	9.4	107	3.6
77	20.1	93	8.8	108	3.3
78	19.2	94	8.3	109	3.1
79	18.4	95	7.8	110	2.8
80	17.6	96	7.3	111	2.6
81	16.8	97	6.9	112	2.4
82	16.0	98	6.5	113	2.2
83	15.3	99	6.1	114	2.0
84	14.5	100	5.7	115 and older	1.8
85	13.8				

Table IV: MDIB Survivor Benefit Limitations

Excess of Employee's Age Over Beneficiary's Age	Applicable Percentage	Excess of Employee's Age Over Beneficiary's Age	Applicable Percentage
10 years or less	100%	28	62%
11	96%	29	61%
12	93%	30	60%
13	90%	31	59%
14	87%	32	59%
15	84%	33	58%
16	82%	34	57%
17	79%	35	56%
18	77%	36	56%
19	75%	37	55%
20	73%	38	55%
21	72%	39	54%
22	70%	40	54%
23	68%	41	53%
24	67%	42	53%
25	66%	43	53%
26	64%	44 and greater	52%
27	63%		

Index

CATALOG

...more from nolo

	PRICE	CODE

BUSINESS

	PRICE	CODE
Avoid Employee Lawsuits (Quick & Legal Series)	$24.95	AVEL
The CA Nonprofit Corporation Kit (Binder w/CD-ROM)	$59.95	CNP
Consultant & Independent Contractor Agreements (Book w/CD-ROM)	$29.95	CICA
The Corporate Minutes Book (Book w/CD-ROM)	$69.95	CORMI
The Employer's Legal Handbook	$39.95	EMPL
Firing Without Fear (Quick & Legal Series)	$29.95	FEAR
Form Your Own Limited Liability Company (Book w/CD-ROM)	$44.95	LIAB
Hiring Independent Contractors: The Employer's Legal Guide (Book w/CD-ROM)	$34.95	HICI
How to Create a Buy-Sell Agreement & Control the Destiny of your Small Business (Book w/Disk-PC)	$49.95	BSAG
How to Form a California Professional Corporation (Book w/CD-ROM)	$59.95	PROF
How to Form a Nonprofit Corporation (Book w/CD-ROM)—National Edition	$44.95	NNP
How to Form a Nonprofit Corporation in California (Book w/CD-ROM)	$44.95	NON
How to Form Your Own California Corporation (Binder w/CD-ROM)	$39.95	CACI
How to Form Your Own California Corporation (Book w/CD-ROM)	$34.95	CCOR
How to Form Your Own New York Corporation (Book w/Disk—PC)	$39.95	NYCO
How to Form Your Own Texas Corporation (Book w/CD-ROM)	$39.95	TCOR
How to Write a Business Plan	$29.95	SBS
The Independent Paralegal's Handbook	$29.95	PARA
Leasing Space for Your Small Business	$34.95	LESP
Legal Guide for Starting & Running a Small Business	$34.95	RUNS
Legal Forms for Starting & Running a Small Business (Book w/CD-ROM)	$29.95	RUNS2
Marketing Without Advertising	$22.00	MWAD
Music Law (Book w/Disk—PC)	$29.95	ML
Nolo's California Quick Corp (Quick & Legal Series)	$19.95	QINC
Nolo's Guide to Social Security Disability	$29.95	QSS
Nolo's Quick LLC (Quick & Legal Series)	$24.95	LLCQ
The Small Business Start-up Kit (Book w/CD-ROM)	$29.95	SMBU

	PRICE	CODE
The Small Business Start-up Kit for California (Book w/CD-ROM)	$29.95	OPEN
The Partnership Book: How to Write a Partnership Agreement (Book w/CD-ROM)	$39.95	PART
Sexual Harassment on the Job	$24.95	HARS
Starting & Running a Successful Newsletter or Magazine	$29.95	MAG
Tax Savvy for Small Business	$34.95	SAVVY
Working for Yourself: Law & Taxes for the Self-Employed	$39.95	WAGE
Your Limited Liability Company: An Operating Manual (Book w/Disk—PC)	$49.95	LOP
Your Rights in the Workplace	$29.95	YRW

CONSUMER

	PRICE	CODE
Fed Up with the Legal System: What's Wrong & How to Fix It	$9.95	LEG
How to Win Your Personal Injury Claim	$29.95	PICL
Nolo's Encyclopedia of Everyday Law	$28.95	EVL
Nolo's Pocket Guide to California Law	$15.95	CLAW
Trouble-Free Travel...And What to Do When Things Go Wrong	$14.95	TRAV

ESTATE PLANNING & PROBATE

	PRICE	CODE
8 Ways to Avoid Probate (Quick & Legal Series)	$16.95	PRO8
9 Ways to Avoid Estate Taxes (Quick & Legal Series)	$29.95	ESTX
Estate Planning Basics (Quick & Legal Series)	$18.95	ESPN
How to Probate an Estate in California	$49.95	PAE
Make Your Own Living Trust (Book w/CD-ROM)	$34.95	LITR
Nolo's Law Form Kit: Wills	$24.95	KWL
Nolo's Simple Will Book (Book w/CD-ROM)	$34.95	SWIL
Plan Your Estate	$39.95	NEST
Quick & Legal Will Book (Quick & Legal Series)	$15.95	QUIC

FAMILY MATTERS

	PRICE	CODE
Child Custody: Building Parenting Agreements That Work	$29.95	CUST
The Complete IEP Guide	$24.95	IEP
Divorce & Money: How to Make the Best Financial Decisions During Divorce	$34.95	DIMO
Do Your Own Divorce in Oregon	$29.95	ODIV
Get a Life: You Don't Need a Million to Retire Well	$24.95	LIFE
The Guardianship Book for California	$34.95	GB
How to Adopt Your Stepchild in California (Book w/CD-ROM)	$34.95	ADOP
A Legal Guide for Lesbian and Gay Couples	$25.95	LG
Living Together: A Legal Guide (Book w/CD-ROM)	$34.95	LTK
Using Divorce Mediation: Save Your Money & Your Sanity	$29.95	UDMD

	PRICE	CODE

GOING TO COURT

Beat Your Ticket: Go To Court and Win! (National Edition)	$19.95	BEYT
The Criminal Law Handbook: Know Your Rights, Survive the System	$29.95	KYR
Everybody's Guide to Small Claims Court (National Edition)	$24.95	NSCC
Everybody's Guide to Small Claims Court in California	$24.95	CSCC
Fight Your Ticket ... and Win! (California Edition)	$24.95	FYT
How to Change Your Name in California	$34.95	NAME
How to Collect When You Win a Lawsuit (California Edition)	$29.95	JUDG
How to Mediate Your Dispute	$18.95	MEDI
How to Seal Your Juvenile & Criminal Records (California Edition)	$34.95	CRIM
Nolo's Deposition Handbook	$29.95	DEP
Represent Yourself in Court: How to Prepare & Try a Winning Case	$34.95	RYC

HOMEOWNERS, LANDLORDS & TENANTS

California Tenants' Rights	$27.95	CTEN
Contractors' and Homeowners' Guide to Mechanics' Liens (Book w/Disk—PC)—California Edition	$39.95	MIEN
The Deeds Book (California Edition)	$24.95	DEED
Dog Law	$14.95	DOG
Every Landlord's Legal Guide (National Edition, Book w/CD-ROM)	$44.95	ELLI
Every Tenant's Legal Guide	$26.95	EVTEN
For Sale by Owner in California	$29.95	FSBO
How to Buy a House in California	$29.95	BHCA
The Landlord's Law Book, Vol. 1: Rights & Responsibilities (California Edition) (Book w/CD-ROM)	$44.95	LBRT
The California Landlord's Law Book, Vol. 2: Evictions (Book w/CD-ROM)	$44.95	LBEV
Leases & Rental Agreements (Quick & Legal Series)	$24.95	LEAR
Neighbor Law: Fences, Trees, Boundaries & Noise	$24.95	NEI
The New York Landlord's Law Book (Book w/CD-ROM)	$39.95	NYLL
Renters' Rights (National Edition)	$24.95	RENT
Stop Foreclosure Now in California	$29.95	CLOS

HUMOR

29 Reasons Not to Go to Law School	$12.95	29R
Poetic Justice	$9.95	PJ

IMMIGRATION

How to Get a Green Card	$29.95	GRN
U.S. Immigration Made Easy	$44.95	IMEZ

	PRICE	CODE

MONEY MATTERS

101 Law Forms for Personal Use (Book w/Disk—PC)	$29.95	SPOT
Bankruptcy: Is It the Right Solution to Your Debt Problems? (Quick & Legal Series)	$19.95	BRS
Chapter 13 Bankruptcy: Repay Your Debts	$34.95	CH13
Creating Your Own Retirement Plan	$29.95	YROP
Credit Repair (Quick & Legal Series, Book w/CD-ROM)	$19.95	CREP
How to File for Chapter 7 Bankruptcy	$34.95	HFB
IRAs, 401(k)s & Other Retirement Plans: Taking Your Money Out	$29.95	RET
Money Troubles: Legal Strategies to Cope With Your Debts	$29.95	MT
Nolo's Law Form Kit: Personal Bankruptcy	$24.95	KBNK
Stand Up to the IRS	$24.95	SIRS
Surviving an IRS Tax Audit (Quick & Legal Series)	$24.95	SAUD
Take Control of Your Student Loan Debt	$24.95	SLOAN

PATENTS AND COPYRIGHTS

The Copyright Handbook: How to Protect and Use Written Works (Book w/CD-ROM)	$34.95	COHA
Copyright Your Software	$24.95	CYS
Domain Names	$24.95	DOM
Getting Permission: How to License and Clear Copyrighted Materials Online and Off (Book w/Disk—PC)	$34.95	RIPER
How to Make Patent Drawings Yourself	$29.95	DRAW
The Inventor's Notebook	$24.95	INOT
Nolo's Patents for Beginners (Quick & Legal Series)	$29.95	QPAT
License Your Invention (Book w/Disk—PC)	$39.95	LICE
Patent, Copyright & Trademark	$34.95	PCTM
Patent It Yourself	$49.95	PAT
Patent Searching Made Easy	$29.95	PATSE
The Public Domain	$34.95	PUBL
Web and Software Development: A Legal Guide (Book w/ CD-ROM)	$44.95	SFT
Trademark: Legal Care for Your Business and Product Name	$39.95	TRD

RESEARCH & REFERENCE

Legal Research: How to Find & Understand the Law	$34.95	LRES

SENIORS

Beat the Nursing Home Trap: A Consumer's Guide to Assisted Living and Long-Term Care	$21.95	ELD
The Conservatorship Book for California	$44.95	CNSV
Social Security, Medicare & Pensions	$24.95	SOA

SOFTWARE

**Call or check our website at www.nolo.com
for special discounts on Software!**

	PRICE	CODE
LeaseWriter CD—Windows	$129.95	LWD1
Living Trust Maker CD—Windows	$89.95	LTD2
LLC Maker—Windows	$89.95	LLP1
Personal RecordKeeper 5.0 CD—Windows	$59.95	RKD5
Small Business Pro 4 CD—Windows	$89.95	SBCD4
WillMaker 8.0 CD—Windows	$69.95	WP8

Special Upgrade Offer

Get 35% off the latest edition off your Nolo book

It's important to have the most current legal information. Because laws and legal procedures change often, we update our books regularly. To help keep you up-to-date we are extending this special upgrade offer. Cut out and mail the title portion of the cover of your old Nolo book and we'll give you 35% off the retail price of the NEW EDITION of that book when you purchase directly from us. For more information call us at 1-800-992-6656. This offer is to individuals only.

Order Form

Name

Address

City

State, Zip

Daytime Phone

E-mail

Our "No-Hassle" Guarantee

Return anything you buy directly from Nolo for any reason and we'll cheerfully refund your purchase price. No ifs, ands or buts.

☐ Check here if you do not wish to receive mailings from other companies

Item Code	Quantity	Item	Unit Price	Total Price

Subtotal	
Add your local sales tax (California only)	
Shipping: RUSH $9, Basic $5 (See below)	
"I bought 3, ship it to me FREE!"(Ground shipping only)	
TOTAL	

Method of payment

☐ Check   ☐ VISA   ☐ MasterCard
☐ Discover Card   ☐ American Express

Account Number

Expiration Date

Signature

Shipping and Handling

Rush Delivery—Only $9

We'll ship any order to any street address in the U.S. by UPS 2nd Day Air* for only $9!

* Order by noon Pacific Time and get your order in 2 business days. Orders placed after noon Pacific Time will arrive in 3 business days. P.O. boxes and S.F. Bay Area use basic shipping. Alaska and Hawaii use 2nd Day Air or Priority Mail.

Basic Shipping—$5

Use for P.O. Boxes, Northern California and Ground Service.

Allow 1-2 weeks for delivery. U.S. addresses only.

For faster service, use your credit card and our toll-free numbers

Order 24 hours a day

Online	www.nolo.com
Phone	1-800-992-6656
	1-800-645-0895

Nolo
950 Parker St.
Berkeley, CA 94710

Visit us online at

www.nolo.com

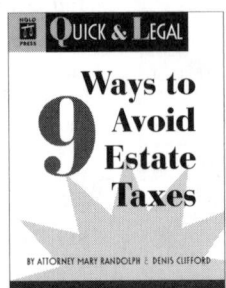

Take 2 minutes & Give us your 2 cents

Your comments make a big difference in the development and revision of Nolo books and software. Please take a few minutes and register your Nolo product—and your comments—with us. Not only will your input make a difference, you'll receive special offers available only to registered owners of Nolo products on our newest books and software. Register now by:

PHONE
1-800-992-6656

FAX
1-800-645-0895

EMAIL
cs@nolo.com

or **MAIL** us
this registration card

REMEMBER:
Little publishers have big ears. We really listen to you.

fold here

REGISTRATION CARD

NAME		DATE

ADDRESS

CITY	STATE	ZIP

PHONE	E-MAIL

WHERE DID YOU HEAR ABOUT THIS PRODUCT?

WHERE DID YOU PURCHASE THIS PRODUCT?

DID YOU CONSULT A LAWYER? (PLEASE CIRCLE ONE)   YES   NO   NOT APPLICABLE

DID YOU FIND THIS BOOK HELPFUL?   (VERY)   5   4   3   2   1   (NOT AT ALL)

COMMENTS

WAS IT EASY TO USE?   (VERY EASY)   5   4   3   2   1   (VERY DIFFICULT)

DO YOU OWN A COMPUTER? IF SO, WHICH FORMAT? (PLEASE CIRCLE ONE)   WINDOWS   DOS   MAC

We occasionally make our mailing list available to carefully selected companies whose products may be of interest to you.
❏ If you do not wish to receive mailings from these companies, please check this box.
❏ You can quote me in future Nolo promotional materials. Daytime phone number _____.

RET 3.0

NOLO IN THE NEWS

"Nolo helps lay people perform legal tasks without the aid—or fees—of lawyers."

—USA TODAY

Nolo books are ..."written in plain language, free of legal mumbo jumbo, and spiced with witty personal observations."

—ASSOCIATED PRESS

"...Nolo publications...guide people simply through the how, when, where and why of law."

—WASHINGTON POST

"Increasingly, people who are not lawyers are performing tasks usually regarded as legal work... And consumers, using books like Nolo's, do routine legal work themselves."

—NEW YORK TIMES

"...All of [Nolo's] books are easy-to-understand, are updated regularly, provide pull-out forms...and are often quite moving in their sense of compassion for the struggles of the lay reader."

—SAN FRANCISCO CHRONICLE

fold here

- -

Place
stamp here

nolo
950 Parker Street
Berkeley, CA 94710-9867

Attn: RET 3.0